CHASING
THE DAYLIGHT

CHASING THE DAYLIGHT

One Woman's Journey to Becoming a U.S. Army Intelligence Officer

JOANNA RAKOWSKI

Copyright © 2023 by Joanna Rakowski.

Library of Congress Control Number:		2023905205
ISBN:	Hardcover	978-1-6698-6941-2
	Softcover	978-1-6698-6940-5
	eBook	978-1-6698-6939-9

All rights reserved. No part of this book may be reproduced or transmitted in any form or by any means, electronic or mechanical, including photocopying, recording, or by any information storage and retrieval system, without permission in writing from the copyright owner.

All photos in the book are from the author's personal archives.

Special thanks to: Wendy Dale, Brenda Smit-James, Casey Kaiser, Alyx Ramos, Maria Barselotti, Alexandar Bonev, Alec Rakowski, and Donna Wlezien for support and helpful input during the creation of this book.

This book is a memoir, and it reflects the author's recollection of events to the best of the author's knowledge. To write this book, the author relied upon her journals, notes, personal documents, books, and online resources. There are no composite characters. Some details, identities, names, characters, businesses, places, and events have been changed or altered, and some dialogue has been recreated for literary effect and to protect the privacy of the people involved.

Cover design Joanna Rakowski
Photos on the front cover Joanna Rakowski
Images on the back cover:
Ballerina by OpenClipart-Vectors from Pixabay,
Female soldier Copyright:<ahref='https://www.123rf.com/profile_belchonock'>belchonock</a>

Print information available on the last page.

Rev. date: 06/06/2023

To order additional copies of this book, contact:
Xlibris
844-714-8691
www.Xlibris.com
Orders@Xlibris.com
833956

REVIEWS:

Chasing the Daylight by Joanna Rakowski is a captivating memoir which provides a unique insight into the life of a dainty ballerina turned army interrogator.... **Her story is one of grit, determination, and self-transformation...** Joanna Rakowski's writing is surprisingly well-written, well-edited, and very well-organized, which sets it apart from many other autobiographies in today's book market. The inclusion of photographs throughout the book adds interest and credibility to her written life history.

Hollywood Book Reviews

Chasing the Daylight pulls no punches and tells it exactly like it is. Author JoAnna Rakowski describes in vivid detail the mental, emotional, and immense physical effort required to achieve success in the Army training courses... **This is a solid read and finding out the nuts and bolts of military service is something I enjoyed immensely.** I can highly recommend this read.

Readers' Favorite

In author Joanna Rakowski's Chasing the Daylight: One Woman's Journey to Becoming a U.S. Army Intelligence Officer, is a memorable journey of one woman as she forgoes the preconceived idea of men going to war by showcasing **a story of strength, courage, and determination....** The author did a wonderful job of capturing the hard work and determination the path of those in the military must follow. **The attention to detail the author gave to every step of the process, really drew me into her story and made for a relatable and memorable atmosphere...** The balance of personal storytelling on the author's part with the information gives readers a better idea of what life in the military is really like making this such a compelling book.

Pacific Book Review

Told in an intricately detailed memoir style (...) Joanna's story nearly runs the entire gamut of the human condition on her quest to become an officer. (...) The passion for her adopted country practically oozes off the pages, and **it's the author's wholehearted belief in her American dream** more than any fast-paced action that keeps you turning the pages (...) Regardless of how you feel about the US as a country or any of its military organizations, Joanna's enthusiasm and hope for her career and what becoming a member of the US military means to her are **so heartfelt and honestly written** that it isn't difficult to overcome your own reservations and simply enjoy a novel about a fiercely optimistic and driven woman achieving her dreams. (...) a **memoir written with passion, grit, and not a small amount of feminine power**...

Chicago Book Review

The largest section of the book – army training and service – was riveting. I read late into the night, needing to find out what happened.

The Bookbag

(...) While proud of her service, Rakowski doesn't shy away from the "heartache and loneliness" of military life (...). Also emphasized is the way the military impacted her personal life (...) **this is a well-written, intimate account that breaks the norms of war memoir** in its focus on the sacrifices of soldiers who never step foot onto a battlefield. **It's also an important reminder of the centrality of immigrants to the U.S. military in the modern era. A poignant story of an immigrant's experiences in the U.S. Army.**

Kirkus Reviews

Atmospheric writing blends with vivid interior emotions to create a roller-coaster ride that mingles pride, fear, doubt, joy, humor, and sheer determination... Rakowski's narrative is studded with specificity, breathing life into the author's grueling, self-selected search to be part of something bigger than herself... Rakowski paints a vivid, detailed portrait of the mental, physical, and emotional challenges she faced in becoming a U.S. Army intelligence officer... Her inspiring tale is not to be missed.

The US Review of Books

In direct but often richly emotional prose, Chasing the Daylight recounts the day-to-day challenges of transformation, as Rakowski faces the rigors of training, the trials of being paired with less dedicated members of her cohort (...) The account is arresting—her English is polished and touched with an original sense of idiom—with jolts of surprising detail Takeaway: **Tough-minded, inspiring account of a Polish immigrant's U.S. military training...**

BookLife by Publishers Weekly

U.S. Army veteran Joanna Rakowski's memoir of training to become an intelligence officer in the early 2000s presents **a deeply felt case study in perseverance and determined self-transformation...** What makes Rakowski's story especially compelling is that she transformed herself on several different fronts... others who have served may find Rakowski's experiences resonate with theirs, and the loved ones of young men or women considering doing the same should find her words instructive and revealing.

BlueInk Reviews

Written by a former ballerina and trained linguist, the memoir Chasing the Light covers an unpredictable military rise... **Scenes from Rakowski's army life,** including of basic training hardships and of following orders later on, **are compelling because of their authoritative details...** She communicates her emotions and experiences in evocative figurative language.

Foreword Clarion Reviews

From ballerina to soldier, experience the bittersweet journey of a woman as she finds the courage to chase her dreams. Joanna Rakowski's debut memoir, Chasing the Daylight, sparks a will in its reader to keep pushing and chasing their dreams... **This memoir is a captivating and inspiring experience that leaves a lasting impression...** I would recommend Chasing the Daylight to anyone seeking a reminder that anything is possible with determination and perseverance and to those who would use the book as a form of inspiration to keep chasing their dreams.

Independent Book Review

Rakowski's story especially compelling in its focus not just on rigorous army training and life, but how trust and confidence develops between officers and soldiers as training develops. (…) women who are also considering military service will find Rakowski's experiences to be candid, thought-provoking, and revealing… Perhaps this memoir's strength is because these experiences come couched in an analysis of military culture that is powered by lessons Rakowski learns along the way. **Chasing the Daylight is eye-opening and captivating. Libraries and readers interested in accounts of women in service** who hold officer positions and training that leads them to be all they can be both within the army and in civilian life **will find it involving and hard to put down.**

Midwest Book Review

CONTENTS

Prologue xv

Enlistment: The Beginning Of My Journey

Chapter 1   I, do solemnly swear 1

Prebasic Training: Military Appetizer

Chapter 2   I can 9

Basic Training: Becoming A Soldier

Chapter 3   Broken into pieces 27
Chapter 4   Accepting the status quo 35
Chapter 5   Blending in 49
Chapter 6   The victory starts here 56
Chapter 7   Relying on others 76

Advanced Individual Training: Learning My Job As An Enlisted Soldier

Chapter 8   I am a soldier first 85
Chapter 9   Rebuilding myself 99
Chapter 10   Emotional roller coaster 105
Chapter 11   Re-validation of myself 131
Chapter 12   The power of healing 138
Chapter 13   Fragility of human life 167
Chapter 14   MI Specialist 179
Chapter 15   A promise of perseverance 183

Officer Candidate School: Becoming an Officer

Chapter 16   Intimidation and discouragement 189
Chapter 17   Trusting my instincts.. 202
Chapter 18   Patience, leadership, and kindness 236
Chapter 19   Looking death in the eye... 280
Chapter 20   A leader within the greater profession................ 297

My First Overseas Training: U.S. Army Emergency Deployment Readiness Exercise, Poland

Chapter 21   Something bigger than myself 305

Military Intelligence Officer Basic Course: Learning My Job as an Officer

Chapter 22   Heartache and loneliness....................................... 317
Chapter 23   Life in slow motion 326
Chapter 24   Survival by volunteering.. 336
Chapter 25   Disconnected cog 344
Chapter 26   Broken and vulnerable... 354
Chapter 27   Intelligence professional second to none........... 363

My Second Overseas Training: Danger Focus II Exercise, Germany

Chapter 28   Belonging and fitting in... 369

Enduring the Darkness: The End of My Journey

Chapter 29   Broken kaleidoscope 377

Epilogue 387
References 389

To my Mom, for her love and support.

Chasing the Daylight

One Woman's Journey to Becoming a U.S. Army Intelligence Officer

> *I will love the light for it shows me the way, yet I will endure the darkness because it shows me the stars.*
> —*Og Mandino*

PROLOGUE

Sometimes you love what you do so much that your profession becomes you. You constantly think, breathe, and live your work. I am not talking about being a workaholic. I'm talking about being deeply passionate about something and doing it daily with ever-growing, evolving joy as you learn more about it. As you grow with it and within it.

That's what ballet was for me. Since I was ten, I've been practicing dance on a full-time basis for nearly fifteen years dancing, then also teaching ballet. I was a professionally trained classical ballet dancer and a lover of anything dance. From 1979 until my departure to the U.S. in 1995, I practically lived at the Great Opera in Warsaw, watching every single ballet and opera stage production up to fifteen times per month. I was listening to classical music only and writing poetry, writing about ballet, painting, and drawing ballet. Ballet defined me so deeply that I was, like ballerinas who are typically perceived on stage as fragile, sensitive, and ethereal. I was a perfect example of this stereotype because I was raised as an artist. Being sensitive and delicate was part of the job. And it made sense. To dance well to beautiful classical music, you have to understand and interpret it. To do that, you need to be receptive to this type of music. Which leads to being sensitive to it and everything art in general.

When I immigrated to the U.S. I was too old to start pursuing a ballet dancer career from scratch, so I was teaching ballet at the local YMCA for a while. I quickly realized that this wasn't enough to pay the bills, so I went to college to learn graphic design and desktop publishing. However, deep down in my heart, I was still this fragile ballerina. The big void after stopping practicing ballet became unbearable. For a few years, I was struggling with the dilemma between staying true to myself and the inability to find myself in an unfamiliar country, culture, and language. Since everything dear to me, especially my friendships, was now left behind, I was torn between whom I used to be in Poland and whom I needed to be in America. Except, I had no idea what I wanted to be. The only thing that became clear to me in this turmoil was the fact that I needed a drastic change in my life. And it wasn't about a career or a job. I needed to do something with my life and become someone I'd never been before. I needed to reinvent myself.

1988: I was typically perceived on stage as fragile, sensitive, and ethereal.

Eventually, by the end of 1999, I received some help from the universe in discovering what I needed to become. It happened somewhat by coincidence, but I'd like to think it was fate. One day at the school, I noticed a table in a hallway covered with literature about all branches of the U.S. Armed Forces. As I browsed the flyers, it dawned on me that I was now in America, living a life of new opportunities and dreams I couldn't realize in Poland. And I was extremely thankful for these opportunities and hopes. At that moment, I decided to transform from a delicate ballerina into a hard-core U.S. Army soldier.

PART I

ENLISTMENT:
THE BEGINNING OF MY JOURNEY

CHAPTER 1

I, DO SOLEMNLY SWEAR

It was the early morning of September 2000. The skies were mysteriously dark. Right in front of me, a shadow of a lonely tree was moving in a sinister wind. I was sitting in my car in a deserted parking lot, in front of the Military Entrance Processing Station, about to enlist in the United States Army National Guard. I was writing a painful goodbye letter to my dearest friend and mentor of twelve years, Chris. Swallowing my tears, I was recalling the last year of the last century.

A massive tornado of thoughts about the ending of my relationship with Chris was invading my mind while I was waiting in front of the building. I desperately needed some closure with my situation with Chris. I needed to accept the fact that this friendship was forever lost. I needed hope. I needed peace. I had to move on and pursue my new dream of joining the U.S. Army. Even though I knew that being of Polish origin and not speaking perfect English could be a big problem, at last, I decided and there was no looking back. In a few hours, after my final in-processing at the station, I would come back to my car as an enlisted soldier.

I was ready for this new journey for a long time. I dreamed about this day even though it never crossed my mind that it would look like this. Deep down in my heart, I was hoping when I joined the army, it would be a beautiful, sunny, and glorious day, my family, and friends with me, happy and proud. Instead, the world around me and within me was submerged in the deepest darkness when the daylight was not coming fast enough or was gone too soon. I was alone, as if my enlistment was a secret that needed to be hidden from the world. As if I were against the world.

Suddenly I looked in my side-view mirror and I noticed an American flag on the pole behind me, unfolding proudly its stripes and stars, caressed by the calming fall wind. I felt an instant relief, and the most wonderful inner peace overflew my entire body. It was a hope of finding my long-lost daylight. From now on, everything would change for the better.

* * *

I left the car a few minutes before 5:00 a.m. and went into the building to complete my in-processing. For a moment, I held the doorknob as if hesitating. Was I doing the right thing? Would I be able to live with this decision for the rest of my life? Would my new military journey help me cope with the loss of my dearest friend? It was impossible to find the answers to all these questions. My heart was telling me to proceed.

I realized that the big unknown of my new journey would soon reveal to me a new mysterious world. I would step into a reality that in a span of the next several hours would put me on a fresh path. Without knowing what to expect, I entered the building. Upstairs, the second floor was filled with young sleepy recruits ready to join the U.S. Armed Forces: Army, Air Force, Marines, Navy, and Coast Guard. Most of them were recent high school graduates, perhaps leaving their homes for the first time in their lives. Some were in their early or mid-twenties, so being thirty-one, I definitely felt the oldest in this crowd. It didn't bother me at all, and I figured it would probably be like that from now on, and I'd better get used to being "old."

I spent the majority of my time waiting for my name to be called. Occasionally, one of the military personnel would yell at these poor young people to wake them up, as sleeping was not allowed. Every couple of hours, a group of twelve to fifteen new recruits was leaving the premises in a single-file line, with a large yellow envelope in their hands, scared, guided by one of the recruiters. They were going to the white school bus in the parking lot, which would take them straight to the airport. From there, they would all embark on their new journey. Later that day, I learned that they were being "shipped to basic training." Like packages via mail. One day, I would become a package as well and be shipped.

As I was waiting my turn, the surrounding crowd was diminishing. More buses went to the airport and came back for more recruits. Eventually, my name was called and along with a group of ten other people, I got through my in-processing. After a couple of hours, my medical and physical examination was completed, and all I had left was to negotiate the contract, sign the papers, and take the oath of enlistment. Because of my four-year college degree, I was enlisting with a rank of "specialist," skipping three ranks: private, private second class, and private first class. I was told that with a college degree, I could enlist as an officer and then directly after the basic training attend the officer training. I briefly considered it, but eventually opted to begin my journey as an enlisted soldier to gain some experience in the army before leading others.

I was the only person enlisting that day in the military intelligence job (interrogator) so I needed to fill out an additional long application for a security clearance and get fingerprinted. Then, I had to wait for approval from Washington, D.C.. I didn't understand much from the conversation I witnessed between my "counselor" and her boss in D.C., but I knew that the military job I was about to get assigned to, was special and that approval was necessary. So I waited another few hours, almost all by myself, in the big windowless room that just this morning was full of recruits—and now seemed deserted. At least I knew that since my enlistment was a "Delayed Entry Program" I was going home tonight. It meant that they would ship me to basic training in three months because my intelligence job (97E) required a special "booking," which had to be coordinated with the basic training. I was going to be "shipped" at the beginning of January 2001.

I was trying to picture all these future events in my mind: leaving Chicago, flying to Fort Jackson, South Carolina, and the basic training, the flight to Arizona to the Military Intelligence School and Center in Fort Huachuca—all this would take about seven months. Suddenly, I heard the counselor calling my name. I went to her office hopeful.

"We got the approval from D.C.. Congratulations. Now you may take the oath in room number eight, right by the main lobby." I didn't know what to say. It was overwhelming.

* * *

Around 4:00 p.m. I entered the "Oath Room" cautiously. It was a completely different world: in the back, I saw a shiny oak podium and a dark, heavy curtain in the background. In the middle of the stage was a speaker's stand, just like the one U.S. President has in D.C., with an emblem of the Armed Forces on the front. In the corner, an American Flag was mounted in a giant brass stand reflecting dimmed lights on the back. I found myself in a magical world where a wizard was about to cast his spell on me and change my life as I knew it. I wanted to be part of something bigger than myself. America gave me a chance for a better life than I would have had in Poland. I was committed to becoming the best human being I could be. There was no going back.

It looked like I was the last one to join this last group of seven recruits of the day. They gave us brief instructions regarding the ceremony. Shortly after that, an officer came on the stage through the side entrance wearing a decorated formal dark-blue uniform. All recruits jumped up to the position of attention as we were told. It was the first time in my life I stood at attention so close to the American flag, my right hand raised, saying the words that would change my life forever: "I, do solemnly swear that I will support and defend the Constitution of the United States…, I will obey the orders of the President of the United States…. So help me God." I knew that these words, carved in my heart, were now my guiding light for the years to come.

It was already late afternoon when the ceremony ended. The main room, full of life twelve hours ago, was now empty—until the next Wednesday when another couple of hundreds of new recruits enlist and ship out…

As I was proceeding down the stairs, suddenly five gigantic round emblems mounted on the wall right in front of me caught my attention. Somehow, I didn't notice them before, but this time I took a good look at them wondering what they would mean to me very soon, what mystery they would reveal—Army, Air Force, Navy, Marines, Coast Guard… Behind every emblem, there were countless lives of those who had perished, those who were now serving, and those who had enlisted today. My name was now encapsulated within the emblem of the army. Looking at these proud signs of greatness, power, and honor gave me unexplainable but strong feelings of security, peace, and belonging.

When I left the building, the heavy rain and thunder tousled the world, tree branches were being thrown around by the fierce wind dancing mischievously in all directions. I ran through the parking lot as fast as I could and finally found myself in my car. My heart was full of excitement, anxiety, and a sense of accomplishment in the face of a new challenge—much bigger and more serious than ever before. My mind was racing, trying to figure out what would be next, how to prepare myself for this journey, and how to succeed. Would I be able to endure the physically demanding training? Although I had experience being away from home while in ballet school so many years ago, I had some doubts about surviving separation from Alec in a completely unique environment. Would being from Poland and barely speaking basic English be an obstacle? Were my spirit and my resolve strong enough to survive the psychological pressure? However, in this chaos of thoughts, one thing was clear to me: I just made the first step in my new journey; I was about to reinvent myself and transform from a fragile, romantic ballerina into a hardcore soldier. It was important to me to prove to those who were teasing me about me joining the army that being a fragile and sensitive artist didn't have to be equal to a weakness of character or lack of physical strength. My ballet shoes were about to be swapped for combat boots, despite those who doubted my capabilities.

By the time I arrived home, the skies had cleared, and everything calmed down: the rain, the wind, and my heart. As I was walking to the house carrying enlistment papers and documents, I noticed the letter I wrote to Chris this morning on top of the pile. I probably grabbed it along with everything important from the car. I sat down, my back leaning against the purple-painted post of the porch and read the last couple of sentences of the letter: "There is nothing left from our friendship but distant memories. I don't mean anything to you anymore." I folded the paper, kissed it, and pressed it against my heart. "Goodbye, Chris," I said out loud. My rift with Chris was now official.

The sun was setting lonely and peaceful far beyond the trees, leaving golden-red contours on the scattered clouds. The day was over, slowly falling asleep, tucked in a fragile September evening mist.

PART II

PREBASIC TRAINING:
MILITARY APPETIZER

CHAPTER 2

I CAN

A couple of weeks later, I found out that the National Guard had recently introduced an additional step for the recruits in their military career. All new soldiers were strongly encouraged to attend "prebasic training to better prepare them for basic training." Instead of going to my regular first drill in the Chicago unit, I would go to Springfield, Illinois, for this weekend of training.

I was so excited and anxious to go that I wasn't able to sleep the night before departure. My first real military training was about to finally happen. It was hard to believe that almost a year passed already since I thought about pursuing this path: becoming a soldier. It seemed like yesterday when I shared this idea for the first time with my husband, Alec, a year before. One December afternoon, we were both in the kitchen talking casually about the upcoming Christmas. The snow was gently covering the landscape of the backyard. I was sitting on the kitchen countertop, looking through the window. Small outdoor lights mounted on the ground along the back fence were almost completely submerged in the snowy fluff. Their subtle yellow glow formed a bizarre combination of triangle-shaped reflections and shadows on the snow around them and the fence.

"You know," I said to Alec, "I would like to join the Army National Guard. I heard on the radio that a linguist unit in Chicago is looking for Polish-speaking soldiers."

"Cool, go for it if this is what you want." I was relieved that he wasn't surprised. Although he sounded casual, it seemed like he appreciated the significance of my choice. I loved him so much for not making a big deal of decisions like this one, for standing by me, and for his talent of making hard choices seem easier on the heart. He was not only my husband but also my friend and an ally. Admittedly, our first year together in America was rough. I was struggling with adapting to my new life and new family. The language was an immense challenge. Despite studying English grammar books, absorbing dialogues around me, listening to the American radio and TV news, watching movies in English, and trying to communicate, it seemed like I wasn't learning English fast enough. I also had trouble finding reasonable work with an English-speaking company. Frustrated and mentally exhausted, I was pressing on because, after all, I came to America for Alec. We had met in Poland when Alec, an American-born man, was visiting his Polish grandparents near Warsaw in December 1993. A year later, after exchanging letters and phone calls, we met again and got engaged. Four months later, we met for the third time, this time for our wedding. Shortly after that, I received my immigration visa and left Poland to start our new life together. It was a self-explanatory decision because bringing Alec to Poland to live with me was out of the question. I, on the other hand, wanted to leave Poland because I couldn't realize my dreams: having my own business and pursuing a PhD in ballet pedagogy. The rules were too strict and irrational. In addition, the housing in my situation was dreadful. Even with a relatively good salary while working for a global French company, I wouldn't have a chance to buy even a small apartment in Warsaw, where I lived. The mortgage interest rates were around forty-five percent, and it would take three generations to pay the place off. Even though Poland was a democratic country for six years now, I had no future in a place where personal freedoms and choices were still fairly restricted. I came to America, to Alec, with a new energy and high hopes. We eventually became a couple admired by Alec's friends. We were respecting each other's personal freedoms and goals, we were making decisions together, and there were no pressures or jealousy. I had gladly accepted all of Alec's friends without having my own. Our social life flourished, and we were happy.

After a brief discussion about the details of my new career, I showed him some literature regarding the U.S. Armed Forces that I had picked up a while ago from Oakton Community College, which I had been attending for a couple of years. We both knew that I wanted to be part of something bigger than myself, and now as a U.S. citizen, truly be part of my new country, which I admired so much. We also thought it was a good plan for me and for us. I would have monthly weekend drills in Chicago and one two-week training per year. In the meantime, I would continue to run my marketing consulting business from home.

This time, before going to my prebasic, Alec was there for me, just like that December evening in the kitchen. He volunteered to drive me to the North Riverside Armory, far south of our home, where new soldiers were meeting with the recruiters before the departure to Springfield for the prebasic training.

* * *

The first step in my journey was the Riverside Armory. We left the house around 4:00 a.m. The world was still immersed in a deep and peaceful sleep. The deserted highway took us directly to the location where we stopped in front of an enormous gate: the Illinois National Guard Northern Area. I'd never been to any military installation before. Since the welcome meeting was not scheduled until 5:30 a.m., Alec and I spent the last half an hour together before my first military adventure. We were wandering around the hallways of the building, admiring the memorabilia and history of the National Guard. While watching the displays, it dawned on me that all these objects, now proudly displayed, once belonged to soldiers, to units, and some even saw the battles in faraway lands. They were here now to inspire those who believed in their message and their power.

The welcome meeting began exactly at 5:30 a.m. after the families left. We were now in the hands of a sergeant who called us into a gym for a formation. I stood in formation a few times during my girls' scouts days years ago while in ballet school. But this was different. It was serious and ritual. About sixteen of us stood there at attention when the sergeant was explaining to us the training process and procedures in Springfield. I realized that it was my very first military formation of hundreds yet to come. I felt like a child on Christmas day lining up with my siblings in front of a decorated pine tree to receive a perfect gift from Santa.

Indeed, although unexpectedly, I did receive a perfect gift, not from Santa, of course, but from the Army itself. We were each presented with a handsome black overnight bag and a gray T-shirt with a beautiful National Guard logo. The logo was a small, white, wavy square with a miniature U.S. flag. The word "Army" was placed on a blue background instead of the stars. Underneath, an inscription: "National Guard." Next to the square, a decisive and strong capital lettered the motto, "YOU CAN", which made me believe that, indeed, I *could*, and I would become part of this new world. It was the first piece of my army "uniform" that I was putting on my back that morning. I was so pleasantly surprised by these welcome gifts that I wanted to celebrate, but I decided to keep my composure.

* * *

Just after 6:00 a.m., we left the North Riverside Armory in three government vans. We drove through isolated areas of scattered small villages and cornfields. Everything looked abandoned and gloomy. I had ample time to ponder my recently broken connection with Chris. I thought about the goodbye letter I wrote to Chris on the morning of my enlistment.

It bothered me that my relationship with Chris had fallen apart. Since I came back home from my last visit to Poland in 1999, everything in my relationship with Chris seemed to be deranged. In our last phone conversation, Chris told me, "It was never really a good time to talk." I was lost and thought that perhaps I was too romantic, and I was getting hurt because I was giving to those I loved, everything I had. While writing my painful monologue, I wondered if, for all these years, I saw Chris as a character from a fairy tale. Was I too sensitive and fragile and therefore jeopardized our relationship? Chris hadn't even noticed that I hadn't written a single letter for the past six months. And since my move to America, we were writing to each other almost daily. Now, a deep crevasse was separating us. The truth was that Chris didn't care about me anymore. Our friendship was over. I realized that I had to accept the situation and move on with my life.

As if nature wanted to show me that she was on my side, she gave me a glimpse of a most beautiful sunrise. Around 7:00 a.m. the sun started rising cautiously and soon the world was finally waking up. While the majority of people in the car were fast asleep, I was too excited to let any moment of this journey slip away. It was my first "military sunrise". I wondered how often I would be able to see them. Would they bring me hope in moments of loss and despair? For now, however, this sunrise symbolized the rising of my will. The will to succeed.

Three hours later, in Springfield, I was completely astonished by the dimensions of this base. It was called "Camp Lincoln," and everything here seemed so much bigger than the North Riverside Armory: gates, streets, parking lots, buildings, and countless spaces filled with all kinds of military vehicles. I was mesmerized by seemingly endless brown arrow-shaped signs pointing to the various buildings: State Area Command, Sixty-fifth Troop Command, Thirty-third Area Support Group, Sixty-sixth Infantry Brigade, 129th Regiment (RTI), and more. So far, none of them, though, represented anything familiar. However, at this very moment, I knew that one day, I would belong to one of those units in my pursuit of a crucial step in my military career.

Just before 10:00 a.m., we spilled out of several government vans parked in a row in front of a gray building. We all looked alike: a little scared and insecure, all wearing the gray Guard T-shirt "You Can" and blue jeans and carrying black bags. The military in-processing started immediately. Everything began moving like gears of a slowly awakening, well-oiled machinery. We had to form up quickly and drill sergeants were checking our belongings for any "contraband" (illegal items like knives, weapons, sharp objects, drugs, alcohol, cigarettes, and medicine). Then we formed a single file line and ran to the main building as we were ordered. I didn't see much difference between the ranks of military personnel. Some instructors were wearing "drill sergeant" hats, similar to those worn by the state troopers or park rangers—broad-brimmed felt with a high crown pinched at the four corners. (I learned later that it was called "Military Campaign *Smokey* Hat") Other personnel were wearing just a plain "field" cap (or "patrol cap") with a round visor. In a flash, my head was filled with new terminology and military slang. It dawned on me that I had to learn very quickly what the commands meant without knowing the exact significance of the words. For now, I needed to blend in with this crowd.

Eventually, I found myself in a large auditorium with a podium on the back and a so-familiar American flag posted along with other, probably specific units' flags. The room was filled tight with about a hundred young soldiers-to-be, sitting in endless rows. Drill sergeants and other instructors were pacing ominously along the sides and in the middle of the room. Then, one of the sergeants stopped suddenly by the row where I was sitting. I was so intensely concentrated, trying to understand these new situations, procedures, and words spoken around me, I must have caught his attention.

"You, over there. How old are you?"

"I'm thirty-one." I felt awful, thinking that I was old.

"What took you so long?" He didn't give up. I knew he was teasing me.

"I just came to the U.S. five years ago."

He smiled mysteriously and walked away toward the stage. Somehow, I knew that he would remember me for the rest of the weekend, and I wasn't sure if it was a good or rather a bad sign. Of course, I would prefer not to be noticed at all, just go through this training, and hopefully survive it. I anticipated that it was going to be very tough for me.

The man who just asked me a question and now was standing on the podium was the first sergeant of the unit we just got assigned to for this weekend's training. He was the boss of all the drill sergeants and instructors, just like a general manager in a civilian company. His speech was terrifying. He painted in front of our eyes the most horrible two days of our lives that would happen the moment we would leave the building. From his tone of voice and posture, I knew he was there to "get us," which in his language meant "to prepare us to become U.S. Army soldiers" and that he was dead serious about his mission.

It seemed like his "welcome" speech successfully crushed the majority of the new soldiers. The silence prevailed in the auditorium as though we just heard our final sentencing and there was no going back. I just had to get used to this feeling, because from that moment on, every training at any level of my career would most likely start from this kind of "welcome speech".

* * *

Suddenly a loud command pulled me out of my reflections: "Company, atten-tion!" the first sergeant sounded off and the whole auditorium stood at attention instantly. He saluted a very important officer entering the room in a blue dress uniform. The officer saluted back and gave us the sign to take seats.

"I'm General Dewberry and I'm a commander of this post. Today, I have the honor and pleasure of welcoming you all to the Illinois National

Guard Training Institute. I'm very proud of the choice you have made to join the U.S. Armed Forces. The history and tradition of the Guard are very long and full of memorable days."

At this point, I could only hear a comforting and calm general's voice talking about those who gave their lives to this country. It all sounded like legends and mysteries that were revealed here, especially to us recruits, as an inspiration. "I'd like to be there one day," I thought to myself. I noticed that everyone in the auditorium was completely enchanted by the general's speech and many of us were probably thinking the same: "We want to be there one day, in those stories and legends, fifty or a hundred years from now." At this very moment, I felt a release and tremendous courage to do anything, as an inexplicable energy flashed through my entire body.

When I regained clear vision from the blurry fog of my thoughts and imagination, I realized that the entire room was completely immersed in the morning sun. In its powerful beams piercing all the enormous windows on the left wall, I could see the tiny particles of dust dancing in the air. I wanted this magic moment to last forever.

After the general finished his very encouraging welcome, the first sergeant called everyone to attention. The general left the room.

* * *

"Sit down, Privates!" His voice was scratchy and scary. "You are all mine now. You will listen to my drill sergeants and do what they ask you to do. I don't care what your rank in your enlistment papers is. To me, you are starting here from zero. You are nothing—you are all privates." I knew that the rank of private was the lowest in the army. It didn't even have any insignia to put on the uniform. "That's okay," I said to myself. "I can take this temporary degradation."

That is how I became a private for the first time. Life began to look like in those "army movies" where there are a lot of drill sergeants screaming and soldiers running or doing endless push-ups. The sergeants divided us into four groups called platoons, each counting more or less than twenty people. One male and one female drill sergeant were in charge of one platoon. The male was up front where just minutes ago the general stood, and he was calling the privates by their last names. When called, we had to run through the middle aisle so the sergeant could see our faces, and then turn right where a female drill sergeant was waiting. We followed her outside. I ended up in the fourth platoon.

Everything started to happen so fast that at some point I became a robot. There was no time to understand each word the sergeants were screaming, so I decided to follow the crowd and think later. I could only guess what it meant to "double time" (run) or "get down and beat your face" (do push-ups). I executed the commands intuitively. One big noise was filling my head. We were running somewhere, stopping, making right and left turns, half-turns, and doing push-ups. I saw countless unfamiliar buildings, barracks, streets, and a multitude of soldiers everywhere. Finally, we ended up in our platoon's barracks. It was a one-story, long building divided by a wall in the middle into two sections: one for females and the other for males. We arrived in front of the barrack in formation where our drill sergeants introduced themselves. The male's name was Staff Sergeant Cambren (I called him "Camby"). The female was a Staff Sergeant Bloomington (I called her "Bloo"). Hundreds of push-ups later, we run into our barracks, and on command, we started rearranging the "footlockers" (big wooden, black-painted chests situated in pairs on top of each other in front of every bunk bed): top one went on the floor, while the bottom one went on top. Ultimately, everyone was assigned to a bed and a footlocker. I got the first top bunk in front of the doorway. Despite the initial search upon our arrival at the base this morning, Bloo quickly searched again our black bags for illegal items, and then she ordered us to leave all of our personal belongings in our footlockers and lock them using the locks distributed to us earlier. This operation took maybe a couple of minutes and before I knew it, we were bursting out of the barrack into a formation. This time, we formed up in four rows (squads). During the next couple of hours, we learned how to stand at attention or "at ease" properly, how to march in a column formation and how to turn while marching or change directions of the march as a column. It was a lot of fun when we were making mistakes and our drill sergeants had to try very hard not to laugh. One time we even had a contest on who can do more push-ups. Both instructors dropped to the ground in front of our platoon, and we all started "pushing." Obviously, we were unable to keep up with them and we lost the contest.

* * *

Around noon, it was time for lunch. Platoon by platoon, we formed a single-file line and waited our turn to grab a plastic tray with four compartments for food. In the line, we had to assume the "at ease" position, with our arms crossed on the back and feet twelve inches apart, straight as a stick. When the line was moving, we had to snap to attention, make one step forward with our right foot, and assume the "at ease" position again. To relax a little and stop thinking frantically "what's next," I decided to concentrate exclusively on perfecting my movement in the line. Since it was rather a pleasant exercise, I enjoyed the moment very much because it reminded me of a dance routine. Suddenly, after I just executed my "one step forward" routine, I heard a familiar screechy sound behind my left shoulder:

"Perfect! That's how it should be done. Finally, someone has learned something here!" I recognized the scratchy first sergeant's voice.

I stood there like a rock, not sure if he was talking to me. Even if he was, I was not supposed to move in this position. He walked up a step, trying to see my face.

"Ah! That's my favorite private!" He sounded relieved and not surprised. "I remember you from the auditorium."

Drill Sergeant Bloo noticed him talking to me, so she approached him curiously. I kept repeating my routine as the line proceeded. The first sergeant and Bloo watched me for a couple of seconds silently. I could hear the first sergeant saying to Bloo, "See, that's my favorite private. She knows what she's doing. Is she in your platoon?"

"Yes, she is mine." I discerned a touch of pride in her voice.

Eventually, I got through the lunch, and while we were running around in platoons back and forth, in and out of the buildings, marching, and pushing, the ever-dynamic in-processing continued. The equipment issue was one of the more important activities of the day. In minutes, we would cease to be civilians. We were all gathered in a large gym with its gigantic door wide open. Platoon by platoon, we were given a military green duffle bag with a very basic army uniform set: camouflage trousers, jacket, two brown T-shirts, some black wool knee-high socks, a patrol cap, a black web belt with a buckle, and cold weather jacket. We were also issued a green plastic water canteen and a "Smart Book," a pamphlet with basic soldier information (drills and ceremonies, general orders, wearing of the uniform, etc.). Finally, it was time for the army boots. Here I wasn't so lucky. Since they didn't have size 6, I had to grab size 8 and wait for the better times. I was happy to get my first real "army issue" uniform. Since the sizes were assigned rather arbitrarily, we marched all to our barracks, where we exchanged pieces of uniform among ourselves. I was tired and sweaty, so trying on the uniform seemed impossible. Someone gave me the trousers, I gave someone my patrol cap (too big for me), then I exchanged the trousers with another female. Drill Sergeant Bloo was rushing us, constantly screaming to hurry up and finish that "fashion show" finally. I was quite impressed by her professional demeanor, overall appearance, and great memory. She already remembered all females' last names in our platoon. She had, however, a little difficulty with mine:

"Private, what's your name again? 'Ra-kow-sky'?" She tried to pronounce it without success. "Ah, it's too difficult to remember. Is it okay if I call you 'SKI'?" She gave up.

"That's perfect, drill sergeant," I replied quickly, before she could change her mind and decide to call me something else.

"All right then, get down and give me fifteen push-ups, SKI!" she ordered with a big smile. "I'm glad you like your new name."

After we finished fitting our uniforms, Sergeant Bloo pulled out her pocketknife and cut our belts to fit snugly into the metal buckles. Once all our civilian clothes were locked up in the footlockers, we were exploding outside again, trying to put on our caps and setting up a proper platoon formation at the same time.

* * *

For now, everything was about speed, accuracy, and focus. That's why we spent the rest of the day practicing new drills and learning new commands (most of which I wasn't even able to pronounce). We had to execute everything on time and precisely, the drill sergeants would immediately punish any sloppiness with push-ups. I had to get used to these fast pace and ever-changing activities. We were continuously marching through the base to the point when some of the routes and buildings started to look familiar. My canteen full of water kept sticking out of my right cargo pocket, my "Smart Book" from the left one. I didn't think I looked sloppy though, which was to me an achievement considering how uncomfortable I felt in my oversized uniform. But I knew it was a temporary setback and eventually I would be issued the correct size uniform and gear in basic training. This here was just an appetizer.

Every time the first sergeant passed by our platoon, he recognized me with his benchmark call: "Yeah! That's my favorite private, right there, in the fourth squad!"

I was so concentrated on trying not to mess up the flow of the march that I couldn't pay attention to anything else but marching. "Column right, column left, left step, left flank, counter column." As the day was going by, all these commands slowly started to have some meaning. We were all serious. Our faces looked like carved sculptures, full of concentration. I didn't want to breathe too heavily or blink an eye at the wrong moment (and any moment could be classified as wrong), just tried to be a machine.

Eventually, we caught a break in marching and drilling. Our platoon stopped in the middle of a green area under a large solitary tree. Its old branches were spreading widely over us, the new soldiers of the United States Army. The afternoon October sun was gently embracing our faces while we were studying our "Smart Books." We had to learn and memorize the "Soldier's Creed."

I opened the first page of my book and started reading: "I am an American Soldier. I am a member of the United States Army—a protector of the greatest nation on earth." A deep chill overwhelmed my body as I continued: "I will be loyal to those under whom I serve. I am doing my share to keep alive the principles of freedom for which my country stands."

Suddenly, everything around us appeared to calm down. There were no more drill sergeants shouting or soldiers marching. It seemed like the entire world stopped for a moment and there was nothing else, but our lone platoon immersed in the prayer-like lecture, the late afternoon birds singing, and the gigantic peaceful tree.

"I am proud of my country and its flag. I will try to make the people of this nation proud of the service I represent, for I am an American Soldier." The words at the bottom of the page resonated with me. I was proud to be a soldier, and I wanted people around me to be proud of me as well.

* * *

After twilight, we marched to the nearby building where we learned how to prepare the MRE (Meal Ready to Eat). It was a small brown plastic bag whose content included a main course of starch; mystery "meat," crackers; a cheese, peanut butter, or jelly spread; a dessert or snack; powdered beverage mix; an accessory packet; a plastic spoon; and a flameless ration heater (FRH). The FRH was a pouch with finely powdered magnesium metal, alloyed with a small amount of iron and table salt. To activate the heater, we had to add to it a little water. Within seconds, the flameless heater reached the boiling point and started bubbling and steaming. To heat the meal, we simply inserted the heater and the MRE pouch back into the slim carton box that the pouch came in. Amazed, I watched this express miniature kitchen work its miracle in front of me. Ten minutes later, I enjoyed my first military version of "beef and mushroom" dinner. I don't remember the taste, but at this point in the day, I didn't care what I was eating.

Before we headed back to the barracks, we did more marching and practiced more drills. Later this evening, we learned how to make the bunk beds and established a schedule for the nightly "fire guard." Each shift was one hour. Eventually, we went to bed. I wasn't able to sleep, however. This first day of training was longer than I expected, exhausting, and very stressful. Right before 1:00 a.m. I woke up my "battle buddy," a girl assigned to me for guard duty. We threw on our uniforms and settled by both entrance doors on the opposite sides of the building. Since one hour seemed like enough time to catch up with the important things, I started scribbling some notes to transfer later into my journal. My "buddy" took care of her makeup.

"What are you doing?" I couldn't believe what I saw.

"What? I'm fixing my makeup because tomorrow I won't have time for this. I have to look good."

"Of course..." That was about all I could say at this moment.

Both of us were struggling with our activities since the lights were out and we could only use our red-lens flashlights. An hour later, we woke up the next pair of guards and went to bed. I still wasn't able to fall asleep. My brain was racing, trying to remember everything that had happened during the last fourteen hours, confusing the present with the past. I tried to think about something pleasant, relive some events from the past, which that night seemed so distant. I wasn't sure anymore if I would be able to recall them.

I stared at the gray ceiling for a while, thinking about what was happening around me and within me. Prebasic training was a new chapter where, for the first time, I was wearing a real uniform and combat boots and was carrying around a real rifle.

*   *   *

I first met Chris in Warsaw, while reinventing myself after I finished the National Ballet School in Warsaw in 1988. To my ballet career, I added the studies of French philology at the University of Warsaw. I wanted to be an expert in French and linguistics.

My knowledge of French was good because I had practiced grammar and writing while in ballet school, in preparation for entrance exams to the university. My classmates, however, had a considerable advantage over me. Most of them came from high schools where the curriculum was focused on French. In addition, many of them had parents working for the French embassy in Warsaw or other French institutions, which allowed them to travel to France on a regular basis. Without this experience, in class, I felt like an underdog. My biggest issue was the spoken language. Since I hadn't had many opportunities to converse in French, I was shy and anxious about speaking and always avoided it because it was causing stress for me.

To my ballet career, I added the studies of French philology at the University of Warsaw.

The conversation in class revolved around a light subject about making holiday cookies.

"In my family, the tradition is that Grandma Elise bakes all the cookies," someone said without confidence.

"We buy French pastries from "Tête-à-tête" on Marszałkowska Street…" another quiet voice admitted.

"Anyone bakes traditional Polish cookies, like kołaczki or faworki? Would you like to share any recipes?"

When this question was posed to everyone, there was silence. Apparently, at least at the beginning, most of the people were still shy and only two or three students had something relevant to say. I was sitting quietly in the corner, hoping that I wouldn't have to speak. My eyes, however, were on my new French professor. The positive, kind aura around this person intrigued me.

Our new professor Chris wasn't exactly happy with the lack of engagement by most of the students and decided to ask each student one by one. This way, everyone had an equal chance to shine. But my heart dropped. I didn't want to shine because I knew that my spoken French was leaving a lot to be desired. However, I was forced by the situation to muster all my courage and speak out.

When my turn finally came, I was shivering from anxiety, my palms sweating. I tried to say something about putting some fruit inside a cookie and baking it in the oven:

"*On doit placer un fruit en dedans du biscuit et faire le cuire au four…*"

"*En dedans*—it's rather a term from the ballet domain," Chris interjected. "For example, you can say *a pirouette en dedans.*"

I was dumbfounded. When I realized that Chris knew the technical aspects of ballet, my heart grew, and I felt an instant connection with my new French professor. I didn't even hear Chris explain how to build this sentence correctly. All I heard was this amazing kind voice, and all I saw was the handsome figure in front of me in a perfectly tailored blue navy suit. At this point, I was completely enchanted, and more butterflies were dancing in my stomach for the rest of the instruction. I realized that suddenly I was an infatuated schoolgirl, and I blushed profusely, hiding behind my notebook.

* * *

Suddenly, I heard wild noises and all the doors opening in the barracks. It was time to get up and start a brand-new day. In one second, the University of Warsaw disappeared.

This morning was about learning the concept of military reward versus punishment. Doing push-ups and sit-ups for no apparent reason was nothing new. This time, however, doing push-ups was introduced as a form of reward. The training was about taking apart and putting together our M16 rifles. At the end of the class, we had a competition, with each team performing both operations. The fastest would win, and the prize was doing only ten push-ups. The second and third place would do twenty and thirty, respectively. All the rest were doing forty. My team was second, which in this case wasn't a terrible deal. Although push-ups were normally a corrective action (a punishment) having to perform "only" twenty instead of forty did seem like a reward after all. So we were pushing, happy that we won second place instead of the last one.

The prebasic training was slowly ending. I learned that after each such training on the military bases, the entire field had to be cleaned and left the way it was at the beginning of the training. It made perfect sense. And so the last few hours were designated for cleaning the training area and the barracks, including rearranging the footlockers again, collecting the keys, cleaning latrines, and cleaning the grass. Finally, we formed up in the small area by the barracks, facing the midday sun. We had to "drop" the last time for some "goodbye" push-ups. To my surprise, there was even a final ceremony during which the National Anthem was played by the cassette player while we stood proudly at attention. We all received a diploma certifying the "Successful Completion of Pre-Basic Training." And just like that, suddenly everything was over. It felt good to be appreciated, even for this minuscule event. The army was about celebrating even the smallest achievements. I guessed it was to maintain high troops' morale and to keep the new soldiers motivated and excited. Not only was I excited, but I felt invigorated and young at heart.

I found myself confused by mixed feelings: the regret that something was over, the enormous joy, a sense of a true accomplishment, and most of all the feeling of being a soldier. I stood there alone on the green field and watched the small groups of recruits leaving our training area with their recruiters in the government vans. The time stopped for a brief moment: the drill sergeants left, noise disappeared—it was time to go home, except, where was my "home" if I felt like my heart belonged here, in the field, in the barracks?

Finally, the familiar government van pulled over and took our small group back to the North Riverside Armory. By the time we arrived there, twilight was slowly fighting off the scraps of daylight. Soon, I recognized the main gate and the parking lot, which now seemed like such a distant memory. In the rain, I noticed Alec waiting for me in front of the building, soaking wet and so proud.

This brief chapter of my military career was a wake-up call. In a good way. I had my first taste of a new life and I liked it. After this experience, I could imagine myself taking on a new challenge. I knew that one of the biggest obstacles would be my English. During this short weekend, my brain was overloaded with new terminology and I felt like a mute, unable to utter a word. For now, I was blindly and instinctively following the commands, like a well-trained circus animal. But I had to trust the system and believe that one day I would find my language and my new identity.

PART III

BASIC TRAINING:
BECOMING A SOLDIER

CHAPTER 3

BROKEN INTO PIECES

By the end of November, I did a lot of studying before my shipment to basic training: I knew more military terminology and was familiar with the organization of the army. I had a much better idea about the expectations of new recruits and what the basic training was all about. The more time I spent at the library reading about the military life, the more eager and ready I was to meet the challenge. The pressure to learn fast was enormous.

Since mid-December, the entire Chicago area was deeply submerged in a thick layer of snow. Our dog Sznurek (a five-pound Yorkshire terrier) was so small I had to dig some routes in the backyard so he could run around without sinking in the snow. It was already the second day of January 2001, my last day before leaving Alec, Sznurek, and our house for the long nine months. Late afternoon, when Alec was still at work, I went outside to pick up the garbage cans standing by the curb. I knew that in South Carolina I would miss those everyday activities around the house. I loved so much being here with Alec, making a fire in the backyard during the summer, or in the winter watching Alec blowing the snow after the snowstorm to clean the driveway. Those days, as I watched him from the kitchen pushing the snow blower, he would purposely direct the stream into the window to create a thick white cover on the glass, trying to scare me. Then I would jump outside laughing and throwing the snowballs at him—always missing. The next day we would both watch the snow melting on the window in the morning sun and then freezing again in the evening. Now I stood in front of the house, trying to remember every single detail, as I wanted to take with me the most precise image of my world here and now. It looked so unreal, like a miniature castle from a fairy tale. Last summer, Alec and I painted the house, the patio, and the fence with three shades of purple and pistachio green. We had planted bushes, roses, and all kinds of blue, white, and purple flowers, and Alec created a little vegetable garden—a perfect feasting place for all the neighborhood rodents. On the back, by the fence, a combination of wild blackberry, raspberry, and gooseberry shrubs just planted themselves. While I was going through these fond memories of these so-recent precious moments, I started missing our magical world.

It was time to say goodbye to my next spring, summer, and fall in Chicago. I took one last good look at the purple house as it was getting ready for the late afternoon nap, all wrapped up in a snowy glittering cover. Through the front windows, I could clearly see our Christmas tree and the colorful shades of the Christmas lights. Later that evening, Alec promised me to keep the tree decorated until my return. I wanted to preserve that moment and this last Christmas before my long absence. This would give me the feeling that I never left home.

It was also time to say goodbye to Alec's family. Since his father was at that time in Florida and his sister was out of town, we invited his mother to give her the news. She wasn't aware yet that I had joined the army. We were afraid that we would face her vehement opposition to the idea that I would be gone from Northbrook for several long months. We decided to keep our low profile until the last moment, to avoid unpleasant confrontations or judgment.

"I joined the army and tomorrow I will go to basic training in South Carolina." I tried to make my voice sound as neutral as possible. "I will be gone for several months."

"I wish for you to break your neck," Alec's mother replied, completely caught off guard.

My heart was cramping from shock, because so far we had a decent relationship. I always tried to be nice to her and not to show up as a threat of any sort. We liked each other to a certain extent, I would say. However, Alec's mother didn't exactly understand me, it was obvious to me that she simply didn't know me much. In addition, I wasn't long enough in Alec's life to develop any bond with his family. After hearing her words, which to me sounded like a curse, I was asking myself if she really meant that, but I didn't have the courage to ask her. Even though Alec took my side and ended the conversation, then promptly cut short his mother's visit, my mind was going crazy with questions. What did she really want from me? I wondered. I instantly imagined myself gravely injured, coming home from basic training, defeated. It dawned on me that I could indeed die during training. Should I really go to Fort Jackson to die? Was it even possible to actually die during basic training? I was hoping not, but I knew that serious accidents could happen sometimes.

While all these thoughts were swarming in my mind like enraged wasps, I was certain of one thing. I wasn't going to change my mind because of the risk of dying in some accident. I wasn't about to change my mind just because someone wished badly for me. I wasn't about to change my mind just to lead a comfortable life at home as a housewife, with no goals or dreams of my own.

* * *

The next day, Alec drove me to the MEPS station, where I enlisted a few weeks ago. As usual, it was still dark outside. He waited then with me at the station until 6:00 a.m. when the pre-shipment in-processing began and he couldn't stay there any longer. We exchanged a quick casual kiss without making a scene. I wanted to be strong and not think about how much I would miss him. About twelve hours later, I was a passenger on a military white bus taking me to the O'Hare airport in Chicago. From that point on, everything started happening really fast.

Since I left Chicago, I didn't see any daylight, as I was spending endless hours on airplanes, airports, and military lounges. At some point, I noticed that I was becoming a part of a continuously expanding group of recruits flying into Columbus, South Carolina, from all over the country. In the middle of the night, another white bus took me from the airport on the endless ride to the base.

We finally arrived at Fort Jackson, the U.S. Army's largest Basic Combat Training Center. At the entrance there was a statue of Andrew Jackson, U.S. President from Tennessee. Behind the statue, a gigantic banner was displayed, 'Victory Starts Here', the motto of TRADOC's (Training and Doctrine Command).

We stopped in front of the reception building. Soon, I was one of several hundreds of recruits—all tired, sleepy, and confused - sitting on the floor, in rows, with their legs crossed. It has been more than twenty-four-hours already since I had any sleep, and there was not much hope of getting any rest for at least another forty-eight hours. I had heard before that the first three days and nights, the sergeants would keep us awake at any cost. Soon we received our PT (physical training) uniforms in a green laundry bag, some additional paperwork, and shots. They also took our blood and urine samples to check for diseases. We also had our first official army photos taken. People were falling asleep or fainting, which aggravated the sergeants tremendously. Some recruits got famous for falling down every couple of hours and eventually almost everyone knew they were faking just to get out of the reception battalion. This was the beginning of phase 0 of basic training. Since we were not allowed to use our enlistment ranks, our uniforms were sterile (no rank insignias). I was a private again.

Eventually, it didn't matter what day it was or how many nights had passed because they all seemed the same. I tried to keep myself busy to avoid unnecessary stress and, most of all, taking anything personally. I used every opportunity to write my notes and letters to Alec, as it kept me calm and focused.

* * *

"Dear Alec,

I can't believe I just heard your real voice on the phone. Our sergeants gave us a chance to call the families to let them know we were all right. Even those three minutes of our conversation were like a blessing. I feel so much better. Since I haven't slept for the last seventy-two hours and I have to stay awake no matter what, I have trained myself to disconnect my mind from Fort Jackson and let it fly! I stand in formation with my eyes open and it looks like I'm here, but my heart and all my thoughts are with you in Northbrook. Once, I even saw you next to me so close that I thought I could touch you. You came home from work; I was holding Sznurek in my arms, and he was squeaking gently, happy to see you. This vision was so realistic, I almost started talking to you...

Yesterday we went to the chapel on base—I needed some distraction from the tedious in-processing. It was supposed to be the "blessing" before the basic, a preparation for difficult and stressful situations, tough daily routines, and overall mental and physical struggle. A golden Latin inscription on the back of the stage read "Pro deo et patria" ("for God and country"), which gave me the sense of consolation that I am now part of something bigger than me. During this powerful ceremony, I thought I was going to war, not to training.

Our platoon sergeant was in a bad mood tonight. So in order to avoid her, I volunteered to give my blood to the Red Cross. For some reason, my veins were very thin and the blood thick, so it took me a good couple of hours to get through the process. I ended up in the last small group of donors and we barely missed the dinner. As we were marching back to the barrack, we noticed from a distance a lot of commotion and we heard our platoon sergeant screaming her lungs out. It was again about some girl that kept fainting every few minutes and our sergeant prohibited anyone from touching or moving her. Apparently, there was a big verbal fight over it in the ranks and at some point, it got physical. It is obvious that the tensions are growing. Some people just don't want to be here and will use any means to get out.

I completely lost touch with reality… I know that you and Sznurek are so far away from here, but there is no single moment that I don't think of you. Here, I'm in a totally different world: the days pass by one after another exactly the same: wake-up call, formation, eating time, formation, processing, formation, eating, formation, sleep time, and fire guard at night. We are allowed to do only what we are told, no questions asked, and no comments. It doesn't bother me that much because I'm still able to write to you whenever I get a chance. Everything I knew and everything I cherished the most—you, home, our friends—it all seems so distant. I'm not sure anymore if the things happening here are reality or just a dream. The word "January" doesn't mean anything to me. The weather is "military": wind or rain doesn't interrupt our daily routine. Soon, we will have to pass our diagnostic physical fitness test to qualify for shipment from the reception battalion to basic training. I heard that sometimes soldiers are stuck here for three or more weeks if they are not fit.

On the last day at the reception battalion, we finally received our "dog tags" and finalized the paperwork and overall in-processing. It was also a very important day because we were officially ready to be shipped to basic training. For this occasion, we were given an opportunity to participate in a surprisingly heartwarming "good luck" ceremony before our departure. I saw everything from the front row of our giant formation: all highly decorated dignitaries, the reception battalion commander, and the chaplain.

It was a big production that reminded me of spectacles at the Great Opera in Warsaw in the 1980s. Everything started with posting the U.S. flag along with other flags of all the units from the battalion. Then a military band with the most wonderful brass section played the national anthem. At the sound of it, I was already tearing up, for this song was always pulling at my heart. Especially when played by a military band. There was something hopeful in it, like an announcement of a better life so hard fought for by the braves who came before me. After a series of solemn speeches from which I could understand very little, there was a history of the U.S. Army presented by soldiers. They would enter the ceremony stage in their historical uniforms, symbolizing all the wars in which the U.S. had participated. In the end, the orchestra sounded again and this time the entire battalion was singing the Army Song: "March along, sing our song with the Army of the free... we're the Army and proud of our name!... The Army's on its way. Count off the cadence loud and strong: For where'er we go, you will always know that the Army goes rolling along." While I was standing at attention, hopelessly trying to join the singing crowd without knowing the lyrics, I wasn't able to hide my tears of powerful inspiration: they were flowing slowly down my cheeks to disappear on my brown T-shirt under my uniform. At this moment, I knew that I needed to memorize this song not just because it was a requirement, but also because I wanted to sing along next time the opportunity came.

* * *

The last twelve hours of the reception battalion went by like a blink of an eye. During my six days spent at the reception battalion, Phase 0 of basic training, I'd gotten used to a certain routine and the order of the day, which provided some comfort. Suddenly, everything had changed. We had to leave our barracks and got reassigned to a building across the quad. We also had to pack our duffle bags and all the uniforms which were issued earlier. All the duffels were stenciled with our last names and the last four digits of our social security numbers the night before and left outside, stocked up in the long parallel rows. I said my quick goodbyes to the friends from the "reception" because I didn't know in which platoon I was going to end up with, and if I would see any familiar faces there. It wasn't easy since I already liked a couple of them. In all this chaos of packing and relocating, I almost forgot my journal at my "old" barrack. After all, I ended up with one of the girls from the "reception" in a third platoon of the D ("Delta") Company, 2-13 Infantry Regiment. The name of my new unit was as new to me as everything else that night. I felt suddenly uprooted and lonely, so after getting ready for bed, I started writing my notes feverously to capture everything I saw and felt so far. Most of all, writing was a perfect antidote for my stress resulting from yet another disconnection. At some point, I felt like a walking recording device. Even when I was on the move and couldn't openly write, I was recording in my head everything that was happening around me, scene after scene, people, voices, sounds, and smells. In my mind, I was taking notes of various images: long rows of duffle bags being loaded into military trucks, officers, and enlisted personnel walking between endless rows of soon-to-be soldiers, "shake downs" and the tension. I was genuinely scared, as if taking a breath or blinking an eye were a crime. I was executing commands like in a spell. The basic training was about to show us what we were made of. We were about to, as drill sergeants would often put it, be "broken down and rebuilt stronger than ever..."

We also had our first official army photos taken.

I wasn't sure if I wanted to be broken down, but I guessed this was the only way to get through the program. It was unavoidable to experience the overwhelming disintegration of myself, the lingering loss of my current being, to live through parts of me, watching them being stripped piece by piece to reveal my core. What would be left of me, the fragile ballerina, after the basic training? If anything, who would I become?

CHAPTER 4

ACCEPTING THE STATUS QUO

That afternoon of January 11, it was time for my platoon to get on the white bus. The moment we filled up the vehicle, our new drill sergeant got in, closed the door behind him, and started screeching: "You are mine now! No talking, no laughing, no thinking. You will listen and do what I say. And don't let me catch you looking through those windows. Put your faces down and start praying."

Just like in the movies, I thought. With my forehead pressed against the duffle bag sitting on my knees, I was hugging it tightly, as if it was the closest companion on the road to becoming a true soldier. I wanted to be there and run away at the same time. Although I wouldn't qualify as a religious person, I actually started praying. I needed to calm down before my biggest performance yet. So far I still had fairly minimal experience with the army life. Prebasic training in my home state was just the first taste of it, and I was extremely happy that I could be part of it. It had introduced me to some basic concepts of soldiering, like military drills and courtesies, which played a major role in the army. The reception battalion was a week of more exposure to the military life, but it was more about paperwork and general in-processing activities. From this experience, I've learned about the concept of "hurry up and wait", where we had to rush into formations just to wait for instructions either standing outside as platoons or waiting in lines in the buildings while each individual's paperwork was being processed. Now, I was about to start a full nine-week training cycle. I needed to brace for a powerful impact this would have on my mental and physical health. Would I be able to endure the physical demands of this course? How would I hold mentally, knowing that all these young people around me were more physically capable than I was? Most importantly, I knew that the pace would be fast and quickly learning the military terminology and all technicalities of our daily routines were the key to survival in this environment. On the bus, I prayed that I was ready for this challenge.

We drove around the base for a while and by the time we got to our new home; it was getting dark. Again, I found myself running out of the bus in a new crowd of young people with nothing to hang on to. My mind was ready to explode from trying to understand and follow all new commands and military jargon. They assigned us temporarily to a barrack for one night until the final breakdown into platoons. At least we had a chance to call home and speak for thirty seconds, just to say that we arrived at basic training okay. The upcoming nine weeks of training were divided into three consecutive three-week phases: red, white, and blue. Now, phase I of basic training (red) officially started. Therefore, our initial platoon flag was red.

* * *

"Dear Alec,

Finally, my dream is coming true! I officially started my Basic Combat Training. My company's nickname is "Delta Dogs" and my platoon's "Mad Dogs." Our barracks are big and beautiful, and there is plenty of military stuff all over. We have two new Drill Sergeants: DS Reaves and DS Girard. We were told that the first week of training we would spend mostly in the classroom learning military policies, army values, history, etc. Military drills and commands are something we are quickly getting familiar with.

"Yesterday, I had my first official PT (physical training) test. I was so anxious the night before, worrying that I will not make the two-mile run that I wasn't able to sleep. You know that I couldn't let myself 'fall out.' The first five laps on the field were very tough; the surface was sandy and wet after last night's rain. When it got extremely difficult to keep running, I was thinking about you, and how I was training a few months ago, running on Techny and Pfingsten Roads in our neighborhood. I remembered dreaming about this moment and trying to picture it in my head: how would it feel to run on the military track… And finally, here I am, living my dream."

* * *

Two days after arrival at basic training, we received all the field gear necessary for our future adventures: a rucksack (military backpack) with the frame, LBE (load-bearing equipment—kind of heavy-duty web belt with buckles), water canteens, ammunition carriers, first-aid kits, Kevlar helmets, sleeping bag, shelter-half, poncho, NBC (nuclear-biological-chemical) protective uniform, pro-mask (for teargas protection), poly-pros (sort sweatshirt and sweatpants for cold weather), and E-tool (entrenching tool—a small folding shovel).

That day, they assigned each of us a "battle buddy"—a soldier companion of the same gender to watch for one another. I wasn't so convinced that my new battle buddy—Carla—would be able to watch out for herself, not to mention for me. She was a seventeen-year-old who just got her GED and, for the first time in her life, left her small hometown somewhere in Georgia. She had no idea what it meant to belong to an organization, follow instructions, or simply pay attention. She wasn't able to stand or sit still and had her own "way of doing" things. I was trying very hard not to pay attention to her attitude or loud, pretentious voice as long as it was possible. Unfortunately, at the same time, I realized that I was responsible for her well-being, just like she was for mine.

We were all privates again regardless of our official enlistment rank. In my notebook entitled PVT Rakowski, 3rd PLT, D Co 2-13 Inf. Reg., I wrote: "Basic training is about forgiveness and the truth." It was the time to forgive myself for who I was up to this point and face the truth—that change is inevitable. It was also about forgiving those who did me wrong or had cursed me in the past and those who would do me wrong in the future. In order to achieve success, it was necessary to forget the past and concentrate on the present. It was also time to verify the truth about my own limits—both physical and mental. It seemed to me that I'd been fighting my limitations for most of my life.

* * *

Especially challenging in the past were my intellectual obstacles while learning French. That one time in February 1989, I'd experienced them firsthand with Chris as my French professor. It was the beginning of my second year of French studies at the University of Warsaw. Our professor was expected in our classroom. I already knew that Chris was a very demanding subject matter expert, with a double master's degree and a PhD, and a tough grader. I quickly realized that the latter was all true. The presence of Chris in front of the class was paralyzing me from day one. For almost a year, I was in the classroom like a first grader, unable to say a word, enchanted by this amazing person speaking the most beautiful French I'd ever heard. Eventually, at the end of the semester, I was approached by Chris.

"Miss Joanna, unfortunately, we will have to meet for additional consultation before I can give you a passing grade for the semester. I never hear you speaking in the class. I would like you to prepare a short paper about the subject of your choice and make an oral presentation in my office next week." Although I didn't expect to be successful this semester, my heart dropped. Being singled out like this immediately made me feel like I wanted the earth to split under me and swallow me whole. Embarrassed would be an understatement.

However, I got to work as soon as I could and selected the subject of the big bang theory. Since I wasn't that great in relating the cookie-baking process before, I figured that nuclear physics would be a more exciting opportunity to learn something new and significant. I prepared my notes thoroughly and showed up in Chris's office.

The office was tiny. It was getting dark outside. The dimmed light from the stylish table lamp was giving a vibe of intimacy. With my hands trembling, I pulled out my notes and started talking about how the present universe was created as a result of a massive explosion. This explosion generated the majority of matter and the complex physical laws governing the continuously expanding cosmos.

I talked about what happened after the initial expansion of the universe, that the new period had begun… and I couldn't remember its name, even in Polish, let alone in French.

"The Big Bang nucleosynthesis period," said Chris.

In shock, I blushed and looked Chris deep in the eyes. I felt more connection between us than I ever felt before. "What else do you know?"

I asked in my head. My heart was already pounding with delight when I realized that this was the first time I was in the room with Chris all alone.

* * *

Army respected soldiers' needs for religious services. Being in church was our refuge, as drill sergeants could not "touch us" there. We could relax and stop thinking about drills, orders, and commands. When, on the first Sunday of basic training, our drill sergeant announced a trip to the church for a Sunday mass, I immediately took the opportunity to leave the barracks. In groups of fewer than ten, we jumped on the backs of Humvees and held on to anything possible to avoid falling out of them when drill sergeants drove on the rough roads. It was a magnificent, sunny morning when we got dropped off on the hill in front of a little church in the middle of nowhere. That Sunday, I volunteered to join the church's choir. During the mass, every time I was standing up to sing to the sounds of an out-of-tune old church piano, the loneliness and struggle of basic training were diminishing. Finally, I had something to hang on to.

The first week of basic training went fast because we were preparing for combat activities, which was huge. We learned how to fight with the bayonet, how to put together our shelter for the night out and how to prepare a "tankers roll" (slipping pad and shelter half rolled together with the shelter stakes inside, bound with the rope). All this was to prepare us for our ultimate experience: the "Victory Forge." At this time however, I didn't know much about this last event, and I had to concentrate on basic survival: how to get through the day when every night I had to pull some sort of duty, like fire guard at the barracks, kitchen patrol (kitchen-cleaning duty and serving meals), or CQ (company quarters, sitting at the company front desk) duty. My other goal was to improve my physical condition and achieve a level where I could blend in with those who were ten to fourteen years younger than me. That's why every night before going to bed, I practiced my sit-ups and push-ups. Fortunately, even though my English wasn't as good as my buddy Carla's, I noticed that I had less and less difficulty understanding and following the commands.

* * *

Very quickly I got used to the early morning wake-up and quite often I would get ready before the reveille played loudly from the tape through our barracks speakers, fully awake and alert. Mondays, Wednesdays, and Fridays, we always ran. Other days, we exercised our muscle strength on the nearby field in the wooded area. Those cold mornings regardless of the weather, always in deep darkness, we would march to our exercise area singing cadences (military songs), and before sunrise, we would come back to our barracks to continue our day. We were constantly on the move like a massive volcano lava of green, brown, and black.

* * *

A special event to which I looked forward to, but not without a certain amount of fear, marked the end of the first full week of basic. It was a Victory Tower, a structure composed of several obstacles combined in the form of a sixty-foot-high wooden tower. Each obstacle was called a "station" and was supervised by two drill sergeants. They would demonstrate how to negotiate the obstacle and supervise us for safety reasons. Just standing in front of this monstrous configuration of wood, ropes, and nets was intimidating.

It was still dark when our long day at the Victory Tower began. The entire Delta Company was standing in formation in a small area covered with white gravel. The company commander and the first sergeant gave us a brief description of the exercise and platoon by platoon, we were dispersed over to the different stations.

"Who is afraid of heights?" Drill Sergeant Reaves asked our platoon right before we started. Half of the people raised their hands, probably hoping that there was their chance to skip the event. I had a feeling that it was a trick question.

"Great!" His reply was quick. There would be no more questions. "Now is a good time to get rid of these fears!" I wouldn't admit openly to my fear. But deep down, I would rather be doing something closer to the ground. But now, all I could do was to take a deep breath and go with the flow. Somehow I knew that the Victory Tower was just the beginning and there would be more frightening obstacle courses in the near future.

Everything started at the ground level, as a warm-up activity before climbing and rappelling. First, we were jumping on the rope over a small sandpit, which was replaced later with a several-feet-deep opening reminiscent of an abyss. For the first time, I realized how tough and painful it was to hold on to the rope and to throw my body at the end of the pit. With serious doubts, I moved to the next obstacle, a three-rope "bridge": two ropes at the shoulder level and one lower, to walk on. The trick was to maintain the balance by stretching the ropes as much as possible away from the body and try not to think about shaking. I walked through the bridge trembling, far from being in a vertical position, but it didn't matter. I just had to cross without falling into the net below. It seemed like this bridge was miles long. After the bridge, I crawled on my knees to the middle of the tower. Here the next station caught me by surprise: jumping on the rope over the "abyss." My heart stopped for a couple of seconds, but there was no other choice. A drill sergeant across swung the rope toward me and barked: "Jump, soldier!" In a split second I grabbed it and without thinking, farther jumped over. "I can't believe I just did this," I thought to myself in deep disbelief. There was no time to acknowledge this minor victory because the soldiers behind me were done with the rope, so I had to move forward. I climbed more wooden stairs to find myself on top of the tower where we were crawling on our knees again (there were no safety barriers around!). On the edge, I noticed Drill Sergeant Girard, my drill sergeant, and felt an immense relief, but this did not change anything. This time I was climbing down the gigantic cargo net, which I saw many times before in the photographs and in the movies! This wasn't a movie, however. My fear was as true as it could be.

"Victory Tower" Just standing in front of this monstrous configuration of wood, ropes, and nets was intimidating.

"Just don't look down. Keep your head up. Hold the net tight and take your time. The net ends eight feet above the ground. When you reach it, let go and jump on the mattresses, then roll out." Drill sergeant Girard recited the instructions like a recording.

Drill Sergeant Girard's calming voice and his gentle French accent sounded like music. Suddenly I wasn't so afraid anymore, just chilled to the bone and stiff. I followed his directions as if they carried a magic power to assure success. Toward the bottom, I could barely feel my hands from pain and cold. After the last jump, touching the ground was the most liberating feeling of the time being.

The last two obstacles were rappelling towers: a small practice one (just over ten feet high) and the actual tower (a sixty-footer). By the time I was tying up my "Swiss knot," it was already raining. The knot was forming a sort of harness around my thighs and stomach. On the front, I was connected with a hook and rope to the top of the tower. I hoped the knot would be strong enough to hold me hanging without undoing itself for any reason. While getting ready to rappel, I met a drill sergeant who was famous for being very easily irritated. He told me how to position myself before jumping down on the rope and started yelling impatiently: "The small of your back! Put your right hand on the small of your back!" He was steaming and spitting on my face. "The small of your back, soldier!" I had no clue what he meant, and my puzzled face wasn't helping either of us. Finally, a tall fellow waiting his turn in the line behind me screamed: "It's in the middle of your lower back, SKI!" It was Private Lewis who saved my day, realizing that I didn't understand the expression of the drill sergeant. I was really grateful.

Soon, I was in line for my last obstacle of the day: the great victory tower's rappelling wall. First, I had to roll over the giant airbags on the ground toward the "ladder." Its first part was simply a flat, almost-vertical wall with wooden planks mounted every couple of feet. Holding on to the rope with knots mounted in the middle section, I climbed the first twenty feet. After that, it was just a "regular" ladder with widely spread "steps," completely vertical, as if it was going straight to heaven. I struggled to the top and thought that I would rather go straight to hell than climb and jump from this tower. Perhaps this was the place where a dreadful accident could happen to leave me paralyzed? There was no going back, however. Once on top of the structure, I crawled on my knees again to the other edge with my "Swiss knot" around my legs. Here, yet another drill sergeant explained to me how to release the rope while jumping and kicking off the wall at the same time. First, he hooked me to the rope, and then I had to stand on the edge facing up. After that, he lowered me on the rope until my body was parallel to the ground below me. I looked at the open skies above my face and tightened up my grip on my back. A few seconds later, I was flying, kicking off the wall, and releasing the rope, seeing my dear ground level closer and closer. Lewis was already there, waiting for me and cheering. Finally, I had it all behind me.

I went to the bleachers to join a group of those who just completed the obstacle course and were waiting for the rest of the company. At this point, I barely felt any emotions: there was no fear anymore, no tension, and no surprises. I watched in amazement how soldiers were fed through different stations as if on conveyor belt, coming out on the other side of each obstacle, stronger and more confident. It was a factory of courage and determination. As my feelings cleared up, I realized that I was extremely hungry. My well-deserved MRE for lunch was delicious. At that point, probably a fist of dirt would taste just as good. My stomach was completely cramped up from all the stress and enormous effort. As I was heating up my food, I noticed nearby a girl. With both hands covering her face, she was weeping quietly, desperately trying to hide it from the world.

"What's wrong?" I was a bit concerned. "Are you hurt?"

"No, it's just so much stress, I can't take it anymore."

"But it's all over now. Look, the others are still up there on the ropes, struggling, and you are here, sitting, on the ground, safe." I could only offer so much consolation.

"I know. Thanks, I just have to cry now."

I figured that she needed some time to relax and calm down, so I left her alone. I was looking forward to marching back to the barracks for more late afternoon classes on how to take apart and put back together the M16 rifle. Soon we were about to start the Basic Rifle Marksmanship (BRM) course and practice shooting.

* * *

Dear Alec,

I have fire guard duty again, so I can write to you. It's hard to believe that another week just passed by. We have already started our normal schedule, especially the PT (physical training). I was running with the slowest group called "D," but people always try to walk there. As a result, we would get constantly dropped and had to "push" (do push-ups). I needed to move up to group C, which was a little faster and was actually running. I love marching to our exercise area in the morning. It's always dark and sometimes I can see the stars and the moon in the black sky. We have to use our flashlights to see the roads. A couple of days ago, we had an obstacle course with rifles and bayonets. We ran through the woods and attacked the "enemy" made of old tires for easy piercing. It wasn't a lot of fun but rather an exhausting exercise. As a preparation for the "victory forge," a three-day camping in the woods at the end of the basic, we practiced setting up our shelters and putting on the "camo"—military camouflage "makeup." We also went through the victory tower, a series of height-related obstacles. I heard so many horror stories about this—apparently, people would fall down or get injured if they didn't pay attention. I was extremely scared. I was climbing the walls and crossing the rope bridge, which was shaking tremendously, and I was shaking along! The last obstacle was the most intimidating because of the height: when I looked down from the sixty-foot tower, everyone on the ground seemed so small that my heart stopped. But I survived. The last two days we were road marching to a training area in the woods, on top of the hill. We learned all kinds of things like first aid, resuscitation, stopping the bleeding with a tourniquet, and putting the splint on a broken leg. Then we had land navigation classes and the test. Again it was freezing up there, so I was incredibly happy to go back to our barracks in the late afternoon.

 Today was the happiest day so far because I received a letter from you! During the mail call, I saw Drill Sergeant Reaves holding the blue box with a USPS logo, and I knew instantly that it was mine. I had to open it in front of the drill sergeant, as he is always checking everything for contraband items. This time, he made us do ten push-ups for every postage stamp on the envelope. So if someone got three letters, and each had two stamps, the person had to push sixty times! Thank you for using *one* thirty-four-cent stamp! A few days ago, we had a TDC (Team Development Course) consisting of six obstacles that we had to negotiate in eight-person teams. I had a lot of fun crossing "destroyed" bridges, walls, and holes, and transporting a casualty using two planks and a rope. We also were transporting a "barrel of fuel" (a barrel filled with sand, actually) or an extremely heavy ammunition box.

Two days after, instead of regular PT in the morning, we went marching to my beloved woods again, this time for the "endurance course." It was a timed event, so we had to hurry (uphill, of course) and negotiate twenty obstacles. Some of them were a bit scary, like the double cargo net (mounted on both sides of a slim vertical twelve-foot wall). Then it was some crawling in the dirt or under the barbed wire, running on the balance beam, swinging on the ropes, or jumping through and over a variety of barriers. I was struggling and thinking about how I would perform if I was eleven years younger. Sometimes it seems like I'm "too old for all this." But so far I am managing.

Immediately after the course, we had a class about the PRO-Mask, gas chamber, and other explosives. Then we practiced reacting to a "bomb blast": a sergeant was making an explosion in a barrel, and it felt, sounded, and looked like a bomb! After that, it was time for the gas chamber. We were entering a small building filled with smoky tear gas, with the masks on our faces, sealed. Inside, we would move along the wall, and I could barely see in the thick clouds two silhouettes crouching in the middle, dispersing the gas from a container. One drill sergeant was asking us one by one to break the seal, take the mask off, and state our name and social security number. Then we would put the mask back on, clear the air inside it, and wait a few more minutes. At the end of the wall, we had to remove the mask completely and breathe in some gas. It was burning my lungs out! We were asked again some simple questions to keep us distracted. At this point, some people were getting sick or were simply running out of the chamber. As I was leaving the building, I overheard behind my back one guy talking to another: "I was right behind her and I see that she's walking without the mask, like nothing was going on, so I thought it must be really nothing!"

It's getting harder and harder to run early in the morning in complete darkness. I switched to group C, but the guys are sprinting uphill to show off and the entire column formation falls apart. The drill sergeant coaching us said that males should not be running in this group because it's too slow for them. But they still do it, anyway. Yesterday, we were supposed to have "an easy run" because of the PT test the next day. In fact, we were running faster and farther than ever before since Drill Sergeant Girard wanted to push us and added a small extra loop uphill to our routine. On my way back with the group, I was struggling tremendously to avoid falling out of the formation. Suddenly, I felt my calf muscle popping and hardening in a split second. By the time I got ready for breakfast, my leg was twice its size, and I couldn't walk anymore. I called Drill Sergeant Girard and after inspecting my leg, he wanted to send me immediately to "sick call" to see a doctor, but I refused. I said that I will walk it off and he didn't oppose it. All day, I suffered. It was too painful, so the next morning I finally went to see a doctor. It turned out I had pulled my calf muscle and needed rest, so he gave me a "profile" (a sheet stating what the injury was and what I could and couldn't do physically: no marching, running, or jumping), some painkillers, and Cepacol for my sore throat. I couldn't afford to fall out of training for physical therapy, as it would be too much of a setback. I had to exercise through the pain and discomfort.

Thank God today was an "easy" day because we had no PT. Instead, we spent all day outdoors taking all kinds of theoretical and practical tests to pass from phase I (red) to phase II (white) of basic training. At this point, I'm only worried about the upcoming rifle training.

* * *

The night of 26 January, excruciating pain was bursting out of my right calf like a hot volcano. Carla, who was normally excessively preoccupied with her own business to notice anything that was happening around her, this time was helpful and when asked, she brought me a bag of ice from the kitchen. Of course, since she was eating her dinner first and then met some girls from the fourth platoon that she had to chatter with for a while, it took her an eternity to show up with the ice.

* * *

When I was lying on my bed alone, surrounded by the marvelous brief silence before everyone returned from the dining facility, I thought about so many moments when I was in pain before. Like twelve years ago, I went through a scary episode of physical pain during one of my classes at the University of Warsaw.

I was a second-year student at the University of Warsaw, the most difficult yet. During my Practical French class, I became extremely sick. My stomach was cramping in agony, and I needed some relief quickly. I wasn't able to listen or hear anymore Professor Chris who was teaching the course. I was sitting in my chair looking dismally at the desktop in front of me, shivering from fever. I covered my face with my hands, trying to stop this horrible pain, but the situation was hopeless: my hands contracted and rolled up in fists. Before I could answer the professor's question, "Are you all right?" I hit the table with my head and collapsed. I didn't remember what exactly had happened. The emergency room was where I woke up. The pain was still shaking my body as the nurse was administering the anti-inflammatory shots and painkillers in my veins. Through my foggy consciousness, I heard Chris's velvet-like voice asking the nurse: "Is she going to be okay? What's wrong with her?"

I didn't care about the nurse's answer. I knew that I would be okay because Chris was here, sitting next to me, and holding my left hand all cramped up and stiff like a rock, trying to bring it to life.

The entire episode was quite a scene I found out from my fellow students. Professor Chris's quick reaction was to have Andrew carry my lifeless body out of the room to the nearest parked vehicle and go straight to the hospital. Chris was my savior.

This time during my basic training, however, I didn't have anyone nearby to take care of me. My only friends and companions in the pain of the strained muscle was this fantastically cold garbage bag filled with ice and a brief but magical silence in the gloomy barrack . . .

* * *

Extensive rifle training entirely consumed the last few days of January. First, we started practicing in a classroom with laser equipment to learn how to aim and hold the rifle in a steady position. Then, the entire company marched five miles to the woods for a full day of outdoor training with overnight bivouac. Since I was not able to march because of my calf injury, I stayed behind with a group of fifty people (non-marchers) in the barracks, pulling kitchen duty. We still were part of training operations though. The only difference was that our rifle practice took place just outside the buildings in the physical training area where we were to camp overnight. We had to set up our tents out there to mimic an overnight exercise of the rest of the company, which was camping in the woods a few miles away. Naturally, we also had a fire guard duty in the middle of the night, during which, along with my always-whining battle buddy, I walked around the camp looking for anything suspicious. Suddenly, I noticed a shadow moving by one of the tents. I thought it had to be a drill sergeant trying to check on us and see how we would react to an enemy.

"Halt!" I stopped with my rifle aiming forward. "Who's there?!"

"It's me, SKI!" Trinidad's voice was shaking.

"What in the world are you doing here in the middle of the night? Can't you sleep?" I asked in disbelief.

"I had an accident. I peed in my pants," she admitted, all scared.

"Are you okay?"

"Yeah, I just couldn't hold it anymore and I panicked. You won't tell anybody . . ." Trinidad was now trying to hang her wet trousers over the tent.

"Of course not. Let me help you with this." I threw the trousers as high as I could at the top of the shelter. "Hurry up, Carla is coming from the other side. Go inside the tent. Good night."

In the morning around 4:00 a.m., we were all transported to the woods only to join the rest of the company doing "rifle PT" in the rain. It consisted of several exercises where we had to hold our rifles parallel to the ground and perform all kinds of excruciating movements with our arms, legs, and the entire body. After this "warmup," we went to the nearby shooting range and spent the rest of the day aiming at the cardboard figures. Drill sergeants were teaching us all procedures and calibrating our M16s.

This part of basic training was very crucial as a graduation requirement, and our instructors made it very clear that many soldiers before us couldn't go anywhere without completing this part. I was relieved when my first day of practice went well.

A glaring truth was that this stage of training was for me about survival and self-preservation. I had to fit in while embracing a considerable age difference between me and my fellow soldiers. Being more mature and experienced was helpful in accepting the status quo of this new reality. I didn't question any orders from drill sergeants and understood that everything we were doing was part of the game called "soldiering". On the other hand, being surrounded by all these young people made me feel younger and non-apologetic about my shortcomings, like my English. If someone got in my face trying to intimidate me, I would simply tell them off in Polish and the scene would end instantly. In a world where I had so much to learn, it was my survival mechanism.

CHAPTER 5

BLENDING IN

The following morning was the beginning of phase II of basic training: the rifle training. Before our departure to the range, we had a "phase change" ceremony. The entire company was called to attention, and each platoon had to ask the first sergeant for permission to change. After permission was granted, each platoon replaced their red flag with a white one, an official symbol of phase II. The skies above us were black and clear. The stars were the greatest witnesses to our achievements. Even the smallest progress in training was appreciated, and it made me feel like I was part of something truly significant.

When I first started researching the idea of joining the army, I'd looked through countless books at the library captivated by fantastic pictures of U.S. soldiers in action or at the parade fields during important celebrations. I loved the pump and circumstance and wanted to be part of that. I was especially impressed by the photos of the West Point Military Academy graduates. They looked fantastic in their white hats, gray jackets, and white pants. Their beautifully adorned uniforms reminded me of the toy soldiers from the ballet *Nutcracker*, nostalgic, almost historical. I imagined how it would feel to study at this prestigious academy, perhaps become an officer, and wear that amazing uniform at the graduation. If I were eighteen, I would definitely aim for the West Point.

The academy had a special sentiment for me for one specific reason. The West Point's history had a connection with a famous Polish general, Tadeusz Kościuszko. In 1776, Kościuszko, sympathetic to the American cause, moved from Poland to North America, where he took part in the American Revolutionary War as a colonel in the Continental Army. During the Revolutionary War, George Washington regarded West Point as the most important military post in America. He appointed Kościuszko, an accomplished military architect, also trained as a knight in Poland and in France, as an engineer-in-charge of West Point fortifications and defenses. He designed and oversaw their construction between 1778 and 1780. Kościuszko then advocated the establishment of an American military school for officers. After Jefferson established the academy, General William Davie requested Kościuszko write the manual, Maneuvers of Horse Artillery, which became a textbook at the academy. In America, Kościuszko was admired for his kindness, personal commitment to freedom, and for his technical knowledge. And now, I was part of Kościuszko's legacy of fighting for democracy and freedom as a soldier in the U.S. Army.

After the phase change, I was already able to march six miles to the range with the entire company. We had more exciting shooting exercises. We first practiced the prone position, lying flat on the ground with one leg cocked. The prone position was the most accurate of the four shooting positions, we were told. It had some disadvantages, though. The low shooting angle was somewhat limiting the view of the target, especially when the vegetation was present. It also took more time to assume it and you had to be careful with the muzzle, which couldn't touch the ground, otherwise it could get dirty, and shooting would be compromised. In addition, before standing up, the rifle had to be left flat on the ground to avoid accidental shots if, for some reason, there was a bullet left in the chamber. After standing up, you would pick up the weapon. These rules were very strict and drill sergeants made sure they were followed to the letter. They took safety extremely seriously.

I was lying in the prone position with my M16 when it hit me that the smell of the gunpowder, the popping sound of flying bullets, and the moist sandy ground hugging my body were more and more comforting. During those moments on the range, I had this great and irreplaceable sense of belonging where I didn't have to speak to be heard. I enjoyed having my hands all gray from the dirt mixed with the rifle lubricant, and countless bruises, scratches, and cuts on my hands didn't bother me at all. Despite having to maintain a constant focus on my shooting, which was quite stressful, being on the range was enjoyable.

At the end of each training day, we would clean our weapons for hours and, after satisfying the drill sergeant inspecting them, we would stand in long lines to return them to the arsenal number by number, chronologically. The night before the third day of the rifle routine, Drill Sergeant Reaves reminded us about the importance of the shooting qualification and designated the best shooters to help others the next day.

"SKI, you'll be the coach tomorrow. Just don't explain too much—you confuse people." Drill Sergeant Reaves was evidently referring to my obvious Polish accent.

The next day was less hectic. I relaxed a little. In the morning, we actually had our regular physical training. I almost missed it already—almost . . . The all-so-familiar white bus took us yet to another range where, for the first time since I left Chicago, I saw a *dog*. I was so used to being around soldiers in uniforms, or in the barracks where everything was brown, green, or gray, that I completely forgot about the "normal world." This dog made me realize how much I was disconnected from reality and how little I really missed it. I was focused on shooting and coaching. I enjoyed the coaching activities and helping a fellow soldier with calibrating his weapon and aiming. He was extremely stressed out and had trouble concentrating. I kept assuring him that if he just concentrated on steady breathing and pulling the trigger after breathing out, he would be fine. He wanted to qualify and not become recycled. We were a good team. I finally calmed him down and he practiced his shooting with less stress. I was glad I didn't confuse him after all.

During the night, I had a fire guard again, which was an excellent opportunity to catch up with writing to Alec. Since I had my little red notebook filled with everyday observations from the field, it was very pleasant to write about all my emotions to someone who actually cared.

* * *

Dear Alec,

I'm so happy that you are doing okay, and you have submitted the paperwork for your next patent. It worries me that you haven't received any of my letters. I write to you every Saturday and Sunday. How was the conference in Atlanta?

This past week, we were training with rifles every day. We use ten different ranges. Some of them are huge—100 firing posts! During the practice, they direct everything from the tower, where the sergeant in charge has his observation post. He watches everything and everybody, and no shot can be fired without his specific command. It was so weird when I fired the first time: the smell, the noise, and the kickback. The "zeroing" was fun when we were shooting the "guy" on the white target board. Then I was a coach designated by our drill sergeant, because I fulfilled the exercise requirements for the first three days. I was firing in a supported position (standing in a hole) from 75m, 175m, and 300m and then the same distances from a non-supported position—prone—(lying flat on the ground). I got the following results: 75m (7 out of 10), 175m (16 out of 20), and 300m (9 out of 10). Can you believe this? I'm so happy!

I still have a severe cold and I'm generally bruised up from handling the rifle. Finally, we were shooting the moving targets, called "pop-ups." They are exactly the same as the ones in the qualification range: they are set up in five different distances and stand up randomly on the left or on the right side, so I had to constantly move my body and adjust firing position. It's quite exhausting but also very exciting. Today the day was so beautiful. I looked at the perfectly blue sky and I thought about you, hoping that maybe I can see your airplane flying from Atlanta to Chicago . . . Did you see Fort Jackson from the top? I'm sending you some great pine needles from the shooting range so you can be closer to me. Take good care of Sznurek . . .

* * *

The rifle training continued through the beginning of February. I even started to like my weapon. Training became more intense and stressful as we approached the time of basic rifle qualification. Eventually, the only time when I could relax a little was when we were cleaning our weapons after the daily practice on the range. It quickly became my favorite activity. I was getting better at shooting my targets, but still, the pressure to qualify and possibly get the best score possible was great because the next phase of basic training depended on passing the qualification. I was hopeful.

On Thursday, February 8, it was time to face the truth. Since we were practicing the routine for qualification for the last few days, there weren't any surprises. When my turn came, I took my position in the sandpit and tried to picture where my targets would pop up and went through the motions of moving my body to adjust to different distances. I was shaking from the stress and damp sand beneath me. I rubbed my pin, "The Victory Starts Here," attached to the interior of my pocket to bring me luck. Before I knew it, the series of "unsupported prone position" was over and I had a few seconds to jump into the foxhole right in front of me to start the series in "supported standing position." Through the barrage of thoughts running in my head, the noise and smell of flying bullets, I could barely hear any of the ranger's commands. Eventually, I caught a fragment of a sentence: "We have a possible Hawkeye in firing position number one." It was only after I finished when I realized it was me in the first position, but I looked to my left just to make sure that there was no one to my left. After the shooting, I was marching back to the tower for the weapon inspection (the sergeants were making sure there were no bullets left in the rifles and we returned the magazines), I noticed members of my platoon applauding and yelling, "You go, SKI! You made the Hawkeye in the foxhole!" I couldn't believe this, but eventually, it came to me when I received my expert badge.

I felt genuine relief the next day when I knew that the second big part of basic training was coming to an end. It wasn't getting any easier, however. I was constantly struggling with the morning running because of my injured calf, physical exhaustion, stress, cold weather, and lack of decent sleep. All this started taking a toll on me. I had to go to a sick call to see the doctor and get some medicine.

That Friday morning, I went to a sick call, and they sent me to the nearby clinic for evaluation. I packed an overnight bag (we had to do it every time we were sent to the hospital to see the doctor, just in case) and went to the bus stop. For the first time in the last five weeks, I was separated from all these soldiers, daily routines, and accountability. I hopped on the white shuttle bus, and everything felt like a dream—normal streets and intersections, people wearing blue jeans, colorful vehicles covered parking lots—where all these elements of a regular civilian life seemed to vibrate in the morning sun.

By the time I saw the doctor and had all the lab tests done, I was barely breathing, and a severe headache was killing me. I had bronchitis, therefore the infirmary on the tenth floor became my home for the next forty-eight hours. I joined a small group of newcomers from other basic training units. They instructed us on how to keep our beds and how to breathe, cough, and sleep. I was assigned to room 1016, bed D, where I immediately noticed a shiny white floor, bedsheets in peach color, and white soft blankets that reminded me of home. No more olive green. I looked through the window to admire the peaceful day, hoping that this was a reality. For the time being, I wanted to absorb the bits and pieces of a temporary "normal" life. Things that I'd taken for granted: the serene view of the hospital window, pastel colors, and peacefulness. On the fourth floor, when I went to dinner, another surprise awaited me: the dining facility looked like a restaurant with single tables and real flowers throughout. I was in paradise. After dinner, I went upstairs and directly to bed, hoping that I could catch up with writing my journal or perhaps write a letter to Alec. The late afternoon sun was caressing my face as I was looking again through the window at the perfect blue, clear sky.

My stay at the clinic ironically felt like a vacation: the surrounding life stopped for a full forty-eight hours. There was no yelling, no formations, or running around in a hurry—it was a different world. Our sergeant on duty kept reminding us about getting as much rest and sleep as possible. The only time we had to get out of bed was early in the morning for the vitals checkup and regular meals.

While resting, I thought a lot about my parents in Poland. They already had received my letter announcing my new military career in progress. Although a little worried about my physical capabilities for such training, they were proud of me. My dad even revealed that when he was in the Polish Army, he wanted to become an officer, but his family circumstances prevented him from pursuing this path. Now I thought that one day, when I become an officer, I would make him proud again by carrying on his dream.

After the first day, I felt much better. I could breathe almost normally, and my sense of taste came back. On Sunday morning, it was time to go back to my unit. As I was leaving my room on the tenth floor, I looked through the window for the last time: a red-orange circle dressed in a foggy veil was drifting above the perfectly smooth horizon. I stood there enchanted, waiting for my daylight, not knowing when the next opportunity to see it would come.

* * *

I returned to the barracks gladly, relieved that I wouldn't have to miss any training, rejuvenated. By now I became used to being part of this enormous crowd constantly on the move. I didn't want to attract any attention to myself, especially doing something wrong, like failing tests or not fulfilling requirements. I wanted to blend in and focus on conquering the obstacles instead of thinking about my shortcomings, like my physical fitness. I was making progress, but struggled. My English was slowly improving, yet remembering all the technical military terms was still a challenge. I just couldn't connect with it and it continued to feel like a strange language. My pronunciation was often questionable. So I didn't talk much with other people and my communication with the world around me was minimal. Blending in had, however, its negative side. My identity was lost in a human mixture where I was merely an ingredient. This massive human machinery was moving steadily toward a seemingly elusive point in the future and I was just one of its multitude of gears, spinning along.

CHAPTER 6

THE VICTORY STARTS HERE

The following week, another change of phase ceremony took place to bring us to the final, phase III of basic training, the most intense because of the amount of activities. We received the blue guidon. From this point on, for the remaining four weeks of the training, we were negotiating a variety of obstacle courses with encouraging names like "Fit to Win", "Confidence Building," or "Omaha Beach." We were training more in the field with all kinds of weapons, grenades, and mines.

We also had the measurements done for our "class A" uniforms for graduation, which was a good sign, as it meant that we would most likely all graduate in March. This gave me a boost of confidence and I knew I would successfully complete the remaining training.

The last event of basic was the FTX (field training exercise), also called the "victory forge," a three-day camp in the woods during which we would have the opportunity to use all the skills we had learned. It was a culmination of basic training. It was supposed to be a gigantic battle simulation combining physical endurance, negotiating various obstacles, shooting, throwing grenades, reacting to tear gas, building fighting positions, and applying tactics. In order to prepare for this event, we had to go through several training days in the field where we would practice all these crucial components of the "victory forge."

The ultimate preparation for this final event was a two-day training at the "Anzio" shooting range and obstacle course. This obstacle course was designed to instill confidence in the mental and physical abilities, ran for time. We were first using blank ammunition before going through the live fire run, practice throwing hand grenades, while reacting to fire from artillery simulators, and small arms.

The first day we marched about nine miles to the location and practiced low and high crawling in the giant sandpit, moving under the fire, firing on the run, and hiding from the enemy. The next day we were brought to the same location on the white buses and this time we learned how to secure the perimeter, set up a Claymore Mine, and use the machine gun and grenade launcher. We were running through the woods with our M16s aiming at the enemy, then through a small valley straight into the pre-dug fighting positions at the range, reacting to live fire.

I used three full magazines and was about to load another one when I heard the alarm signifying the tear gas bomb. Without turning around to verify if the white gas cloud was indeed behind me, instinctively I grabbed my PRO-mask and sealed it on my face. I noticed that the mask was full of sand since we were constantly crawling, but there were only nine seconds to put it on before the gas would become unbearable. Through the fog in the mask, I could barely discern the silhouettes of soldiers around me. "This is the true battlefield. There is no time to evaluate the situation for too long. Split-second decisions. Breathe through the mask and hope that the filter works," I thought to myself. After a few minutes of fire exchange, there was an "all clear" command, meaning that it was safe to remove the mask. We spent the rest of the day in the nearby bunkers, training with the grenades. The dinner was delivered to us, and we ate it in the field waiting for the sun to go down. At dusk, we found ourselves running through the woods again to settle on the large battlefield area. This time we could not only clearly hear the barrage from the opposing forces, but we could actually see the bullets flying, leaving traces of red and blue lasers.

I was moving forward with my platoon buddies along the small ridge line, surrounded by the fierce noises of machine guns and bursting bombs. Far ahead, I could see the silhouettes of half-burned, distorted military vehicles, abandoned fighting positions, and the fire divulging the enemy lines. For a moment, I was overwhelmed by this spectacular yet blood-blood-curdling spectacle, but there was no time to think, so I loaded another magazine and started shooting at the blinking lights up front.

My buddies next to me were in firing mode as well. For the first time, I noticed that my M16 was spitting fire like a ferocious dragon. Until now, I was always shooting during the day, and I was never able to see the actual sparks coming out of the weapon. At night, everything was different. It seemed more dangerous and malignant. Accidents were more likely. I didn't want to be part of an accident. Once the final live fire run was made, a mock explosive device was detonated, and we scrambled to take cover behind the range's walls. It was frightening, but I tried to stay focused on the task, especially when the speed of movement and quick reactions were critical. When the bullets from all the rifles were exhausted, we could see the red flare shot in the skies by our sergeant, the signal for "ceasefire."

Suddenly everything went quiet, and I could only see the soundless flames engulfing the wracked enemy tanks. My platoon was then moved to the waiting area to observe other teams in the same action we just completed. I was lying on the ground securing our perimeter with my rifle aiming toward the enemy lines, saturated with the smell of burned grass, fire smoke, and deep forest moisture. Right above me, the skies were smiling, with millions of stars hanging so low that I could almost reach them. I found the Orion and the Big Dipper, which brought memories of home. On hot Sunday nights in Northbrook, I used to sit with Alec on the deck behind our purple house. We were burning wood in the outdoor firepit, drinking red chilled wine, and listening to the opera on the white portable radio. We also looked at the stars, wondering if our friends or families in other parts of the world could see the same stars at that same moment. And here I was, in Fort Jackson, thinking the same thing: Was Alec looking at the skies in Northbrook? Did he know how much I missed him?

* * *

February 19 was a very special day for the majority of soldiers in my company: family visitation day. It was like a holiday: the wake-up call was late (6:30 a.m.); the weather was perfect, and hundreds of families were pouring in. The base was filled with civilian vehicles, and everyone was running around frantically looking for their loved ones. There were tears of joy, lots of homemade pies, balloons, candies, and picnic blankets all over the field. Small children were running with their big brothers and sisters, touching their uniforms, and wearing their hats. I didn't expect anyone to visit me, so my plan was to stay in the barracks and write some letters. Kyle, a girl from my platoon, was there with me. Our drill sergeant wanted us to go to our auditorium and watch the movie *Apollo 13* if we had no guests, but I considered it too depressing, so I went outside. Kyle joined me since she didn't want to be alone. We sat on the curb, pretending that we were waiting for our families. This reminded me of my time in Warsaw, when, as a ten-year-old, I was in a boarding ballet school. On Sundays, the parents would come and visit us for a few hours. Sometimes my parents couldn't make it. It was an almost four-hour drive from my hometown. On Sundays like this, I would roam the main school lobby, mingling with other girls, pretending that I was waiting for my parents. However, I knew they were not coming. But there was a silver lining in this situation. At the end of the evening, the parents were going back home, leaving their crying daughters behind, waving in the lobby. I didn't have to cry because I wasn't saying my goodbyes. I would go upstairs and pretend like nothing happened.

And now I found myself pretending again. I knew Alec wasn't coming. Pretending was my best option to survive the day.

Kyle started to write a letter home as I was watching the joyful crowd around us. Before I knew it, Kyle was in tears. She missed her family tremendously. It was her first time away from home, so the visitation day became unbearable for her. I didn't know how to console her. She was just a kid, fourteen years my junior. The best I could do at that point was to take her for a walk around the parking lot filled with colorful cars and try to blend in with the overwhelming happiness which we couldn't share.

* * *

It didn't make sense to pretend all day long that someone was coming to visit me, so I went back to the barracks. Since everyone was busy with their families, it was a perfect opportunity to spend some quality time alone writing my journal and reading the letters from Alec. As I was sorting through my notes and letters, I stumbled across a small photo with a Post-it note on the back laminated together. I recognized immediately the handwriting in purple ink: "Jo, we keep missing each other again. Wednesday, 10 a.m. Kisses. C." Maybe I kept this little Post-it note instinctively as a symbol of my past relationship with Chris. Years ago, when we were very close, we would leave each other Post-it notes behind the windshields of our cars. It was our way of discreet communication since we were both busy and usually in different locations at the university. Sometimes a note would be an invitation to meet during a break in a nearby coffee place, or it simply meant that we constantly thought about each other. The picture on the reverse carried a lot of wonderful memories as well. It was taken in a forest preserve, near Chris's house, where we used to walk in the early spring of 1993. We would stroll without any disruption of civilization and talk for hours. The smell of leaves burning in the backyards was spreading its magic through the woods, carried freely by the Sunday morning breeze. Then we would head back to the house because Chris's father was always visiting on Sundays. He was coming from the city with a box of pastries, followed by freshly brewed coffee. It was a true celebration of life and its simple pleasures, a ritual that for a few precious hours would bring the entire family together, reconnect their lives constantly dispersed in their daily routines, and slow down the pace of reality. As I looked at this laminated picture, all the little perfect moments were flashing in my mind like the colorful pieces of a broken kaleidoscope, fragments of the past life, which were gone forever. It was much too painful going through these memories, so I put the photograph away between the pages of my notebook, hoping that I would forget about it soon. At that moment, I realized I was grieving the loss of a very special, long friendship.

* * *

As the last days of February were passing by, I got to know more deeply my fellow soldiers from my barrack. While at the clinic, I had plenty of opportunities to hear countless stories about their private lives, and some of them were pretty colorful and chilling. One day, a twenty-year-old redhead just decided to tell me about her adventures before joining the army and admitted that she did a few stupid things in her life. She didn't finish high school because she had to stay at home with her dogs to protect them from the boyfriend-intruder. Then she added innocently that she'd been married for five years now, but it wasn't probably a legal marriage because they were both fifteen at that time. Another girl maxed out all of her credit cards to buy clothes. Her mother paid off the debt under the condition that she join the army to pay her back. A young girl across from me got married recently, but she was unhappy with her new husband, so she ran away from him straight into the army. We also had quite a few aspiring "PT Queens"—those who wanted to achieve maximum scores in the physical training—at any price. Micah was one of them. She trained so hard during the last six weeks that she completely tore her hamstring and now was walking on crutches without a chance to even pass the run at the next PT test. Most of us had already suffered from several more or less serious injuries—some of them were actually real. One night, I caught one of the girls crying in the bathroom and depressed because she missed her perfect PT score by two push-ups. I could only imagine how hard it was for a swimming champion with ideal athletic body strength to take this. She said that she was a failure. We were all pretty beaten up, but we still had to go through two weeks of demanding training in the field and several road marches to prepare for the victory forge.

* * *

The short month of February was finally over. So far, I received several letters from my parents and my friend Joanna from Poland. It was kind of funny, but not that unusual that we had the same name. In Poland, Joanna was a very popular name for my generation. As far as my memory goes at every stage of my life, not only I knew, but was friends with at least one Joanna; kindergarten, preschool, grade school, ballet school, university, music academy, and later work. My maid of honor was Joanna. Fortunately, people were always coming up with nicknames for me, which were beneficial for everyone's sanity. These were usually variations of Joanna (Joasia [yoashia], Asia [ashia], Joanka [yoanka], Dżanka [djanka], Jeanette, or Juana), or names unrelated to Joanna, like the endearing Little Chick. With this Joanna, I had a special bond for several reasons. We first met in 1989 while assigned to the same room in a university dorm. We had hit it off from the get-go, once I found out that she was studying Czech language (she was of Czech origin but fluent in Polish) at the University, as well as musicology at the music academy. I was studying French and ballet pedagogy in the same schools, so our itineraries were the same. Naturally, we shared our love for classical music. We were the same stature and the same age. Both redheads, both playing piano. Both, away from our families in a big city. She gave me a nickname of Little My—a small but fierce friend of the Moomin family—because at that time, I was a redhead sporting a high, short ponytail, just like Little My. I loved that nickname. After our graduations we had rented an apartment together. She had helped me find my first full-time job with a French company, and I hired her as my helper. My heart shattered when I was leaving Poland, but we had managed to stay in touch. I loved receiving her beautiful, thoughtful letters, especially now, when I was separated from everyone and everything familiar to me.

Now, I was in a survival mode: countless nights of fire guard, staff or kitchen patrol duties, spring cleanings of our training area, barracks inspections, shake-downs, and Sunday trips to the little church up on the hill in the woods. I enjoyed singing in the choir and being away from the barracks. My body was covered with bruises and scratches, and my uniforms and boots lost their original crispiness and color. I wrote over one hundred pages of memories—my red pocket notebook was filled to the brim with notes from the field training.

At this point, my primary goal was to pass the final PT test and survive the last three-day camp in the woods. The vision of the final PT test was paralyzing: I wasn't sure where I was standing regarding my run because I had not been running for a long period due to my calf injury. However, the passing score was a condition for graduation. That's why in the evenings, whenever we had some "free" time, I would run around the barracks, frantically measuring the distance in my head and comparing it to the two-mile requirement. Every night before going to bed, I took the opportunity to practice my sit-ups and push-ups without realizing how strong my mind and body were becoming. "I have to get much stronger or I won't be going to Arizona," I kept telling myself to keep my motivation going.

* * *

The beginning of March brought a brief distraction from all these thoughts about physical training. I was facing yet another excruciating event called "Confidence Course," a set of several clusters of obstacles grouped in the shape of a five-arm star. Each arm represented a colossal wooden construction, considerably higher and more complicated than the "victory tower" from the first week of training. Each arm represented a unique challenge.

The first one was a fifteen feet reclined wall with attached all-so-familiar rope with knots to hold on to. After climbing it, we were sliding down on two other ropes attached to the vertical walls. On the second obstacle, we climbed a set of five consecutive walls (six, eight, ten, twelve, and fourteen feet tall) set up in a row a couple of feet apart from each other like dominoes. This time it was all about teamwork—instead of ropes to hang on to, we had our buddies. As we progressed to the consecutive stations, the tasks were harder. The third one was a thirty-five-foot-tall tower. First, we had to climb a nearly vertical ladder with the steps spread out as wide as almost the entire height of my body. At the top, a drill sergeant was instructing us individually how to wrap our feet around the rope on the opposite side of the tower and slide down to the ground by moving our hands. The rope was stretched several feet forward, so the slide was almost parallel to the ground. Of course, in case of an emergency, we could always let go of the rope and fall to the net below, but it wasn't a very appealing solution. The drill sergeant told me that the best way was to slide on the boots because the line can tear the uniform and damage the skin. I instantly imagined my torn, blood-stained pants. At the beginning of the descent, I was hanging correctly, but as the slide was gaining speed, my feet started coming apart, so I crossed them swiftly and the line ended up directly against my knee. Since I had no intention of letting go, I kept going in this position. The burning heat under my knee was unbearable, so I slowed down, which added more effort to my semi-frozen bruised hands. After this long and painful ride, I dropped to the ground with no life left in me. I moved on to the next station called a "skyscraper," another tower composed of five platforms about eight by eight feet large, stacked on top of each other like a giant stool on four legs. "How in the world am I going to climb this thing, being only 5'4"?" I was wondering in panic. Again, we could only hang on to each other as we were scaling this monster, floor after floor, up to the very top. The tallest guys from my team would always go first, and then they would drag the rest of us to the next level. I honestly thought it was the last event in my entire life and I was going to fall off this thing and die. Somehow, thanks to my buddy Lewis, I found myself at the top. Afraid to sit up, I was lying flat on the platform without any borders or rails. Unfortunately, it was just one-half of the success because we still had to go down as a team the same way: supporting one another from the lower level and holding tight from the upper one. When I finally ended up on the ground level, I gained an entirely new appreciation of my teammates. The "skyscraper" wasn't an obstacle for an individual.

"Skyscraper." "How in the world am I going to climb this thing, being only 5'4"?

After lunch, we faced the ultimate startling giant, a split-level tower combining three sections of different tasks. The first section consisted of a cargo net on which we had to climb to the "first floor." At that point, I had to negotiate a several-foot-long balance beam (a log was hanging about twenty feet above the ground). I crossed it very slowly with my arms spread out to keep the balance, but still, it seemed like the entire construction was resonating from my shaking body. After that, I climbed a few more steps to a little cabin on the top of the structure where I was immediately instructed to put on the harness and connect it to the rope stretching endlessly ahead of me. With my hands interlocked tightly behind my neck, my drill sergeant positioned me in a small "doorway" facing open space and said,

"As you fly down, keep your hands close to your head and legs stretched in front of you. And now, on my count of three, you will make a step forward through the door."

"But there is nothing behind the door, just an open space . . ." I was not ready to zip down.

"One, two, three . . ."

There was no time for discussion, however, so I closed my eyes and made a step into an abyss before the drill sergeant would push me. I could sense the adrenaline rushing through my body. I had to take that step forward. For the next several seconds, I was flying on the zip line and was almost enjoying the moment when a sudden jolt of the line brought me back to reality. It was the end of the ride and in order to stop the descent; the line had to be jerked up by the people on the ground controlling the landing. I hung there, several feet above the ground, until the giant ladder on wheels pulled up and they finally disconnected me from the harness. The relief was so great that I could barely walk. At last, the obstacle course was conquered.

* * *

Dear Alec,

Packing for the victory forge made me very nervous: the list of equipment was quite long and I was afraid it wouldn't fit in my rucksack. We had very specific instructions on where every single item was supposed to go. I finally finished and calmed down so I can write to you.

I never thought it would be possible to be in the actual army. And now thanks to you I'm here. I'm living my dream because of your support and belief in me. You know that my career in the army is not only my personal obligation toward America, who gave me a chance to pursue my goals, but it is also a step for our future, better life and fulfillment of our biggest task ever: to build our own dream house. This is our American Dream. I think about you all the time, what you might be doing at a specific moment of the day, or where you might be. A couple of days ago during the night fire training, when this beautiful, fantastically black vault of heaven was hugging the forest, I looked at the stars, thinking that maybe you were looking at the same skies at that moment. It felt so warm in my heart.

Tomorrow morning we leave for the victory forge. I admit I'm scared because it's a long and exhausting event—three full consecutive days in the field and two long road marches. At some point in the day or night, I will be digging my firing position in the ground, all sweaty and tired, but with joy in my heart, because it's for us. Sometimes I will be lying in the dirt with my rifle loaded and pointed out, waiting for my invisible enemy. I will be fighting my fears, shooting them off one after another. I will look mean, fearless, and dangerous with the dark camouflage on my face. For these three days, I will become a powerful monster conquering my new invisible land of freedom—the land where we'll find our peace and dreams. One night I will die in flames like a phoenix, only to be reborn the next morning from the ashes, stronger than ever, powerful, and invincible . . . Thinking about you and our new house keeps me focused and excited. I dedicate everything to you, my efforts, sacrifices, pain and loneliness, sadness from being different from most people around me. You should be very proud of me. I want you to have something that other people don't have—a true, loving life partner, a warrior who will protect everything precious to us: our values, our beliefs, and most of all, our dreams. I always write to you about the everyday events at Fort Jackson but almost never talk about my feelings because I went through so much here and faced so many fears and obstacles, and tomorrow is the last time when I have to push myself to do things I despise and go beyond my abilities in order to survive. My anxiety is something I want to share with you. I'm tired of marching, running, carrying the rifle, being dirty, eating the MREs, and rushing all the time. It's almost over though, and I will see you soon at my graduation. You will be my biggest reward and the greatest medal. I miss you tremendously, but at the same time, I feel your continuous presence. I carry your latest letter in my trousers' cargo pocket or keep it under my pillow at night. I will be going soon to Arizona to face new challenges and a few months later we'll be home together. You are my strength and inspiration.

* * *

 We left the barracks just before 4:00 a.m. We marched in the darkness with the stars as our guides scattered along both sides of the road, quietly, our rifles pointed outward. I knew that this was not the last several hours of marching with all the equipment on my back. Every time we stopped for a break, I was getting colder and the pain in my feet wouldn't allow me to stand up afterward and continue. I fought it with all my heart because I knew that in three days, I will come back to the barracks for the graduation. I got used to my sweat-drenched T-shirt drying on my body and getting wet again.
 The sun was barely rising when we finally arrived at our training camp in the woods. The next half of the day, we spent digging our fighting positions and setting up the shelters. My battle buddy Carla didn't feel like doing anything, so she asked the guys next to us to dig for her. For lunch, an unexpected treat was awaiting us in the woods: We got hot chicken soup

and fresh apples. I promised myself that I would never take hot soup and fresh apples for granted.

The company chaplain was there with us to cheer us up and to make sure we stayed positive for the next three days. This time, the mass in the field was more powerful than ever before. We were sitting in a large circle praying in our hearts for strength for our minds and bodies, while a distant and subdued sound of artillery reminded us of the upcoming events. This time, I truly felt like I was going to war. It was so real. From this point on, everything was entirely tactical and mission oriented. No time or place for personal conversations or casual moves.

At dusk, I proceeded to the foxhole prepared a few hours earlier. The night was calm, a perfect time for guard duty. The enemy could come from any direction, so I concentrated all my senses and waited. It seemed like time stopped and I would stay there forever.

I looked upon the skies, cold and shivering, curled up in the deep and sandy hole. It was the beginning of spring in South Carolina when a freezing and unforgiving night was about to reveal the beginning of my life's next chapter. I looked at the moon, full, smiling in his white and cynic glory, and I saw my purple house in the middle of the night. Suddenly, I woke up from my live dream and I realized that I would have to go to a battle very soon. I could get hurt or die. And I might never see my purple house again.

Before I knew it, the morning sun was up, and we were running through the woods confronting our always-present but invisible enemy in fierce combat. I could only hear the monotonous, distant noise of bursting bombs, exploding grenades, and the rhythmical cracking sound of several machine guns in this big, never-ending symphony of a battle in which we were becoming the ultimate warriors.

There was no time to think about obstacles, fear, or cold. As I faced the "destroyed bridge," I climbed instinctively on a nearby tree to negotiate the ropes, which were replacing the regular bridge over the imaginary river. I hung on the top rope above my head while walking on the bottom one. However, everything was moving around, and I ended up just using my hands to cross the rest of the obstacle. Shortly after that, I found myself crouching in the bushes along with my platoon members, looking out for the enemy, and preparing for the next step. I glanced at my swollen, bleeding hands. They were painfully exploding from a sudden heat caused by holding the metal rope and by the cuts. But it was time to go. I hurried with my platoon to face several obstacles, like crawling under the barbed wire near the enemy bunker or scaling a fifteen-foot cement wall and other structures. Eventually, we had a chance to reinforce our relationship with the PRO-mask when the Fourth Platoon's drill sergeant ambushed us and offered a hefty helping of tear gas.

After a quick MRE for lunch, we continued digging our fighting positions in four-person teams. Carla, of course, volunteered immediately for the easiest job, which was pulling the guard duty. But she couldn't even do that as she fell asleep immediately after taking her position on the ground. Naturally, the "enemy" spotted us easily and attacked from up close. Carla finally woke up by the shots fired right by her when our team scrambled to chase away the intruders. Finally, when it was her turn to dig, she conveniently disappeared into the woods, looking for the latrine for the next three hours.

By twilight, we set up our shelters and left the camp on the white buses, deeper in the woods, for the ultimate soldier experience: the "NIC night"—night infiltration course. We were told that part of the course was an "Omaha Beach," which was supposed to mimic the operation during the U.S. Normandy invasion in 1944. After a ten-minute ride on the bus, which this time felt surprisingly comfortable and cozy, we were dropped off on the top of the hill covered with thick foliage. We could see the vast area of woods just beneath us, where the mystery of NIC's night was awaiting us soundlessly. The anticipation of this exercise was taking my breath away, as I was starting to struggle in the chilly wind. A few people from my platoon were feeling this unforgiving cold more and more intense, so we kneeled in a small circle on the gravel to keep warm, waiting for the sunset. I was hoping for a moment that it was just a bad dream, and it would be over soon if I could only wake up.

But everything was only starting. Once the sun died quietly beyond the silver horizon, the darkness wrapped the world around us in a bitter night. Immediately after that, the first platoon was given a command to go, then the second, then mine—the third platoon. We were disappearing into the darkness of the woods without knowing where we were going and what was waiting for us inside the woods. I ran very close to Lewis since he was very tall and easy to spot. It wasn't too hard to get lost as we didn't use flashlights. I wanted to keep up with the group at any price, especially at the big log wall, which was extremely hard to scale without any ropes or tools. With my rifle in the sling banging around my back, I managed to climb up. I thought with relief, "Now just jump down," and I let go, but my feet were still in the air. Apparently, my belt got caught on a huge nail. "Don't panic!" I thought as I was wrestling frantically to liberate myself from this predicament. The group was slowly disappearing into the woods. Eventually, I touched the ground and ran toward the burning truck, shedding some light on the scene where I saw the soldiers from my platoon. Before I could recognize any of them, I found myself in the low concrete tunnel, moving on my knees behind someone just to catch up. The obstacles seemed endless, but our mission was to "rescue the lost parachute squad" somewhere in the woods. There was no time to waste. Endless sandpits, minefields, yards of small and large barbed wires, walls, and "contaminated areas" were multiplying in front of me constantly. But I was already with my platoon. I felt a genuine relief when a tall silhouette of Lewis was just a few yards ahead. One more ditch and we were all safe in some kind of abandoned enemy bunker. We gathered in this dark building, all forty of us crouching tightly next to each other. As we were waiting for the drill sergeant's sign to move out, I realized that my uniform was completely drenched. A small, hot stream of sweat was running down my spine. I grabbed my rifle and, hugging it, I supported the edge of my Kevlar on the barrel. Extreme exhaustion after all this running was taking a toll on me, but we were not allowed to sleep.

* * *

I made a tremendous effort to keep my eyes open as my thoughts took me far away from the battlefield. At this moment, I wanted to connect with someone that I loved. I needed a friend with whom I could share my current emotional state, my insecurities, and my fears. I remembered how I was in that state of wanting to have a close relationship in the spring of 1990 in Warsaw. Back then, I was constantly thinking about Chris.

We saw each other in class at least twice a week, not to mention other accidental meetings everywhere else. One day, I was going to school earlier than usual to take care of some paperwork before the classes. In my mind, I was continuously talking to Chris. We had so much in common, and we were attracted to each other. Our relationship was subtle, mysterious, and unspoken. While on the bus to school, I decided to break this silence and express the feelings I had for Chris. Using a piece of paper impulsively torn out from my French notebook, I wrote a brief letter about my admiration with an audacious question at the end: "Can we talk?" My heart was racing as I was planning in my head how to approach my favorite French professor with this spontaneous letter. Fortunately, destiny took care of it for me. As I got off the bus, I found myself negotiating the crowd around the bus stop by the university's gate. Instinctively, I was hoping to find a familiar face, when suddenly I saw Chris, right in front of me. I almost fainted. Completely speechless, with a piece of paper folded in my hand, I froze. It took me a good few seconds before I finally caught my breath and spoke up, "I just wrote a note for you . . ."

Looking straight into my eyes, Chris took the letter from my hand and read it right away.

"Let's meet at this corner café. I still have some time before my next faculty meeting."

This was our first private meeting, which gave our relationship a whole new significance. I didn't even remember what the subject of our conversation was. I felt inspired, uplifted, and enchanted. The most precious souvenir of this meeting was Chris's business card.

"Call me or stop by anytime if you need anything." I heard the magic words as Chris was drawing a little map with directions on the back of the card. "And don't forget to keep me posted about your upcoming French literature exam."

How could I forget? Two weeks later, I was on the bus again, this time going to the suburbs to bring the good news to my favorite French professor. I passed the exam. Nothing counted anymore. Anxious to see Chris as soon as possible, I almost ran from the bus stop through the forest preserve in full bloom. I probably didn't even notice the most wonderful nature unfolding its colors, sounds, and scents. I finally slowed down by the gate, where for the first time I saw Chris in a casual setting, reading a book in the garden among flowering bushes. For a moment I stood there, holding a bouquet of white roses, without taking a breath or making a move, afraid that I could ruin the most magnificent, peaceful painting of life. I was looking forward to my new friendship.

* * *

"Get up, move out, time to go!" The drill sergeant's voice abruptly brought me back. We marched silently to the ridgeline and ended up in a gigantic concrete trench. Flares shooting in the air were signaling each platoon's departure into the enormous sandpit.

When my time came, I climbed the wall of the trench to find myself among hundreds of soldiers crawling in the sand. The live ammunition was flying low, marking the air with a bright laser light like miniature spaceships. I was terrified to the bone.

The first several yards were called the "low crawl" under the thick barbed wire, where I was merely dragging my face on the ground. I wasn't even able to look up and verify if I was going in the right direction. Suddenly, the earth beneath me trembled, throwing my whole body a couple of inches up in the air. The noise was atrocious despite my earplugs. Apparently, I passed by the artillery simulator, which certainly felt real. I gasped in disbelief. The live bullets just above my head made me think that even the smallest mistake could cost me my life or a horrible injury. "Don't look up. Taste the sand. It's better than the taste of blood," I was saying to myself. My imagination was ruthless. I could see my helmet flying off my head after getting shot, then my brain exploding into pieces. "Stay low. Don't look up. Just keep moving forward, wherever it leads," I kept repeating to myself like a prayer. Eventually, the "low" area ended, and everything became rather chaotic. Soldiers in front of me were speeding up, kicking the sand in panic, trying to get out of this pit as fast as possible. I could finally use my elbows and knees more efficiently and didn't mind the sand in my face and boots and rifles bouncing off my Kevlar. My only focus was to stay low, avoid getting shot, and definitely get to the end on my own. For several minutes, which dragged like hours, I couldn't even see the end of this commotion. In my mind, I was going through the images from the TV program *20/20* describing this experience of basic training soldiers. At this moment, I knew there were no theatrical tricks in this program. I also thought that this must have been how the troops felt on Omaha Beach in Normandy during the 1944 invasion.

It seemed like the end line was disappearing on me. My aching body was refusing to move. But there was no place for weaknesses. I continued and eventually reached the dirt, which felt refreshing compared to the sand. The last log to cross seemed in my tired mind like a building. I dragged my rag-doll body over it and collapsed on the other side. I barely stood up and immediately went toward the buses. I needed a few moments to process this "crawling on the beach." As I stood there shaking, my brain was still spinning in survival mode, adrenaline rushing through my body.

Eventually, I escaped from my trance, dusted off my uniform, and removed the sand from my helmet. Once on the bus, I reached into my cargo pocket for my notebook, now completely yellow and covered with sand, which became my ultimate souvenir from the basic training. I was writing through the rest of the trip despite my shaking hands, exhaustion, and cold.

We arrived at the camp after midnight. The last few hours of the night, we spent wearing the anti-chemical MOPP (mission oriented protective posture) suits, protective gear used in a toxic environment. In fact, in the morning, a thick white tear gas fog covered the entire area, and we had no choice but to put on the PRO-masks. But that was okay with me, because I had already gotten used to the mask and the MOPP suit was providing an additional layer of comforting warmth.

* * *

The last day in the woods was passing by quickly, as we swept the camp clean and covered all the fighting positions with dirt, without regret.

While eating my last MRE of the day, I was admiring the most exotic sunset ever. The majestic, perfectly round golden-red circle was hanging on the horizon. I thought perhaps Alec was seeing the very same sun as he drove home from work. Perhaps at home, the last few gleams of the sun were coming through the half-shut blinds, creating a combination of light and shade stripes throughout the living room. And maybe our dog Sznurek was enjoying this afternoon sun lying on one of the sunny stripes. Or maybe he was just sitting on the couch by the front window, waiting for Alec to pull into the driveway.

But I was here in the woods, and just like the last day of the victory forge, something was definitely coming to an end. The rush was over. The only thing left was the nocturnal march to the base, our home away from home. I couldn't help the uneasy feeling of conflict in my heart. Part of me was enchanted by the innocent beauty of the forest and the powerful nature around me. I was fascinated and excited by the soldier's fairy tale, which I was living to the deepest extent of its every detail—the smell of the gunpowder, flares at night, moisture of dirt on my uniform, and never-ending sounds of the battle. On the other hand, I felt anxiety that this long ruck-march home could break me down. I joined a few girls from my platoon, and, for a couple of minutes, I listened to their conversations about homemade pies. We all wanted to come home just like the soldiers returning from war with victory. Talking about pies made this home just a bit closer. I could only imagine how nice it would be to have this twelve-mile march behind me and see the lights on the dark horizon at the end of the road.

Before I knew it, the memories of the day were gone and we were marching in silence, scattered on both sides of the road. Again, surrounded by complete darkness, we had the moonlight and the stars as our guides. In my mouth, I felt a bitter taste of the sand as if it became a part of me these days. Around midnight, I noticed a familiar shape on the side of the road—it was a shooting range. This meant that we were getting close to the end. The entire formation accelerated as if we all wanted to get it over with. However, our drill sergeant decided to take a "shortcut," which took us in a completely unknown direction, and which afterward came out to be an extension to our road march. Apparently, our counterpart company was struggling, and drill sergeants didn't want our group to finish first, so we had to make the extra mile, literally. On this alternative route, I was completely lost and couldn't tell how far from the end we were. Suddenly, a monstrous hill grew right in front of me. Despite my disbelief, I leaned forward and climbed it while biting my teeth and using my hands to support the rest of my body. It was hard. In my mind, this was the last thing I did in my lifetime.

*   *   *

At the top of the hill, the drill sergeants told us to form up in the original non-scattered formation. I moved up to the front, struggling to see above the heads of the soldiers in front of me. I couldn't believe my eyes when I saw a barely visible row of lights far in front of me in the background of the dark large structures looking like buildings.

We fixed our uniforms and Kevlars, aligned the lines and columns of the formation, and took a breath before the last stretch of the march. With the song on our lips, we marched proudly home from the victory forge, the conclusion of the basic training. "And the Army goes rolling along" never sounded more meaningful and clearer, and never made more sense than this very night. We wanted to wake everybody up on base to let them know that we came with victory. When we reached the barracks, everything around seemed so dear, and I realized how much I missed these buildings. We set aside our equipment and formed up for the last time to move in front of the company building for the conclusion ceremony. As we marched toward the front, I heard the military songs blasting through the outdoor speakers. The U.S., Army, and Regiment flags were proudly posted in the center in full lights. The battalion and company officials were there on the podium, waiting for us. After several speeches about the tradition of our regiment and countless achievements of soldiers for whom "the victory started here," we received personal tags with the army values: loyalty, duty, respect, selfless service, honor, integrity, and personal courage. This was our rite of passage. We officially carried on the mission of the heroes from the *Saving Private Ryan* motion picture. Then the company commander congratulated each of us individually.

* * *

I took the elevator and found myself on the tenth floor. I was hoping to get the same room I had before—with the sunrise view. It had been only a few weeks since I came here for the first time, yet it seemed like several centuries had passed. Here I was again at the clinic, this time because of my shin splints and a very bad blister on my heel. When I came here before, my feelings were mostly fear of the unknown and uncertainty of surviving the basic training. But those disappeared a long time ago. I was now a different person—exhausted, beaten, and relieved. This sense of enormous accomplishment made the pain in my feet almost pleasant. This time I stayed at the clinic for one night only until I could walk normally in my tennis shoes. Saturday morning, I watched the sunset for the last time through my window on the tenth floor.

Sunday morning, I rushed limping from the hospital back to the barracks. I wanted to visit my little church on the hill, where ten weeks ago I was praying with all my heart for survival. Now everything was so different—the spring was finally here, nature was well awakened from the winter frost, and the woods looked greener than ever. My heart was filled with joy and pride as I was singing in the choir with genuine passion. I felt uplifted and inspired. My last Sunday at Fort Jackson was fading in the evening breeze when I decided to donate my blood, just as I did at the beginning of my journey. As I reflected on these past ten weeks, I realized that the big mystery called "basic combat training" was finally resolved.

My last PT training was not typical. Since I wasn't able to run yet, I was prescribed weight training. Our company's first sergeant ordered me to take all the fitness equipment outdoors. For the first time in my life, I was lifting free weights under an open blue sky. This reminded me of my summer days spent with Alec on our deck—he would take outside his bicycle racing equipment ("rollers") and my Total Gym gliding bench. We would both work out right there in our backyard.

* * *

It was time to stop for a moment at the lending before conquering the next flight of stairs of my transformation. Now some of the vivid recollections of my climbing struggles were behind me, yielding space for new experiences. These memories were stored deeply in my mind like building blocks of the new me. Surviving the Victory Forge meant crossing the point of no return. Without a doubt, after shedding my artist's wings and fragility, I finally morphed into a soldier.

CHAPTER 7

RELYING ON OTHERS

Before I knew it, another three days had passed, and it was the day before graduation: the family visitation day. I couldn't wait to see Alec. I was so excited and energized that I decided to participate in a battalion run. All graduating companies and other training units, including battalion and company commanders, first sergeants, staff, and instructors, were running. It was a special ceremonial run, very slow and majestic. We were all saying to the world that today another group of brand-new soldiers was born. Hundreds of people in front of me and hundreds behind me. We were all running "dressed right" in tight columns, proudly displaying at the front all the battalion colors, like the athletes carrying the Olympic fire. We were told that these types of runs were a tradition.

I looked at the skies. The airplane right above me was flying toward the airport in Columbia, South Carolina. I was hoping Alec was on board, maybe even glancing through the window at the ground, looking for Fort Jackson. He was supposed to fly into Columbia the day before graduation and drive to Fort Jackson to see me at the ceremony.

That afternoon, we received our freshly pressed and starched BDUs to wear during our family visit. We were then transported to the cultural center where drill sergeants released us for the rest of the day.

As I heard the word "dismissed," I started to look frantically all over the field, where soldiers were greeting their loved ones. Everybody was dispersed in seconds—going in different directions and creating gigantic chaos. Everything was suddenly mixed up: soldiers, children, adults, dogs, colorful clothes, and uniforms. As I was desperately trying to find Alec's face in this commotion, I heard a deep and soft, familiar voice right behind me. "Are you looking for someone?" It was Alec, wearing his favorite purple polo shirt. My heart melted as I was hugging him, my face against his chest, listening to his heartbeat, which I missed for so many weeks.

We spent the rest of the day together touring the base. I showed Alec my barracks, my bed, the famous PT field, and the training area. We walked the streets where for several weeks I was running in the darkness of the early frosty mornings. I showed him where I pulled my left calf muscle, where I dug my first foxhole, and where I shot my first rounds from my M16. We drove through the training camps, admiring again the huge pine needles and the splendid look of the woods. We visited all the obstacle courses, towers, and ropes, taking endless pictures of my dearest and painful memories. I saw all these places for the last time, remembering all the conquered fears and unknowns.

At dusk, we had to say goodbye, and I went back to the barracks. Everyone was packing their belongings because the very first morning after graduation, we were all leaving the base. I hated the hasty packing and changing locations. I had already gotten used to all this routine, people, and places. But there was no time for a comfortable transition.

* * *

The anticipation of seeing Alec again and the graduation ceremony kept me up almost all night long. It was hard to believe that this moment finally came. Finally, I was marching on the green parade field, among all my "brothers and sisters in arms," proudly saluting the world. It was a perfect spring day, the day my dream came true. I was standing there in my "class A" uniform facing the bleachers filled with families waving their little American flags and taking endless pictures. Nothing counted for me at this point. Alec was here for me and with me. I completed my mission. We were sworn in again and promised to protect our country, and then the American anthem was played by the military marching band. I couldn't and didn't try to escape my tears.

After the ceremony, the buses took us back to the barracks, where the families were already waiting for us. We marched in front of them in a tight formation, proudly presenting ourselves to hundreds of flashing cameras. Before we were released to our families, Drill Sergeant Reaves gave us some pointers on how to behave off base while enjoying the family day. I could see that he was indeed proud of us, even though he tried to stay very serious.

This time, I didn't have any problem finding Alec in the crowd of families downstairs. We drove to Columbia and went to dinner like the good old days. Alec took me to the park, which looked so much like the park in our hometown of Northbrook. A small brook passing through was making a wonderful familiar noise of water caressing the stones like it was telling a magical tale about a lone soldier somewhere away from home. We walked around a neighborhood filled with homes in which an ordinary life was going on. People were walking their dogs, children were playing outside, and others were washing their cars in the driveway. But for us, life couldn't be any farther from the ordinary. We were finally reunited, at least for several hours.

We spent the night together at the hotel talking. I didn't want to waste this time on sleep. I tried to stay awake, as if I were afraid to wake up and realize that seeing Alec was just a dream. But the reality was catching up with me and the next morning, I came to a brutal realization that our time was over, and I had to go back to the barracks to prepare for my trip to Arizona. I hated saying goodbye so early in the morning, in the dark. The only consolation was the fact that, while in Arizona, I would be counting the days not just until graduation but until my return home for good.

* * *

While packing my duffle bag, the laminated photo of Chris fell out of my notebook. I wondered what Chris would have thought about my accomplishment of finishing the basic training. Would it be appreciated? After all, I didn't fail like those many times in 1990, while at the University of Warsaw, I had failed my French class.

It was the time of the final exams ending my second year at the University of Warsaw. The Practical French exam had three parts: French grammar, specialized French, and conversational French. First was the written exam from all three, and if passed successfully, there was an oral exam. On my first attempt, I failed the written exam miserably. I was worried, but I had high hopes that the retest in July would go better. I studied hard for two weeks, doing grammar exercises, and reading. The written retest gave a borderline result, but the oral part was as disastrous as the first try. Just like the first failed exam, the second one had to be signed off in my student book by all three professors of practical French. Chris was one of them. I felt embarrassed that I had managed to have Chris's signatures next to two failed exams. I was trying for so long to make the best impression in French class, but my efforts had proven futile. In my mind, I was worthless. In addition, I was desperate because I was running out of time. The new academic year was starting in October, and I needed to start it fresh. So, I requested a third chance for September, which, in my case, because I had eventually passed the written retest, consisted of an oral examination only.

It was a sunny Saturday morning when I arrived at the university. The building was empty, but in one room, there was an academic board waiting for me. All three French professors and the dean of the entire department were sitting behind a long table. I could tell that Chris was a bit nervous. I, on the other hand, was frightened. Until then, I never had to present anything in French in front of a board of faculty.

From the start, I was struggling. I was confusing and misusing words, building some awkward expressions, and not understanding the questions. I was more and more embarrassed and avoided looking at Chris at any cost. At some point, a question was posed related to a press article that I knew very well. I did not satisfy one of the professors with my answer, as she was looking for me to use a specific expression. Despite numerous tries, I couldn't come up with what was expected. Eventually, I froze and wasn't capable of uttering a single word. With tears in my eyes, I finally gave up. Then I was told that the expression was "le temps sclérosé" [sclerotic time], which was referring to the times of resistance to change. For the third time, I collected several signatures next to my failing grade. I had to be "recycled" and repeat all French classes from my second year of studies.

Everyone eventually left the building, and I stood there alone in the hallway. I didn't know what to do with myself. In my desperation, I needed to talk to someone. I ran out of the building to see a departing white sedan. I recognized Chris's car. Instinctively, I started running behind it, hoping to catch up with it before it disappeared for good. I didn't know what I was expecting, catching up with a car? When I followed the car around a corner, I noticed it was already parked in front of a staircase of a building. To my surprise, no one was in the car. I sat on the steps nearby, devastated.

Chris emerged from the building, and without being too surprised to see me there, quickly provided the words of support.

"It's not the end of the world. While repeating the second year's French, you can study all other subjects from the third year in advance. In the fourth year, everything will be evened out because in the fifth year, there is no practical French."

"Are you sure?" I asked, my voice shaking through tears.

"We do it all the time. You just have to decide if you want to continue studies in advance. You don't have to let French hold you up."

"I like this option. How do I proceed?" This was my last hope for continuing my studies.

"Just submit a request for the advanced continuation and I'll approve it. I have the authority to do so. After all, I am the dean of Academic Student Affairs, remember?"

"I do remember." I wiped the tears with my sleeve like a schoolgirl. "I voted for you."

* * *

With my heart heavy as lead, I was in the barracks, depressed. I just realized how much I already wanted to leave. I finished packing my duffle bags and took them downstairs to align them with the others going to Fort Huachuca. Throughout the day, the groups of soldiers were leaving the base on luxury coaches. Our group of eleven soldiers going to Fort Huachuca, a military intelligence center, was waiting in the sun on the sidewalk. Since our bus wasn't coming, I went back to the barracks to say goodbye to these buildings and take a last look at the bay with a gigantic painting on the shiny and now empty floor: "Mad Dogs, 3rd Platoon."

Our group was the last to leave Fort Jackson. All three of our drill sergeants came by to say their last goodbyes. When the bus pulled up, Drill Sergeant Reaves immediately started organizing the baggage lockers as if he wanted to cover his emotions. I could see that he was sad to see us leave like we didn't need him anymore. I tried to say something nice to him, but he turned it into a joke. It was hard even for him to laugh. He shook my hand and said in his short and chilly voice, "Good luck, SKI. Go and do great things up there in Arizona." I got on the bus and couldn't take my eyes off Drill Sergeant Reaves. He stood there and turned sideways, looking somewhere far in the endless woods, and pretending that he didn't care that we were leaving. I knew he could see the bus from the corner of his eye, just like he always did. Suddenly, he started walking away as if he had some pressing matter to take care of. I waved to him as my bus was driving off, but he didn't look and just kept going toward the building.

With my heart heavy as lead, I went back to the barracks to say goodbye to these buildings and take a last look at the bay. (My bunk on top.)

Negotiating many obstacle courses, where physical stamina, sheer muscle power, and mental prowess were the key, made me wonder time and again, how conquering them was even possible. What I learned was that in many situations, it wasn't about skills and determination. It was about trusting your teammates to pull you up and pull you through, literally. Sometimes it was about moral support. The trust and kindness, stripped of prejudices and judgments while working together, was what made my platoon a great team. Being part of it made me realize I didn't have to excel in everything on my own, which was a striking contrast with professional ballet dancing, which was all about individual skills and presence. In the incredibly physically demanding conditions of basic training, for the first time in my life, I had experienced what it meant to have no options but to rely on others to help me conquer my own fears.

PART IV

ADVANCED INDIVIDUAL TRAINING:
LEARNING MY JOB AS AN ENLISTED SOLDIER

CHAPTER 8

I AM A SOLDIER FIRST

Now that I was finally a soldier, I was looking forward to my AIT in Fort Huachuca, where the first four weeks of school were called phase IV of training (the first three were basic training). To be fully qualified, I needed to learn the skills needed to perform my specific army job, 97E (ninety-seven echo), the Interrogator. When I mentioned to people that this would be my "military occupational skill," they immediately thought about the torture being inflicted on prisoners of war to extract information. It was probably because of the perception of interrogation in films and literature, I suspected. Just like interrogation, the notion of "military intelligence" typically had a strong connotation with spying. Of course, I was also strongly influenced by these popular views.

Before I was shipped to basic training, however, I did some research and knew a little more about what my future job would entail. I wasn't going to be a spy or torturer. When I discovered the Interrogator also had a more friendly designation, "human intelligence collector" (HUMINT), I had a feeling that there was more to this job than the popular culture had led me to believe. HUMINT collector's role was to screen various intelligence sources (prisoners of war, documents, artifacts) for information critical to the battlefield and perform interrogations. What I didn't know before was that they also were conducting liaison meetings and interviews with sources (civilians like enemy deserters, insurgents, friendly forces, and refugees) during wartime or peace-keeping operations. The interesting part was about creating specialized intelligence reports about enemy forces and potential battle areas to help the commanders in their decision making. It seemed like a highly intellectual job, which, to me, was always very attractive. What struck me the most in their job description was the required proficiency in at least one foreign language. Humint collectors were interrogating or interviewing people not only in English but also in foreign languages, serving as interpreters and translators of foreign documents. This was the most enticing to me, as linguistics were my passion, and I was already part of a Chicago-based Military Intelligence Battalion with the "Linguist" designation. Every soldier in my unit was fluent in at least one foreign language and many in two or even three. The best part about learning this job, however, was that I already was fluent in Polish and French and had a basic knowledge of Russian, which was a requirement in ballet school. This meant that I wouldn't have to attend the Defense Language Institute in California to learn a language for the next couple of years. After six months of AIT and studying the interrogator/humint collector job, I would be fully qualified and hopefully an expert in that field.

These job descriptions sounded pretty foreign to me, as my English at the time was pretty basic. My biggest upcoming task was to understand this new language, learn to use proper terminology to function in the military intelligence environment. I was ecstatic to be entering the elite of the U.S. armed forces, as at that time, there were only, we were told, 570 people with this MOS in the entire country. It was a wonderful challenge.

* * *

Although winter was never my favorite season, December 1990 in Warsaw had a special meaning. My existence was saturated with the feeling of loneliness and longing for some mysterious and undefined notion of happiness. It seemed like any traces of daylight were hiding from me among the deserted streets of Warsaw.

For several days, right after Christmas, I was outlining in my mind the entire course of action—step by step, location by location, how and where to see my favorite French professor.

The anticipation of this unexpected result of my encounter with Chris felt like a fresh stream of energy that was making my heart race. I attempted several times already to find Chris, but we kept missing each other. My last option was eventually quite simple: since it was the evening of the ballet *Nutcracker* at the Great Opera, I was hoping to find Chris there. All day long, I was thinking about placing a brief note on Chris's car with best wishes for the upcoming new year and a small gift. I wanted to be a ghost and watch everything from behind the scenes, without being seen. Just imagining Chris finding my note, a little smile, and a discreet look around in search of the mysterious protagonist was a delightful exercise for my mind. I was in a hurry to see this moment realized and I couldn't afford to lose this last chance of the day. All my thoughts were chasing each other in a chaotic maze of images streaming through my head like a blast of sudden light pursuing this potential moment of brief and fragile happiness.

Getting to the opera on this snowy and windy evening was a challenging task. Without a single minute to spare and completely dependent on public transportation, I was switching buses several times to eliminate the waiting at the bus stops. The urge to move forward at any price and getting to the end of this frantic race with time kept me going.

I ran as fast as possible through the mounds of snow on the pavement, passing by the empty front stores closed up for the day. Barely catching my breath, I finally arrived at the Great Opera Plaza just to see it completely abandoned, with no sign of life. Ferocious winter was blowing snow all around. An enormous maze of countless fresh tire tracks was covering the plaza. Everyone had left already, and I missed Chris. I stood there in disbelief, disappointed. My worst nightmare just came true. I was too late.

* * *

A sudden bump on the ground shook up the vehicle and woke me up. A golden glow of the desert blinded my eyes. My group from Fort Jackson was approaching Fort Huachuca, Arizona.

This time at the gate, I saw the monuments of the Buffalo Soldiers, the nineteenth-century predecessors of the U.S. Army soldiers in this area. The base was beautiful—at least at first sight. All the buildings were brand-new, clean, and contemporary. "Fort Huachuca - Est. 1877 National Historic Landmark" was proudly embossed on the sign by the gate. As we were passing through the base, I spotted countless radars, a variety of gigantic electronic equipment, and airplanes set up by the clusters of windowless buildings dispersed through this desert.

For the next several months, I would wake up with the bright sun warming up my face. I lived in a three-person room equipped with real homelike furniture, decorated with pictures and window curtains, and with a private bathroom.

It dawned on me that the first few weeks at Fort Huachuca would seem like a never-ending struggle with the most powerful feeling of depression ever. Being uprooted again from everything that was already familiar to me at Fort Jackson and felt like home, was unbearable. This time, however, I was staying at my new base for at least twice as long. Deep down in my heart, I knew that eventually Fort Huachuca would become my home and I hoped that at some point I would enjoy my stay there. In the meantime, I was desperately looking for something meaningful and inspiring in this new reality.

Despite the beautiful barracks and access to the movie theater and a choice of stores on base, during the first weekend, I felt lonely and lost. The surrounding people were too young—my roommates could only talk about guys, movies, and physical training. It was impossible to find someone to share my thoughts with, not to mention have a decent conversation about something other than plans for the upcoming weekend. Since my classes didn't start for almost two weeks after my arrival at Fort Huachuca, I was mostly busy pulling a variety of duties like overnight twelve-hour shifts at the company quarters, kitchen patrol, or barracks' maintenance during the day. There was too much time for anxiety and constant worry about the slowly approaching tough school program.

One good news was that I could finally wear my rank on the uniform. I was a specialist at last.

It was extremely hard getting used to the thin mountain air at over 5,000 feet above sea level, especially during the morning runs. I was constantly blinded by the scorching desert sun, and the hot, dry air was causing me quite frequent nosebleeds and headaches. The only consolation to this predicament was the most magnificent nature surrounding the base. Despite the deep feeling of disconnection from my last "home" at Fort Jackson, eventually, I felt inspired by the most magnificent view of the majestic Huachuca Mountains with their peaks adorned by snow. I looked through the window in my room in disbelief that it was indeed a reality, not a painting on the wall. From now on, the Huachuca Mountains would be there for me like the omnipresent guardian angels.

As the days went by, I continued to fight the feelings of detachment and growing anxiety. The second Friday, I was assigned to barracks' maintenance duty. Since the tasks were not clearly specified, I found myself in the laundry room equipped with brand-new washing machines and dryers. What a refreshing difference compared to the equipment I used at Fort Jackson. In the corner, a utility sink caught my attention because it was unusually dirty and seemed like an enjoyable challenge for the rest of the day. The sink was covered with colorful acrylic paint and, by my quick assessment, had not seen the scrubbing brush for a while. I jumped at this opportunity to do something useful. It reminded me of the art studio at my college in Chicago, where I worked as a facility supervisor on the weekends. I painted my best artwork those days, as the atmosphere in this beautiful, spacious studio was casual and relaxing. In the early spring, the morning sun was always entering the room through the large windows like a long-expected friend, the best partner of artists seeking the natural light. After each painting session was over, I would put away all the easels, canvas, and paints. The brushes were then cleaned with bar soap in the sink, covered with various paint colors. This memory of artistic adventures in Chicago brought me closer to the barracks. Ultimately, I had something to relate to. While scrubbing the blue, gray, and yellow paint off the sink surface, I was thinking about what could possibly be painted around here with these colors. Eventually, I discovered that it was a gigantic emblem of an eagle—the E Company mascot posted a few days later in the building's main lobby. I missed the painting tremendously. I thought that perhaps one day I would have the opportunity to paint a company mascot as well.

* * *

Dear Alec,

The forsythia shrubs are blooming right by my window, just like the ones in front of our house in Northbrook, and exactly the same as those in Poland. Here in the Arizona desert, this unexpected beauty of spring makes me feel so much better.

I guess you are getting sick of seeing the picture of a drill sergeant on my letterhead. I'm sick of it too, but unfortunately, it's my reality. We have plenty of drill sergeants here too, at least two for each platoon. They have their offices in a separate building adjacent to the barracks and they take care of soldiers' paperwork and other things. Some days, I see huge lines in front of certain drill sergeants' offices. I wonder why?

A couple of days ago, we had a meeting in the main auditorium on the base for those new arrivals who had bachelor's degrees. Our battalion commander, Colonel Keller was encouraging us to become U.S. Army officers. He randomly picked me from the audience and asked me to say a few words about myself, where I was from, what my degree was, and so on. After the meeting, a captain sitting nearby approached me. "Hello, I am Captain Zubr, E Company commander. I'm Polish too. We should talk one of these days. Ask your drill sergeant to set an appointment for you to see me this week." I was ecstatic. Can you believe this? A U.S. Army captain of Polish origin in Fort Huachuca!

Our company, "Echo-Eagles," is the largest and the best company in the Military Intelligence Village. We have only two specialties: 97E (interrogators), sometimes called "military detectives," and 97B (counterintelligence agents), "Spooks." Last week, I was finally transferred from the First to the Second Platoon as we started the school cycle. Our platoon is called Marauders (what a creepy name!), and we received our official Class 003 guidon—a platoon flag we carry everywhere we go as a formation during the school hours.

Every day we bring to school about thirty pounds of load: laptop, LBE, and books. Out of my thirty books, some of the titles are *Military Intelligence Activities, Worldwide Weapons Systems, Military Law and Justice, Intelligence in Combating Terrorism, Commander's Handbook on Intelligence, Intelligence Preparation on the Battlefield,* etc. No wonder I'm overwhelmed and stressed out. Yesterday, after my first full week of school, I fell asleep at 7:30 p.m. and slept for twelve hours! Despite the stress and the overwhelming amount of new knowledge to digest, the academic lifestyle suits me better than barracks maintenance. I am a little disappointed with people around me—kind of flat, thinking only about watching TV or going to the movies. They are not like you—intelligent, educated, and sophisticated. I also hate the fact that for the first four weeks of school, I am not able to go anywhere by myself since I still need a battle buddy with me. I can't wait until phase V when after school I can slip into my civilian clothes and go anywhere without the buddy. Phase V+ (the last two weeks of training) will be even better: we can drive civilian cars, go off post, even for an overnight stay (with a pass, of course), and have internet in my room! The only conditions for phase privileges are satisfactory academic progress, passing PT tests, and passing phase tests. It looks very appealing to me.

* * *

The school absorbed me so deeply that the feeling of disconnection eventually began to fade away. I devoted every evening to homework and studying, still mysterious to me, military language. Since my English was limited to a common language and rather basic military terms, the terminology used in the interrogation course posed a tremendous problem. Ultimately, as I went through the course, I was creating my own dictionary of military terms. This gave me even more purpose and strength. Slowly, from the deepest depression, I transitioned into euphoria. I loved being in school, doing homework, and stretching my brain to the limits. It didn't matter that all this pressure of succeeding gave me ferocious headaches. Sometimes I would think of the days when joining the army was my biggest dream. Back then, I wanted to be part of something big and meaningful. I imagined all these unknown places I would have to go to for training. And here I finally was, in the largest intelligence school and center in the country, a specialist in the United States Army. My only challenge was to understand and conceive these complicated new subjects I was trying to learn. Every morning while marching to school in formation, I was watching our class's guidon proudly waving in front. For the first time in Arizona, I felt like I was in the right place, and nothing could disturb my newly found inner peace. I loved our early morning running routines, when we would stop at 6:00 a.m. in the middle of the desert to salute the invisible flag as it was pulled up on the pole, somewhere in the historical district of the base. The flag rising was always accompanied by the military trumpet playing reveille, unfortunately very hard to register in the barracks area.

One day, however, this moment was extremely special. Since our Friday runs were usually long, our drill sergeant took us to a new, more challenging location. On our usual stretch of the route, we passed an impressive platoon of marines in their green sweats running at a fast pace, carrying a huge log resembling an electric pole. We continued our slow run until the lights of the military intelligence village disappeared behind us. Soon we were swallowed by the darkness of the cold desert morning. Suddenly, I noticed an ancient-looking shield on the nearby bridge: "Heritage Mountain." My heart almost stopped because it meant that we were about to run uphill!

Since I was in the first row of the formation, setting the pace, I slowed down to regroup and keep a slow and consistent tempo for everybody behind me. I'd heard about Heritage Mountain before. People were falling out of formation, unable to finish the run because of the height. Failure was not an option, however. Definitely not when I was up front. The drill sergeant next to me was cheering me on, as if he could see my struggle and a battle of thoughts in my mind. "Just keep this pace and you'll make it, SKI!" His words resonated with me. As the pavement was closer and closer, my body slanted forward, and I lifted my chin up as if I were trying to grab the air and lift myself up to the top. I heard people crying in formation behind me, our drill sergeant yelling, "Do not stop! Not now! We are so close! Keep going! Do not stop!" Although we were not allowed to stop, a few runners on the back were dangerously close to expire. As a pace setter, I slowed down the entire formation and kept running in place so others could catch up. By the time we finally got to the very top of the hill, the skies started clearing to let the impatient sun reveal its shiny face through the clouds. Prompted by our drill sergeant, we stopped running, fixed the staggered formation, and stood there at attention facing the area where the reveille signal was normally coming from. On command, "Present arms," we saluted the flag. For the first time in my life, I heard the reveille signal so clearly, echoing off the glorious mountains. At this very moment, the sun finally broke through the clouds like a breathtaking symbol of victory, announcing a new day, and the end of struggle, bringing hope for the days to come. I felt like I was reborn, stronger than ever, my heart pounding from happiness and the strenuous run. Arizona was slowly becoming my home.

* * *

I dusted off the orange fine particles from my freshly polished combat boots. The day was slowly waking from a deep sleep in the chilly Arizona desert. I was guarding the road from vehicular traffic for the soldiers who were about to run through the intersection as a part of their daily physical training routine. I was anxiously waiting for the dawn to break through the darkness and breathe new life into the nature around. A dense fog on the ground was lethargically disappearing in the air. I remembered marveling at the same type of fog one day a decade ago, one early morning in the spring of 1991.

I was on the bus to the Warsaw-East train station to say goodbye to my dearest friend. As the bus was crossing the Vistula River, I watched a delicate mist slowly disappearing in the air, revealing the innocent reflections of the rising sun. A morning breeze was gently kissing the river and announcing a brand-new day. It appeared so close and incarnate that I could almost touch it.

I found myself at the deserted train station, on a solitary bench in the middle of track number two. Submerged in a deep ocean of thoughts about the upcoming days, I stared blindly at the overhead sign announcing the departure of the train to Nuremberg, Germany, scheduled at 8:15 a.m. I was wondering how I would survive not seeing Chris for several days. I would miss our secret meetings. I would have no one to leave little Post-it notes behind their car's windshield. I would have no one to wait for around the corner of the building after classes. Suddenly, a familiar silhouette appeared next to me and brought me back to reality with a soft voice.

"You're already here. It was so nice of you to come." Chris's silver and elusive voice sounded like the sweetest melody of life.

I kissed gently Chris's cheek and whispered, "Thank God it's only two weeks. I miss you already." I desperately wanted to move the time forward and have this time of separation behind me already.

"Would you do me a favor?" Suddenly I came to life from my gloomy mood, eager to do anything for my friend. "For the last few days, I was trying to rent this book from the university library without any luck. Could you please place an order for it so they would put it on hold for me when it becomes available?" Chris handed me a piece of paper with the name of the author and a title.

A few minutes later, I watched the train slowly fade away in the morning haze, pressing this piece of paper against my heart as if it was my only lifeline connecting me with Chris. At this moment, ordering the book was like a mission and my primary purpose in life. The next day I ran to the University of Warsaw Library and with my heart pounding from excitement, I meticulously filled out the order form for *The Presentation of Self in Everyday Life* by Erving Goffman.

The rhythmic sound of a running platoon brought me back to my early morning road guard duty. I turned on my flashlight and proceeded to the middle of the intersection, making sure no vehicle would pass through.

* * *

As time went by, I noticed that my new journey in Arizona was revolving around two very distinct worlds. One was the life in the barracks—a very mediocre equivalent of what I so desperately wanted to be my home away from home. The other was school life, by definition independent of the one in the barracks. Despite the rule that our drill sergeants were not to interfere with our school and the school instructors to stay away from the barracks, sometimes these two worlds were overlapping. For example, in order to transition to phase V and get more privileges, a spotless academic record was required. On the other hand, to qualify for any distinction at school, spotless records outside of school were required. With the class material more challenging every day, it was harder and harder to balance the requirements of both worlds.

I already felt like an underdog because of my—not always so obvious to others, but painful to me—weakness. I was an ESL (English as a Second Language) from Poland. As I progressed in the classroom, it felt more and more unbearable to be an outsider. One day in school, one of my instructors made an ethnic comment about Polish people. Regardless of my internal rage at the moment, I bit my tongue and remained quiet. Sergeant Poracek apparently didn't realize that his joke might be offensive to others, so he followed me after class to the door and made a comment to me in Russian. I responded to him politely that I was not Russian. What I heard after that would make anybody's blood come to a boiling point. That afternoon in the barracks, I talked to my drill sergeant, and he recommended to either file a formal complaint or confront Sergeant Poracek and clarify why I found his jokes offensive. I chose the latter because I didn't know any better, and of course, it didn't help. I had to stop being naïve and believe that the school instructors would have some integrity. The ultimate price I paid for this brief confrontation was a failed exam and therefore I lost the chance to graduate with distinction. I retook the exam the next day and got the optimum score, but I wasn't nearly done paying the price.

After this incident, my natural love for school diminished dramatically, and I couldn't help my growing distaste for Tallmadge Hall (our school building). Instead, I put all my efforts into preparation for the upcoming fitness test. My goal was to pass it the first time around since my transition to phase V depended on this. My other upcoming nightmare was unfortunately school related—the infamous IPT: Interrogation Performance Test. If failed, there was no possibility of a retest except by repeating the course up to this moment: the entire two-thirds of the school cycle. The IPT was a breaking point for most of the interrogators, and many of them ended up being "recycled." The term itself was making me nauseous because it suggested that we were garbage. I eventually met several "recycles" from previous classes and noticed that the majority of them were Hispanic, Polish, or Russian. Without thinking too much about it, I devoted all my free time to the preparation of the "Interrogation Notebook," a tool required to conduct an interrogation according to very specific, quite often nonsensical, and unrealistic rules.

I devoted all my free time to the preparation of the "Interrogation Notebook."

After a couple of weeks, my initially fearless roommates lost their feisty spirits. Diane fell into serious money problems: her spending was out of control and her parents had no money to send. She was buying movies and music CDs as if her life depended on them, draining every single penny earned while in training. Eventually, she asked me to be her "bank". This, however, didn't last very long because she still kept "withdrawing" her money from me. The money, however, was not the only problem. Diane was slowly losing focus, failing fitness tests, overeating, and being late for our routine company formations. One Saturday, she was late for PT. As a punishment, her drill sergeant had her report to him every single hour wearing a different uniform: class A, class B, BDU, and PT.

Kate, on the other hand, had long lost her dream of becoming a "PT Queen" as she had failed her PT twice already. I could see her spirit breaking while she was eating more cakes, candy, and chocolate every day. In the afternoons, she would still exercise, but apparently it was never enough. Sometimes after lights out, from the top of my bunk bed, I could hear Kate crying into a pillow, her body quivering in deep spasms.

Before the end of April, I found myself homesick as never before. Time was not on my side. I made a calendar and taped it to the wall to count off the days until graduation and the departure home. Since March 17, I crossed off approximately four weeks. The remaining half of April, May, June, and half of July were overwhelmingly blank, cynically staring at me every day. The vision of staying at school this long was horrendous, so I added to my calendar the months of January and February, with the days already marked off and taped them on the wall as well. It made me feel much better knowing that not everything was still ahead of me.

I couldn't help feeling exhausted from all the brain activity at school, late nights devoted to homework, and constant marching to Tallmadge Hall with all thirty of my books. I wasn't alone, though. Half of the people in my class were injured—their backs, knees, or feet had given up already. Some of us started bringing to school only books directly related to a current subject. However, we would never know for sure what would be on our agenda since the instructors wanted to humiliate us in front of other platoons and always told us to carry all of our books. One Friday, our class sergeant (principal instructor and advisor) decided to conduct a surprise test at 4:30 p.m. He was infuriated after discovering that six people didn't have the appropriate book with them. Fortunately, our drill sergeant showed up like a guardian angel in the doorway to march us back to the barracks because on Fridays the school day was supposed to end at that hour. I was never so happy to see a drill sergeant before. "Pack your shit and get the hell out of here!" Sergeant Reinhardt, the instructor, was enraged, as we were leaving the classroom swiftly. I would have taken marching back to the barracks over any test at school any day.

*　　*　　*

Exactly one month went by since my arrival at Fort Huachuca. The afternoon was peaceful after another exhausting day at school. As usual, I was sitting by the barracks on the giant pole used by the marines in their running routines. The sun was slowly setting behind the dining facility. I watched with envy small groups of soldiers in phase V wearing their civilian clothes, getting into their private vehicles, and driving away amused. I wondered how it would feel to be in a private vehicle with a little scent-tree hanging off the rear-view mirror. Perhaps that little tree would have a scent of a "pine" or "daisies"? I grabbed my journal to let my feelings flow on paper like a river of consolation and defiance.

"Yesterday's news about yet another test necessary to advance to phase V irritated me greatly. I'm already frustrated with the school and now this. Despite my greatest efforts, I fail to comprehend what is the reason for all these negative things going on around me. Maybe there is a sign somewhere that things will get better, and everything indeed happens for a reason. Meanwhile, I feel like some powerful force is against me instead of rewarding my hard work and dedication. My discouragement grows deeper every day. It seems like the limits of my patience are holding strong and I'm still far from absolute despair. I'm still hanging on asking myself the same question every morning: 'How long am I going to have to endure this nonsense at school?' Despite all the pressure, constantly changing rules, being locked up in the barracks, or having to rely on a battle buddy to go anywhere, I want to get through this. My ultimate dream is to become an officer and come back to Fort Huachuca for my intelligence officer training. It will be a completely different battle. Maybe here and now is the true preparation for my career. I'm so overwhelmed and tired. I know it's hard, but I also know that I'll stick it out and move forward . . ."

*   *   *

As usual, we were waiting over half an hour for our drill sergeant to come to Tallmadge Hall and march us back to the barracks. While sitting on the curb, I noticed on the ground an ant carrying a hefty chunk of building material. He was moving forward decisively, as if he knew exactly where to go. I doubted an insignificant creature like this would be able to navigate through the asphalt routes in the middle of the desert. Curious to see where this little fellow was headed, I followed him for nearly fifty feet along the curb. He disappeared in a small gap between the concrete and the dirt. It was his home! At the entrance, millions of his brothers and sisters were moving around, in and out, carrying various materials to their habitat. I felt relief that he found his home. In fact, he probably was never lost, only drifted far away from home in his quest for the best building materials. I thought about my recent feelings of being lonely and discouraged, but fighting to survive and find my way home. I felt like this little ant, carrying on my mission to accomplish and build my future. It occurred to me that one day I would find my way home just like the little creature.

*   *   *

"I'm a soldier first, but an intelligence professional second to none . . . With a sense of urgency and tenacity, professional and physical fitness, and above all integrity—for in truth lies victory. Always at silent war while ready for a shooting war; the silent warrior of the Army team." The military intelligence soldier's creed was one of the many requirements for transition to phase V. I loved the pathos and brilliance of this creed and wanted to identify myself with this heroic way of life. I believed in the literal sense of these words and wanted to live them with all my heart, be a true MI soldier, and save the world. My patriotism was highly romantic, supported by legends of Polish warriors like Pulaski and Kosciuszko, who, as soldiers of the U.S. Army during the Revolutionary War, fought for the values of democracy for all. As I was slowly growing up as an American citizen and a soldier, it was more and more clear to me that America, a symbol of ideals and dreams that could be now achieved, was for me, an ultimate country to prosper in, to be part of, and to defend.

CHAPTER 9

REBUILDING MYSELF

Dear Alec,

It's been exactly four weeks since I arrived at Fort Huachuca on March 17. I had an especially good day today. Finally. Since both my roommates had a Saturday PT this morning, I could sleep in peace. I decided to study a little for the phase V test while doing my laundry. I hooked up with a couple from my class—Zealands—and we all went to see our drill sergeant for testing. We all survived the questioning and received our temporary phase cards! For the first time since I left home in January, I reclaimed my civilian clothes and could walk around the base freely all by myself.

Last night I went to bed early, but in the middle of the night, I heard our drill sergeant doing a surprise "bed check." In fact, he went into our rooms assisted by a female soldier to see if we were actually in bed. Apparently, during the weekends, some people were sneaking out through the windows. Later today, I heard that one girl left a dummy in her bed and got caught outside the barracks at night. Unbelievable. She is being discharged from the army for unknown reasons already, yet she's still adding trouble to her military career.

Lately, it's been getting exceptionally hot during the day, so I had to purchase a pair of "desert combat boots." They are so light and comfortable; I can't wait to wear them to school on Monday.

I'm doing well at school. So far, besides this one unfortunate encounter with Sergeant Poracek, all the other tests I've maxed. I'm still worried about the test on Monday. As you know, the instructors are being very difficult and complicate things that are simple, as if they wanted us to fail the interrogation test."

* * *

During our after-school formation, we usually had a mail call. Every letter would "cost" ten push-ups, depending on how many postage stamps were on the envelope. Just like in basic training. For each additional postage stamp, we were looking for one to five extra, and if the stamp was representing a heart or something cute, then the redemption cost would double. One day, however, I found out the cost of receiving a package. It was the first one since I transitioned to phase V, so I was expecting a lot of things, which were prohibited until now. The twenty-five push-ups' price was well worth paying for a piece of home. Alec sent me everything I asked for, including my blue flannel bedsheets, a brand-new purple CD player, and the classical music CDs I was craving for so long.

* * *

I made myself comfortable on my top bunk bed and loaded the CD with *Italian Baroque Concertos* played by trumpeter Maurice Andre. I wanted to hear my favorite piece by Domenico Zipoli again. It was the Suite in F major to which I listened so often in the summer of 1991 in Warsaw when my friendship with Chris was growing strong.

It was the last week of my summer courses at the Music Academy. At that time, I lived in the landmark dormitory for fine arts students. In the early years of the nineteenth century, a famous Polish composer, Frédéric Chopin, studied piano and composition in this historic building. I loved the architecture and the ambiance of this old edifice. The place was filled with strange-looking characters carrying unusual cases with big and small musical instruments. At night, I loved to keep my window open and listen to someone practicing the trumpet concerto. A smooth and lonely sound was gently echoing off the walls of the L-shaped building opening to an old, abandoned garden.

In the afternoons, I usually went to see Chris, who at this time of the year was running the entrance exams to the university. We would meet by the French Studies building and walk to Dynasty Park, near the music academy. Sitting silently on the bench and sipping apple juice from miniature boxes with a straw, we were enjoying the peaceful surroundings filled with the distant and fading sounds of music students playing their instruments at school. Life around us seemed to stand still for those few magic moments of summer, uninterrupted by the prosaic noises of civilization. It was the most enchanting experience to hear the music played so casually yet tremendously meaningful. Secretly, I was excited and proud that I was part of this secret ritual I was enjoying with Chris, away from the prodding eyes of the public.

*   *   *

By mid-May, my chances of successfully passing my IPT exam were very slim. During our recent interrogation practice, I had a problem with understanding some military designations and I expressed my concerns to my role player (playing the prisoner that I was supposed to "break"). Before I knew it, I found myself surrounded by Sergeant Reinhardt, Sergeant Cabbage, and all the instructors in an office, screaming at me for mentioning my "language issues." They believed that since they could understand everything I was saying, there was no "language problem" and I should never mention anything about it. I stood there, amazed by the intensity of the aggression of the instructors yelling on top of each other at me. Despite my best efforts, I was not able to make sense of this attack. I squinted my eyes in an attempt to understand what all this barrage of words meant. The next thing I saw was Sergeant Reinhardt screaming in my face so close I could feel his spit on my skin. Clark was called to the room to be my "battle buddy" and witness the entire scene. On our way back from school, she told me she didn't feel comfortable with me having so much confidence during the confrontation. I could only assure her that in my position, there was no other option but to stand tall and be able to fight for what was right. And I was right because only I could know how hard it was *for me* to understand specialized English. It didn't matter that I could be understood easily. That evening, my drill sergeant asked me about the incident at school. Apparently, Sergeant Reinhardt had already complained about it to him.

"Don't worry. We have the same problem with the 97E instructors at least a couple of times every cycle. The Zealands already told me how you guys are working together on your English. They also mentioned that the role player you had today has something against the females in the army. You just have to adjust and overcome."

It was a genuine relief. I wasn't punished and grounded by the drill sergeant. That evening, I enjoyed a trip to the mall in my civilian clothes. Naturally, the first person I had to bump into at the store was Sergeant Reinhardt. In his torn, dirty jeans and rag-like T-shirt, I barely recognized him. He was probably surprised to see me there regardless of his earlier request to take away my privileges. He was the first to say "Hi" and then quickly disappeared into the crowd as if he was ashamed to be seen looking like a villain beggar. I felt sorry for him.

* * *

Dear Alec,

It's Saturday, but I'm at Tallmadge Hall because we have a study group before our interrogation test. Being here in civilian clothes is better. It feels a lot like a regular college. This weekend, I see so many people getting in trouble for stupid things. Wherever I look, I see some type of "corrective training" going on. The guys from our company were caught having a mess in their barracks, so the entire weekend they had a "GI Party." This means that from 8:00 a.m. to 8:00 p.m. they wear BDUs and clean everything. My roommates also managed to screw up their weekend. One has a PT test every Saturday at 6:00 a.m. because she was not able to pass the regular monthly fitness test. The other one was woken up for training by mistake! Last night, she didn't feel like checking the list for Saturday PT and correcting the mistake. Besides, both of them have to report to their drill sergeant in their BDUs at 7 a.m. on Sunday because their entire platoon messed up something. One of my drill sergeants noticed a girl from the air force wearing these huge earrings, so he wanted to punish her, but he couldn't because the army cannot impose upon the air force personnel. She probably felt that he wanted to do something, so she said to him nonchalantly, "Yep, I'm air force." The drill sergeant was so pissed that he talked to her instructor. Because the air force people can never have PT corrective training, she was ordered to sweep clean all the parking lots and scrub dumpsters in the area. I also have some examples from school. Yesterday, after explaining something in class, our instructor asked, "Everyone is on the train now?" Some smarty-pants replied, "Yes, we just need to get Bradley on the dining cart." Bradley is a little overweight. Besides, our famous, most hated instructor, Sergeant Cabbage, always says stupid things about herself, which are as funny as they are pathetic. For example, she said, "Folks, I'm blonde. Make your report understandable to me. Keep it simple and stupid. I have to get it." I love when she admits to being a moron, especially after all the hard times she gave me a couple of weeks ago during the infamous confrontation. Last Sunday, I heard her saying something even better and this time she was probably serious because she said that to a small group of people. "I could play *Who Wants to Be a Millionaire* because I know all the answers," she said. "But if I had to use a 'lifeline' for help and call a friend, I couldn't because I have no friends. It would be hard for me to admit in front of millions of people that I have no one to call." This time, it wasn't funny. Just pitiful.

Yesterday one private in DFAC (dining facility) got on my nerves. I was standing in line for food, pushing my tray next to me on the counter. For a moment, I stepped a couple of feet away to grab an apple from a nearby fruit basket. When I came back, the guy who was behind me in line skipped the line and moved my tray to the side.

"Hey, what do you think you're doing, pushing my tray away?!"

"Relax, girl."

What a freaking attitude, I thought to myself. I'll give you "girl." "First off, I'm not your girl. Second, I'm not from your hood, and third, Private Johnson,"—I read his name from his uniform tag—"to you, I'm a specialist, so address me properly."

"I didn't say 'girl,'" he tried to backpedal.

"Make way." I grabbed my tray and stepped in front of him.

It's Tuesday already! Time is going so fast; I can barely keep up. I had a wonderful day because of my PT test. I did 35 push-ups, and 65 sit-ups, and ran my two miles in 18'50". I beat my record run of 19'48"! I asked our first sergeant to run with me, and he couldn't be happier to do it. He kept me focused and talked about breathing and relaxing techniques, and how to think about the effort planned to be used versus the effort already used as a method of measurement of how fast to run. He ran the entire time next to me at my pace. Half a mile before the end, I picked up the pace slightly, then by a quarter line, I picked up again. The last hundred yards, he whispered to me, "Sprint, SKI!" I bolted as if some unexpected surge of energy struck my entire body. As we both approached the finish line, I could hear him screaming, "Excellent job, SPC Rakowski! Great work!"

I will never forget what he told me later. "It doesn't matter how you start. What matters is how you finish . . ."

*   *   *

It was time to start my reintegration. Picking up the pieces one by one, I was building the new me. Improving my English, establishing myself in school and in the barracks as an individual, and standing up for myself, all these things were the key to gaining self-confidence. I was like a child learning how to ride a bicycle, graduating from a three-wheeler to wobbling on two wheels. I'd often fall from that bike on my face for yet another wake-up call. It was now critical to relearn how to count on myself for sheer self-preservation of who I was at the core. At the very essence, I was an idealist who believed that once I put my mind to it, any dream was attainable.

CHAPTER 10

EMOTIONAL ROLLER COASTER

The dreaded IPT test was approaching fast. It was crucial to pass it because after that I would move on to phase V+ and gain more privileges. Although my recent iterations were inconsistent, I was hoping to have on the test a role player who would stick to the rules without giving me a hard time like the last one. The test was planned on Thursday before Memorial Day weekend. Everyone was making plans for this four-day trip off post. For me, it was supposed to be a celebration after passing the exam.

I was preparing for and organizing the trip with Coleman—the counterintelligence agent who also became my friend. During the warm spring evenings, we usually sat on the rocky benches in front of our barracks and talked. Since I left home, she was the first person I considered a friend. She was intelligent, kind, and had ambitious plans for her military career. She wanted to become an intelligence officer, then a strategy adviser in Washington, D.C. and eventually secure a high-profile job in the Pentagon. I was impressed and enjoyed her companionship tremendously. That's why I was looking forward to our trip to the Grand Canyon. It was a great opportunity to ride a normal car again, and simply get away from the military reality, take a decent break for a few days.

Then, my worst day of the Fort Huachuca adventure arrived: the Interrogation Performance Test. Contrary to my hopes, I had the same role-player who wanted me out through all interrogation practice sessions. I was mentally prepared for a disaster. And it ultimately happened. I failed my IPT. I was devastated. At the end of the day, I was consoling myself with the thought, that even if my failure meant starting the entire school cycle from the very beginning, it was worth it because it guaranteed a new group of classmates, different instructors, and definitely different role players for the interrogation part (the school rule to avoid bias).

Unfortunately, failing the test also meant losing all the phase V privileges (like spending the night off post) effective immediately. Since the IPT was on the last Thursday before Memorial Day weekend, I expected to be grounded. Luckily, our drill sergeant didn't revoke my phase right away. I was going to be stripped of privileges after my return. "You're good troops, SKI. Have fun at the Grand Canyon. We'll take care of the formalities after you get back." As I thought about the situation at school, my heart was getting heavier.

Our entire trip felt like we were running away from something. Nobody knew for sure our itinerary, just like in the adventures of *Thelma and Louise.* Coleman and I just kept on driving. She wanted to drive the entire trip because she missed being behind the wheel. I didn't oppose it. I was already happy that we could leave the base for a long weekend. We had a great time visiting the Grand Canyon.

After the sunset, the magnificent rocks of Great Canyon slowly disappeared in the evening mist. A miniature silver moon emerged on the dark firmament, attempting to shed some light on the sleepy giant. Everything around us seemed so small compared to the canyon rocks.

We left the park and drove to Flagstaff, hoping to locate a place to spend the night. Neither of us had any luck in making any reservations ahead of time because of the season. The Memorial Day weekend was a big time for the annual festivities in this charming town. We traveled for hours, searching the empty streets looking for a motel, while the entire population was enjoying the evening in the downtown park. Eventually, we left the area and opted to take a scenic route south, toward Sedona. We drove in the darkness through Oak Creek canyon, passing the gloomy distant figures of the Cathedral Rocks. The route was daunting and complicated, and after a while, it seemed like we were traveling in circles. Endless turns, narrow passages between the soaring walls of rocks, and lack of any sign of a clear horizon in front of us. All this was quite startling. We passed countless small ravines right below the edge of our route. Only a shy, barely noticeable reflection of the moon in the water was signaling the unsuspected presence of canyon lakes beneath.

As I was admiring the mystic darkness, all the events from the past few weeks began flashing through my mind like scenes from a movie. I remembered passing another phase test to V+ and enjoying more privileges than before for just a few days. Zealand and I became close friends. We both took the opportunity given to us by our drill sergeant and moved together into the air force barracks because the army ones were overcrowded. This move liberated me from the obscure, filthy room 170, which smelled like cheeseburgers. My previous roommates evidently gave up on their fitness, and despite the rules, they continued bringing junk food to our room. Every afternoon, they would watch TV until late at night, and on the weekends, they would sleep most of the time. The window curtains were routinely shut as my roommates both hated the daylight. Eventually, I was suffocating. The Zealands helped move my belongings to the third floor of the AF barracks. The two-person room there was clean and spacious, the furniture looked brand new, and the carpet on the floor was fresh.

Around midnight, we arrived in Sedona, a charming little town deeply submerged in the sinister hours of darkness. It seemed lifeless and abandoned, lonely in the cold desert mountains. With no success in finding any place to spend the night, we continued our desperate journey. By dawn, we finally found a motel in Phoenix.

After our return to base, with my heart content yet broken, I lay down on my bed and looked at the light blue ceiling. My training would take an additional two months. I also realized that my *Thelma and Louise* adventure was over. I promised myself that one day, I will drive across Arizona again with a happy heart. However, now it was time to face a brutal return to reality at the barracks and at school.

* * *

For the next couple of weeks, I lingered in limbo between two cycles, waiting for my new class to start. They had already pulled me out of my class "003" but hadn't officially assigned me to "005," who was arriving soon from the Defense Language Institute in California. In the meantime, I ended up again in the first platoon, this time called "Psychos." I was sometimes wondering who in the world would come up with these crazy names for the first platoon? The first platoon was the hardest to survive because it "contained" all people who were not in the active school cycle—those with health issues, paperwork issues, conduct issues, and school failures. Some of them were going crazy being holdovers for any reason. Perhaps this was the reason they were called "Psychos." While in the first platoon, I was pulling kitchen duty, barracks maintenance, and waiting for our drill sergeant to walk us to the DFAC (dining facility) fifty feet away from the barracks. I was miserable. I felt discarded and useless.

Although living in the air force barracks was bringing me some joy, I didn't fit in because I was in phase IV. Since I had no battle buddy (everyone in this building was already independent), I was constantly forced to "fish" around for small groups of soldiers walking to and from the barracks, DFAC, or mini mall to avoid getting in trouble by walking anywhere alone. It was so annoying being unable to go anywhere by myself, or relentlessly looking for a stranger to walk with. I eventually stayed in inside, leaving my room only for my company formations by the army barracks.

My roommate, Zealand, was also recently pulled from class 003 because of some paperwork issues. She ended up in limbo as well, however, without losing her V+ phase privileges (she had passed the IPT). I saw her extremely rarely though since she was usually pulling an overnight duty at the company quarters (front desk) in the army barracks.

By mid-June, I finally started school again. With enormous relief, I instantly discovered that the majority of people in class 005 indeed came from DLI. Meaning they had just spent at least a year or two learning a foreign language. They were mostly in their late twenties or early thirties and seemed more mature and interesting than the bullies from 003. Since most of the class came from DLI carrying V+ privileges, the entire class 005 instantly was granted the same phase and instead of the black guidon, we received the gold one. However, as a "recycle," I had to remain in phase IV, which worsened my feeling of being singled out, like a marked outsider. While all the students in my class were driving to school in their POVs, I still had to march with the entire company until I passed another IPT test in two months and earned my phase V+ privileges. This only made my feeling of isolation more profound.

* * *

One day, the company duty driver dropped me off at the military clinic. It was quite early, and the facility wasn't open yet. A warm breeze gently touched my face while I sat on the curb by the entrance. The foggy blanket covering the mountains gave me a feeling of security and comfort. I reflected peacefully on my situation, realizing that this time I would do everything differently. I promised myself to study less, try having friends, and definitely have more fun and take care of myself. My initial motivation changed dramatically, and my goal wasn't to achieve ultimate success at school any longer. Now it was all about being happy with what I had without trying to achieve the impossible.

I was at the clinic to take care of myself and stop sacrificing all I had to school and physical fitness. My health was slowly diminishing. I had to see Major Maadox again because of an ongoing problem with my left heel. Despite numerous attempts to fix it through icing, custom orthotics, massages, ultrasound, and limited running, my plantar fasciitis (inflammation of the bottom of the foot) wasn't improving. The only remedy left was a temporary solution—a regular intake of ibuprofen, also called "army candy." Major Maadox and I talked several times about various topics and became close. She knew everything, not only about my health issues, but also about my school situation.

"I really think you should talk to the inspector general about your recycling." I didn't expect this sudden encouragement.

"What's the point, ma'am? They won't do anything, anyway. . ."

"Look, I see too many people here that were recycled, and almost all of them were ESLs, non-native English speakers. You speak several languages, and I can't comprehend that you wouldn't be able to learn some interrogation techniques. That's so absurd. I deeply admire those who can speak at least one foreign language because I know how difficult it is to learn a language."

"I agree, yet it seems like these people are being treated like second-class soldiers. All the recycles from my class were non-natives: Panama, Poland, Russia, Mexico, and Saudi Arabia. We all failed."

"That's why you need to talk to the inspector general and bring it up, so he can investigate it. You can make a change, so no one suffers again because of language issues. And the school can't fail you again because it would be gross discrimination."

I agreed with Major Maadox entirely and was thinking about doing something for a while, but needed some reassurance. My doctor, her assistants, and nurses gave me much needed moral support. I took a card with the contacts to the IG Office and left the clinic uplifted and inspired. She insisted on keeping her posted about my mission. "Call Major Johnson. If you can't get through, I will call him for you."

Once I came back to the barracks, I immediately reported to my drill sergeant that I would be scheduling a visit with the inspector general's office about the treatment of ESL people and recycling them in almost every single class. He tried to change my mind, saying, "The IG doesn't care about things like that." I just reminded him it was my right as a soldier to talk to the IG, and they will decide if they had a case and how to handle it. I also clarified that I was not asking him for permission to do this, just alerting him to my intentions. He asked if I talked to Captain Zubr about it. I said that I tried to talk to him for the last three months, and I was tired of being dismissed. He still insisted that I should talk to the captain, but I wasn't interested anymore because no one at the company level wanted to do anything about this, even though all the drill sergeants were aware of the problems at school. Eventually, I agreed to meet with the captain, but only after my visit with the IG. My drill sergeant couldn't convince me otherwise. My assertiveness was surprising even to me, but with nothing to lose and tremendous support from the clinic, I was ready for the battle.

* * *

Dear Alec,

I wish I could write to you more often, but I've been pretty depressed lately and nothing new is really going on. My everyday life is the same and uneventful. All days seem alike: get up, morning formation, PT exercise, shower, breakfast formation, academic formation, march to school, lunch formation, march back to school for the afternoon classes, march back from school, recall formation and mail call, dinner, air force barracks, polishing my boots for the next day, homework, reading something, and going to bed.

On the weekends, I usually hide in my room, only emerging to eat at the dining facility three times a day. Sometimes I go to the store across the street, sneaking out without a battle buddy to buy soap or the purple Gatorade. If I am in a better mood, I take a trip on a bus to the main PX for all the change I find on the streets—it's the biggest adventure these days. I spend hours wandering around the store despairingly, just to look at things or people, but most of all, to kill time.

Yesterday we had another blood drive. I gladly volunteered just to break the boring routine of my existence here. Everything went well up to the first half of a pint. After that, I started fading away and eventually almost the entire personnel were preoccupied with bringing me back to life. I got horrible cramps in my hands, and my blood didn't want to drip. The nurses turned my seat upside down and placed a wet towel over my forehead. I felt much better, and the pint of blood was finally full. When they disconnected me from the needle, I started shivering so badly that people around were covering me with everything they could find—jackets, blankets, and sweaters. First Sergeant Owen showed up and was telling me funny stories and jokes to cheer me up. Eventually, I was told to sit down and join all the other blood donors at the table with sweets. They made me drink loads of soda for the caffeine. After a few minutes, the horrible cramps came back and twisted my arms into arthritic curves. I ended up on a bed again. Suddenly, Captain Zubr emerged from the crowd and asked jokingly, "What are you doing, SKI?" I joked as well, "I wanted to be a hero and donate blood." "You are a hero," he said and started telling me the story of his life—about growing up in Argentina, about his Polish roots, about Lvov, Ukraine, and Lithuania. Few moments later, while being transported in the wheelchair to the company van in front of the building, yet another officer showed up. This time, it was our battalion commander, Colonel Keller, who, as a new commander in charge, was roaming around the MI Village, checking on soldiers. He shook my hand and thanked me for donating blood. I was really moved. The people from my company drove me back to the barracks where the air force personnel helped me upstairs and carried my rucksack. Although the entire blood-giving experience was this time a true ordeal, I got to see the first sergeant and my unit commanders, which are normally out of reach for soldiers like me. I got a huge "Real Hero" sticker, and I didn't have to do morning PT on Saturday because the donors were excused, which was a tremendous relief.

I'm constantly listening to the CDs you sent, especially the Glenn Miller band. My windows are finally open so I can hear the familiar sounds of the crickets at night, which reminds me of our Northbrook home.

I counted all the fruit bars I received from you in the last package. I will eat one every Thursday as a special treat and something to look forward to. The last one will fall on September 20, exactly one week before my graduation!

* * *

The skies cleared up after a brief and lavish spring rain. For a few moments, quite unusual-in-the-desert humidity filled the air. It seemed like nature took a fresh, deep breath of life. The early morning sun was gently caressing the Huachuca Mountains, suddenly awakened by a brand-new day.

I was at the Old Post waiting for my meeting with the inspector general. I drifted away in my imagination, envisioning the cavalry soldiers who had resided here over a century ago. In my mind, I saw the cavalry soldiers formed up in front of the pale wooden barracks surrounding a sloping field. As the reveille echoed in the mountains, the American flag gracefully raised on a flagpole was guarded by the small cannons in the middle of the parade grounds. Almost immediately after the morning formation, the soldiers proceeded to the routine bayonet training and the preparation for the next mission. At last, they mounted their horses and disappeared in the dusty clouds of the deep Arizona desert. They were most likely pursuing the Chiricahua Apaches led by Geronimo. As the sandy dirt settled down, I could hardly perceive the sound of the hoofbeat fading away.

Now, I was surrounded by the historical post buildings at the foot of the Huachuca Mountains, residences of garrison officials, and the old barracks—now the administrative offices. This historic district seemed so small compared to the contemporary military base built around it. It was a mysterious capsule of time. I could almost smell the history and see the events that took place here in the late 1880s. The wooden buildings have not changed a bit—still standing proudly around the small parade field, tacit witnesses of the times gone by, their faded pinkish surface blending with the desert behind them.

Sitting at a worn-out picnic table by the inspector general's office, I felt calm and optimistic. Regardless of the outcome of my discussion with the inspector regarding the situation at school and the discrimination of the ESLs, I have already resigned to the idea of being recycled. The fight didn't matter anymore, and I was convinced that my visit here was just a formality.

Somehow, I knew I would be back in Fort Huachuca again, perhaps in a couple of years, as an officer. To commemorate my visit to the historic district, as well as my feeling of liberation, optimism, and a newfound inner peace, I wrote my initials and the date 6.20.2001 on the picnic table.

* * *

A few days later, our company commander resolved the situation with the ESLs. He finally agreed to meet with all the people who were recycled because of the Interrogation Performance Test. During a feverish discussion, which was mostly unfavorable remarks about specific instructors, unfair evaluation procedures, and unclear rules, the captain listened for the first time to students' report of the situation at school. As a result, shortly after the meeting, a new procedure was established for all the new arrivals attending the interrogation course. A spacious drill sergeant's office upstairs in the barracks was transformed into a classroom designated for a preparatory course called "97E Head-Start." The course was an introduction to interrogation terminology and map-tracking techniques, which almost always were the underlying cause of IPT failures. A gigantic military map of the area was laminated, framed, and placed on the wall for practice. Soldiers could also use this room as the study hall whenever they needed it. From this point on, all the new soldiers arriving at E Company from basic training, instead of pulling endless kitchen patrol or barracks maintenance duties, took part in these preparatory workshops. I was impressed by this quick change in the company. It made better sense for the new arrivals to spend time with the maps than patrolling the kitchen.

* * *

Shortly after the beginning of the astronomical summer, a heavy rain season arrived. The desert—exhausted from the scorching heat and the omnipresent piercing sun—was demanding relief. Nature finally answered its cries. The rains began more frequently and eventually became a full-blown monsoon season. One afternoon, I watched a real thunderstorm in the desert for the first time. In front of my eyes, the firmament darkened in seconds, while ferocious clouds were cascading down the Huachuca Mountains. The skies descended low and intimidating in their grandiose thunder fury, stabbing the desert with continuous electric shocks. I watched, fearful that the world was coming to an end. The earsplitting thunders continued to illuminate the darkness with their countless golden spears along the entire horizon, trying to split the trembling earth into pieces. Each time multiple thunders hit the ground, the most magnificent brightness revealed for a split second the angry black clouds and their golden red contours, fighting fiercely with their electric swords, discharging the sparks of fire all around. I felt like I was on a battlefield of nature. Suddenly I could hear a single thunder explosion rupture the exasperated skies and release a glorious downpour, submerging the entire world in water. The mountains reminded me of distant volcanoes releasing vicious rivers of water coming down their spurs, like deadly lava frantically abducting everything on their way downhill at the speed of light. Instantaneously, all streets and parking lots of the MI Village became enraged watercourses. I wasn't going to run for safety, although I probably should have. I was too enticed by the beauty and fearlessness of the unstoppable nature. I wanted to be just as fearless. After several minutes of heavy rain, the clouds cleared up and the wall of water faded away. Perfectly blue skies smiled, thankfully revealing an evening sun setting majestically behind the horizon. After the enormous and refreshing drink of water, the desert could finally rest.

* * *

At the end of June, they officially promoted one of our drill sergeants from staff sergeant to sergeant first class. The entire E Company was celebrating his promotion and reenlistment at the midday formation. After the ceremony, I was chatting with a small group of soldiers under the skimpy shade of a young tree. The battalion commander, Colonel Keller, was passing through, sneaking behind the platoons, annoyed by the soldiers saluting him every step of the way. Eventually, he stopped next to me as if he found something he was looking for. I greeted him with a salute and a smile.

"How are you, Specialist Rakowski?" He saluted me back and shook my hand. He took off his sunglasses as if he wanted to see me better. "I remember you from the auditorium. How is everything going so far?"

To the great disbelief of my fellow soldiers, the colonel spoke with me as if he knew me for years—he asked about school, my family back home, and my military career plans.

"My intent is to become an officer, sir. I will apply for the Officer Candidate School next spring," I announced without hesitation. This was the first time I actually said something like that out loud. By doing so, I made it official. I was relieved the colonel didn't seem surprised and that I wouldn't have to explain my choice any further.

The signal to form back up and return to school for the afternoon classes brutally interrupted the conversation. I was uplifted by this personal encounter with our battalion commander, who somehow was often finding me in the crowd to have a casual conversation. It felt like with the colonel's blessing, I made a genuine commitment to become a professional soldier, an officer in the United States Army.

* * *

The time was slowly passing by as I was negotiating the interrogation course, getting through all the tests with excellence. I had gotten used to the new reality. However, because of my declining physical condition, my daily marching to school and back several times a day turned out to be an ever-growing challenge. In the mornings, I could only run twice a week with the slowest group, struggling with increasing pain in my heels. My biweekly visits to the clinic became a routine necessary to provide me with the indispensable supply of ibuprofen.

Eventually, a long Fourth of July weekend provided some relief from my physical exhaustion. The MI Village seemed abandoned. Still in phase IV, not being able to wear civilian clothes, I barely left the barracks during the entire four days. I missed home tremendously. In my mind, I pictured the festivities in Northbrook celebrating Independence Day with the fire engine parade passing through the village, outdoor concerts, and a Ferris wheel at Village Green Park. In the evening, the Anetsberger Golf Course was packed with crowds on blankets, admiring the most spectacular fireworks. While thinking about it, I could almost smell the sulfur in the air and the burned grass at Meadowhill Park where the show was taking place.

* * *

Dear Alec,

I just received five letters from you all on the same day. It's great that they all came right before the long weekend. I read them repeatedly for four days. Indeed, I needed some consolation after the past week. In a few days, the company command will change, and we will have a new commander and a new first sergeant. The rumors are spreading at the speed of light that apparently, there will be quite a few changes in our company policies. For example, the POV (privately owned vehicles) privileges will be taken away. This means that there will be no driving around the base, even on the weekends, and the males from Riley Barracks will have to take the bus several times a day. Some people will have to move to the marines' barracks because army buildings are filled to capacity. I was already notified by my drill sergeant that I will move back to the army barracks, but with no specific orders to do so, I'm staying at the air force. It's really confusing and disturbing, all this uncertainty and nonsense. Phase IV soldiers can have only one picture on the wall in the room. Those in phase V and V+ can have only one pair of civilian shoes under the bed, one CD player, and a TV or PlayStation per room. The worst news is that at the beginning of August, we will have a "GI party"—take outside all of our personal effects and clean the barracks all weekend long. It will be an enormous mess if we have a downpour while all our belongings are in the parking lot. People are more and more depressed, and some were moved to our day room for a suicide watch. Last week one suicidal person was finally discharged from the army and left the company. Other people are still struggling. When the announcement was made about all these upcoming pointless changes, some soldiers started screaming, "Welcome to the red phase," "Basic Training 101," "Can we still make a phone call once a week?" "Ooaah—motivation down!" or "Can we still eat three times a day and keep three pairs of socks?" This last one was mine. I was infuriated and couldn't help it.

Recently, the residents of the army barracks had to pull the "smoke guard" for the entire weekend. It was to stand on the evacuation stairs in twelve-hour shifts. According to the grapevine, someone was smoking cigarettes there and left cigarette butts all over the place. Apparently, some soldiers have had enough, and they don't even hide while smoking because they want to be caught and eventually discharged from the army. A friend of mine from basic told me he is going home soon. As far as I know, he keeps being punished—they'd already demoted him once. He continuously pulls some kind of "corrective training," was withdrawn from his counterintelligence agent course, and will probably receive a dishonorable discharge. Some of those who have been waiting for their security clearance paperwork to be processed ended up in the Psychos platoon for nearly a year! No wonder they are going crazy.

I revamped my "class A" uniform by attaching the real brass buttons and insignia instead of plastic ones—the regular issue. They are really nice and shiny. The uniform is hanging on my locker to cheer me up and remind me of graduation. I look forward to this moment and feel so much better when I think about finally seeing you in September.

* * *

By mid-July, I became used to my daily routine of sneaking out of the army barracks without a battle buddy and jumping over the boulders behind the building leading straight to the air force barracks. I was always very careful not to damage my impeccably polished combat boots and, of course, not to twist my ankle in the process. My rucksack filled with books only made the matter worse. However, there were only four weeks left in phase IV, and after that, I wouldn't have to worry about the battle buddy and just use the sidewalk.

My morning running routine became more challenging than ever and having passed all the required physical fitness tests, I had no reason to aggravate my foot injury. One day, however, was very special, and I decided to participate in the company run. It was a "change of command" ceremonial run.

That Friday, we departed the barracks area earlier than usual. It was still foggy and drizzling. Our gigantic formation of nearly five hundred people strong was moving rather swiftly along our usual PT route at the foot of the Huachuca Mountains. For the first mile, I ran with the entire company, but once they turned left uphill at the intersection, I wasn't able to continue with the group. With the E Company ahead slowly disappearing in the dark, I kept going at my own pace. A few other people who fell out of the formation joined me. Fortunately, Drill Sergeant Messinger came to the rescue of our small struggling group. "Stop right here. The company will turn around at the top of the hill and come back down. Drink water and wait for the formation on this field, right here." A tremendous joy and relief filled my heart. I would expect just about every drill sergeant to spare us but Drill Sergeant Messinger.

Just before 6:00 a.m., the entire company was in formation waiting for the reveille to salute the flag. The day was just waking up, slowly emerging from the morning drizzle. The entire landscape was saturated with flickering vibration, the echoing sound of the military trumpet playing the morning song for the soldiers called to duty.

The ceremony began immediately after the reveille. The outgoing commander transferred the company colors to the incoming commander. Then, unexpected daylight broke through the picks of the glorious Huachuca Mountains, revealing the most magical, enormous double rainbow, a grand symbol of the transition of power. As the new commander led the company running downhill, I was hoping this was also a sign for me. From this point on, my journey would take a turn for the better.

Later that day at school, I went outside on break to get a snack from our civilian friend Mike. He had an ice cream truck loaded with sandwiches, junk food, and ice cream. It was very refreshing to talk to him, as he was quite amusing and always in good spirits.

"Here are your pretzels, Captain Rakowski." I looked at him with a big question mark on my face, pointing at my rank. He didn't utter a single word, just smiled and shook my hand. I walked away puzzled and wondering, was it possible that I had some kind of "officer aura" around me?

At the end of the day, I felt uplifted and inspired, and I had to share my happiness with Alec. I had so much to tell him about my days as a "recycled" person. My GPA so far was 97%, and I had promised myself to stay on this track until the end. I wanted to tell him how things were better this time around because I already knew the entire material for the interrogation portion of the course, and I also had an experience with the final test itself.

Lately, I didn't call Alec much because of the timing. Despite my ongoing problems with the "disappearing minutes" on my calling card, I was finally able to talk to him for a while, without being harassed by other people waiting to use the phone. Still, I was often getting disconnected without a warning, and I mentioned to him I didn't know what I would do if this happened again.

"Just walk away," he said, and a sudden long continuous signal followed his voice. The conversation was over.

With my heart heavy, I remained in the phone booth for a while, replaying in my mind the last few seconds of our chat. I felt like a bird in a cage trapped by an unfinished conversation. I couldn't just walk away.

* * *

Dear Alec,

It's hard to believe but I'm still hurting after yesterday's PT test. The night before, I wasn't able to sleep having nightmares about it. Since 4:00 a.m., I was just lying in bed waiting for the day to start and hoping that the test would go well, so I could have peace of mind for a while. Unfortunately, the proctor was unfair. He didn't count all my push-ups using an excuse that my entire body wasn't moving, so I ended up with a score of only 37. Same with sit-ups, which I like a lot better than push-ups. He didn't count all of them and gave me a score of 69. The two-mile run was exhausting, but I kept running and still made it my best at 18'48". At least this time was called when I crossed the finish line. When I think about all my results, however, compared to my initial fitness evaluation at the beginning of basic training in Fort Jackson, when I could barely do five push-ups and eleven sit-ups, and run a quarter of a mile in twelve minutes, yesterday's results are nothing to sneeze at and not too shabby for a thirty-two-year-old woman.

Today all my breathing muscles and legs hurt like crazy. Thank goodness I had some samples of cooling gel from you, so I immediately used it all up. Now I just have Bengay cream to use every night to survive the pain.

With the new company commander, life at the barracks sucks more than before. I just found out that the new order is that people who have a medical "profile" because of an injury or illness (which means restricted physical activity for all fitness training) now, as "punishment," have to do mandatory fitness training on Saturdays. Where is the logic here? Doctors give profiles for a reason, yet no one seems to respect their decisions. It irritates me, but that's okay. I'll do some PT on Saturdays because I don't care anymore about things like this. All I'm thinking about right now is to pass the upcoming IPT.

* * *

Life in the barracks with new leadership was annoying. Some rules had changed. For example, since drill sergeants didn't supervise phase IV morning formation before marching to breakfast, the situation was slowly getting out of control. Many soldiers from that phase (mostly new arrivals) were skipping this drill. The new order from the company commander was to take the names of everyone who showed up, and those who didn't would be on a special "no-show" list and, therefore, would be punished with corrective training on Saturdays. Apparently, one day, the list of the "no-shows" contained over one hundred names. Thankfully, my name wasn't on it because I attended the darn formation ever since I restarted phase IV after my May IPT failure. That meant that I was invisible, just as I wanted. Some time ago, one of the school instructors, Mr. Orsky—who was favorable to me after my ordeal with IPT and my visit to the inspector general (clearly, the word got out that I had filed a complaint against the instructors' discrimination against ESLs)—approached me during the break between classes and gave me a word of advice. "SKI, low key is the key." I decided to follow Mr. Orsky's advice and just be quiet and not stand out. That's why with new rules in the barracks, PT on Saturdays, and corrective training for not showing up at phase IV formations, I knew that this time I would not be making waves.

Another nonsensical order from the company was about the monthly ruck march by the entire company to make our lives more "interesting," meaning miserable. Ruck march was usually at least twelve miles long and took place early in the morning before school, without time to change into fresh uniforms afterward and minimal time for breakfast. Pure torture. Last time, the route selected by the company's first sergeant was so difficult that the company didn't make it to breakfast at all and was late to school. So the solution was to add marching time instead of correcting the route. Because of this, the next march would begin at 3:30 in the morning instead of 4:30. That meant that we had to rise at 3:00. Luckily, I had a "profile" for long-distance marching because of my foot injury. Nonetheless, I still had to wake up with everyone else for the formation and show my paperwork from the doctor.

There was one good news in school though. It made me realize the secret of successful IPT passing for a class. I saw it with my own eyes. One day, when our class's senior faculty, Sergeant Cruchene, was explaining the interrogation process during a lesson, the civilian instructors sitting at the back of the room started questioning his interpretation of concepts, introducing the ambiance of disrespect and general chaos. Sergeant Cruchene politely replied that his role as a senior faculty was to assure rules' consistency, so everything during the IPT was clear for every student and that everyone needed to be evaluated according to these rules only. There would be no change of rules during the test, like with previous classes, and no other surprises. The instructors opposed it, so Sergeant Cruchene took them outside the classroom and put them in their place. Since then, during the preparatory interrogation exercises in booths, everything went smoothly and according to Sergeant Cruchene's rules.

* * *

The days in the desert were hot, and the daily marches to school and back became unbearable. Fortunately, some of my classmates in phase V+ of our training already enjoyed their POV privileges and could drive to school their own vehicles. With one of them, Sparks, I entered into a secret agreement that whenever possible, she would take my rucksack filled with schoolbooks and drive it to school so I wouldn't have to carry the load. It was an immense relief for my painful plantar fasciitis, but I still had to march to school and back daily. However, sometimes there were some unexpected benefits of this marching.

One day, on my way to school, I was at the end of our formation because I was in pain and couldn't keep up with the class's fast pace. Suddenly, I noticed flowering bushes on the side of the road. Flowers in the desert, at least in Fort Huachuca, were not very common. I stopped for a moment and immersed my face in the leaves. The smell was divine and brought a smile to my face. I collected a small bunch of tiny blue flowers and placed them in a buttonhole in the left chest pocket of my uniform. I could still smell them from there. It provided a temporary feeling of happiness, and I imagined that somewhere in people's backyards in gardens, the bushes were in full bloom, and it was normal. I would never take flowering plants for granted.

Flowers in the desert, at least in Fort Huachuca, were not very common.

* * *

Similar flowers were covering the shrubs in Chris's backyard at the beginning of the fall of 1991 in Poland. The flowers all around always made me feel like I was in a magical garden in a faraway land from fairy tales.

"I'm so happy to be back," I said to Chris with relief. "I hope that we will never have to be separated for so long."

Chris and I were just reunited again after my trip to Ravensburg, Germany, where I had spent two months teaching ballet in a private ballet school. No matter how much I loved my job, I still missed Chris tremendously and couldn't wait for my contract to be over. Immediately after my return to Poland, I went to see my dearest friend. Chris's house was the most charming place in the heart of the Kampinos National Park in the suburbs of Warsaw. While visiting Chris at home, I always had a feeling of being transported to a transcendental reality, where everything was happening in slow motion, without any regard to time or space. From my perspective, as a spectator or as a participant, even the most mundane activities performed around the house seemed magical and breathtaking. That day wasn't any different. I was raking the leaves in the backyard, captivated by the peace of the surroundings, breathing deeply the smell of burning leaves by the house next door. For a moment, I stopped what I was doing, and with my chin supported on the handle, surrounded by flowering azaleas, I watched Chris hanging a fresh load of laundry on the twine stretched between the trees. Speechless and enchanted by this serene image, I was trying to carve it into my heart forever. My mind was replaying the two years of the most precious moments of our friendship, like little puzzle pieces of our history. Our relationship was growing stronger and more intense than ever. I was still Chris's student, which made the whole situation so much more challenging as we were not able to communicate freely at university. We both had to keep our guard constantly and carry on our relationship hidden from the formal academic world.

I saw a barely noticeable, mysterious smile on Chris's face, causing my heart to fill with joy and a comforting, fuzzy feeling of warmth.

"How did your teaching go in Ravensburg?" I suddenly heard the silver voice behind a blue-striped shirt waving gently in the summer breeze.

"It was quite exciting, actually. The students in a private school are used to a distinct atmosphere. They take ballet classes for pleasure, not for professional development. You can't discipline the students as we do it in Poland. I really liked that. It was a relaxed and peaceful setting. No stress like in Warsaw school."

After the sunset, we continued the conversation inside. There was always so much to talk about. The house was quiet, so we both sat by the baby grand piano in the living room and played four hands the *Polonaise in G Minor* by Chopin. Occasionally, we would take brief moments to sip cognac from the glasses resting on the lid of the piano. Before I noticed, the candles on the table died out and the dawn was presenting a brand-new day. It was time for me to go back to my place in Warsaw. As I drove through the early morning fog, I could hear the longing sounds of the piano.

* * *

Dear Alec,

I had such a great week! I received your letters and package with sports gel, for which I am very grateful. Despite some recent bad news about having to move to marine or navy barracks in August (army barracks are still overflowing), for the time being, I am staying in the air force barracks. I like it here because I have only one roommate and we both have normal beds (instead of bunk beds). Our room on the second floor is spacious and sunny, and the building is quiet.

I also had a couple of tests in school, and I maxed them both. My last PT test didn't go too great, but I passed easily anyway. The next will be better once I start running regularly again. The most important thing is that I currently weigh only 129 pounds, and I am in pretty good shape. I can do forty push-ups in two minutes and eighty-two sit-ups in two minutes as well! I look quite good, especially in my class A uniform.

Tonight, I will listen to some Wynton Marsalis playing his trumpet. They have a smooth jazz program on the radio every Saturday evening. On Fridays, they play classical music, so yesterday I was listening to Wagner's *Tristan and Isolde*. It was refreshing. The other day, they played a transmission from the Ravinia Festival, which reminded me of home and times when we used to go to this festival together last summer.

I continue to find money on the streets of our MI Village. Practically, wherever I go, I end up finding some change on the ground. I collect these "tokens of fortune" and keep them in a secret place in the barracks. Perhaps in a short while, I'll have enough to take a taxi to the Clothing and Sales store on base to pick up my class A pants and new shoes to complete the uniform."

* * *

Another Saturday came by. I changed into my BDUs and went to the army barracks for my CQ (company quarters) twelve-hour night-shift duty at the front desk. As usual, it was exhausting. People were constantly crowding up the entrance, and I had to keep chasing them away and taking their names. There were many people coming from basic training in the middle of the night, still stressed out, tired after the long trip, and lost. Drill Sergeant Messinger was torturing them relentlessly with tons of paperwork to deprive them of sleep. He even told me to wake them up if I saw them snoozing in the billiard room near the CQ desk. I didn't notice anyone snoozing. They were enduring everything bravely.

Some other people had gotten into trouble during the week, so now as a "corrective training," they had to write dissertations in the middle of the night. Others yet had extra duties, like cleaning the laundry room and polishing the hallway floors. I saw a few people getting Article 15 for being caught smoking cigarettes under the fire stairs outside the building. In the late-night hours, some of my classmates in phase V+ were returning to the barracks from their outings on Friday night, happy, relaxed, and careless. It was hard for me to watch their cheerful faces, wearing jeans and flip-flops, while I was stuck on night duty in my uniform. However, it wasn't all that bad. Sparks brought me coffee, then my roommate joined me because she couldn't sleep after pulling her dose of the night CQ for the past several days. I gladly agreed to order some Chinese food (we could eat at any time during the CQ duty—usually takeouts).

Drill Sergeant Messinger would occasionally stop by our front desk and get on everyone's nerves by messing with us. When he finally exhausted everyone around me, he approached me. Anticipating some mischief coming from him, I caught him off guard. I proposed a game I knew he wouldn't win. Since he was always bragging about knowing Polish, I asked him to say the sentence *"chszqszcz brzmi w trzcinie"* (in Polish: "a beetle makes sounds in a bush"). I added that if his pronunciation was correct, I would do ten push-ups. He quickly backed off, saying that he had a lot of work to do, and left our perimeter. Shortly after that, he brought me a pile of paperwork and gave me a pleasant task of sorting the documents.

Occasionally, because the front desk area was buzzing with life, I would go outside and stand in front of the barracks to smell the late-night rain and listen to the calming noise of raindrops. The humidity was a delightful break from the constant desert heat. That night, I had a fantastic message from the universe. The fortune cookie that came with my Chinese food stated, "You will pass a difficult test that will make you happier." Although I normally didn't believe in fortune cookies' predictions, this one was spot on, so I gladly accepted it and taped it on page 599 of my journal.

The next day, the recall formation took place in the moonlight, the stars shimmering in the cool air. I was unusual, and I loved it. It meant that the sun began to set early in the evening. Days were shorter, and fall was approaching. It also meant that school would be over soon, and I could finally go home. I was overwhelmed with so much on my plate. The exhaustion causing my injuries, physical training, IPT at school, constant tests, homework, endless uniform and room inspections, then the approaching collections after IPT (the counterintelligence block of instruction after the interrogation part) and field training at the end (several days spent in Huachuca Mountains interrogating insurgents). I was fatigued, but I had to endure only two more months at Fort Huachuca, so after nine months away from home, I could finally be reunited with Alec. I believed God would help me get through all this and first pass the infamous IPT test. Everything after that would depend on it. Regardless, I felt like giving myself a pat on the back. I realized that I've done everything in my power to set myself up for success. I was doing excellent in school. My practice interrogations were spot on, to the extent that I had become a tutor to some students in my class, including a couple of sergeants. People were notoriously copying the structure and the content of my interrogation notebook, even designing the same bookmark I created for myself. I thought perhaps they did it for good luck.

*   *   *

At the beginning of August, my worst nightmare came to its realization. One day, during the company meeting with the commander, they announced that those of us who lived in the air force barracks would now move back to the army. Apparently, after one of many platoons graduated, leaving a bunch of space in the army barracks. I was furious, but had no other option than to pack my things and move the same day. I ended up with a classmate who was a troublemaker, and who had already got caught (and punished for) forging her weekend overnight pass. I didn't want to be around people with criminal inclinations, so when I walked to the room, I stated to her,

"Here are some rules that I am asking you nicely to follow: Don't speak to me at all because I'm pissed that I have to be in these barracks. Don't play your music too loud and don't bring here any of your friends to chitchat and distract me from my schoolwork. Capiche?" Maybe I was too harsh, but I didn't care.

"Okay," was all she could utter, stupefied.

"We're squared then."

After unpacking, I threw myself on the bottom bunk and stared for a long while at the springs above me and pondered my faith and my destiny. I decided I wouldn't believe in God anymore because, to me, he ceased to exist that day. If he was indeed around and aware of my situation, he would spare me this constant stress. The entire nightmare with moving was repeating itself. Just as I was shocked one week before the infamous IPT over two months ago with my move to the air force barracks, this time it was happening again, ten days before the IPT. I didn't appreciate this distraction. As much as I liked them initially, now I hated the army barracks with a passion. They were loud; the rooms were dark and overcrowded, two dreadful bunk beds per room (meaning four personnel per room as opposed to two in the AF). Constant commotion, people everywhere moving in all directions, arriving from basic training in the middle of the night, shipping out after graduation, coming back from the field, doing corrective training, laundry, gathering at the CQ desk, drill sergeants screaming and "smoking" people, abuse of intercom, etc.—all of this was irritating. I was living in an anthill or, worse yet, in a factory of 97 Echoes and 97 Bravos. My room was dark, humid, and too small for four people and all their gear. It felt like a prison cell on a decrepit ship in the middle of the ocean.

I was seriously depressed and since Coleman had already graduated and left the base, I wasn't able to talk to any people except my old roommate from the AF barracks, who also had to move to the army. She said that I was her only friend in the entire company of over five hundred people strong. On weekends, I gladly agreed to accompany her to the Shoppette on base just to get out of the barracks. Sometimes we would order a takeout Chinese to bury our sorrows in it. This gave me a feeling of a somewhat "normal life."

* * *

I went to the DFAC for some coffee to release some stress related to my recent move. They had chocolate chip cookies. As I was dipping the cookies into my coffee, I realized it has been over twelve years since I did that. What a silly thought. Yet, dipping cookies into coffee seemed like a special ritual for me. It also required certain skill. I had to be careful not to dip for too long so the cookie wouldn't fall apart or not to pull it out too soon without absorbing enough coffee to be moist. It had to be just right. And all these years ago, I was an expert in dipping Italian biscotti in coffee.

In Warsaw, at the beginning of the spring of 1992, I was in the middle of my fourth year of studies at the Chopin Music Academy in Warsaw. Ballet pedagogy was my second master's degree, which I was pursuing in addition to my French philology studies at the University of Warsaw.

"It's been a while since we had coffee together," said Chris, sipping the hot liquid.

"It seems like an eternity, actually. But I have a good excuse: I've been extremely busy at the academy. I had quite a few final exams this semester. We had wrapped up the classes that are not directly related to dance subjects: psychology, sociology, or political sciences. All we have left are some practical exams from ballet and writing the master theses."

"Have you been able to transfer the credits to the university? After all, there is no need to study these subjects twice."

"Yes, thank goodness. This gives me more time to concentrate on the research and on writing my thesis."

"Speaking of which, have you chosen your subject yet?"

"Yes, indeed. It is going to be about the ballet jargon in ballet environments in Poland. As you know, the strict ballet terminology is French, but the jargon is actually a mixture of French and Polish. It sounds like a 'Polifrench' language and is incomprehensible to nondancers. I want to explain how this jargon is formed and the meanings of these expressions that describe ballet movements, positions, and figures."

"Your French philology knowledge, especially linguistics, will be very helpful."

"Exactly!" I exclaimed enthusiastically. "After all, ballet terminology and jargon are forms of language, so we could study them in the context of linguistics. Dance as the art of expression is a subject of esthetic or philosophical nature. However, it's never a subject of purely linguistic considerations." I was definitely rambling, but I couldn't help it. I had a listener that could take it.

The waiter brought a fresh pot of coffee and poured it into our cups.

"That's why there is virtually no research, any books or dictionaries, about this matter," I had to add, as if my rambling wasn't enough already.

"It seems like you have an opportunity to write something completely new, unusual even," Chris interjected. "It all sounds intriguing. Tell me more, please."

"I think that dance can be considered a fusion of two complementary language systems." Since Chris volunteered to listen, I felt encouraged to continue passionately. "On one hand, the dance is a language of forms, meaning pictures expressed by movements. To a person without professional or specialized knowledge of dance, this language is the only one they can see. On the other hand, dance is a system of dance vocabulary. It's about words that are considered a symbolic code because they signify movements, poses, and positions. It's understood only by professionals. Finally, this code has two aspects: strict terminology and everyday dance jargon. So that is the framework of my thesis." It definitely was a mouthful again. I was not only enthusiastic but also nervous. This was my first chance to explain to someone my interest in ballet linguistics. Someone who really understood.

"It seems like a very good approach," said Chris, playfully dipping an almond biscotti into my coffee. I found it endearing, and I dipped mine as well.

"To your master's thesis." We touched each other's biscotti.

"A ma thèse de maîtrise! (To my master thesis)" I repeated in French, and we took bites of our cookies. To me, this gesture was our secret code of communication. It was also my tacit promise to Chris that I would succeed with my thesis.

* * *

It was the beginning of August. The end of day formation was dragging, but I didn't care anymore. Drill sergeants were talking about some German Badge, which can be earned after successfully completing several types of sport competitions, tests, and shooting qualification. I thought that this wasn't for me because all this fitness stuff would probably be at the Olympic level. I wasn't a "PT Queen," by any means. In my mind, it was simply unachievable. The following morning was the official beginning of the German Armed Forces Proficiency Badge (GAFPB) competitions. I found out that my platoon would inaugurate the entire event and it was the day of the sprint. Out of curiosity, I checked the description of the sprint posted by the CQ. There were categories per gender and age, and we could pick the distance to run (50m, 75, and 100m). I joined the sprint group to avoid that morning's regular, boring fitness training. We went to a track field, and that's where, for the first time in my life, I felt the spirit of sport. Sports disciplines, people at the start line, then run, then the finish line, time count. I'd never run on the track or heard someone calling my time in a competition. Everything was new, and the mystery of the unknown, if I could meet the standards, was suddenly exciting to me. I thought that since there was no obligation or pressure here, it could actually be fun. I was unfamiliar with track and field because, in my high school years, I was in ballet school in Warsaw. We didn't do sports to avoid contusions. We were dancing, we were artists, and speed was not on our menu. Only physical stamina and grace.

But this time, I wanted to run as fast as I could and qualify. At least I wanted to try, experience the air beating my face, heart pounding from effort and joy. I chose 75m and did as I planned. At the finish line, I had no breath, but had an exhilarating sense of accomplishment. I received a "GO." I made the sprint in 12.7" which meant I made the qualifying time of 13' and was approved for the next competition. I was so elated, I ran around the track half a mile to cool off and for this new accomplishment to sink in. My hamstrings were on fire, my heart was pounding, and I was trembling from this experience. I just achieved a tiny goal. It was enough to get me inspired and motivated to continue pursuing the German Badge.

The following day was a distance run. My age category and distance I selected of 2000 meters (1.24 miles) called for the timing of 13 minutes. I woke up excited and forgot about my heel and hip pain. This time I ran methodically at my pace, knowing from my routine morning runs that I could easily make the distance in my prescribed time. I decided to sprint the last 100 meters just in case, which gave me one minute and 20 seconds to spare. It was magical. I had a hard time believing that in two days, I'd already successfully completed two events. Was I slowly becoming an athlete? Probably not, but for the time being, it felt good to play this role.

* * *

Roller coasters always scared me to death. Every time I'd drive on the Tri-state 294, passing Six Flags Great America (the paradise for coaster fanatics), I would speed up to have it behind me as soon as possible. Just the thought of standing close to a roller coaster would give me nausea. That's why I never rode one and avoided them like a plague. Emotional roller coasters, however, were unavoidable in the army, and I faced them with great difficulty. Often feeling cornered, in all this turmoil, I had to fight for myself in school and in the barracks. Compelled to follow my instinct, I refused to relent under the enormous pressure of authority. Since my sanity and my dignity were at stake, I needed to continue to grow stronger on my journey to transformation.

CHAPTER 11

RE-VALIDATION OF MYSELF

Time was flying fast, and now the GAFPB absorbed me completely. I was eagerly waiting for more competitions. I was anxious about the upcoming swim. I knew how to swim and survive in the water for some time, but I wasn't good enough to compete and make a specific time. I wished that I was in phase V, so I could be free to go practice my swimming after school and not worry about having a battle buddy to accompany me wherever I went.

One Friday, however, the universe was on my side. That day was called Organization Day, meaning that the first formation was at 7:00 a.m. (late!), and there was no morning fitness training or school. It was a fun day to be spent at the track field where all six of our company platoons were competing in various activities with other companies from the battalion.

Among all the commotion, I noticed that a class behind my class (006, who started a month after mine) was suddenly in phase V+, despite not having their IPT test yet. That meant that everyone in my class who was recycled because of IPT should at least be in phase V. This made me think that something with the rules in the barracks wasn't right. On the first appropriate occasion, I approached one of my drill sergeants and inquired about it. He brushed me off, saying that I needed to go through a "soldiering process." I had no idea what he meant by that because last time I checked, a soldiering process was the basic training, which I finished nearly five months ago. Puzzled, I decided not to press the issue and walked away because the drill sergeant didn't want to continue our conversation. Since I was convinced that what I was told was a complete BS, I took a different route. I grabbed Sparks and Willis, who were both in my situation, and we approached our company commander, Captain Hamilton, to explain our situation. To our surprise, he agreed with us. We had been in phase IV for too long (over a required month). Since we didn't have any disciplinary issues and we had already passed our phase tests, physical fitness test and room inspections, he decided to give us our previously earned phase V back. It elated us when he said, "It's on me," because he was, after all, the company commander and no drill sergeant could question his decision. "So, we can enjoy our phase V today?" Sparks cautiously asked. "Of course," said the captain, and we left him alone. We almost ran to the barracks to change into our CVs (civilian clothes). It was freedom at last. I could finally walk around the base alone. In my jeans, I went back to the stadium to continue observing the company competitions. The first was the Guidon Race (race with platoon guidons). The view was breathtaking. Nearly five hundred troops in six platoon formations were sprinting before my eyes, flags fluttering in the air. For the first time, I was genuinely happy for our company. I especially admired Rios sprinting and leading our platoon to victory. I was moved to tears when she crossed the finished line. For a moment, I was inspired and thought about getting involved in sports. Then, my short dream ended when I realized I was almost thirty-two years old and my time for sports had passed a long time ago. For now, however, I could still dream about my German Badge as there were no age limitations in this competition. Uplifted by my newly regained phase V and no need for a battle buddy anymore, I kept thinking about my swimming competition and couldn't wait for Organization Day to be over to go practice my swimming. I wanted to go to the swimming pool right away, but on Organization Day, we were to either participate in the events or observe, not go wherever we pleased.

* * *

Early in the morning, after fulfilling my unexpected duty of mopping the hallways in our barracks, I went straight to the swimming pool. I ended up sharing the line with a female who was an excellent swimmer. I asked her for advice on how I could improve my swimming in four days. She explained the technique of front crawl stroke, and we practiced for several hours. Misty was an excellent coach, and thanks to her, I was making fast progress in the next few days. I was obsessed with swimming faster every day, because my minimum qualifying time for 200 meters was 8 minutes. My present timing was still not sufficient as I was swimming 1 minute and 30 seconds per lap. On top of that, I had never in my life swam 200 meters continuously. Swimming with my head underwater was downright frightening. My breath was too short and uncoordinated with my strokes. I was training relentlessly, practicing every move, breath, and vision, and pushing off the pool wall while changing direction. At one point, Misty let me borrow her swimming goggles so I could see underwater and keep myself swimming straight. Then I saw a blurry pattern of tiles on the pool floor. Seeing the bottom of the swimming pool was new and terrified me to the bone, and that distance was nauseating. I had to overcome my fear because using a proper form of crawl with head underwater was my only chance to swim faster and more efficiently. Despite all my shortcomings, my training with Misty was exhilarating and motivating.

* * *

Dear Alec,

Constant commotion in the barracks and lots of new people coming in from basic training from all over the country makes it impossible to concentrate on anything. Despite this chaos, I'm trying to stay focused on school. I run in the morning with our platoon as much as I can. I'm even excited about running because I imagine that when I come home, we'll be running together.

Recently, we started receiving our mail only two times a week, that is, if we get lucky. Apparently, there are not enough qualified personnel in the company to sort the mail. I would like you to send me more samples of the "energy food" you use for your bike riding escapades. I might need it soon as I compete now in various sport disciplines to earn my German Armed Forces Proficiency Badge. Physically, they are very demanding events. I still have the Skittles and the special "fruity bars" from you. Thursdays are my special days because I eat one bar every Thursday. I even put the dates on them, so I know when to eat one. This makes me feel like I'm closer to home in all this organized chaos, stress, and pressure related to school. Now, I just have to pass this awful IPT test, which is only in two days.

Every day at school, on the large white board in our classroom, I draw and sign his name underneath: "SZNUREK." By now, everyone knows him already, and I taught all my classmates how to pronounce his name correctly.

I am thinking of you all the time. I hope you are taking advantage of your break between jobs and you're relaxing a bit. Everything will come back to normal once you find something appropriate for you. Then we can start again to work on building our dream house. I'm sick to my stomach thinking that I have to imagine what you look like, what preoccupies you, and the sound of your voice. It seems like a very long, bad dream not being able to be with you and Sznurek . . ."

* * *

After my Sunday swimming practice, I was physically exhausted but extremely satisfied. I felt like I was making progress, and perhaps I would qualify for the next stage of GAFPB competitions. Just when I thought I could relax a bit, I realized we had a mandatory study hall at school before the fast-approaching IPT test. Reluctantly, I packed my purple backpack and went to school. The only consolation was the fact that I could wear my civilian clothes. I kept pondering my situation, and how, so far, I did everything in my power to assure the successful passing of the IPT test. I studied hard, my interrogation notebook was in order, I passed with flying colors all my interrogation iterations at school, and I had mastered the process almost to perfection. I was comfortable, although a little anxious, because I never knew which role-player-instructor I would have for the actual exam.

When I was leaving the classroom for a break, Sergeant Cabbage (who had previously given me a hard time at school several times) approached me out of nowhere. "I saw all your interrogation reports and interrogation evaluations." That worried me. What did she want from me now? "You were kicking butts! Just keep doing what you're doing, and you'll pass this time. You've made amazing progress and your interrogations are excellent." I stood there, dumbfounded. "Just treat the test like one of the iterations and everything will be okay," she continued. "Keep kicking to kick butts and take names." She finally finished.

"And take no prisoners." I had some sense of humor left in me despite being suspicious of Sergeant Cabbage's sudden outburst of kindness.

"No, you'll already have one prisoner in your booth on Tuesday. Interrogate the hell out of him! You know, now you're good enough to stay here in school to teach classes full time after your graduation. We need people like you."

I was now frozen in disbelief. Was this the same Sergeant Cabbage who, weeks ago, was teasing me and making fun of my interrogations? What could have had possibly changed her so drastically?

* * *

This time the letter from Alec was sad, and that made me worried. Then I found out that he actually called the company commander earlier, looking to speak with me. I had no idea why he called the commander instead of the company quarters. Perhaps something important happened, perhaps an emergency? I was a nervous wreck.

I kept reading his letter, helpless. From Alec's writing, I could sense that he was sad, lost, and perhaps needed my consolation. After all, his job search had proven unsuccessful. We needed each other more than ever before, but a distance of nearly two thousand miles was separating us for over seven months now. I couldn't discern from the letter what might have been going on at home. Deeply concerned, I went to the Mini Mall near the barracks to call home from there. Alec told me that nothing wrong was happening at home. He was just missing me because he hadn't heard from me for a couple of days. We weren't able to talk for long, however. A massive storm came from Huachuca Mountains, shaking the ground powerfully and throwing dangerously low thunders all around. All personnel around the building were ordered to evacuate inside.

For the rest of the evening, I shifted my thoughts toward swimming for the German Badge, which was more optimistic. While reflecting on my recent swimming efforts, I realized I had my laps timing calculations all wrong! It turned out that if I had eight minutes to swim 200 meters, I would have two minutes for each of 50 meters (a lap). Since one length of a swimming pool was 25 meters, I had one full minute for each length of the pool, not for an entire lap, as I previously had thought. Thus, with my current speed of 1 minute and 30 seconds per lap, I should have about 30 seconds to spare on each lap. That, multiplied by four, would give me around two minutes' safety margin over the minimum prescribed time of eight minutes. I was ecstatic because of this finding. With a big smile on my face, I went to bed.

*   *   *

The night before the IPT, I wasn't able to sleep from anticipation and anxiety. Just two and a half months ago, I failed this test, and I was devastated and desperate for another chance. Now finally, this chance was here. I thought about my most recent successful practice interrogations and felt a relief and hope.

We went to school earlier than usual, missing breakfast altogether. They assigned me to the group being examined in the first half of the day. While setting up my booth for interrogation, I kept replaying in my mind the words of Sergeant Cabbage: "Just treat the exam as any other iteration." It was helpful. My biggest concern at this point was who would be my role-player-examiner. When Mr. Orsky entered the room, my first instinct was panic, because he was very strict. Then I remembered that previously, he was favorable to me when he gave me a hint that my previous IPT failure was a setup of some sort. He was the one who gave me encouragement by saying, "Low key is the key."

The beginning of my interrogation was hard. Orsky wasn't a pleasant individual to begin with. During the exam, he was grumpier than usual. I pushed forward, collected from him the information for my first report, and stopped looking for his sympathy. As the hours flew by, I was doing map tracking, more questioning, and more reports. I did everything I was supposed to, forgetting that all of this was actually a test. I felt comfortable. Even though I still had almost an hour left to finish my interrogation, I had full control over the situation in the booth. I filled the rest of the time asking more "control questions" and obtaining more detailed information for my fourth and the last report. Before I knew it, the sound of a school bell indicated the end of the test. Until the end, I maintained my military bearing despite the lingering stress and trembling. The four-hour test was finally over.

Mr. Orsky kept his neutral composure as well. He didn't give me a single clue about how I did on the exam. I packed all my books and materials and removed my overlay from the map. I left the booth, relieved. After everyone from my group finished, we were escorted to a waiting room far from the building entrance and classrooms. They had prohibited us from having any contact with the second group of our classmates, who were just arriving for the afternoon test, as well as instructors and role players. Once the second group started their test, we went to our old classroom to receive our scores.

I maxed all the sections of the interrogation test and received the highest scores from the class on all four of my intelligence reports. But the most exciting were Mr. Orsky's comments on my score sheet. In every section of the test, he wrote, "Exceeded expectations!" "Excellent job!" I was elated. Sergeant Cabbage gave me two thumbs-ups. "I told you, you will pass!" she exclaimed.

For the first time in such a long time, I felt indescribable liberation and lightness. As if I just entered the garden of Eden and was floating in the air, a white fluffy cloud. At that point, my self-confidence skyrocketed. I felt like I could move the magnificent Huachuca Mountains. I pictured myself running out of the building and actually doing just that. They seemed light and firm, like plastic Lego blocks. After all, my fortune cookie told the truth.

After lunch, I met with Mr. Orsky to sign my test paperwork. When he told me I did a "phenomenal job" that morning, he sounded casual, as if it was a routine.

Because I had passed the IPT I attained my V+ phase and was finally enjoying the same privileges as the rest of my classmates.

After the entire day of stress and emotions, I was trembling until late evening. I had a hard time believing that the infamous IPT was finally behind me. I felt like a new road appeared ahead of me, encouraging me to walk on this fresh path through a flowering meadow. Then I realized that the following day was my swim test.

* * *

Fighting to redeem my self-esteem after the infamous IPT and to save my dignity was one thing. Finding a new passion to pursue in this turmoil was an entirely different story. Instead of going with the flow through the motions, I needed a challenge bigger than anything I'd attempted before, to test my physical and mental limitations to re-validate myself as a human being. The German Badge was not only an ambitious goal, but it became an ultimate chance for establishing myself as an individual soldier. It was the key to my transformation.

CHAPTER 12

THE POWER OF HEALING

On my first day of phase V+ I woke up with a throbbing headache. I barely made it to the company bus taking us to the swimming pool. It turned out we didn't have to swim front crawl after all, so I opted for the backstroke. I felt more comfortable and confident swimming on my back. I ended up sharing the line with one sergeant who was making so much splashing I could barely swim straight. I had to stay focused on my swimming, so I passed her and could finally relax and swim at my pace. From the corner of my eye, I saw people in lines next to me, struggling. It was stressful, so I concentrated on the flags above me marking the swim lines. It felt like I was mowing in slow motion, passing each flag gently waving at me. These flags reminded me of the amusement park during the Northbrook Days celebrations back home. But I had to focus on my breath, a steady in and out, like a well-oiled engine. Second push for the wall, then fifth, and the final, seventh. I landed back at the start line at exactly 6'30", with a minute and a half to spare. Being in the water never felt so good. I wanted to hug everyone around me as if I had just won an Olympic medal.

Leaving the pool, I bumped into Colonel Keller. "Are you changing your specialty from interrogator to a swimmer?" he joked.

"No, sir." I was trying to sound a bit mischievous. "I'm competing for the German Armed Forces Proficiency Badge. Swimming is my third event in the competition. After that, I have five more to go."

"Congratulations then, Specialist Rakowski." He shook my hand, and we parted. Shaking hands was not typical because, usually, senior officers kept their distance from the lower-ranking enlisted personnel, especially trainees. I was always pleased to have a quick exchange with the colonel. Although he was the commander of the entire battalion of nearly eight hundred personnel strong, somehow he could always take a few seconds of his time to talk to me. I felt appreciated as a soldier and as a human being.

* * *

By mid-August, the monsoon season was in full swing. Some mornings, we didn't have our usual physical training because the thunderstorms were too dangerous. The usual orders were to clean our rooms instead. The GAFPB competitions on the track field had to be canceled several times. I kept thinking about the upcoming shot put and jump (either long or high). I was seriously concerned because I never in my life had experienced these disciplines. I was anxious to go to the field and practice as much as possible, but the track was off limits.

In the meantime, the competition in shooting targets for the badge was scheduled for Saturday, on our day off. The entire company was going to the water park in Tucson, except those who were competing for the German Badge. It was an early morning when I donned my BDU, LBE (load-bearing equipment), and Kevlar and one of the drill sergeants took me to the shooting range.

The desert heat was unbearable, and nearly fifty people were standing in lines for target practice and for the qualifications. I was lost, but a sergeant from the range encouraged me to take a short shooting class. For the first time in my life, I saw from up close and had in my hand a 9mm pistol Beretta. Suddenly, I was apprehensive about shooting it because it seemed quite heavy and challenging to handle. My small hands could barely handle the weapon. At this moment, I thought it would be nice to have enormous hands and a muscular torso for better balance. The sergeant taught me how to position my body, lock my right knee and right elbow, and support the weapon with my left hand. I got excited and took my place in line.

I donned my BDU, LBE (load-bearing equipment), and Kevlar and one of the drill sergeants took me to the shooting range.

In order to qualify for the final GAFPB competition, a road march, one had to have a minimum shooting score of 3 out of 5 targets in a row. That meant the marching would be for a bronze medal. For the shooting score of 4 out of 5 targets, one could choose to march either for a silver or bronze medal. Scoring 5 out of 5 targets meant marching for gold, or silver or bronze.

In my first practice, I shot two out of five. Those who quickly qualified for bronze were sitting on the bleachers, bored and waiting for the rest of the company to qualify. There was a lot of pressure on timing and accuracy. It was getting hotter by the minute. I felt I was wasting bullets. Desperately, I was trying various lines, new shooting instructors, different firing positions. All my efforts weren't paying off, and I was getting worse, scoring only 1 out of 5, and then 0 out of 5. Others around me were growing more desperate as well because they were at the range since early morning. More people were leaving the range after their successful qualification. After several more failed attempts, I was devastated and ready to give up. I was stressed out, my hands were shaking, and I lost my focus. When all the bullets were used up, someone offered to buy more of them in the nearby store. There were only about ten of us who still needed to qualify. Although heartbroken, I wanted to score at least the minimum 3 out of 5. I went to the first shooting position I used at the beginning to try my luck. The ranger told me I was aiming too low, and my bullets were hitting the sand, so I adjusted my aim. I shot 3, at last.

It suddenly dawned on me it was not the shooting position or the instructor that mattered, but more experience, practice, and knowledge, which I was gaining slowly. Then I scored 3 again. I placed my score sheet, "Rakowski 3/5," on the table with other score sheets and sat down on the bleachers to take a break. I was almost the last one to qualify. However, there were still about twenty people who wanted to upgrade their minimum scores so they could have a chance to march for silver or gold. Chang was complaining about the weaker shooters using up all the bullets, so she volunteered to collect money and buy some more. I realized I had nothing to lose, so I could try some more. I remembered that in my basic training I wasn't doing that great at the beginning, yet at the end, I gained the nickname "hawk eye." After all, perhaps I had some potential. Feeling guilty that I wasted so many bullets, I added $5 into a hat. A short while later, a lieutenant brought a new batch of 650 bullets, which was enough for about twenty people, six tries each.

Again, my struggle with shooting began. It was a scorching afternoon. Majestic Huachuca Mountains were all around me in a protective embrace. I was sweaty, and the desert dust and sand were sticking to my face, hands, uniform, and boots like peanuts to a caramel-dipped apple. But I was fighting fearlessly. In my attempts, I shot 3, then 1, then 0. As more people were satisfied with their scores, it was harder and harder for me to get back in line without feeling enormous pressure. I decided to stick around until I shot 4 or until I would get kicked out of the range, whichever would come first. Finally, I got 4 and felt an amazing relief. Thinking that I had no bullets left in the magazine, I was about to put down the weapon. But my gut told me to continue shooting. When a target of 25 meters popped up, I took all my energy to stay focused to aim correctly. I got it with my last bullet! A little person-villain on the target collapsed into the clouds of dust. Now I had a chance to march for the gold medal. Looking at my scoresheet, I couldn't believe my own eyes, my heart pounding with joy.

I succeeded and earned my "hawk eye" again. My hard work and sweat finally paid off with this small, yet amazing victory.

We cleaned up the range from all the bullet casings and left on a Humvee to the barracks. Although I was bone tired, my spirits were high. I didn't even mind when our drill sergeant selected me to clean the weapons. It felt like a reward, actually.

* * *

Dear Alec,

After yesterday's successful shooting for the German Badge, I started mentally preparing for the 25 km (15.5 miles) road march next Saturday. This will be the last competition. I am seriously anxious as I never marched this kind of distance. The longest I have accomplished so far was 12 miles. Before the march, however, we still have to complete the track and field events, none of which I am familiar with. They just announced that tomorrow is the last chance for these events because the forecast shows thunderstorms every day of the week except tomorrow. I hope they won't cancel these events. That's a lot of pressure.

I fed the ants today. I'm sure they are struggling to find any food in this desert, just like many other critters. I gave them some popcorn. They organized themselves in small groups and carried the kernels along the curb, going in the same direction to their home far away. As I watched little white dots disappear on the road, I thought about how courageous and tenacious these ants are. I admired their dedication and physical strength. Their efforts remind me of my own struggles in all the competitions for the German Badge, in my morning runs, and previously in school.

They issued our laptops again for schoolwork. This is great because I can finally look at the pictures you sent me on the colorful floppy disks two months ago. The house looks so beautiful, surrounded by spring-flowering shrubs, and I miss it so much. Sznurek sleeping on your lap is just precious! It made me cry. When I come home from this desert, it will be the fall. I like this season in Northbrook when the air becomes cooler in the mornings and evenings. Trees are colorful. It will be a fairy tale. So much time has already passed since January when I left home. I can't believe that it's already been eight and a half months . . ."

* * *

That Monday after school the recall formation was dragging, which made me anxious because I wanted to go to the stadium and practice and qualify in my jumps and shot put for the German Badge. I had to select to compete in either long or high jump. Whichever was first successful, counted as "GO." At first I selected long jump because it seemed more doable. However, after about a dozen tries, I wasn't able to make my distance. I was still short of about a foot.

The sun was setting slowly, enveloping splendid Huachuca Mountains, the field, and all competitors with a bright red blanket. Although the day was ending, my fight had just begun.

I went to check out the high jump. A swarming crowd surrounded the station. Nearby the males were practicing the shot put. I couldn't imagine myself performing either. The crowd started thinning. Many people were done with their jump and shot put and went to the barracks. After some brief instructions from a sergeant on how to throw the ball, I finally had to try. The ball for females weighed 4 kilograms and was painted gold. I was hoping the gold color would bring me good luck. I had to throw 20'5". It seemed very far. I kept trying again over a dozen times. Every time I hit the cones nearby, the crowd was teasing me, shouting, "SKI, this is not a bowling alley!" I had to admit it was quite funny, so I laughed it off and just kept on trying. After a while, only three females were still throwing. The pressure was tremendous, as I still had to complete either of the jumps. At once, I collected all my physical and mental energy and tried again. I could see the company first sergeant and a couple of drill sergeants carefully checking the landing spot of my ball. Finally, they unequivocally confirmed that it was a "GO"! My joy was indescribable.

Now just one jump, I thought to myself with a newly regained enthusiasm. I dashed to the high jump station. Again, I tried numerous times, but my form was deplorable. For a moment, I was thinking about giving up. I stood there observing Ambrosio, her tenacity and form. She seemed unstoppable. I worried that since my landing form was pretty bad, I could easily break my bones. Then I had a vision of falling and actually breaking my neck, then being sent home in a wheelchair, defeated. That would mean that my mother-in-law's curse would be fulfilled. I couldn't let that happen, so I did my best to shake off that image. Eventually, it was just Ambrosio and me. Suddenly, I heard a squeal on the landing mattress. She got injured and wasn't moving. I felt guilty that perhaps my worries about breaking my neck somehow got transferred onto her. I ran up to her and called for help. Drill sergeants surrounded her and were trying to provide first aid. She was in agony.

They shut the station down because of Ambrosio's accident. The night was quickly falling. Huge stadium lights provided some comfort. Alone, I returned to the long jump, my only chance to qualify in track and field. Drill Sergeant Britting was manning the station and taking scores. As I started my tryouts again, he was cheering me on with all his power. "Fly, SKI, fly far!" he screamed. I was still short, about six inches. I really needed to fly.

After another twenty tries, I was nearing full despair. I was so close to the marker, yet still too short a couple of inches. I kept pouring tons of sand out of my shoes. I was all sweaty, covered in sand. Drill Sergeant Britting was patiently raking the sand after each of my jumps. He was giving me pointers on how to improve my run and launch. "I'm not leaving here until you qualify, SKI." Every ten jumps or so, I was collapsing desperately in the sand. "Keep trying. You are so close! You'll make it soon! Don't stop!" I could hear him shouting as if through the fog. I had to take a brief break to calm my breathing. My hamstrings were on fire, and I was trembling from the effort. "What can I do to actually fly?" I wondered. I needed wings. But for the time being, I only had my regular human body, which was simply too short.

Far away silent thunders were piercing the skies. The stars were shimmering in a perfectly black firmament right above me. "Gold stars," I thought to myself. "Be my lucky stars!" I prayed.

I stepped on the runup line one more time. The runup and take-off mark were clearly visible. In my head, I heard the famous music from *The Chariots of Fire* by Vangelis, the scene of a run on the beach. The run on the sand. Now it was my turn to fly above the sand, as far as I could. I imagined how quickly I had to run, how strongly to bounce off the marker, how far to fly. The qualifying distance for my gender and age was 10'7". Everything was taking place in slow motion, full concentration, steady breath, sweaty palms. Suddenly, I felt an amazing power and took off like a cheetah pursuing her prey. As I ran, I could feel my hands slashing the air like aircraft propellers. "Bounce and fly," I thought to myself again. Clouds of sand.

The drill sergeant quickly ran up to me and started measuring my prints. "That's it!" he screamed. "Exactly 10'7"! You qualified! Congratulations!" We hugged each other, filled with an exhilarating joy.

I went to the grassy area and let myself collapse flat on the ground. With relief, I lay there panting. I was getting satiated with the earthy scent of the night. I felt new strength and new hope that I got so much closer to earning my German Badge.

The raindrops started falling on my body. I heard a massive sound of a thunder right above me. The field lights went out. It was time to go.

* * *

The next day, during the first morning formation, my classmates were curious about my competitions the day before. They seemed excited when I told them that I had passed both the shot put and the long jump. Maloy asked me jokingly, "Should we call you 'Air SKI' from now on?" I took it as a compliment. Then Chang admitted, "Rakowski is actually a much better athlete than we had originally thought." Being called an "athlete" was even a bigger compliment and sounded so much better than a "romantic ballerina." It was exhilarating because despite my classmates' doubts, I went so far in the competitions, and it was noticed. Most of the participants fell out of the German Badge during the first two events: sprint and long run. I felt good about my achievements. That's why I wouldn't put up with one of the guys teasing me later during the morning PT.

"SKI, you're doing your 'close hands' push-ups incorrectly," he said. What the hell, I thought. Who does he think he is to correct me?

"At least I can swim!" I remembered when I was training for the swim, I offered him to practice together. But he never showed up, claiming that he was tired. So he didn't make the swim and fell out of the competitions. "You have all these great push-up muscles, but somehow can't use them properly." I couldn't help myself put him in his place.

My classmates laughed and applauded my comeback. The conversation was over, and I couldn't care less if the guy felt offended.

Drill Sergeant Britting congratulated me in front of everyone, saying, "See? I knew you would make it. You just need a little more confidence in your own capabilities."

"Sometimes all I need is to have someone nearby to believe in me." I felt like giving him a barely noticeable wink and a smile would sufficiently express my appreciation for being there for me. Although he was my drill sergeant, I would prefer for him to be my friend. But friendships with the cadre were out of the question.

* * *

The following day, after the usual morning training, I was barely moving. The pain was unbearable. I couldn't walk or sit down or get up. At the nearby Shoppette, I purchased some menthol oil, Absorbine. It brought at least a temporary relief, so I started using it regularly. I smelled like a walking eucalyptus cloud. I was worried that in five days, I would have to ruck-march 25 km (15.5 miles), if I was to select to compete for the gold badge. I had to be in the best physical shape I could be to conquer this task. After two days, I realized again that the pain was actually getting worse. My upper legs, shins, shoulders, and back were on fire. It was most likely from the shot put and the long jump trials. Every day I would ice my legs. Desperate for relief, I was performing various strength and stretching exercises and massages with a little plastic porcupine toy I received from Alec. The Absorbine didn't help much anymore, and even walking was a challenge.

It was another day of running. I was thinking and stressing about it all night long. I couldn't imagine how someone could run while unable to walk. As counterintuitive as it might have been, I realized that my only option to get rid of this horrible pain in my legs was to actually run. I took the position of the rearguard of the formation. I was running at my slow pace all the way to Heritage Hill and back. Geraldo was constantly falling to the ground, out of breath and stamina. I thought that if I was still capable of running despite my pains, she could do as well. She just needed a bit of encouragement. I told her to stop giving up and that falling down on the asphalt was not an option. Eventually, she got up again. I grabbed her elbow and ran with her. She didn't fall once throughout our run all the way to the company.

* * *

Absorbed by the GAFPB, I wasn't thinking about the school anymore. We only had theoretical classes on counterintelligence. The instruction was mostly endless recounts of our instructors' personal adventures and successes in their careers as the military special agents. Although some stories were fascinating, sometimes it was hard to discern what was the actual focus of a class. At times, however, we were learning skills necessary to conduct collection of information properly. Some were interesting, like how to "case"—a tactic used to select places around the post suitable for secret meetings with "informants," how to hire the "sources" of information (role players), how to obtain from them critical battlefield information through interviews or interrogations, and how to write various intelligence reports. Eventually, to start our "Collections," we got grouped into small teams, assigned our team leaders-instructors and one classmate. The interrogators (97E) were paired up with counterintelligence agents (97B), in teams of two. I ended up with Crowder, an easygoing and brilliant young woman from the fourth platoon. We had our instructors to play the roles of informants in various scenarios. We were to meet with them all around the post and collect various types of information from them. Crowder's specialty was interviews, while mine was interrogations. Then we had to write gazillions of different reports and submit them to school for grading.

Every day after school, my thoughts went to the fast-approaching road march for the German Badge. I was still concerned about my aching body. When I spoke about the march with the company first sergeant, he mentioned that the terrain picked for this event would have some paved and unpaved roads, some flat terrain, and some mountains. The latter was worrying me tremendously, as I couldn't imagine myself climbing mountains in full military gear. Another reason for concern was the timing. The posted schedule showed that marching began at 5 a.m. This meant that we would have only two hours of march before the sunrise, in darkness, and therefore in the cool morning air. Typically, this time of the year around 7 a.m., the heat was unbearable, simply dangerous. The remaining two hours of the march would have to take place in scorching heat.

Friday night before the road march, the company commander organized a preparatory meeting for those competing for the German Badge. We all had to declare the levels we had selected. This time, the distances assigned were in three age categories: 18–29, 30–39, 40–44 for both females and males. I selected the gold medal, which meant I had to conquer a 25 km (15.5 miles) distance in 4 hours and 10 minutes. We received our packing list for the rucksacks, which had to weigh 10 kilograms (22.5 pounds), which equaled 17 percent of my body weight without the combat gear I had to wear. The good thing about the march was that everyone could walk or run at their own pace, alone, without worrying about formation or battle buddies. It was like a marathon. We also could walk in our soft caps instead of Kevlar helmets, to prevent heat stroke.

Another good news was that my sore legs were getting better, and I was finally able to sit on and get up from the toilet.

* * *

Saturday, the big day finally arrived. The night before the big marching event, I was restless. I had to wake up at 3:30 a.m. and prepare everything. I was ready mentally and physically. The formation was at 4:00 a.m. In the darkness, shadows in uniforms were swarming around the company entrance. People were checking the weight of their rucksacks to make sure the weight was exactly 22.5 pounds. Eventually, we mounted a white school bus, filling it to the brim. Once we arrived at the Range Control, the starting place of the event, we fell out of the bus like Lego blocks. Most of the people lay down on their backpacks because it didn't seem like we would start any time soon. The starting time, 5:00 a.m. had passed, which made me very nervous. The stars in the firmament were slowly disappearing. I didn't know what to do with myself. We were wasting the best marching time on some administrative stuff. Some people still had to weigh their rucksacks. There was no way anyone could escape the mandatory 22.5 pounds of load. Eventually, we were given our scorecards and timing markers (where and at what time we should be to make it) to help keep the pace. The company chaplain said a prayer for us as we bowed our heads and looked at the pavement for the last time before marching. After this brief and solemn moment, we were finally ready.

I turned on my timer and crossed the starting line, along with a fairly sizable crowd of soldiers. After several steps, I decided that keeping up with the group, especially tall males, was pointless. I needed to find my pace. I wouldn't run right off the bat like some people. With time, the column started stretching. More and more faces were passing me, and I was slowly falling to the very end. But I kept a good pace of 16 minutes per mile, running downhill whenever I could and leaning forward while walking uphill. After the first hour, I ate one energy bar and drank lots of water. For now, everything was happening as planned. The sun rose too quickly. Drill Sergeant Britting ran up to me and walked with me for a while, cheering me on. After five miles, the asphalt pavement disappeared, and the terrain changed into a dirt road. I knew it was going to be harder and harder, just like it once was during my basic training.

Regardless, I was pushing forward, constantly wiping my face and neck with a brown washcloth. I was looking at my watch; the timing was still good. Every mile-marker (container with water) was appearing on the horizon according to my planned timing. Soon, I started seeing some people marching back after they had met their half-distance marker at 5.5 miles. I had a lot more to go since my turning point was at the 7.8-mile marker. I was walking fairly comfortably along the bush line on the red sand. However, after about 6 miles, the route changed again, this time into rocky terrain uphill. I could barely move forward on these rocks, watching not to twist an ankle. I needed to walk on the sides of the road with a bit of sand. It was helping.

Captain Hamilton drove up to me in a military jeep and gave me a banana. I nearly swallowed it in a split second. I continued to push forward, constantly checking my time. It was getting harder and harder to move quickly.

I passed another turning point of 6.25 miles. From this point, I was marching exclusively on rocks, as there were no other options. The water in my canteens was warm from the heat. Then I walked on the red sand again. Finally, I noticed an SUV on top of the hill fairly close to me. I recognized this red vehicle of a sergeant from my class. I nearly ran up to him, knowing that he was my turning point at 7.8 miles marker. When I reached him, he quickly signed my scorecard and told me I "had a good timing so far," and to keep up the pace. Up to this point, I was walking for exactly two hours, which meant I had another two hours and 10 minutes till the finish. Excited, I started shuffling back.

When I reached the darn rocks again, my enthusiasm melted considerably. It seemed as if I were walking in place. I was desperately expecting to see mile-markers. With disenchantment, I finally reached number seven. Seven more miles to go. This meant that I conquered a mere 0.8 miles. I continued to push forward, just to reach yet another marker and check my timing. I was constantly tripping over the rocks, ankles twisting, barely keeping my balance. My feet were hurting from these acrobatics. I started feeling that something strange was going on in my boots, but I couldn't put my finger on it. My imagination was showing me pictures of popping bloody blisters. I fought it. I didn't need to see them. I had moleskin, so I thought I should be safe.

The scorching heat was slowing me down. The relatively smooth sand that I was walking on previously was now trampled. It was nearly impossible to walk on it, because I was sinking. The captain drove up to me again and gave me an orange this time. With my hands swollen like balloons, I could barely peel it. I fought the rocks again, running uphill. My watch showed that I should be soon arriving at another marker. However, I couldn't even see it from the distance. The sixth marker simply didn't want to show up. When I finally ran up to it, according to my timing, the previous mile took me an entire 18 minutes. "Too long," I said to myself. "I have to catch up on the paved road. It should come soon."

The sun was burning me alive, so I unbuttoned my BDU top and folded my cap into my cargo pocket. I was doing everything in my power to conquer this scorching desert, yet it seemed as if I were walking in place again. The bush line should be around the 5-mile marker. I still couldn't see it, though. I passed one female sitting on the side of the road, probably after giving up. I didn't want to give up. As I walked, I turned around a couple of times to see if she was marching, but eventually I didn't see her anymore.

At some point one of my classmates, Tsami, walked up to me and we marched together until the next marker. It was uplifting to have a living body accompanying me for a while. At the marker I felt the immense pain and swelling in my feet as if they were crushed. I also felt something wet inside my boots. I immediately regretted stopping at the marker for just a few seconds to get water. At that spot, an army ranger was resting on the ground, exhausted. He advised me to keep running downhill once I reached the top of the hill. Tsami was already far away in front of me. His silhouette soon disappeared. According to my watch, I had about an hour and 10 minutes to traverse 5 miles. I moved on forward, encouraged by the captain's words from earlier that the last five miles were downhill. However, after claiming the hill, I realized it wasn't so. All I saw were rolling hills. My feet were on fire. I wasn't able to run anymore. I checked my watch. "I have an entire mile too much to walk. There is no way I will make the time." This intrusive thought was blasting in my head. It took everything I had to keep on advancing as fast as I could, as far as I could. "Don't give up," I kept repeating to myself like a prayer. "Perhaps the terrain will flatten, and I try to run?" I was passing more and more people who had given up and were sitting by the side of the road waiting to be scooped up by the cadre. My end was nearing quickly. I remembered the ranger from the 5-mile marker. He was also waiting there to be saved from the scorching desert. Otherwise, he would have already passed me. Ahead of me, small groups of people were getting into SUVs, driving up and rescuing those who couldn't walk anymore. I promised myself that I would not volunteer to get into one of these cars under any circumstances. So when they were approaching me and someone would ask how I was doing, I would reply persistently with a smile, "I'm still hanging." They would wish me luck and drive away.

The miles continued to stretch relentlessly. A three-mile marker was nowhere near me. I was forcing myself to drink the disgusting, almost hot water from my canteens. My uniform was soaking wet, hands swollen, a thin layer of salt dried up on my face. I became a dry, salty potato chip. It didn't stop me, however, from jogging whenever I was approaching downhill terrain. My feet were rebelling against me. At last, I saw the 3-mile marker. "I needed a miracle to make it in time." I passed O'Haver, who was sitting on the ground exhausted, waiting for the ride. I started running with all the energy I could squeeze out of me, but it wasn't the run comparable to the one from the beginning. Again, it felt as if I were running in place. I could feel my feet cracking and breaking, blisters popping, and wetness in my boots. But I kept telling myself that as long as I was moving forward and had gotten used to the pain, everything was okay. I would worry about my injuries later.

The captain drove up to me again, and I asked him if I still had a chance to make my time. He said, of course. It was encouraging, so I kept pushing forward. By then, the heat was unbearable, and boiling air was pouring from the sunny skies. I didn't know what to do with my swollen hands. The rucksack seemed heavier by the minute. I knew I had only a half hour to conquer the last 2.5 miles. On my good days without a full gear and loaded rucksack, I could run two miles in 19 minutes. However, now the situation was hopeless. At this moment, I decided to march for the distance, not for the time, just to prove to myself that I could do it. With resignation and a heavy heart, I said goodbye to my German Badge. I just wanted to reach the finish line and save my dignity.

When I approached the third building of the range, I stopped my watch. Measuring my timing was unnecessary anymore. Suddenly Sergeant Thomas drove up to me and yelled from her Jeep, "Come on, Rakowski, you have twenty minutes for one and a half mile! You can do it!" I thought she must have had the distance all wrong. It was simply impossible for me to run one and a half mile at this point of the game.

Because no one was trying to pick me up from the road, I was courageously pushing forward for another twenty minutes. By the time I reached the last mile-marker, I knew I didn't make the time. The only thing on my mind was to reach the finish line and take off the wet uniform and my boots, dirty despite pouring water on them. I gave everything so far. I had no regrets. Although I had gotten used to the overwhelming pain, my feet were crushed. I sped up again, regardless.

I finally noticed in front of me the familiar Range Control buildings. It was a good sign. The last heel, the last run. When I approached the hilltop, about half a mile from the finish line, the captain drove up to me again. He didn't have any words of encouragement or any fruit for me anymore. "Come on, Rakowski. Your time is up. Hop in!"

I wasn't in any position to argue with him. My dream of earning the German Badge in gold was officially over. The only thing I had left for me was the satisfaction that I just completed fifteen miles of marching in extreme conditions, pain, and insufferable heat. I barely got into the captain's vehicle. My entire body was in agony. I was suddenly shivering from the cold. Everything in my pockets—some chewing gums and one last power bar—had melted. We quickly arrived at the finish line where everyone was waiting for me, the last woman standing. I nearly fell out of the truck. Someone took my rucksack. Someone else helped me remove my load-bearing equipment and the BDU blouse.

I collapsed under the shade of a skimpy little tree surrounded by the conquerors and the conquered. It was miserable to be picked up so close to the end. "My ranger" from the 5-mile marker congratulated me for making it so far. I needed every bit of consolation I could get. After all, we were all winners for even trying.

Once I took off my boots, I nearly passed out from the view and agonizing pain. The boots came off with socks, which were attached to my moleskin, which was attached to the flesh on my heels, which were now raw and exposed. Bloody blisters were covering all my shattered toes. I felt dizzy and sick to my stomach, so I lay down on some concrete nearby with my feet on my rucksack. The concrete offered a pleasant warmth to my shivering body. The sun was suddenly pleasant on my face. I lay there for a while, but I felt so physically sick, I wanted to die right then and there.

It was a devastating blow. I should have been stronger. I could only find some consolation in that I hadn't given up, that I gave everything I had. I fought, but I lost. I went the farthest from all of those who didn't win. My heart and my body were broken. Perhaps the German Badge wasn't meant to be mine after all.

* * *

I was barely able to get on the white bus. My classmate Maloy helped me with my rucksack. Barefoot, I dismounted the bus by the company barracks. My blood-covered feet were pulsating with pain, my entire being was broken and shivering violently. I threw my uniform off my body with disgust. This uniform had all my sacrifices and my fight in it, all of which turned out to be in vain.

At that point, I felt lonely in my defeat. I needed Alec more than anything.

For the rest of the day and Sunday, every time I walked by the front desk, people were expressing their admiration toward me. Apparently, the news about my heroic marching had spread out fast. Everyone was curious about my "battle wounds" and deeply disappointed for me for not having won the medal despite my fight.

It took me several hours to realize that everything was over, that the only thing left for me was this excruciating pain in my feet and the pain in my soul. I was depressed. Despite the raging throbbing in my feet and exposed skin on the heels and toes, I finally worked up the courage to take a shower to wash off not only my blood, sweat, and tears but also all my hopes and dreams about the badge.

I was not able to wear socks, so the DFAC, where socks were mandatory, was off-limits for me. Thus, for lunch, I had to buy pizza at the Mini Mall. Later, instead of dinner, I took care of my feet and popped all the blisters I could find. Although it provided some relief, every time I was in the sun, the burning was unbearable. I thought I would never heal from my broken spirits and mangled feet.

* * *

On Monday, first thing in the morning, I went to sick call to get my wounds checked. Major Maadox and a nice sergeant from the other clinic were there. For a few moments, we were all joking about my marching adventures. The sergeant looked at my feet and said, "I know that if you had a chance, you would do it all over again."

"Oh hell, no!" My reply was purely instinctive. "Never in my life. It wasn't worth it. I would rather not have that chance again." I barely believed my own words. What if I did have another chance? Would I have it in me to do it again? These thoughts seemed too far out at the moment, so I shook them off.

They soaked my feet in some mixture and told me I had stress fractures in both feet. They gave me crutches, ordered to wear heel-less sandals, and gave me a "No PT" profile. My uniform pants had to be rolled up, exposing my heels, to keep them dry and let them heal faster. Not being able to wear socks without the risk of aggravating the wounds was just as exasperating as walking with crutches. I had to rely on other people to bring me food, to carry my school computer, or to drive me to school and back. Even my instructor-team leader, Mr. Bonvillain, would walk me out of the classroom carrying my laptop and asking my classmates with cars to give me a lift to the barracks.

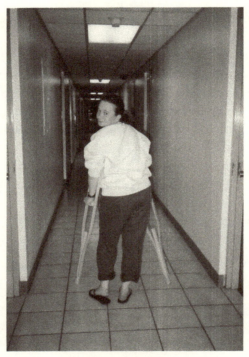

Not being able to wear socks without the risk of aggravating the wounds was just as exasperating as walking with crutches.

I was desperate for relief. Nothing seemed to work—ointments, dressings, icing, rest. My feet were so swollen, I couldn't see my ankles or veins. To make things worse, I had some flu symptoms that were keeping me up at night. I was dealing with a horrible cough, headaches, and fever. After being pushed to the limits, my body was breaking down.

* * *

Meanwhile, Intelligence Collections at school were in full swing. My partner Crowder was constantly anxious about our meetings with our "source" played by Mr. Bonvillain. She lacked self-confidence in her interviewing skills and in writing intelligence reports. She would bombard me with questions about everything we were doing. Despite being on crutches and "on quarters" (no school), I wanted to be as helpful as possible and not miss any of our meetings. At least schoolwork was an excellent distraction from my agonizing feet.

At the recall formation, they awarded the first round of German Badges to several soldiers in our company. However, I could hear behind my back that Scully and some people from Fourth Platoon found it unfair. Apparently, some awardees hadn't completed all the competitions and somehow slipped through the cracks. I was hoping this time someone other than me would make waves about it. To my relief, they did. They went to the company commander and brought the issue to his attention. They also suggested that the marching event was unfair because we had started it too late, and it was dangerously hot. That's why many people weren't able to finish. "Like Rakowski, who gave everything at every competition, and she wouldn't get the medal." I overheard the entire conversation. The captain seemed caught off guard and a bit frustrated. Perhaps he thought something went horribly wrong with the German Badge.

As I stood there with my crutches, watching the medals being awarded, deep in my heart, I was crying. To get some relief, I convinced myself that I never really wanted this badge, anyway. I didn't want it, even if I had an opportunity to fight for it again. It was the only way to gain some peace of mind.

* * *

Surprisingly, the school-related work was more enjoyable, mainly because it didn't involve any physical work, and being on crutches, I was always lucky to get a ride either in someone's private vehicle or in a company van. Mr. Bonvillain was very thorough and fair, had a great sense of humor, and was authentic. I felt like I was learning a lot from him during our Collections. It was always intriguing what he had to say in school and the field.

Crowder also had a very colorful and easygoing personality. She would make us laugh sometimes. Like that time when before one of our morning meetings, she had "stolen" three coffees from DFAC, and on the way to the meeting place, she had spilled most of the coffee. Later, however, she suddenly fell sick to her stomach during the meeting and had to vomit behind a fence several times. Each time, she would return to the meeting as though nothing happened and continued the interview. She persistently refused to seek medical help. I found it brave.

During one meeting, somehow, we even started talking about ballet. Crowder had revealed her secret out of the blue. I was shocked listening to her vast experiences with this art. Apparently, she had studied ballet for several years in Washington, D.C.. At some point, she even spent months studying it at the Moscow Ballet Conservatory on a scholarship. She knew a lot about the "Vaganova technique," enough to convince me she wasn't making things up. She was the real thing. I was deeply impressed and immediately developed a new admiration for her. And so here we were: two former ballerinas, now sisters in arms—Counterintelligence Agent Crowder and Interrogator Rakowski, the Dynamic Duo of the Military Intelligence. Mr. Bonvillain had a great time with us. He appreciated our efforts and successful interviews and graded our reports highly.

"You ladies are a tough team. You don't give up despite obstacles. All the males in your place would cry and run to bed!" I liked that he called us "ladies," instead of soldiers. It reminded me that we were women in this male-dominated world.

*   *   *

On Thursday before the long Labor Day weekend, I heard an interesting rumor. Apparently, the next Saturday, those who didn't complete the road march for the GAFPB would have another chance. I was told that Captain Hamilton admitted that the first time around, we started the event too late in the day, and the extreme heat caused many failing to complete it in time. One person from the second platoon was roaming the barracks, collecting the names of those interested in marching again. It made me think these rumors were true after all. A bit shocked by this turn of events, at first, I was skeptical about doing it the second time. But the proposition proved tempting.

I had chaos in my head. Endless questions were bombarding my head. Would I be able to heal in time and get used to wearing socks and combat boots? There were only eight days to accomplish that. Would I be capable of marching long distance again? Would I be allowed to march at least for silver (judging from my first attempt, gold had proven not doable)? After all, it was "only" 12.5 miles for the silver.

Regardless of it all, since a new energy and fighting spirit filled my body and soul, I needed to expedite the healing of my feet. With all my heart, I wanted to bring home a medal and show it to Alec. He would be proud of me.

The night of August 31, I was still pondering why the captain would allow only bronze. What difference did it make for him? I wanted to have the option to choose tough goals, not easy ones. I wanted to go for silver. Unfortunately, Scully from my class confirmed that it was all true about the bronze. I found it unfair and demoralizing that we were not allowed to reach for the stars far away. I told myself that if I didn't try the silver march, I would not forgive myself for the rest of my life. That's because I would never know if I was indeed capable of conquering the 12.5-mile distance in 3 hours and 20 minutes. However, the hope alone for marching again restored my will to fight.

From all this barrage of thoughts in my head, the next morning, I woke up with a throbbing headache. Luckily, I didn't have to do the morning training because I was still on crutches. The good news was that my heels were almost healed. At the beginning of the long weekend at breakfast, I met Izzy from class 006. I told her that next Saturday there would be another march for the GAFPB.

"Are you going?" I don't know why but she seemed excited.

"I don't know. I'm not happy with what happened to me the last time. Besides, I'm still barely walking on these damn things." I pointed to my crutches.

"You should go. You owe it to yourself. I know you are strong." My face now looked like a big question mark. "You're not one of those who give up. I saw what you went through here, and I know you can do anything you want and achieve success," she continued enthusiastically.

"Where do you get all this?" I didn't even know her. I couldn't believe how much she knew about me.

"I see it on your face for the past two months since I've been here, and I know you very well by now. Besides, you're a legend!"

Me? A legend? What the heck was she talking about? Despite being surprised, I took her words as a compliment. I suddenly felt uplifted and inspired.

"Do it again and you will win this time," she insisted.

After this conversation, it was time to ditch the crutches and start slowly walking around the barracks. In my head, one thing dominated: to heal faster. I imagined my marching again, exactly a week from now. Perhaps this was my last chance.

I called Alec. We were both a bit down. "Buy yourself a six-pack of beer," I said, "and I'll do the same. I'll sit somewhere in the corner and have some while you drink yours. We'll enjoy it together."

* * *

Dear Alec,

As planned, yesterday, I packed my purple backpack and went to the town of Sierra Vista. I had enough money saved from change I've been finding on the streets to cover my transportation for the entire day. It's good to be roaming freely around different stores and look at the colorful people around me and eat Chinese food. How refreshing! Because hours go by slowly and because of the holiday, I have more time for schoolwork and for myself. After the entire day in Sierra Vista, I had my two beers and read a book about cowboys, which I had borrowed from our instructor at school.

It's amazing how our MI Village looks different during the long weekend. Parking lots are practically empty and even the air seems cleaner and cooler. I can hear better the sounds of the night, which I never have time to hear on regular nights.

For the past few days, I've been sick with some virus I've probably caught from my roommate. She always goes places off base and who knows what she can bring back from her escapades. I'm coughing up a storm and something is in my lungs. It's rather painful, but I'm not worrying about it too much.

After frequent icing and applying various healing substances, my feet are getting much better. Although my Achilles tendons are still aching, the swelling went down considerably, and my veins are finally showing. I can even sleep with my feet under the covers or on my back without pain or discomfort.

Guess what? It looks like I will have another chance to march for the badge! I still worry about my strength and beaten feet, but I'm slowly getting excited about it. Everyone in the company is very supportive and they encourage me to try again.

I'm excited that there are only twenty-four days left until graduation, which is planned for the twenty-fifth of September. The anticipation of seeing you and our sweet home fills me up. I am obsessed with the thoughts about going home and about what awaits me there. I'm trying to remember how our house looks like, the smell of the air in Northbrook, how Sznurek's fur feels like or touching real green grass, how it is to drive the car again, or what clothes are in my dresser.

* * *

There were only four days left until the second iteration of the infamous road march for the GAFPB. Many people at the company were asking me about my feet and looking at my wounds. The healing progress collectively impressed them. My feet were indeed healing fast, and the only thing left to do was to fix my toes, which were still in pretty awful shape. I had to cut off the dead skin from old blisters and remove four toenails, which were also dead. I needed space for brand-new ones. The most important thing, however, was that I could walk almost normally without crutches and wear socks.

Crowder and I were both doing well in school. In the mornings, we were meeting our "informant" in the field and after collecting intelligence from him, we would go back to school to write endless reports. In the afternoon, our small team would meet with Mr. Bonvillain for a quick lecture and evaluation of our reports. Mr. Bonvillain often complimented our work as extremely detailed and according to the rules. Indeed, Crowder relaxed a bit, could organize herself and concentrate better on her tasks. She eventually gained some confidence. I liked her as a partner.

In the afternoon, I found out that there was one thing to be completed before the road march for the German Badge. It was a first-aid test. Since I had an hour to spare, I went to my room to study. I knew most of the questions. However, I had to be careful with my answers because more than two mistakes would disqualify me from marching for silver, which I still hoped for. Thankfully, I passed the test with no problems.

Two days before the marching day on Saturday, I finally could wear my combat boots instead of heel-less sandals. At the beginning, it was quite hard, but I knew the discomfort eventually would pass. Besides, if I wanted to march, I had to get used to wearing combat boots quickly. I was running out of time.

* * *

On the Friday before the event, I had decided for sure that I was marching. Maloy, who already had completed his march for gold the first time around, helped me to prepare properly. He recommended I put the moleskin directly on the skin, then the nylon socks (to reduce friction), then the wool socks (to keep moisture away from feet), and it should work. It was his recipe for success. This solution reminded me of my ballet-dancing years. Back then, I was using nylon socks to wrap my toes to avoid friction while dancing in hard, pointed, ballet pointe shoes. Without nylons, I would end up with painful, bloody blisters on my feet and blood inside my shoes. It made perfect sense to use nylons in combat boots as well, to avoid injuries. Why didn't I think of that sooner? After all, dancing ballet was for me as physically demanding as marching in the military. The only difference was the footwear. I was grateful for Maloy's advice, so I ran to the Mini Mall to get the nylons and super thick and fluffy wool socks. I polished my combat boots from basic training to use instead of the desert boots, which I had used last time. The basic training boots were heavier and more stable because they didn't have cloth sections on ankles like the desert boots. In addition, they were more comfortable and had "tractor" soles, which were attached in Fort Huachuca at the beginning of my stay on base. Finally, unlike the desert boots, they had a lot more mileage on them, thus they could better withstand treacherous roads in the Huachuca Mountains.

Ultimately, I placed moleskin on all my toes and the heels and packed my rucksack with all the required elements plus some rocks to meet the weight. Later I would decide to keep one of them as a souvenir. That's how my pack became the "ROCKSACK."

* * *

I was wondering all night how far I would be capable of marching this time. The evening prior to the second march, I had asked Captain Hamilton if I could go for silver, the longer distance. Since I had shot five of five shots correctly on the shooting qualification day, the captain agreed I could march again, but one grade lower. He knew that, because the first time around I walked for the gold, this time I could do silver, 12.5 miles. This was good news and contradicted the rumors that everyone would be "downgraded" to bronze.

I was set to go for silver, and this decision was unnerving. My brain, however, was still going places I didn't want to go to. What if I fail again? What if I mess up my feet again? What if I fall from the heat? These intrusive thoughts kept me up all night as I was doubting my capacities.

Early in the morning, just like two weeks earlier, several shadows in uniforms were moving back and forth around the assembly area in front of the barracks. Last preparations, weighing in the rucksacks, and checking the equipment. This time, there were barely a dozen of us. I was better prepared this time around and felt calm and comfortable.

Once they dropped off at the familiar Range Control, I collected all my courage and will to survive and win this time. Exactly at 4:20 a.m., I took the scorecard for the silver.

A few minutes later, I started my stopwatch and began my march at a fairly fast pace. Everything seemed comfortable: my "rocksack" was tightly packed and close to my body. My supportive kidney belt was in the right place, boots tight but comfortable. The group started stretching from the very beginning. Soon I ended almost at the end. I wanted to catch up with the shadows in front of me. It was Chang, Sergeant O'Haver, and someone I didn't know. They welcomed my company, and for a mile, I walked with them. After the first mile and a half, I was already sweating profusely, but it wasn't too bad because the darkness hadn't given up yet to the morning sun. While running down one hill, I lost my handkerchief I used to wipe my face and neck. "Let it be my gift to the Huachuca Mountains. A memory, that I was here," I told to myself and kept on advancing. We marched faster, using the "airborne shuffle" (jog with a rucksack), about 9 minutes per mile. It was a healthy pace. Now and then, a crisis and doubts were crushing my brain. Perhaps I should have aimed for the bronze? I had to fight my mind. Energy bars devoured here and there kept me going. I caught up with O'Haver and Chang because I needed and wanted to stay with them. It was always safer and easier to run with others by your side. The miles were slowly passing: 3-mile marker, 4-mile marker, 5-mile marker. It was harder and harder to keep up with my companions, but I had to conquer my aching body and my racing thoughts. Our goal was to reach before sunrise the 6.25-mile marker, the turnaround point, bronze for O'Haver and Chang, and silver for me. We didn't want to see the sun too soon. At dawn, the still red fresh sun wasn't too dangerous, so we pushed on. At last, we reached the half point, but we were a few minutes short. Our company commander was cheering for us, shouting to hurry because we still had good timing. After the mid-point, I wasn't able to keep up anymore with my companions. In agony, I was trying to catch up with them, but didn't have it in me. They were too fast. As the two shadows were slowly disappearing in the morning fog, I was fighting the red sand and rocks again, alone.

I thought about Alec and our home in Northbrook. I dedicated my march to Alec and everything I cherished the most. Our house, our Sznurek, our peace, and our dreams. Suddenly, I felt lonely. With my sleeve, I wiped two hot tears from my cheeks. But I kept fighting the time, the pain, and eventually, the sun. To lift my spirits, I forced myself to eat a power bar and started jogging.

By the 5-mile marker, I had 1 hour and 20 minutes to make it on time. Exactly 16 minutes per mile. Still doable, but with jogging. The captain was passing by in his Jeep every few minutes, encouraging me to keep going faster. I knew that this time around I was in better shape, and I also knew the route. Only the scorching heat was getting unbearable. I started feeling my toes swell up and my leg muscles on fire. "Move your hands back and forth, SKI!" The captain was now driving right next to me.

I started moving my hands, and it proved helpful. After another half a mile, I conquered the highest hill. However, I was exhausted physically and mentally and wanted to quit. I still had about four miles to go. In sheer desperation, I threw my cap behind me and pushed on. Until the 3-mile marker, I was still fighting my lonely battle with the elements, myself, and time. Even though everything was against me, I was determined to win. Soon, I started seeing the instructors passing me by in their private vehicles, manning the road, and checking for casualties. I could hear them screaming, "Good job, SKI!" This kept me going.

When my captain showed up again, I asked him for water. He dismounted his car and took my two empty canteens, then he drove off about fifty meters, filled the canteens, and encouraged me to run and grab them without stopping. It worked. I got the canteens and immediately poured one over my head. The captain drove off again and, standing by his car, shouted for me to catch up with him. Every time I had run up to him, he would drive off and call me again. We both fought for my success together, a perfect team. We played this game for about two miles. I was spent but still moving, walking, jogging, and running. I was doing everything in my power to resist slowing down.

"Just a little more, SKI! After this hill, you'll see our white bus. Hurry!"

With my soaking-wet BDU unbuttoned and both hamstrings cramping, I started running again. Everything was pulsating in me, my heart like a giant bell trying to break free from my chest.

Suddenly, on top of the last hill, Drill Sergeant Britting appeared out of nowhere. I thought it was the finish line, so I ran up to him.

"The finish line is right there!" He pointed at a group of people about 100 meters in front of us. "We're gonna run together. Ready?"

"As ready as can be!" was my breathless reply. I lied. I wasn't ready. But there was no time to ponder if I still had it in me. My clock was ticking.

From this point on, my struggle became a real run for the medal. Nothing else mattered. As in a dream, I felt everything was happening in slow motion. The silhouettes of my fellow soldiers were pacing around the finish line in anticipation. Another 20 meters. Suddenly, a group from the finish line started running toward me. Through my foggy mind, I could hear them cheering: "SKI never gives up! Hard-core! You can do it!"

Two more meters and the white line was finally behind me. It was over. I could barely realize what I had just accomplished. My legs were giving in, but people wouldn't let me fall. So, with my heart pounding stronger than ever before, I was still standing. Someone gave me my canteen with water, which I gulped, spilling half of its content on my neck and shirt. Someone took my "rocksack" off my back. Two people were holding me under my arms to prevent me from falling. "Walk around the tree in the shade to slow your heart rate," I heard Drill Sergeant Britting.

As I paced around the tree, wobbling, I took my BDU top off and poured more water on my head to cool off. People around me were hugging me, congratulating me. Because I never gave up, because I was the last person to finish this race successfully. Although I was mostly trembling from this enormous effort, I was also shaking from joy and disbelief that I actually had accomplished my goal.

"I cheated you of two minutes," the captain said with a mischievous smile. "You made it one and a half minutes ahead of your time!"

"That was really kind of you. Thanks for believing in me." I barely squeezed the air out of my hurting lungs and smiled.

Everyone helped me get on the bus. They were carrying my pack, my BDU top. Someone brought me my cap found on the road. Once I sat down, the realization hit me that it was all finally over. My dream came true, and I won the silver 100 percent. I swapped my combat boots for heel-less sandals. I poured some water over my mangled feet. They didn't look too bad. The entire bus was celebrating. All winners were relieved that the toughest competition was finally over.

I barely got off the bus by the company and walked to my room. To my surprise, I discovered it was only 8:00 a.m.

Someone knocked on my door. It was Izzy.

"I heard you made it. Congratulations! You are my hero!" A hero? I thought I didn't deserve it. So many people before me had conquered this march. All I did was persevere, thanks to everyone supporting me. Perhaps in Izzy's mind, this was enough to be a hero. Regardless, I blushed, but it was probably indiscernible on my roasted face.

"I knew you would do it," she added.

"You did, but I still don't know how you knew it." We hugged each other like sisters.

* * *

I changed into my civilian clothes and went to breakfast. On my way there and at DFAC, I was meeting people congratulating me and expressing their admiration for my exploits. It felt like I'd just come back from war. Indeed, it was a veritable war against the elements, time, pain, my body and mind, and finally, my doubts and insecurities. Miraculously, after such tremendous effort, I could still walk on my own. My victory in GAFPB competitions was slowly sinking in. I needed to share it with Alec as soon as possible. I told him everything about my morning fight for the silver. My dream finally came through. After all, I would bring home the medal. I was so emotionally charged; I cried like a child who just received a puppy for Christmas.

My classmates Young and Chang invited me to join them in Sierra Vista for the Oktoberfest celebrations in town. We went to a German restaurant and had some good German beer. I danced the polka with the Germans. It was the perfect way of celebrating my German Badge.

* * *

Because of my uplifted spirit, everything around me seemed more colorful and fresher. Even the air smelled good. Monday seemed like the most exciting day of the week. After the morning formation, every person who took part in GAFPB march was released from physical training.

Relieved, I went back to the barracks and mopped all hallways with enthusiasm.

After a busy weekend, Crowder and I had to hurry and catch up before meeting our source at the commissary. As we walked to the meeting place through a deserted area of the post in extreme heat, I was coughing and barely breathing. My head was on fire. I was convinced that I had caught the flu that was apparently spreading around the MI Village. Regardless, our meeting with Mr. Bonvillain went well. He came dressed up as a cowboy and let me borrow his belt with two pistols and a brown Stetson hat. It was a fun distraction from the mundane school activities and from the scorching heat.

Later at school, we had an evaluation of our meeting and Mr. Bonvillain said that it was nearly perfect. We were extremely happy as this was our last meeting in Collections. The chief instructor was so impressed by our work that he complimented us in front of the entire class and asked us to perform a demonstration (of a meeting with "source") for class 006. It was one big, successful improvisation.

He let me borrow his belt with two pistols and a brown Stetson hat.

* * *

Throughout my training, I had experienced many ebbs and flows, often my spirit and my body broken. I could endure a fair amount of pain. Sometimes it was borderline unreasonable. And that was okay, as long as I could continue pushing on with my goals. However, when I had reached my limits of physical and emotional brokenness while pursuing the German Badge, enduring the pain wouldn't get me anywhere, I had to learn the power of healing. Healing was the only reasonable thing to do, so I could start my fight again, stronger and liberated from pain and open wounds. And, unlike in ballet school, where dealing with pain was the only option in pursuing a dancer's profession and no time to heal, this time around, it was my choice to continue the competitions for the Badge, against all odds and in unbearable conditions. That choice alone was the power and the chance for renewal.

CHAPTER 13

FRAGILITY OF HUMAN LIFE

September 11 was supposed to be one of the happiest days in my military career. It was the first anniversary of my enlistment in the U.S. Army. I wanted to celebrate it all day long and everywhere, during the morning run, at school, and in the barracks. I wanted to sing and dance from the joy and satisfaction of achieving an important milestone. Just a year ago, I was writing a goodbye letter to Chris, mourning our extinct friendship. I was eager to begin my new journey and promised myself that I would achieve a definite transformation from being a ballerina to a soldier. And here I was, proudly wearing my army uniform daily. I had a new way of life, and this felt like I was on the right path. I felt like someone.

It was also a special day for the entire Fort Huachuca. That morning, a change of command ceremony was scheduled on Browns Parade Field, near the track field where just three weeks ago I successfully completed my sprint, the first competition for my German Badge. A three-star-general, a new garrison commander, was taking over the post.

The morning formation at 5:00 a.m. was going on as usual. Accountability. Warm up before the exercise. Jumping jacks, push-ups, and sit-ups. Around 6:50 a.m., Drill Sergeant Britting stood in front of us and in a somber voice announced, "There has been a tragic accident in New York. A plane crashed in the North Tower of the World Trade Center.

Go to the dayroom and watch the news." For a moment, I thought it was some kind of cruel joke.

We rushed into the barracks. The day room was packed. We turned on the TV and watched the burning building in horror. I was wondering how an accident like that could have happened. The view was heartbreaking. Those of us from New York were stunned and grew anxious about our loved ones.

Ten minutes later, yet another plane crashed, this time into the South Tower, right in front of our eyes. Everyone in the room gasped in disbelief. People were tearing up, covering their faces, and cursing. It seemed perfectly warranted to curse. The sound of pounding hearts was almost palpable. We watched in dismay as people working in WTC in windows were screaming for help, some jumping to their death, barely visible in thick clouds of smoke and debris. At this moment, I knew that these were not accidents. We soon found out that it was a terrorist attack. Apparently, some terrorists had hijacked two commercial planes to hit the Towers.

I immediately called Alec to reassure him I was okay. I asked him to call my parents in Poland to reassure them as well. I imagined they were worried, in a faraway country, knowing that their daughter might have been in danger. Even though they would still worry, I was hoping the news from me would provide some relief.

By the time we made it to school, more information was available. Before 8:00 a.m. a third hijacked plane crashed into the military wing of the Pentagon in Arlington, Virginia, causing its partial collapse. Soon, we were devastated by more horrifying news pouring in. We were pacing around the classroom, disoriented. My head was spinning from guessing why these attacks happened and what was coming next. Were we in danger?

We were told that all the big cities around the country started mass evacuations of people from their downtown areas, and air traffic was canceled, except for the military aircraft. People were fleeing New York City. There was still one commercial plane missing with which the radio contact was lost. The street traffic on the base closed.

Around 8:00 a.m., a sergeant briefly entered the classroom with more bad news. He also brought us a small radio. We heard that another hijacked flight flew toward Washington, D.C.. We soon found out that alerted of the previous attacks, the plane's passengers attempted to regain control, but the hijackers ultimately crashed the plane into a field somewhere in Pennsylvania. This flight most likely was targeting either the U.S.

Capitol or the White House. At about 8:50 a.m., both towers at the World Trade Center collapsed, burying thousands of people in fiery rubble. This triggered the collapse of other World Trade Center structures, including 7 World Trade Center, and the severe damage of nearby buildings. It felt like we were at war.

Everything and everyone were on high alert. The orders came in for all personnel to stay at the school hall only in the areas without windows. I heard before that all modern buildings in Fort Huachuca had been built with slim windows, like bunkers, in case of enemy attack, so the soldiers could use them as defensive firing positions. For a few seconds, I saw in my mind the war scenes that could take place in Fort Huachuca. "What if we got hit by some hijacked aircraft or a bomb?" I thought. The buildings with slim windows could quickly become our graves. All the bad news was making me nauseous. The post was officially on lockdown. No civilians were allowed on base except for former military personnel—school instructors. Everyone's IDs were being checked at all gates and various points of post.

Our instructor for that day, Mr. Bonvillain, made it to school after waiting in line at the gate for four hours. The recent developments visibly shook him up.

"It's Bin Laden," said Mr. Bonvillain, deeply disturbed. "We've had him under surveillance for so many years." The tears were trying to burst out of his eyes, but he kept his composure. He was trying to be strong for himself and all of us.

It was too hard to concentrate on any school material, so we listened to Mr. Bonvillain's stories about intelligence efforts during President Clinton's times and how much we knew back then about Al-Qaeda. It was overwhelming.

At 9:00 p.m. Warsaw time, I had an opportunity to call Poland. I could briefly speak to my dad to let him know I was okay. I could sense that he was relieved. Perhaps he still had some doubts. What if I was in danger but didn't want to worry my parents? I wasn't sure if I was indeed safe, either. It was hard to wrap my head around what was happening in the United States.

The chaos and full alert in the country continued. The civilians working on post were sent home and only essential personnel (trainees and all military personnel) were to stay on base. The rumor had it as a U.S. Army Intelligence School and Center; we were the next target. As frightening as it sounded, unfortunately, it made sense. However, I would prefer that it didn't make sense so we could have an illusion of being safe.

Everyone had almost forgotten about the change of command. The ceremony had to be scaled down to a minimum—no parades, and all festivities canceled. Instead, by the end of the day, Fort Huachuca was covered by concrete barricades. All trainees had to wear full combat gear and march in formations to school or DFAC. It was now martial law. Only military vehicles were roaming the base. All privileges were gone, and we were all in phase IV again. This had a tremendous impact on my morale because the phases were a symbol of status, the "classes of citizenship", so to speak. The highest phase, V+ was the hardest to achieve because it required a specific amount of time in training, adequate academic progress, and passing of all fitness as well as "phase" tests. It had the most privileges. Being constantly tossed between these phases was mentally tiring for me. I felt like a piece of furniture being moved between different rooms depending on the phase—in IV in a dingy prison cell, in V+ in a royal castle chamber.

Ultimately, it didn't matter that this day was my first anniversary of service in the army. Worries about my safety on base were overwhelming. I felt trapped and could do nothing about it.

* * *

Because of what happened the previous day, the spirits were down. The images of tragedy in New York haunted all of us. We lived in constant insecurity, the terrorist threat accompanying our daily activities. I was mentally spent thinking constantly about New York. I kept replaying in my mind the disturbing images I saw on TV, which were now constantly running in the dayroom. Fresh reports about the terrorist attacks kept coming. People from New York were shaken up and anxious. We were like shadows somberly roaming the base.

Fort Huachuca looked like never before. More concrete barricades appeared throughout by the day. The internal roads were closed and vehicle traffic minimal. Since we had to march everywhere as a company, all the personal vehicles were filling the parking lots, as if abandoned. Everything and everybody was in a state of high alert. The guards in full combat gear were posted by every building, and they checked the military identifications at every entrance. We were not allowed to wear our civilian clothes after school. If we weren't in school or DFAC, we were confined to the barracks. I was dazed by everything that had happened. I thought that all these nightmarish movies, thrillers, and horrors about burning buildings, hijacked airplanes, and explosions had come true in just a matter of a few hours, except we didn't have a happy ending. This wasn't a movie. We were in Threatcon Delta. This meant threat condition declared as a local warning after a terrorist attack to place or intelligence pointed to expected terrorist activity against a specific location. I had never been in Threatcon Delta, one of the most serious levels of threat. Now I was living it, not knowing what to expect and how this situation would be resolved.

Apparently, many National Guard and reserve units throughout the country were already sent to New York to help in disaster relief. We knew that soon the rest of the armed forces would be involved in some way. As the war on terrorism was surely approaching, everyone on base talked about the possible deployments. As trainees close to graduation, we also were growing anxious about being sent to war to pursue Bin Laden, now the most wanted criminal in the entire world. Despite the general turmoil, I sensed that something would be done to alleviate the situation and combat the terrorists.

Although it was hard to function with all the new restrictions freshly imposed on us, life had to go on. In school, we were about to begin the last block of instruction, called CHATS (Counterintelligence/Human Intelligence Automated Tool Set). During CHATS, we learned how to use this portable military equipment in the field for the upcoming FTX (field training exercise).

I was stressed out and distracted in school because we still had to submit our last reports from Collections, then pass the last test from this block. But I was sad that Collections were over because I enjoyed working with Mr. Bonvillain tremendously and being able to move freely around the base was a pleasant bonus. Besides, I was lucky to have been on his team because I had learned a lot about collecting intelligence.

For several days, I continued to struggle with the flu. My morning visits to TMC (Troup Medical Center) became more frequent. I was running a fever. My body ached more than ever before. I had headaches keeping me up at night, and my cough grew to be unbearable. Once I received a syrup with codeine, I felt slightly better, but it didn't last too long. That same evening, I came down with horrible stomach cramps and was vomiting violently for several hours. I wondered if my symptoms were worsening because of stress about terrorist attacks. After all, I was under a lot of pressure. At some point, Drill Sergeant Messinger came to my room to check on me, which was unusual. Normally, the male cadre wouldn't visit the rooms of female soldiers. They would send the female drill sergeant instead. I guessed he was concerned enough to bend this rule. He had me pour the syrup into the toilet and go to sick call again first thing on Monday morning. I was in excruciating pain sitting on my bed, rocking back and forth. Eventually, my suite mate gave me Mylanta, and it seemed to help. I made a mental note to self to avoid codeine and any drugs containing it to spare me serious misery.

* * *

That Monday at the recall formation, I found out that we would receive our German Badges. I donned my best polished boots and a fresh uniform. It was already dark outside. On the low firmament, a friendly moon was gently caressing our faces. The entire company was present. The German colonel gave a solemn speech. For the first time in my life, I appreciated the gravity of the words, "Attention to orders." As I stood there in the second row, ready to receive my Silver German Armed Forces Proficiency Badge, I was reminiscing about my entire crusade leading up to that moment. My sprint on a rainy morning when my hamstrings were bursting from the effort. I remembered with pleasure my distance run at dawn, accompanied by a rising sun on a brand-new day. At that moment, I had committed to pursuing the medal until the end. That success inspired me to undertake my independent training for swimming competitions. I remembered how right before the big IPT test, I realized I had made an error while calculating my swim timing requirements. I smiled to myself at this thought. Then there were two track-and-field events. The shot put finally was conquered after several attempts. After all, the golden ball had brought me good fortune. The long jump, alone on the empty stadium, solitary moon as a witness to my struggle, starry night, and rain on my body. The worst, however, was the infamous first road march, my attempt to walk for the gold, and a bitter failure. It cost me multiple injuries and crutches. I was broken down. But then, a glimpse of hope, another chance, this time for silver. At last, an overwhelming victory.

Now everything was concluded and encased in this medal of a silver German Eagle, shining proudly on my chest, and a colorful certificate with emblems. Finally, a firm, friendly handshake from the German colonel and our company commander, who supported me during the road march, Captain Hamilton, crowned my success.

I looked at the dark skies and instinctively thanked God for leading me to this victory. Just three months ago, in my darkest moments after failing my first IPT, I had nearly lost my faith. Now I thought about everything I endured in Fort Huachuca.

Months ago, I was struggling to keep up with the nonsensical, ever-changing rules, and with the infamous IPT test's repercussions. I was wondering then, where was God when this turmoil was happening? Why did he allow all that to happen? I thought he wanted me to doubt his existence, to lose my faith altogether. What else was I to think about my ordeal in the barracks in phase IV and being "recycled" in school like some trash? Where was God then? I often pondered. What were his plans for me? At that time, I had concluded that he didn't exist and that I wouldn't believe in him. I had to admit, on some occasions, there were glimpses of his presence, and I was grateful for his brief interventions. But all these months, I was confused and lost with my faith because it was never clear to me what God had prepared for me.

Until now, while receiving my GAFPB. I realized that had I graduated with class 004 (my original assignment), I would have missed the opportunity to take part in GAFPB, which was announced a couple of days after the 004 graduation. I finally understood that I had to be recycled and stay longer in Fort Huachuca to earn my German Badge. I also found out that this badge was quite special because all the activities had to be performed under the auspices of senior German officers physically present on post. We were lucky because Fort Huachuca, as the nation's main intelligence school and center for operations and training, was also hosting personnel from all over Europe to provide intelligence instruction to ally countries, hence the presence on the base of German liaison officers who had the authority to offer the GAFPB to all personnel who wanted to take advantage of this opportunity.

That day, everything became clear. After all, God had some amazing plans for me. I just hadn't been able to see that back then.

* * *

Dear Alec,

Since the big national tragedy, life in Fort Huachuca is not the same. We have a lot of restrictions, and the entire battalion is in phase IV again. I'm still sick and my cough is so violent it chokes me at times. I'm extremely tired of school and these barracks. It feels like I'm in prison. So far, the classes at school are taking place as scheduled. As they say, "the show must go on." The company commander took Saturdays away from us and we have to go to school on a weekend. It doesn't make any sense.

At school, we were issued amazing equipment to use for interrogations in the field. The case has a bulletproof laptop inside, a portable file phone, and a digital camera. The computer can apparently be run over by a tank, and nothing would happen to it. I have never seen anything like that.

I'm sorry to hear that your grandmother is dying. Hopefully, she's not suffering. It would be nice to see her after my return. Perhaps she will wait for me.

My last days at Fort Huachuca are dragging forever. Fortunately, the time of our graduation is close enough (exactly ten days!) for us to begin making arrangements for the trip home. I was worried about coordinating this trip for both of us so we can fly together. It's great that you had American Airlines. I talked to a gracious lady in the Transportation Department, and she booked my plane ticket on your flight! How awesome! I had no idea this could be done.

*   *   *

It was 5:15 in the morning when my class was ready to depart to conduct the field training exercise. It was our last event before graduation. Three days of camping and working in the woods of the Huachuca Mountains seemed like a wonderful distraction from the high-alert nightmare on base. We were issued more equipment like tents, sleeping bags, bulletproof vests, and, of course, the M16 rifles.

Luckily, Crowder was on my team. We'd put up our tent and were awaiting further instructions from the leadership. I was coughing up the storm when out of the blue Chang approached me.

"Hey SKI, are you OK? Are you ready for the FTX?"

"I'm ready, just need to survive this damn cough," I replied, catching my breath.

"You'll be fine. Everyone knows that you're not a wimp." With her friendly pat on my shoulder, I suddenly felt like someone cared about me, and this brought me closer to my home.

Our camp was in a beautiful wooded area, high in the mountains. It was protected by layers of concertina wires (barbed wire and razor wire that is formed in large coils, which can be expanded like an accordion) for security reasons. We were working twelve-hour shifts in small wooden sheds throughout the area. We jokingly called them our "offices." Each shed was equipped with multiple sets of the CHATS kits for interrogations and interviews conducted with "insurgents" and "informants" (civilian and military role players). Each gate to the compound was manned by the posted guards in full gear.

We were working twelve-hour shifts in small wooden sheds throughout the area.

At first, Crowder and I had some free time to sit quietly in our tent and admire the peaceful nature around us, but I was growing anxious about my upcoming shift at 6:00 p.m. Our scenario to interview the refugees from Bosnia and Herzegovina was complex and convoluted. It wasn't exactly clear what kind of intelligence we needed to collect from these people and how they were supposed to end up in our hands. Finally, I worried that in the middle of the night the higher-ups, like the battalion commander, would show up to debrief us about the latest intelligence. I found debriefings to be always stressful. In these situations, because of my nervousness, I tended to mix Polish and English when giving oral reports.

As the hours were passing by, my worries melted away. Everything became clear, and the briefings were going well. We worked in teams all night long, in extreme cold, interviewing various personnel, and sending reports to the command. In the morning, we had a visit from the battalion sergeant major for a "sensitivity session" (interview to determine the morale, if soldiers' needs were met, and how they are being treated). Luckily, we were all awake. This was a perfect opportunity to complain about our Echo Company abusing the threatcon to take away all our phase privileges, and we were confined in the barracks in our free time. The good news was we received positive feedback from the sergeant regarding our intelligence-collecting efforts during the past twenty-four hours.

I was still in terrible shape when it came to my physical health. Sometimes I would cough so hard that I was vomiting half of the content of my stomach, mostly water anyway. The days were so hot that it was impossible to sleep in oven-like tents between shifts. I often had to lie down on the ground with a wet cloth covering my face and a rifle by my side. Nights, on the other hand, were extremely cold, which was typical for high elevations in this area. Sometimes the temperature would plunge to 50 F, causing thermal shock to our bodies. These changes in temperature were not helpful.

At some point, our company commander showed up and talked to us about our future military life. He said that having our MOS in intelligence, we would be treated with respect, especially if we had a mastery of any foreign language and knowledge of operational areas in other countries. For a moment, I thought about my first year in the army. It was now clear to me, life in the military, which once was a big and fascinating mystery, now became my new routine, a normal way of living. I was learning a lot, and I was changing, almost being reborn as a new human being. It felt good. I was in the right place at the right time. I believed with my whole heart that there was so much more waiting for me in my career. One day, I would become a U.S. Army intelligence officer.

"SKI, your time will come," suddenly said Captain Hamilton, as if reading my thoughts, as if he knew I wanted to realize myself as a soldier.

Then he gave me a long, symbolic handshake, wishing me the best. It was a handshake of trust and confidence.

*   *   *

The last night in the field seemed uneventful. Our team worked hard in our wooden "office" interrogating "prisoners" and "sources," writing notes, and taking photos.

I just finished one of my reports and had Sergeant Robinson approve it. She promptly sent it to the higher-ups. Suddenly, I heard a loud noise next to me as the door to our shed opened wide. In a matter of seconds, two people in foreign uniforms stormed into the shed. They grabbed me violently and threw a cloth bag on my head. Before I knew it, my hands were tied behind my back with zip ties, and they forcefully escorted me to an unknown location. I could hear Sergeant Robinson screaming as she was dragged behind me. As we were pushed through the woods, I was trying in vain to wiggle myself out of custody. The enemy's grip was tight. Blindfolded, I was tripping over the branches and rocks. My heart was trying to burst out of my chest. I was completely disoriented, shocked, and scared.

Finally, we stopped, and they pushed me onto my knees. I heard angry voices around me, most likely in Serbian or Croatian. The bag covering my head smelled like rotten eggs and mud. In the tumult, I could discern a weapon being locked and loaded. Something hard was pressed against the back of my skull. At that point, I was trembling with pure panic and fear. My entire life flashed before me—lots of green, brown, and black. I was convinced that these were my last moments on earth. I heard more voices shouting something. Then a brief silence. Click between my ears. The weapon didn't fire. The vigorous pounding of my heart was palpable. I was certain that there would be another attempt and this time I would die for sure. I said the quickest prayer in my life. "God, please save me." Silence. The voices stopped and the commotion around me subsided.

Suddenly, the cover from my face was violently removed, and I found myself and Sergeant Robinson kneeling next to each other, surrounded by our entire platoon, watching this execution-style scene. From stress and complete mental exhaustion, I fell to the ground. I could see in slow motion people running up to me to free my hands from restraints. Someone cut the zip tie too close to my skin, the blood flowing. Instinctively, I wiped my sweaty face with my bloody hand, and I was now covered in blood. I tested a warm metallic liquid in my mouth. Although I was still shaken up and in shock, I realized that all this was an exercise. "Too darn real for an exercise," I thought to myself.

"This is to show you all that when you assume something on the battlefield, people will die," said the instructor role player stoically. "Never put a source's address on the reports. The enemy will find them and kill them, and you will go down with them."

I was now sitting on the ground under a tree, breathless, and spent. I was trying to think about what I might have put in my last report. At that moment, thoughts of guilt and shame were bombarding my brain. I felt embarrassed in front of all these people, as a terrible example. "How in the world did I let myself get caught like this? What was I thinking? Not thinking enough. I should have known better not to put sensitive information in this darn report. If I could only go back in time." I was too mentally exhausted to figure it out. I was just happy to be alive.

Two people grabbed me under my arms to help me get on my feet. I was definitely alive, but couldn't think straight. In my mind, I could only see brown, green, and black. And I'd still smell the awful mildew and rotten eggs stench of the bag.

It was nearly impossible to get the execution scene out of my mind for a long while. With time, as I was analyzing the horrifying details, I felt more traumatized, but I didn't want to show it. I pretended as though nothing had happened, but deep down in my heart, I felt like I just survived my death.

* * *

We never know where our limits are until we get tested by circumstances. It wasn't enough to hear or read about terror. I've seen it in the movies, I've imagined it. However, for what I had gone through this time, my imagination was inadequate. I could never be prepared for that. The FTX showed me what it was like to be captured, judged, and executed. "Show don't tell," they say about good writing. Except this was not the art of creating a story. This WAS the story. That was how the army training was conducted. Realistic and surreal at the same time. Reasonable and insane. Being able to live through it, experience this adrenaline rush, hopelessness, and fragility of human life, was for me the key to understanding what it meant to be a soldier.

CHAPTER 14

MI SPECIALIST

When we were leaving the compound, a sudden melancholy descended upon me. Of course, on the one hand, I was glad that everything was over. I had just endured the FTX, the last event at school in Fort Huachuca. On the other hand, I started feeling some sort of void in my heart. As we were taking our last ride on a white bus, I realized that my fast-paced life was ending. There was no more rushing, yelling, and marching everywhere. Everything started happening at a slow, relaxed pace. We regained our phase V+ privileges and could now take care of some administrative tasks on post freely.

First thing on my agenda was my airplane ticket home. Transportation Department was at the "Old Post," with historical pinkish buildings surrounding a small parade field. I took my ticket and went to find a picnic bench by the inspector general's office, where just a few months ago I was sitting, broken and devastated after failing my IPT. Looking at my initials and the date 6.20.2001 carved on the table, I pressed the ticket to my chest and thought about the last six months I had spent in Fort Huachuca. There were multiple moments when I hated this place with a passion. There were also moments of tremendous victories and triumphs. Now everything was closing in this one plane ticket. Out of my cargo pocket, I took the last fruity bar that Alec had sent me so long ago. For the first time, it truly tasted like home.

* * *

Finally, my last weekend at Fort Huachuca arrived. The stress of the past several months was slowly subsiding. That time was marked by many "lasts" before my long-anticipated trip home. For the last time, I went to my swimming pool to swim my last laps. I still had in my mind vivid images of my solitary training for the GAFPB, from two months ago. I had my last hard run after nearly four weeks of not running due either to GAFPB, my physical state, or my illness.

I returned the last pieces of my military gear, my faithful companion of the past six months. I attended the last briefings about the return to "normal" civilian life. Although I was craving life at home, I wasn't sure if the real "normal" was being a soldier or a civilian back home with a regular job. Was I really ready to live without my uniform daily? Of course, I would still have my monthly drills with my unit in Chicago, but it wasn't the same as being a soldier every day.

Since I needed to look good for the following day at the graduation, I also bought some basic components of makeup. For the past nine months, I only wore military camouflage makeup. I hated using the greasy sticks of brown, green, and black on my face. But it was necessary to blend with the tactical environment. Now, I wanted to stand out, look like a human being, and look like a woman again. I felt elated when, later, sitting on the curb by the barracks, I tried the new makeup on my face. To complete my look, I painted my nails with pale pink nail polish. I knew I looked good because it felt good.

Finally, our class had the first and the last dinner off post with Drill Sergeant Kilbourne. The ambiance was light and friendly. We drank beer, laughed, and recollected our times in Fort Huachuca. My mind and heart, however, were with Alec. At that moment, I realized now we were separated by merely eighteen hours.

* * *

It was a beautiful morning in Fort Huachuca. The weather wasn't too hot. In the September breeze, the shrubs around the barracks were barely moving. The commotion in the barracks was indescribable. My classmates were running around, saying last goodbyes, greeting their loved ones, and giving them tours of the barracks.

I was standing at my designated spot by the curb of the north parking lot when Alec pulled up right in front of me. In some way, he seemed different from what I had remembered when I had seen him in January. He looked taller and more handsome. His voice sounded like music. Because of that, the world around me seemed more colorful.

After I showed him my barracks, I took him on a tour of Fort Huachuca to visit all the places that were my home for the past six months. We drove the entire route of my road march for the German silver medal and visited the shooting ranges along the way. Finally, I took Alec to the Old Post to show him the historic buildings and the antique cannons and howitzers from the WWII era. We walked around the field with the proudly posted American Flag. From this spot since March 17, I heard every morning the reveille and the taps every evening. Finally, I had to show Alec the famous picnic table by the inspector general's building.

We met each other again the next day at the graduation. There was true pomp and circumstance. Everyone was wearing their crisp army greens with medals and crests, civilian instructors in suits and ties. This was my first military graduation where I was to walk on the stage as an individual, receiving personal congratulations. It felt more intimate, almost secret, because I wasn't part of an enormous crowd, anonymous, like in basic training. I felt like somebody who achieved something on my own.

Our class's senior faculty, Sergeant Cruchene, presented a brief introduction to our class. Then the commander of the 111th Military Intelligence Brigade gave his short speech, accompanied by the commander of the 309th Military Intelligence Battalion, Colonel Keller. We walked one by one to receive our diplomas and shake hands with our unit's leadership. When the colonel shook my hand, we exchanged knowing smiles. He had me figured out and witnessed some of my toughest and best moments in Fort Huachuca. He was my secret guardian angel.

When the colonel shook my hand, we exchanged knowing smiles.

Completing the AIT meant I was now a full-fledged Military Intelligence Specialist. No longer a beginner-soldier without identity. Now, someone with qualifications designed for a specific mission: collection, analysis, and dissemination of critical intelligence related to military operations. Even though it wasn't easy to get to this point, it felt like it was merely a promising title. I'd suddenly lost the powerful sense of direction and purpose. I couldn't help but feel, as they call it, a "success hangover". And I was extremely thirsty. Thirsty for more. This state of mind reminded me of two buildings connected by a suspended corridor. I was in the first building, "the enlisted career", with three floors: prebasic, basic and advanced individual training. On top of the third floor, I was now facing the corridor leading to the second, taller building. It would be called "the officer career," and its first floor, the Officer Candidate School. The corridor itself was like a chunk of civilian life awaiting me before going to OCS. After crossing it, I'd have another purpose, and a renewed sense of urgency.

CHAPTER 15

A PROMISE OF PERSEVERANCE

Three days after my return to Northbrook, Alec and I were driving my car home from his grandmother's funeral.

"Where are my college graduation tassels?" I tried to sound casual.

"The ones hanging on the rear-view mirror? They were obstructing my view, so I've put them in the glove box."

I quickly opened the box. There they were, tossed like trash.

"I can't even have tassels in my own car? My things don't matter to you? Do I matter to you?" There was nothing casual about my tone anymore. How could he just discard something I cherished, the symbol of my first graduation in America? I never had any graduations in Poland. No walking on the stage, no gowns, no tassels. I felt like he just discarded a piece of me. Perhaps this was a sign that we were slowly growing apart, but I wanted to believe that it wasn't so. "If this is how you welcome me home after nine months, then I would rather go back and die in a war," I added in despair, hoping to evoke a tender sound in his heart.

"Then go to war and die, if this could only bring my grandma back."

This caught me off guard. Until now he was my supporter, writing letters regularly, sending packages. We spoke on the phone as much as it was possible. I thought he cared about me. If there had been any red flags, I had missed them because I was preoccupied with my daily tasks in the army and my health. But now, it seemed as if I suddenly lost my husband's support. My heart imploded.

* * *

Thinking about the past nine months I just spent away from home, I felt like instead of being closer to the light at the end of a tunnel, darkness suddenly overwhelmed me. I felt unappreciated by people who I thought were close to me, like Alec. I also felt lost and insecure, just like that ten-year-old girl back in 1979. That year, I had just begun my education in a boarding ballet school, and I was in the first grade (the equivalent of a fourth grade of elementary school).

One evening I found myself alone in a long hallway of the school, with nine doors on the left-hand side about twenty feet apart, numbered one through nine. Each door corresponded to a classroom for a specific ballet school grade. I stood next to my classroom, number 1, looking at all these doors ahead of me. They symbolized my new journey in pursuit of a classical ballet dancer profession. It was a tremendous goal.

It was overwhelming to realize that I would be in school for nine long years. I was afraid that I could never actually reach door number nine at the end of the hallway, which seemed so distant, barely visible in the dimmed evening lights. For my ten-year-old brain, it was inconceivable how much I would have to endure to reach that elusive end.

I wanted to overcome the overpowering feeling of fear of the unknown, so I started walking down the hallway in silence. I would stop briefly by each door, imagining that from now on, I would be opening these doors as I progressed with my education. Every year a new door, a symbol of new challenges. I would be growing up within these doors. Each of them would become my "home" for one year. Then I realized I had to muster all my courage and willpower to conquer one door at a time. I had to persevere on my own, far from home and from my protective parents, hundreds of kilometers away. I was at the mercy of the world around me, foreign and ominous.

When I stopped by door number nine, I thought about myself nine years from now. What would I look like? What would my voice sound like? What would I know I didn't know now? How would I dance? Would

I have friends? At that moment, I promised myself that no matter what the obstacles I would endure, and classroom number 9 would be my last "home" in my journey until graduation in 1988. This was the first time in my life when I made a conscious decision about my future life.

And now, returning home as an MI soldier after the first nine months of my army training, I was facing new challenges in my military career. I had to promise to this little girl I once was that I would persevere again and follow my dream of becoming an intelligence officer, no matter what the obstacles. I was only halfway through my transformation.

PART V
OFFICER CANDIDATE SCHOOL:
BECOMING AN OFFICER

CHAPTER 16

INTIMIDATION AND DISCOURAGEMENT

November 1, 2001

Dear Sir,
I haven't had a chance to talk to you about my career in the Army. Since I earned my college degree eight years ago and have a lot of experience with managing people, I would like to become a Commissioned Officer.

I joined the Army as an enlisted soldier to gain military experience and learn the basics about the Army. Now, after accomplishing these goals, I am convinced that the officer's career is what I would like to pursue.

I would like to ask you to initiate as my Unit Commander, the process of putting me through the Officer Candidate School program. For the November drill, I will bring my college transcripts, as well as my biography and other documents that might be necessary.

I will be grateful if you could write me a recommendation letter for the OCS. Please contact me at (123) 123-4567 if you require more information from me.

Thank you very much for your time and help with this important matter.

Sincerely,

SPC (Specialist) Joanna Rakowski

* * *

It was February 2002 when the process of admission to the officer candidate school was formally initiated. I received the recommendation from my company commander and the packet was already en route to Springfield, Illinois.

It'd been five months since my return home from the AIT and things were better with Alec. Like the good old days, he wasn't surprised that I wanted to continue my career in the army as an officer. While my application for the officer candidate school was in motion, Alec and I decided to take a break from the bitter cold in Chicago. It was a great opportunity made possible by Alec's parents. Apparently, they had won a pair of tickets for the Pro Ball taking place at the Aloha Stadium in Halawa, Hawaii. They couldn't go, so they gave us their tickets. I thought this was a fantastic gesture, proving that we all had great relations. I also wanted to spend some quality time with Alec and strengthen our marriage, away from the family and always possible judgments. Besides, we both needed to relax and reconnect with nature. Knowing that the upcoming training would be challenging, and many dark moments were waiting for me, I needed to absorb as much of the daylight as possible. I needed peace to collect my thoughts and brace for the next step of my military journey. The beach of Oahu was the perfect place to do that.

* * *

After a short walk on the beach, Alec and I reached the edge of the pier extending into the wide-open space of the Pacific Ocean. Still asleep, merely approaching daybreak, the powerful nature seemed shy and innocent. A feathery fog suspended in the air around the giant volcanic mountains blanketed the island of Oahu. The world was still submerged in a placid, almost lifeless darkness. In front of our eyes, the infinite purple blue waters of the ocean, perfectly undisturbed, were anxiously awaiting the long-anticipated resolution of a big mystery. Paradise was slowly awakening.

The nighttime obscurity slowly faded away, surrendering its power without a fight. For a few moments, a flawlessly linear horizon flickered, announcing the dawn's early light. The immense oceanic water, suddenly awakened from the tranquil dream, traded her nightgown for a heavenly blue dress. A golden red jewel appeared on the surface, bringing the promise of a fresh start. The world, like an empty page of an unwritten story, was ready to inaugurate a legendary journey.

Like a sudden surge, the most powerful, superb sunlight saturated everything around us, proclaiming the celebration of a brand-new day. The air was vibrating with mysterious energy and ecstasy, glorifying the past, the present, and the future. It was like a true beginning of time, a chance to dream unrealistic dreams again, to feel uplifted, encouraged, and enlightened. It was the ultimate time of reconciliation and peace.

Later that day on a boat, the ocean breeze was caressing Alec's face as he was catching the waves. For the first time, I saw him in such high spirits. I had my Alec back and was convinced that our relationship survived the toughest times. Our elusive tale of happiness and liberation continued. At least this was what I wanted to believe. I could only hope for this day to go on forever.

* * *

Shortly after our return from Hawaii, I received an invitation to attend a preliminary meeting at the Army National Guard Regional Training Institute in Springfield, Illinois. My dream of becoming a U.S. Army officer was about to begin to materialize.

During one weekend in March, all the future officer candidates from the entire state of Illinois were going to be introduced to the program and in-processed. Then the two weekends in April—one in May, and another in June—would be the phase zero of the program. Phase I was going to be a two-week training in June, out of state. Phase II would be twelve consecutive months of weekend drills in Springfield, and phase III would be another two-week training out of state. The entire process of becoming an officer amounted to eighteen months of training and driving back and forth to the state capital. With everything proceeding as planned, I would receive my commission in August 2003, just a month shy of my thirty-fourth birthday. Now my chief concern was to be accepted into the program, pass the physical fitness test, and make the proper arrangements at work concerning my future monthly trips to Springfield and annual two-week training sessions.

* * *

In mid-March, I was already en route to Springfield. Over two hundred miles of a lonely drive was quite a challenge, considering that the longest distance I'd driven in my life was 130 miles at most back in Poland. I felt a little apprehensive about getting there in a safe and timely manner. However, the excitement of starting the next step of my military career eventually prevailed. Before I knew it, I was flying through Chicago streets and highways, passing by the gloomy cornfields of the countryside, blasting the music of Mozart's *Requiem Mass*, and singing along with the chorus, the most memorable part, *Confutatis*. It was the song of the approaching Judgment Day when the condemned spirits destined for the bitter eternal flames of hell were desperately pleading for absolution in their final hour. With my heart burned to ashes before the resurrection, humbled and scared, I was like a departing soul praying for strength and forgiveness.

That Friday, I arrived at the base in the late evening. Approaching the main gate, I instantaneously recognized all the major buildings. Nothing had changed there since my last visit merely sixteen months ago when I reported there for my prebasic training. As I was driving through the base, the pleasant feeling of comfort came over me like a warm blanket. All the female candidates were assigned to the same barrack in which I spent my prebasic training weekend. I was back and ready to take my first step to becoming a commissioned officer in the United States Army.

Saturday morning, the in-processing of over a hundred candidates from the entire state of Illinois began at a fast and furious pace. Mostly, we were standing in long lines, verifying various documents and updating records. Then we had various classroom training, military equipment, and some uniforms issues. Several people resigned from the program before the end of the in-processing. In one classroom, the introduction to the TAC (teach-assess-counsel) officers, our new military instructors, the equivalent of enlisted personnel drill sergeants, was brutal.

"Who wants to quit? Say it now. Don't waste our time here. Raise your hand. If you don't think this is the place for you at this time, if you don't think you can come here once a month for the next eighteen months, leave now. Just raise your hand and you'll be free to go. Anyone?"

Silence in the classroom was deadly. The first ten seconds passed like hours.

"Come on! Raise your hand. You? Or you? Officer candidate? Maybe you in the last row? Now is the time to quit this program. It's not for weak people, candidates. If you are weak, you need to go now. Just stand up and leave. Go back home to your family, your kids, or whatever. Sit on the couch, watch some TV, and relax. It will be ugly here, so don't waste your time and energy. There are enough people here to make outstanding officers. In fact, there are too many of you here right now. One hundred twenty candidates. Only about twenty will make it through the program. Maybe. So here is your last chance. Quit now, no questions asked. Raise your hand." He was definitely convincing. I was wondering if this discouraging tirade would be enough to break me. Then I remembered my days in Warsaw ballet school. We were constantly yelled at and reminded that only one of us in the class could be a prima ballerina. The rest of us should quit and change professions. Enjoy a normal childhood. Now, just like those years before, I wasn't about to quit, no matter how harsh the discouragement tactics were.

Another ten seconds passed in silence. This time, soldiers started raising their hands one after another.

"Okay! Now that's better." The TAC officer seemed relieved. "Come up here and put your initials next to your name on the list. Go home. Have fun. Anyone else?"

Again, about ten people left the room.

* * *

The early spring storm caught me off guard just a few miles north of Springfield. I found myself under a vicious barrage of torrential rain. My car, like a lonely vessel, was slowly disappearing under the tremendous waves. The entire highway became an enraged river, ready to swallow anything and anyone. The wounded, broken skies were crying profusely. After losing a desperate battle with the darkness and being unable to continue, I pulled over to the shoulder. For several minutes, I was surrounded by the unpredictable force of water and wind pounding my vehicle like a little wooden toy. I watched this breathtaking, frightening spectacle, with my heart growing heavier by the minute. It was only my second trip to Springfield for my OCS training, and it already felt like a punishment. I couldn't imagine repeating this for the next eighteen months.

However, one thing that was clear to me at this point was that the third degree (the first was the basic training and the second was my AIT in Fort

Huachuca) of my incredible military adventure had begun. The Officer Candidate School was all I could think of. I was convinced that this time around, having some experience, I was better prepared for the mental and physical beating waiting for me.

I spent an entire day in Springfield on various "smoking sessions" and running around from building to building to in-processing activities. Even though I was at the same location where I spent my prebasic training, now I had mixed feelings. On one hand, becoming an officer seemed far in the future, a long route to negotiate. On the other hand, it was an inevitable path. I just thought that becoming a noncommissioned officer (NCO), like a sergeant, was not for me. I was confident in my leadership skills and hoped that as a commissioned officer, I could inspire others and perhaps change their lives.

At some point, I found out that the option of completing the OCS in two months (accelerated program) instead of eighteen months (state program) was available. As soon as I found out that I could apply for this accelerated OCS program, also called "fast-track" or "501," I jumped at this opportunity. The candidates over thirty years of age and who already had a four-year college degree were encouraged to apply to assure their commission before the age of thirty-four. They also had priority. Being thirty-two and a half and having my degree, I was hoping to qualify for the program. However, there were many people interested, and only fifteen spots were available for the entire state of Illinois.

The program seemed intense. It was eight consecutive grueling weeks of training: Phase I (a two-week training period at Fort McClellan, Alabama, focused on the orientation to the OCS program, leadership, counseling, map reading, and land navigation), phase II (four weeks at Fort Indiantown Gap, Pennsylvania, with emphasis on tactics, military law, communications, military writing, personnel management, and logistics), and phase III (another two-week training period at Fort McClellan, which was about patrolling and tactical exercises in the field). After this training, the graduation and commissioning ceremony would take place at my home state capital, Springfield, Illinois. I wanted to go for this option so badly that I completely stopped stressing out about driving to Springfield for eighteen months.

* * *

During the April training weekend in Springfield, compared to over a hundred candidates in March, all that was left was merely a platoon of fewer than forty people. Once again, we were stripped of our ranks and from now on called "officer candidates."

Mathia was designated as our platoon sergeant, so for the time being, we weren't in too much trouble. With over eighteen years of service in the guard and the rank of sergeant first class, she was the most qualified person in the entire group. I truly admired her command presence and general military competence, especially when the TACs were constantly jumping on her to test her leadership skills. We were all tested, of course, but not nearly as fiercely as Mathia.

The other platoon were the candidates who began their OCS (traditional) program last year and would graduate in four months. It was rather intimidating and overwhelming to see them being "chewed" by the TACs. Only eight of them were still hanging in there. That meant that the odds of surviving this type of training were quite slim.

* * *

Before I knew it, three weeks had passed, and it was time for a nearly hundred-mile drive for another training of the OCS "phase zero." This time, in the National Guard Marseilles Training Area (MTA), in Marseilles, Illinois.

Per orders from my company commander, before the training, I had to write a detailed memorandum, known as a "drill preparation letter," listing my activities preparing me for the drill.

Subject: Drill Preparation Letter   May 2, 2002

1. I am a member of a second squad of a second platoon. According to the instructions of my platoon leader and my squad leader, I am preparing myself for the land navigation exercise by making sure I have all the necessary equipment. For this purpose, I've scheduled a trip to the Great Lakes navy base on May 8 to purchase the ranger beads. In addition, I'm making sure I have everything according to the packing list provided during the last drill in Springfield.
2. I receive an e-mail on a daily basis in preparation for the exercises in Marseilles. I also have transmitted an electronic version of the

roster of the entire junior class to both platoon leaders, per their request.
3. SFC (Sergeant First Class) Crouch offered his help in preparation for the land navigation course in Marseilles. I will work tonight on the problems that SFC Crouch distributed electronically through my chain of command.
4. According to the instructions of Captain Kitson, I'm preparing to report to the senior TAC officer about my previous leadership positions and the lessons learned from them. I will accomplish that by studying the appropriate material.
5. I have established a physical fitness plan for myself in order to keep in optimal physical condition. In addition, I have adjusted my diet to maintain my ideal body weight.
6. To make sure I show up in Marseilles at the right place at the correct time, I am also planning on doing a reconnaissance on the location of the training area. I will accomplish that by driving there a day prior to the drill and familiarizing myself with the route.

Joanna Rakowski
Officer Candidate, ILARNG (Illinois Army National Guard)

* * *

It was a rainy Friday morning. After studying the atlas of Illinois and printing detailed directions, I drove to Marseilles, Illinois. It was a big rehearsal. I could not afford the stress of driving there on Saturday morning to report at 8 a.m. without knowing the route. What if I got lost somewhere in the woods of La Salle County? It was important to be familiar with the location and avoid unnecessary stress while landing in a new environment.

The Marseilles Training Area (MTA) was an immense woodland terrain serving as a major training site for combat, combat service support, and combat support units up to a battalion size. At that location, the National Guard units were conducting on the regular basis their annual exercises at the shooting ranges and land navigation terrain. My one May weekend in Marseilles was the last part of the OCS phase zero.

After several hours of wandering in the countryside and passing by the endless inaccessible gates poking through the woods every few miles, I finally arrived at the main entrance. As I rolled down my window, I saw the familiar face of a TAC officer.

"What are you doing here, soldier?" The captain at the gate was surprised. "The training doesn't start until tomorrow morning."

"I'm conducting my reconnaissance mission, sir," I replied resolutely. "Now that I know my route, I'll be back tomorrow by dawn."

Indeed, the next day, I drove to Marseilles again, this time without the fear of getting lost in the middle of nowhere. The brand-new and fresh barracks were inviting and quiet, but we didn't stay long inside. Late Saturday morning, we had a short road march to the woods for our field training (classes and "smoking" sessions). My colleague from the unit in Chicago, Abedi, instantly became a legendary "beacon of light" because he forgot his flashlight. Throughout the day, we practiced tactical exercises while getting lost in the bushes as many times as virtually possible, learning the terrain. The last exercise at night was the infamous land navigation, during which my group, heroically led by an "experienced" candidate and self-proclaimed navigation guru, completely missed the boat. Luckily, this wasn't the test. Still, I had a pretty bad feeling about this land navigation. The instructors were telling us endless horror stories about how the candidates would usually fall out of the program because they couldn't pass this test. Since I haven't learned much so far, at least from the practical perspective, I felt uneasy and more concerned than ever. I could only hope that I would qualify for the "fast-track OCS" and would eventually have more opportunities to practice my skills.

*   *   *

Land navigation wasn't my only concern, however. I kept thinking about my physical fitness. It'd been several months since I came home from Fort Huachuca in fairly good shape. At home, I wasn't doing any marching or running. I had hoped that lifting weights would be enough to preserve most of my muscle strength. The thought of lifting weights brought back a memory of the times in Warsaw a decade ago.

Who knew that at some point in my life, I wanted to become a bodybuilder? Back in the day, it was my secret dream, which I revealed only to Chris in June 1992. We'd been frequenting a fitness studio for several weeks. Those were the times when health clubs in Poland were quite a novelty. Because of this new trend, they were appearing everywhere in Warsaw. We had chosen one that was on the way to Chris's home on the outskirts of Warsaw. It was a friendly establishment, fully equipped with all the newest machines one could dream of. The blue walls were decorated with flower baskets, various landscape paintings throughout, as well as pictures of handsome people with beautifully sculpted bodies.

For a moment, I lost my repetitions count on a bench press. I couldn't help but admire the photos of stunning humans on the walls. To me, it was fascinating how someone could achieve such a silhouette.

It had been a while since I had exercised regularly as a dancer. To some extent, I was missing being physically active. I decided to join the gym to gain some healthy muscle. As a ballerina with a proportional lean and petite figure, I looked decent. However, at least in my mind, I was too skinny. Some extra curvy muscle would do me good.

The most intriguing thing to me was that in ancient times, the sculptures of men showed their near-perfect athletic physique, but they didn't look like bodybuilders. Their bodies were rounded, with firm muscles and little fat, perfectly proportional and harmonious.

"I want to look like a callipygian Venus, the ancient feminine standard of beauty," I said to Chris out of the blue. "Back then, as visual input, her beauty gave pleasure to the mind for sure. Nowadays, sadly, it's not the case, I'm afraid."

"You want to look like a sculpture?"

"Sort of. More like a Venus with muscle definition. A modern Venus," I clarified.

"She wasn't skinny by any means, and having a bit of extra fat was considered extremely attractive on a woman. It also showed her class," Chris added.

"Exactly. I don't want to be skinny either." I pulled a hanging bar toward me to reach my chin level, then released it back up with control. "I'm just not sure if my body type has a potential for sculpting."

"In reality, we all could be athletic regardless of our body shape. You could definitely be athletic, especially having danced for thirteen years. However, I think that the beauty of a woman isn't in the clothes she wears, the figure that she carries, or the way she combs her hair. Experiences, proximity, and caring are what catch my attention. Genuine beauty comes from the kind of person you are, the choices you make, and how you treat other people."

"Then you are the most beautiful human being I know," I concluded.

I realized how deeply I was falling in love with Chris. And that was all that mattered.

* * *

By the end of May, I finally got the news that I was confirmed to attend the 501 accelerated program. Out of nearly forty people in the Illinois state OCS, only six were selected to pursue this type of commissioning. When Alec found out that I would be gone for two months, he seemed happy for me, but at the same time I had an impression that he was looking forward to living his "bachelor life of freedom", as he sometimes put it. He was joking, I was convinced. So, I dismissed it, hoping for the best. That's why I was ecstatic when Alec had agreed to drive me to Springfield for my last qualifying physical fitness test before the departure to Alabama on June 7. Despite the need for a restful sleep the night before the event, I wasn't able to calm my mind. I was nervous that I didn't have enough physical strength to pass the test.

We had left our home in the middle of the night in order to arrive in Springfield early in the morning. Unable to sleep or relax, I was daydreaming about my near future. Suddenly, something brought me back to reality; Alec was suspiciously quiet. I looked at the dashboard and my heart started pounding, ready to explode. Apparently, we were running on fumes for a while. For several more miles, there was no sign of any gas station, the exit, or a city, and my nervousness grew deeper by every yard. Eventually, we took the first available exit and ended up in Pontiac, Illinois. In the city submerged in a deep dream, luckily for us, we found a police officer who pointed us to the only gas station open at this hour. This incident suddenly made me doubt Alec's seriousness in supporting me. We could have easily got stuck in this town for hours, causing me to miss my test. Although alarmed, I thought his recklessness was perhaps an accident and everything between us would continue on the right path.

A few hours later, I took my lonely challenge in Springfield while Alec was patiently waiting for me in one of the buildings. Somewhere, just yards away from him, I was performing my physical training drills, supervised by a sergeant who was taking my scores. I was exhausted by the unexpected spring heat. I was struggling with my push-ups, and I felt weak. By the time I got to the sit-ups, I was drenched from the heat and effort but completed the task without major issues. The two-mile run was a veritable challenge because some time had passed since my last run in Fort Huachuca. I was no runner by any means and was seriously concerned about this event. My running route had been designated within the training area, around the barracks, and various administrative buildings. I had to run five laps of 0.4 miles each. It seemed like each lap would take me an eternity to run. I had to figure out my pace and how to breathe in a relaxed manner. However, there was nothing relaxing or calm about this run. During the first lap, I was anxious about not knowing if I had a good pace. Although the sergeant monitoring my time was reassuring me I was doing well, I still was stressing about being able to keep pace. My lonely run was taking a huge toll on me. With each completed lap, I was losing hope that I would ever complete this run. I could barely breathe. My mind was racing, and I was panicking. But this test would determine if I was going to the OCS, so I had to do everything in my power to pass.

Suddenly, on my last lap, I saw Alec emerging from behind a building, waving to me. He found me at last. I was so happy to see him cheering for me and screaming, "Go, *mysz*! Go, *mysz*" (go, mouse). Fresh energy propelled me forward like a rocket. I felt like I was running for Alec to make him proud. That last lap was the victory lap. I completed the last event of my physical fitness test and was officially qualified to pursue the "OCS 501 program."

With Alec next to me, I walked on my cotton-like, shaking legs to a nearby bench to catch my breath. This was my last time running long distance in Springfield. My mind was absorbed by the intrusive thoughts about my future training in OCS, trying to imagine and rationalize everything that was waiting for me in the new adventure.

In June in Springfield, the midday, sweltering heat was just a small prologue of what was waiting for me in the near future: Alabama and Pennsylvania. However, nothing could prepare me for the 501 program. Certainly, I suspected that all the familiar matters like basic leadership, teamwork, time-management skills, and conducting training at the squad and platoon level would be experienced at the proverbial "next level." The OCS was going to be an uncompromising, demanding-an-extreme-physical-exertion course taking place in a twenty-four-hour-a-day training environment. I anticipated phase I in Alabama to be especially challenging because it was designed to weed out the weakest candidates. The infamous theoretical and practical land navigation tests during the day and night were known as the primary elimination steps. The soldiers in my Chicago unit had warned me about these hurdles more than once.

Thinking about all that was ahead of me, I also felt melancholy. In two days, I was leaving Alec, Yorkie Sznurek, and my home again.

* * *

It wasn't hard to decide about pursuing an officer's path. The hardest part was the separation from Alec and everything I called home. Yet, I wanted to believe I was ready to learn one more time how to function in the new reality. For now, I had a taste of what the OCS would be about, just like I'd once experienced the prebasic training. But was it enough to prepare me for what was coming? The only valid option was to take the plunge and learn how to swim in this ocean of the unknown.

CHAPTER 17

TRUSTING MY INSTINCTS

The plane landed in Anniston, Alabama. As soon as I exited the airport building, the hot steaming air filled my lungs. The bright midday sun blinded me suddenly. Our small group stood there for some time, waiting for our ride. Eventually, the typical white school bus pulled over. I sat down quietly, hugging my duffle bag, trying to picture what the future events would reveal. We drove for an hour outside the city limits through endless fields, poverty, semi-abandoned villages, misery, and sadness. My heart was pounding with angst and excitement, but I was full of hope. After driving around the base, as if trying to confuse us, the driver finally dropped us off in front of two identical barracks facing each other across a vast quad.

It was a typical sultry afternoon in Alabama. Six of us, the candidates from Illinois, were tired, uncertain, puzzled, and totally not ready to jump into the lion's mouth. I was sitting there on the bus and wanted to be invisible. I thought that maybe no one would notice that we had arrived, so we might as well just quietly enjoy the last few moments of normal life. It would be better for all of us to just sit on this bus rather than get out of it and face the monster: the officer candidate school, accelerated program.

Eventually, a TAC officer showed up. It meant that the hell just broke loose. We had to get out of the bus, form up in front, and take accountability. Someone had to be in charge immediately. It all became blurry after a few moments of the TACs yelling and screaming and rushing us through the obscure empty hallways in one of the barracks. That place just became our new home for the next two weeks. We dragged our duffle bags full of heavy equipment into a building nearby and changed into PT uniforms. After a quick in-processing in a small room, where they weighed and measured us, and assessed briefly that we were healthy, we ended up in a somber classroom with small windows. They gave us "Rules and Regulations OCS Phase I" to read and memorize. The room was quiet, chilly, and dark. I sat there immobilized, afraid to breathe, trying to be invisible. "Two weeks—somehow I will survive," I thought to myself. "Just don't think ahead. Live through it one day at a time. All I know now is that life will be going at a fast and furious pace, and before I realize it, everything will be over. Now I'm here and I have to get through it."

Brand-new officer candidates from different states were arriving at Fort McClellan every few hours, in groups of about ten to fifteen people, each on a white bus. The atmosphere was filled with mysterious silence yet saturated with the anticipation of something that will come unexpectedly, catching me off guard. That day was the last day of this uncertainty.

* * *

I got assigned to the third platoon of the Alfa Company, which was to occupy the third floor in the barracks north of the quad. The bay was filthy, dark, and humid, with windows covered with partially broken, dusty, yellowish shades and black garbage bags stretched over and duct-taped to the frames. Steel, rusty lockers divided the space into several two-bunk sections along both sides of the room. Right in the middle of the floor, there was a huge, recently wiped-off puddle created by a leak in the roof. The leaks on the side walls were creeping all over like vines. It looked like time stopped there over two decades ago when apparently it was the last time that place was used. I picked a bed by the wall, strategically as far as possible from the door. After dragging my overloaded duffle bags up the stairs, I dropped onto the bunk and pulled out my notebook. I felt uneasy, exhausted, and apprehensive. For the first and the last time during my OCS adventure, I had managed to actually write some paragraphs in my journal.

"I hate my current situation. It's 6:30 p.m. in Alabama. Tremendous pressure, hassle, heat, and chaotic runs through the barracks as an attempt to establish our newly formed platoons in this new home. At this moment, it's rather unpleasant and depressing. I'm quite stressed out with all the new rules, additional equipment, school materials issued, and elaborate saluting methods that we have to follow. Just after our arrival and initial in-processing, I walked with a few people from Illinois looking for the entrance to the barracks when we got stopped by a male TAC officer. We froze and didn't know how to recite the new formula for the salute, so we got dropped for push-ups and had to do a couple of rounds running around the building to practice the proper salute every time we saw the TAC. Finally, he left us alone. It was rather irritating, but I better get used to it, since this is most likely just a minor prelude to what is coming our way. On top of that, I just realized that I completely forgot to bring with me my biography, which will probably be required at some point. I have no idea how much time it will take for me to adjust to these new conditions. Hopefully soon enough to survive the next couple of weeks without feeling too disconnected.

"We rushed upstairs to our barrack and started unpacking, but apparently, it's possible that we will have to move somewhere else. I'm not even hoping to settle in too quickly. Because I had no chance to collect my thoughts since I left Chicago this morning, I have to find a way to calm down as soon as possible, rationalize the surrounding chaos, and prepare myself for the big unknown. This entire situation reminds me of basic training."

Indeed, it was all similar to basic training. However, the expectations of officer candidates were much higher than those of new recruits. The good news was that my English was much better, and I was learning everything faster than before. I knew I had to function like a well-oiled machine.

"It's Saturday already. Today is officially my first day of OCS in Fort McClellan. From stress, I got up an hour too early, but after getting dressed in uniform, I jumped back to bed to enjoy the last hour of quiet time. My push-ups before breakfast were rather pathetic. We have this strange formula for saluting officers. While facing an officer, we have to stop at attention, salute, and recite: 'Sir/Ma'am, Officer Candidate (last name), good morning, sir/ma'am.' Then, when the salute is returned, we drop our hand to the position of attention. Although it's all hard for me to pronounce the entire formula, I'm slowly getting the hang of it. One sergeant in the DFAC made me eat more for breakfast than I intended to, but I had no choice.

"Some females from the traditional Alabama OCS program are with the accelerated program folks for their two-week annual training. Since they already know some of the Alabama TACs, they keep telling horror stories about how we will be running uphill several times daily, being yelled at, and getting dropped for push-ups in the ditch. It's not helping. I would rather not know and don't expect the worst-case scenarios. The tensions are building up already and we haven't even started the actual training. Arroyo from Illinois is constantly rearranging her stuff in the lockers. She is very stressed out, but I'm not in a position to calm her down while I'm trembling and disoriented. I'm making my best effort not to pay attention to any erratic behaviors in the bay and to keep myself from going insane."

* * *

Later that afternoon, we were marched as the battalion to the vast parade field nearby where, as eight platoons (each company equaled four platoons), we stood at attention in front of the battalion commander and several TAC officers in black caps.

The commander gave a lengthy speech about the role of an officer in the army. Leadership, loyalty, taking care of their subordinates, leading by example, personal courage, and various technical skills. He talked about the challenges of the OCS and how we were about to become the armed forces' elite. We had to show our dedication to the program, the motivation to complete it, and the ability to perform and learn fast in a challenging environment. It all sounded familiar.

The warm and inspiring welcome from the battalion commander was over. We all stood there silent in the "parade rest" positions in anticipation of the second part of the "welcome."

There was nothing warm about this silence. There was no rest after this silence.

"Batta-lion, attention!" screamed the battalion sergeant major, then added in a normal voice to the TAC officers facing the platoons, "They're all yours."

There were two TAC officers (a female for female candidates and a male for male candidates) and one staff sergeant assigned to each platoon. That meant there were twelve cadres in total on the parade field.

Suddenly, as if struck by lightning, the TAC personnel began their "welcome smoking session." By screaming various commands in fast order, they were challenging our mental and physical strength, our reflex, and speed. From attention, to front leaning rest position, to on your back, to attention again. About face, right face, left face, "military left face," then to front leaning rest position again. I started sweating, but I was going strong, keeping up with the pace.

"Start pushing! One, two, three, four... This course is gonna be hard! If you are weak, go back home to your 'fort living room'!" TACs yelled, one after another. "Seven, eight, nine..."

"Quit now!" another TAC added. "We don't have enough space for all of you. On your back! Sit-ups! One, two, three..."

"Front leaning rest position!"

Now, my arms were shaking in agony, and drops of sweat were forming on my forehead. This was anything but rest.

"Start pushing!" a platoon sergeant screamed. "One, two, three... If you've had enough, you can go home now! Quit before it gets worse!"

"Atten-tion!" a TAC interjected. "Side straddle hop! One, two, three, four. Stretch those hands! Six, seven, eight... twenty-one, twenty-two!"

"Front leaning rest position! Start pushing!"

My face was now covered with dripping sweat and my T-shirt under the BDU blouse was drenched. I dropped to the knee position for modified push-ups. "It will be over soon," I kept telling myself. "Just endure this 'smoking.'" My upper back was slowly sagging, barely supported by my aching arms. "They can't keep us on this field forever. At least this is my opportunity to get that beautifully sculpted Venus body I've always dreamed of!" I desperately consoled myself.

"This is bullshit!" I kept hearing the candidates muttering around me.

"Sit-ups!" a TAC officer yelled. "Who wants to watch some TV, have some beers?! Give up now! OCS is too hard. We only need a few of you!" I was already annoyed by these encouragements to quit. I felt like the TAC was trying too hard. It was getting old, but it was part of the game. But the truth was, not everyone was material for an officer.

Several people stepped out of the ranks.

"Side straddle hop! One, two, three . . . seven, eight . . . fifteen, sixteen! On your back!"

A few more sit-ups and I was ready to implode from the pain.

"Front leaning rest position! Push!"

"Fuck this shit, I'm out," someone said under his breath in a rank behind me.

Another handful of candidates stepped out of the formation.

The sun started setting beyond the horizon. The air was filled with chilly humidity. Giant field lights became the quiet witnesses of the war on the parade field. The fight between strength and weakness, the fight between those who could endure and those who would give up.

I was telling myself to breathe, to not think about or be tempted by anything pleasant, encouraging me to quit. It was just a game that I would have to play more than once. I was about to collapse from the physical exertion when I heard, "On your feet! Right face! Forward, march!"

It was finally over. This was my first victory in Fort McClellan.

Once we made it to the barracks, I was immediately assigned to the night CQ duty in our building. I was expecting an entire sleepless night of duty, like in Fort Huachuca. However, after a couple of hours of sitting in CQ and reading the OC (officer candidate) guide with my fellow soldiers from Illinois, I was pleasantly surprised when we were released. The new arrivals from Alabama were taking over the shift, and we were sent upstairs to bed. Since we were not allowed any contact with the outside world, it looked like I would never be able to call Alec while I was at Fort McClellan. I was not surprised.

From what I gathered, we had over two hundred candidates from eight states. That was good because hopefully, all this yelling would be spread over so many people and it wouldn't affect me much. I just had to get used to everything until the end, when we would fly to Pennsylvania.

* * *

My pocket notebook quickly was filling up with daily orders, assignments, tasks, responsibilities, map coordinates, and "enemy situation" descriptions. Writing journals was always a perfect antidote for my struggle with difficult situations and an uncomfortable state of mind. Sadly, this time around, the pace of Alabama Military Academy was too fast for this sort of therapy, and I realized that from this point on, there would be no time for writing. I had to leave something for myself though, so I decided to write only the "good moments" that happened to me in the process. These notes were mostly passages of what someone said to me in a specific situation—a positive comment, a joke about me, words of encouragement, something funny, something to keep in my heart for the rest of my life. It was the only remedy for feeling blue, tired, and lost or when in doubt.

* * *

Dear Alec,

Here we go. I'm assigned to the Second Battalion Officer Candidate School (OCS) 200th Regiment at the Alabama Military Academy, Fort McClellan.

I barely got here, and it seems like I have a moment to write to you, probably the last time during my adventure here. There is quite a bit of confusion, tension, and running around everywhere. I have a lot of unknown names and places to get familiar with and it's overwhelming, but no more than the basic training. For now, anyway.

It's challenging to get myself in this mindset of being away from home in training again. I know this is what I dreamed about for a while, not much of a consolation at this particular moment though. As expected, we are getting screamed in the face and "smoked." Our TAC officers are wearing plain black "soft caps" with their last names embroidered on the back, so we can recognize them from far away. I can barely understand the people from Alabama with their Southern accents, especially the sergeants and officers. I'm still overwhelmed as I am not able to find "my space" in all this hazy reality, which appears to be a perfectly organized chaos.

We got a nice "welcome" from the unit commanders and the cadre. It was a gigantic smoking session of the entire battalion (both companies) on the parade field. Can you imagine a few hundred people being dropped for push-ups, roll-ups, sit-ups, and running around, trying to stay in some kind of formation? I think it was quite funny for the spectators or TAC officers who did all the screaming, but I wasn't laughing. My only goal was to try not to stand out in any way by being too slow or too fast, definitively keeping the stoneface at all times and following the orders. I'm sure they have a lot more events like that in store for us. As my heart is still very heavy, I don't allow myself to think about home. Not yet anyway. I will be more comfortable thinking about that in four or six weeks. Meanwhile, I need to stay focused and get this mission accomplished.

*   *   *

The next day, we were introduced to our cadre: Captain Busbee (platoon advisor), two assisting TACs, Lieutenant Caldwell (for male candidates) and Lieutenant Brown (for females), and the NCO (noncommissioned officer) Sergeant First Class Mathis from Illinois. It was refreshing to have someone around from my home state. We were instructed about our new daily routines, laundry and sick call schedule, and the eating rotations between Alfa and Bravo Companies. Our uniforms had to be "sanitized" of all ranks, tabs, unit patches, combat patches, and American flags. Once again, we were all equal, officer candidates.

The TACs gave us a detailed overview of requirements regarding our military bearing and courtesy, academics, extreme physical conditioning, fitness tests, road marches, and the unprecedented stamina essential to accomplish all the training requirements. The hourly hydration was emphasized more than ever before. For a moment, I thought about my competitive marching at Fort Huachuca in the scorching desert, through the sand and rocks, and up and down the hill, doing my "airborne shuffle" for most of the time. However, here in Alabama, the blistering desert from Arizona would be replaced by the agonizing hot humidity, similar to the one in Chicago in the summer of 1995.

One thing that particularly caught my attention was the leadership assignments rotation. The candidates were going to be placed in various command positions and evaluated during a formal counseling session after a twenty-four-hour duty period. The concept itself was not as new as in Springfield. During my "phase zero" training, we also had leadership positions. However, here, the process was taking a completely new dimension because the size of our units, like squads, platoons, and companies, was quadrupled. Thus, being in charge of an enormous crowd posed a much bigger challenge. I wouldn't dare imagine myself in this type of position, getting screamed at in my face, disoriented, and trying to lead a couple of hundreds of fellow candidates.

During the entire training, we were required to maintain the highest standards possible. The TACs emphasized that "the moral character and integrity must be an inspiration to others and our conduct must be impeccable at all times." As I listened to all this, my heart was growing stronger, more faithful, and uplifted. Everything started falling into place again.

* * *

One afternoon, I was rushing through a small hallway connecting the female and male bays in the barracks when suddenly, a familiar silhouette of Lieutenant Brown appeared right in front of my face. I felt suspended in the air, not sure how to react, but she quickly resolved the situation.

"SKI!" Lieutenant Brown stopped me in my tracks. "You're the only squared-away soldier here. Don't be running with your dog tags hanging out now!" she whispered in my face. "Who is your state TAC officer?" she continued with a suddenly softer and friendly voice. "I want to talk to him about you." I was most likely in trouble, I thought to myself.

I looked down and there were my dog tags, shamelessly out and dangling on my chest. I shoved them quickly under my T-shirt and probably blushed like a little schoolgirl caught in the act. When confronted by Lieutenant Brown, I felt embarrassed and uplifted at the same time. She knew how to catch soldiers, but it was always for a good reason: to correct their shortcomings and keep them focused. At this moment, I knew she was on my side, and I promised myself that I would do everything in my power to keep it that way. I felt compelled to maintain the highest standards possible.

Finally, the day was over. My mind was filled with events, people, smells, procedures, and sounds. All my senses were over-saturated with this new, hard-to-embrace reality.

I got in the shower, hoping to wash off the stress and relax for a few moments, away from the chaos and madness. I closed my eyes and suddenly I started hearing a strange noise—monotonous, hard to define, and continuing as the water was bouncing off the tight cabin walls. After a couple of minutes, I realized it was the water sounding like charging battalions, thousands of soldiers running toward the enemy, screaming heroically. Those "battle calls" were our trademark there. Everywhere we went, we had to rush screaming to emphasize the purpose and urgency of anything we were carrying out. When marching, we would sing the cadences, and while running to the dining facility or bursting out of the barracks before dawn or after dusk for the formations, we would scream.

This sound was embedded in my mind so deeply that it prevented me from truly hearing and appreciating the silence and almost any soothing sound of nature for several weeks.

* * *

On day two, both companies fell out of the morning formation, and squad by squad and platoon by platoon were double timing in a single file toward an "agony pit" where the pre-meal routine was taking place three times a day. While waiting in line for this pre-breakfast drill, everyone was cheering, singing cadences, or simply screaming our "war cries" and clapping hands. We had to look and sound motivated, excited, and pumped up at all times. Since there were a few hundred soldiers in both companies, it took quite a while to get to the pit, and after surviving it, finally, run to breakfast. This routine was a series of pull-ups and push-ups, and immediately after that, a crisp proper salute and a lengthy greeting of the day directed to a TAC officer facing any soldier executing the process. After this, if everything went smoothly, we would run and form a single file on the nearby grass to get our dose of sit-ups. Naturally, the TACs were looking for any minuscule, or even nonexistent, mistakes because they wanted to drive us by punishing us. During the first couple of days, it was a challenge for almost all of us to get this procedure done correctly, so most of us would end up executing a "corrective action" by crawling into an enormous pit filled with sawdust and wood chips. After this maneuver, it was a nasty feeling spending all day itching in a dirty uniform.

It was a fourth day of hell running to the schoolhouse in full gear for the land navigation classes. I barely knew where the other candidates from Illinois were. In each company, there were four platoons of about forty soldiers each, so locating six people in this immense crowd constantly on the move was nearly impossible. Completely cut off from everything familiar, I felt lonely and vulnerable, troubled that I might not survive these two weeks.

But this morning was different. After successfully completing my pre-breakfast routine, I was moving fast toward the Bravo Company barrack adjacent to the dining facility. The day just started, but I felt exhausted already. My mind was racing and was bombarded by these endless questions: What was going to happen next? Will I get through one more day? Will the body ache ever go away? How will I survive this unbearable, steamy heat? It seemed like a desperate struggle to try to keep on moving without bursting into tears, so I kept running and trying not to think anymore. The Bravo Company was running in the opposite direction. I saw soldiers' faces passing by me in slow motion, one after another, like in a lethargic dream where everything seemed blurry and fragile. Everyone was a ghost going through the motions.

Suddenly, I noticed a familiar face. My heart jumped for a split second of exaltation. I hadn't seen Mathia since my last drill in Marseilles, Illinois. She was on a different plane to Alabama and now I saw her again. We could only exchange a weak smile. After a quick look into her teary eyes, I was barely able to keep my bearings. But, it was heartwarming to find Mathia and know that she was here nearby and that one day we may be reunited in the same platoon.

The day continued as always, with relentless rushing everywhere. After breakfast, we ran uphill to the schoolhouse. We were doing pretty good and kept together our formation the entire time. Out of the blue, Lieutenant Brown sprang out in front of us like a rocket and encouraged us to move even faster, screaming, "It's not a punishment. You didn't do anything wrong! Just push harder. Come on!" she continued, leading from the front.

Eventually, the inevitable "time of the ditch" arrived for our platoon. We were lucky for a few days while other platoons were "getting smoked" in the ditch at least a couple of times daily. This time, however, we ran out of luck and our captain decided to drop us in the ditch for endless push-ups exactly when the visitors (future cadets) were passing by. He certainly was amused watching us pounding the ground with our faces on this magnificently hot day in Alabama. Usually, the punishments like that were performed for show or to compete with other units in "who got it worse" game.

* * *

It had been a few days since phase I started in Alabama. I couldn't tell exactly what day of the week it was because they all seemed the same. The same daily routine made the time pass extremely quickly, without specific indications as to what day it could be. Quite a few people from my platoon already had a chance to experience a "leadership position" assignment. So far, I was a team leader and squad leader, but my biggest fear was platoon level (platoon sergeant or platoon leader) or—even worse—company-level position (like company first sergeant or company commander). Anyone in these positions, at least in my platoon and company, was in big trouble—getting constantly "smoked" with or without reason. But that was the game: teach the candidates their responsibility as leaders in the most unbearable conditions. If you played the game by the rules, you could get ahead, but you still would be smoked. The trick was to learn how to take it.

For days now, I'd been struggling with daily runs uphill in Kevlar, combat gear, in formation—from the schoolhouse and back—three times daily. As we were running, I would slip off, rank by rank, to eventually end up in the last row of the formation. Somehow, I couldn't break that pattern. When we were marching to the schoolhouse, every time I heard the command "Double time, march!" my head would start spinning. The only thing I was concentrating on was to stay in formation during the run and not to fall out completely at any price. This would not be acceptable in any circumstances. I knew better.

The evening of the fifth day of training changed everything. I was called by our platoon's TAC officer, Captain Busbee. It was a bad sign, and I knew right away that some unpleasant surprise was waiting for me in his office.

I reported to the captain. He asked me to sit down and said something nice to me. I was so tense already; I didn't even hear what it was exactly. Then, there was dreaded: "Candidate SKI, for the next twenty-four-hour period, you will be our platoon leader."

My heart stopped. However, since I suspected that this leadership rotation would happen sooner or later, I resigned to the idea. At the same time, it was a genuine relief that he didn't make me a company first sergeant or a company commander.

"It will be very challenging, as you already know. But remember, I do not want to see the defeat in your eyes when you run up that hill. You are in charge now and you will have to stay up front at all times as a leader. These people count on you. I know you are capable of doing it."

I probably started breathing again, but my heart was very heavy and my mind went crazy. "So much responsibility. What am I supposed to do for the next twenty-four hours? How am I going to survive this?" Intrusive questions were exploding in my brain like grenades.

"And one more thing, SKI, you are responsible for this platoon's map-reading test at school tomorrow. You better make sure they all pass. I don't want to see any dropouts. We have zero tolerance for these kinds of mistakes." And how in the world am I going to do that? I thought, puzzled.

Then he spelled out more tasks that I was responsible for, including providing detailed reports on the platoon's activities and overall performance. "Don't worry. You can do it. I have no doubts about it."

I left the room on cotton legs, barely catching up with reality. Tonight, after the last platoon formation, there would be an official platoon change of command procedure for my new position. I had to brace for mental and physical impact.

* * *

My day as a platoon leader was hectic. I was in charge of nearly forty people. To make sure my activity reports were detailed enough, I attempted to take notes of everything transpiring that day. In the morning, I had to prepare everyone for the day by briefing them about the schedule and studying hard at school. McFarlan was late to the after-breakfast formation. Apparently, she got lost or stuck somewhere and we had to look for her all over the quad area. Because of her mishap, we were late to school. I was constantly thinking about not leaving anyone behind, especially those sick or injured. Sloan was late for the run as well, and while catching up, he twisted his ankle. We managed to survive the first run to school. It stressed me out tremendously. I delegated the platoon sergeant to stay with the injured and request TAC's help.

At school, I made every attempt to lead by example by asking the instructor pertinent questions and encouraging learning. I also had to keep an eye on everyone to keep them hydrated. After the first lesson, I followed up with Lieutenant Brown about Sloan's injury and she said, "Let us (TAC officers) take care of him." Halfway into the second lesson, everyone in the classroom was so stressed out that the platoon sergeant and I had to conduct breathing exercises for the entire class.

During the first latrine break, we were running toward a row of porta potties about thirty yards from the schoolhouse. We didn't make it there and were turned around halfway. Apparently, we weren't screaming the war cries loud enough. Without the opportunity to use the latrines, we had to crawl back to school in the dirt.

The good news was that we all passed the map-reading test. Everyone was ecstatic and proud. My mission was accomplished, but my hands were full. Martin collapsed from the heat, and I sent her with Coleman to the medics, who were parked with their ambulance behind the schoolhouse. I instructed Coleman to secure Martin's equipment. McFarlan got lost again somewhere in the schoolhouse, mixed up with another screaming platoon. I had to instruct my platoon sergeant to keep an eye on her and make sure she knows where to go at all times. As the day was going on, the heat casualties were multiplying and most of us weren't able to function at full capacity. People were falling out of the formation, collapsing left and right. Another unsuccessful latrine break, then crawling right back to school.

* * *

At last, lunchtime came, and we were leaving the school in platoon formation. Midday heat and humidity were slowly taking a toll on my body. However, this was my time to prove to the TACs that I could lead from the front. With all the power I could find in my lungs, I screamed, "Platoon! Double time, march!"

I kept the formation running, staying ahead, leading from the front. Suddenly, I noticed our captain's face a few steps ahead of me, standing on the side of the road. I said to myself, "See? I'm running and I'm still up front. There is no defeat in my eyes." He just stood there and watched me struggling, gasping for air, as the Kevlar helmet was covering almost entirely my eyes. My uniform was completely drenched, my boots weighed about a ton, and my LBE (load-bearing equipment) was sliding. Barely hanging on, I was leading my platoon up the hill, through a vast woody area, tripping over branches and rocks. Finally, I was there, up on the hill, on the quad, with my entire platoon behind me in formation. It felt great to be there without falling out for the first time. Lieutenant Brown took my report, and she smoked me for a few more minutes, making me do endless push-ups. I dropped and started pushing on my knees, as I couldn't keep my body straight from shaking. I saw the sand on the ground right before my eyes and wasn't able to get up. A sudden throbbing headache felt like my head was frying under the helmet while the chilling cold was shooting through my body. Eventually, I got up. Lieutenant Brown then asked me some questions, but my mouth was producing some incomprehensible statements. Most likely in Polish. I stood there looking at Lieutenant Brown as she was saying something, but I couldn't hear anything anymore. Then I saw a male TAC officer from an adjacent platoon pacing toward me to help Lieutenant Brown smoke me. He looked directly into my face and asked me a question. I repeated the same blurry speech from before. Suddenly, the world around me started whirling like a tornado. Trees, equipment, people, and the bleachers were viciously tousled around by an unexplainable force. I desperately wanted to do something about it, snap out of it, and come back.

"Are you all right, soldier?" I heard through the fog of my mind's uncontrollable spin. I couldn't say anything. It didn't matter anymore. It was so hot, so humid, so bright, and hot . . . and bright . . . and bright . . . I didn't know what to do. I needed to run to safety, but where was the safety? Confused, I launched to the back of the formation to switch my position with the platoon sergeant. I wanted to hide and collapse somewhere behind the ranks in silence. I needed to feel safe. As I was running, I could barely hear Lieutenant Brown screaming behind me, "What are you doing, SKI?! Where the hell are you going?!"

Eventually, I hit the ground with my face. My helmet fell off and the map case with school books slipped off my shoulder. Everything was going in slow motion while I was struggling to stay conscious. A couple of fellow soldiers grabbed me by my arms and dragged me to the ambulance standing by—dark, quiet, and cool. I could barely see or hear anything. The paramedics took off my BDU jacket and began checking my vitals. I was so hot that I felt cold and started shivering uncontrollably. They were trying to cool me off as quickly as possible. With my entire body soaking wet, I was sitting in the vehicle, leaning forward with my head down and a cold wet towel on my neck. Suddenly, through the voices of medics swarming around, I heard a welcoming and noticeably anxious voice: "What's going on? How is she doing?" Lieutenant Brown was inquiring about me.

"We've got a possible heatstroke. She's still sweating, but her body temperature is too high," one paramedic replied. "We need to cool her off immediately."

"Okay, I'll follow up shortly."

After a couple of hours, I was transported back to the schoolhouse by the paramedics' truck called "the bus." As I approached the building, a familiar feminine silhouette caught my attention. "Damn, I'm probably in trouble for passing out," I thought in panic. Still trembling, I smiled softly to counteract a potentially incoming reprimand. Lieutenant Brown jumped out of the nearby bleachers and after a few brief questions about my well-being, she offered me a Gatorade . . .

"What color would you like? Or maybe a bottle of Miller Lite?" Even though I couldn't imagine myself drinking a beer in this situation, every word she said was like a balsam for my exhausted body and soul. "Here, I got a lunch for you from DFAC. You need to eat everything on this plate." Food, on the other hand, was now my best friend. I was starving.

I savored my purple Gatorade as if it was a gift from the heavens because, normally, we were not allowed to drink anything but water. For the rest of the day, I felt dizzy and lightheaded, but I was still in charge of my platoon. It took an excruciating effort to stay alert and think of all the soldiers under my command. I had to report to the instructor before and after every break and keep an eye on those struggling in the classroom.

Despite my heat exhaustion, I still had to go out on the break and face the heat from the sun and the TAC officers. Deep down in my heart, however, I was very disappointed with myself that I wasn't stronger, and the heat took such a horrible toll on me. I felt like I lost the fight and the will to survive. My morale went down.

* * *

At the end of the day, after a one-on-one review of my shift in a leadership position, I regained my confidence. As expected, Captain Busbee pointed out my weaknesses, but he also took note of my accomplishments. It was a true consolation that this morning's test was a success. The entire class passed it with flying colors, something very critical at this point in our training. Another good thing was making it uphill during the lunchtime run to the quad area and successfully leading from the front of my entire platoon. This was my second victory in Fort McClellan.

"How did the eval go, kiddo?" Sergeant Mathis stopped me in the hallway on my way back to my bay. It didn't even bother me that as a thirty-three-year-old woman, I was called "kiddo." I liked that he called me that because I was still a bit like a lost child. But this endearing nickname felt warm and fuzzy in my heart, and I needed that. I craved the feeling that someone cared about me in this crazy chaos. "Something tells me it was pretty good."

"Not too bad. I did my best to keep everyone together and to pass the test as a platoon."

"I know you did. Your actions show what you are made of. Keep up the good work!" Oh yes. If this good work was noticed and appreciated, then I would definitely keep it up. I wanted to prove to the world that I was the best I could be and that I was in the right place.

* * *

In the evening, the change of command took place and Yorker took over as a new platoon leader. Although my day was full of responsibility and the tremendous pressure associated with it was over, my battle with the heat was only beginning. I was banned from any exercise, morning fitness routines, runs, and daily running to school and back, and I had to wear a white engineering cloth tape on my sleeve—a designation for a heat casualty. From this point on, I was driven anywhere I needed to go.

That evening, the entire platoon got yelled at because apparently, some people were not giving a hundred percent in their daily procedures, were failing some school tests, and were pretending to be sick. Everyone, except a few people with profiles ("handicaps"), including me, had to sit on the bleachers and watch our platoon getting punished by endless push-ups on the quad. I felt uneasy and helpless, but there was nothing I could do about it.

"I know you gave it all, and you really fell sick. Since you are now considered a heat casualty, keep me posted at all times about how you are feeling." Lieutenant Brown's words were a relief. I wanted her to know that I gave everything on that hill until I had nothing left in me to give.

Despite my declining health, I didn't want to make any additional waves and remained patient in the classroom, hoping that my miserable condition would somehow go away. But it didn't. The next day, my physical strength was deteriorating rapidly and the entire morning in the classroom became a fight that I just couldn't win. I felt dizzy and nauseous and couldn't concentrate in class. I started seeing double and could barely sit up straight. Finally, I asked my platoon leader to arrange an emergency appointment with Lieutenant Brown. At the risk of getting smoked, I met with Lieutenant Brown during the break in the schoolhouse. I told her everything that was bothering me regarding my well-being. Contrary to my worst expectations, she received me with respect and understanding. She even admitted feeling bad that I had to sit on the bleachers last night with those who were pretending to be sick to avoid exercise.

"I have no doubt you are giving your best all the time." Lieutenant Brown was convincing. "After this block of instruction, you're getting an IV. The medics will pick you up at the school gate." From that point on, I had to eat more than usual, and Lieutenant Brown was watching me like a hawk, making sure I put additional salt on my food to replace the electrolytes. She took care of me and from that moment, I didn't feel like a failure, lonely among hundreds of soldiers.

* * *

Lieutenant Brown pulled into the parking lot and dismounted her Jeep near the ambulance. Just as she touched the ground, I heard her voice: "Now what did you do, SKI?"

"Ma'am, Officer Candidate Rakowski. I dislocated my finger, ma'am," I replied quickly, waving my right hand just decorated with a splint. "I hit it against my Kevlar while taking it off. I wanted to make my move snappy," I answered a big question depicted on Lieutenant Brown's face before she had a chance to ask it.

In the afternoon of day seven, Yorker was still in charge of our platoon. He was so wired up and frantic at times that Lieutenant Brown called him the "Energizer Bunny," the pink furry character from the TV commercial for Energizer batteries. Despite his genuine efforts, some fellow soldiers were not following his orders, and Yorker was trying to take care of everything and everyone at the same time. Lieutenant Brown didn't need much more encouragement to teach him a valuable lesson. He had to march around the platoon with his arms straight in front of him, clapping, like the Energizer bunny, with a drum. He also had to sing along: "I will delegate, I will delegate." Lieutenant Brown's sense of humor would always bring some relief and freshness to our usually serious, demanding routines. One time, for example, our platoon left for school incomplete because one person was tardy. As a reminder that we should never leave a soldier behind, we had to hold hands when going anywhere and stay in a single file like kindergarten children. Although it must have been a rather comical sight, the other platoons were not laughing. Their punishment of choice was crawling in the dirt.

On that day, after our last land navigation test in the classroom, I reported, as ordered, to the ambulance and was given two IVs for rehydration. I was extremely uneasy about missing two hours of instruction and how this would affect my progress in school, but I needed to get better.

The rest of the day was dedicated to practicing our pace count (counting how many steps one takes to traverse one hundred meters on flat and on rough terrain) in the nearby wooded area in preparation for the fast-approaching land navigation test in the field. In the evening, the entire platoon was called to the barracks by our furious TACs. Apparently, eight people had failed the morning test, so we got yelled at.

"SKI missed half of the instruction when she went down from the heat," Captain Busbee screamed through his teeth.

"And she had an injured finger," Lieutenant Caldwell added.

"And she still passed the test," the captain finished his remark. I felt like they were playing a ping-pong game, bouncing my name back and forth.

Unfortunately, it was not only a yelling session. In addition, because it was the army's birthday, we had to throw on our BDUs in the middle of the night and crawl several times along the quad's dirt.

I was a bit flustered about the situation. I also felt guilty that when my platoon was getting punished, I was sitting on the bleachers, watching them suffer. Even though I had no physical activity profile, I thought about the team. I should have been there with them. After the chewing session, the males and females went to their respective bays with assigned TAC officers. On the way there, Sergeant Mathis stopped me.

"Don't worry, kiddo. I admire your dedication. So far, so good." Coming from him, it was always an honor and consolation at the same time.

Later, Lieutenant Brown gave all the females a detailed description of what would be expected from us in the woods, where for several days, we were about to practice map reading, teach classes, and eventually take our day and night land navigation tests. We were merely in the middle of the training, but the sudden change of pace made me feel like we had crossed a certain point of no return. The "cozy days" spent in the barracks were coming to an end. Our daily runs to school were over and we were now preparing for the long-expected field training. I had gotten used to our daily routines. However, sensing a drastic change in the upcoming activities, I started feeling a little concerned about spending most of the time in the woods, only occasionally going back to the barracks.

"Anything else you need at this point?" Her surprisingly soft voice was free from the usual traces of sarcasm.

"A hug?" I replied quietly with a straight face. I was joking, but deep down inside, I felt like I could really use a hug. Or maybe not. That would have weakened my spirit and left me crying. I couldn't allow myself to cry. This was definitely meant to be a joke.

For a moment, she looked me in the eye as if she wasn't sure if I was actually serious.

"Get down, SKI, and start pushing." That was better. I was convinced that Lieutenant Brown took my comment as a joke. Joking was not allowed, so I got punished. Gladly.

* * *

On day eight, we left the quad and barracks area and embarked on a new adventure. After several days spent entirely in the classroom environment, our land navigation training in the field officially started. We were loaded on the deuces (military trucks) like sardines and taken deep into the woods. Although I was aware of the poisonous snakes, spiders, as well as bees, wasps, and ticks common in the training area, it was truly refreshing to suddenly see so much green: to feel protected from the sun and the scorching afternoon heat.

We were required to use a map to cross the woods and find specific landmarks ("points") marked on the map. From my perspective, just getting from one side of this huge perimeter to another would seem like an accomplishment. At the same time, the vision of doing it alone one day and then one night was not so attractive. All the land navigation theory didn't make sense to me even though I'd practiced my pace count for several days, worked with the compass, and was reading the map quite well—on the written tests, anyway. I still felt rather confused by the surrounding people. Somehow, they were always "doing it their way." Just like that time in phase zero in Springfield when we got lost in the woods, guided by an "experienced" sergeant who just "knew better."

My intuition, however, was telling me something different, and deep down in my heart, I believed I could do it on my own—find my points on the ground. I decided not to worry too much about the "smarty pants" around me and just go through the motions during these practice rounds before the final solo test in a few days. I knew that my time would come, and I would succeed. In the meantime, I enjoyed walking through the dense fantastic woods, whispering to me as if they were trying to tell me that everything would be all right. Without a doubt, I needed an ally.

For the following two days, we were repeating the process of finding the landmarks, and every time, the teams were smaller. Although I was trying very hard to feel good about this process, my anxiety grew stronger. People were continually getting lost, and I still wasn't able to correctly locate all my points. One time, I got especially confused when I was negotiating the woods with two teammates. One of them was oblivious to our situation and simply didn't care about anything. The other one was a preacher's son who, for several hours, managed to talk continuously about his not-so-intriguing personal life. I could barely follow not only his mind-numbing story but also his steps. He was walking frantically without any focus or attention to the map and the surroundings, carrying on with his monologue. We were meandering like mad nomads several yards away from the markers we needed to find. I couldn't wait to get out of the woods and be liberated from this annoying company.

* * *

We took a break from our delirious wander, and I drifted away almost instantaneously. Suddenly, my senses awakened and for the first time in Fort McClellan, I became aware of the enchanting, peaceful scenery surrounding me all the time. I looked at the massive trees towering above me like guardian angels and felt an amazing serenity flow through my body like a warm liquid. The early afternoon sunbeams were picking through the branches of the lower shrubbery, creating a fantastic mesh of tiny lines sparkling in the light. The minuscule insects were playing in the glowing air. This natural spectacle with sunbeams reminded me of the time in Warsaw back in the early summer of 1992.

I was sitting at the Ambassador Restaurant, erratically flipping through the pages of my daily planner. A fresh breeze of an early afternoon was coming through the open window like a long-expected friend. The room was filled with sunbeams gently dancing with window sheers moving in the air. A fantastically deep, aromatic smell of freshly brewed espresso saturated the atmosphere. I loved the smell of coffee in the sun. It would make me feel like I was at a small café in Paris in the middle of daily hustle and bustle on a sunny afternoon, with tourists overflowing the city. The smell of freshly baked croissants would remind me of breakfast that I could eat all day, any day.

Suddenly, a new current of air passed through the room as the front door of the cafe opened. I looked up from my notes and saw the person I was waiting for. At the entrance, Chris appeared in a stunning, light-colored classic suit with a briefcase. My heart stopped from exaltation while the entire place instantaneously filled up with shimmering luminosity and bliss. I blushed tremendously, so I looked down, afraid that my feelings might be too obvious. As soon as Chris approached me, I jumped to attention, pretending to be surprised. We exchanged a quick kiss on the cheek and settled down at the little table.

"I spoke to Professor Gorecka about your thesis, and she was quite interested. Now, just come up with the proposal with a detailed outline and discuss it with her directly," said Chris. "I'm positive that she will consider moving forward with this project. And, as you know, you'll be in expert hands since she is an absolute expert in linguistics."

While listening to this soft and melodious voice, I couldn't help noticing the reflections of the sun delightfully caressing Chris's face. This was the picture I wanted to keep in my heart forever. And the smell of that coffee.

* * *

In the afternoon of our field day, in the nearly casual atmosphere, we were taking classes and continued practicing our pace counts in the wooded area. The classes were about basic military operations and procedures like deployment of hand grenades and setting up of claymore mines, construction, and the use of the M16 rifle and the M60 machine gun, when and how to use the MOPP suit, how to decontaminate yourself, and finally, how to react to a nuclear threat. While discussing chemical threats on the battlefield, we discovered that Lieutenant Brown was part of a Chemical Battalion in one of the Alabama National Guard units. We were very impressed by her talk about her unit's mission to "provide decon" (decontamination), NBC reconnaissance, large-area smoke, and staff support to commanders to enhance their war-fighting capabilities or support contingency requirements. Her unit organized special trainings on how to conduct operations to protect the nation from WMD (weapons of mass destruction) and CBRN (chemical, biological, radiological, and nuclear) threats and hazards. It was refreshing to finally have a "normal" conversation with our TAC officer. After all, she was a soldier, just like all of us.

For the next two days, we had to prepare our brief lectures about different topics. I was very nervous about giving my class about evaluating the casualty, mainly because I didn't have much time to prepare for the class. In addition, I wasn't very comfortable speaking in front of a large group of people. Being nervous, I was interjecting Polish words when I couldn't come up with English ones or when I was trying to speak fast.

"Speak English, SKI!" Lieutenant Brown interrupted my lecture, chuckling.

I couldn't help but send her a friendly smile.

"Stop smiling and get down!" I could hear in her voice that she was also smiling. I wanted to bring some lightness into the situation.

"Ma'am, Officer Candidate Rakowski. How many, ma'am?" I responded cheerfully from my front leaning-rest position.

"Give me fifteen. Start pushing, SKI!"

"Tak jest, Pani Porucznik!" (Polish: Yes, ma'am.)

"What the hell does this mean!?" She was now openly laughing, and the entire platoon seemed amused. Looking at the ground, I was laughing too.

"Ma'am, Officer Candidate Rakowski. It means 'Yes, ma'am'!"

From that point on, during our field classes, I would always greet her in Polish and immediately drop, ready for push-ups, asking, "How many, ma'am?"

* * *

In the middle of a break between our classes, Lieutenant Coldwell approached me, saying that I had an urgent call from home. Lieutenant Brown took me in her Jeep to an area on top of a hill where the field command was located.

"Act sad and tell them I had broken my leg," Alec whispered on the phone as if afraid that he could be heard by the cadre. "The actual news is that you just got a job offer from Pfizer! Congratulations!"

"Okay, I understand. Take care of yourself." I played my part and kept the conversation short and fairly somber. But my heart was rejoicing as I had completely forgotten about my interview at Pfizer just before my departure to Alabama.

Later, Lieutenant Brown had me call Alec from her cell phone to check on him. Of course, he was doing great. We were both ecstatic that a new job was waiting for me after my return home from the OCS.

"I can't give you the hug you requested," Lieutenant Brown joked, "but feel free to use my phone anytime you need to call your husband." I appreciated this generosity.

* * *

Day twelve of the OCS in Alabama was our most critical performance of the entire phase I. We knew from the beginning that land navigation was the toughest individual land navigation course in the U.S. military. That's why so much emphasis was put on the land navigation classes and written tests we had in school until now.

The practical test was to be conducted with minimal equipment (a military map, a compass, a protractor, and a pencil, and for the night, a flashlight with a red lens).

It was dawn when we were transported on the white buses to Fort McClellan's' land navigation course. The sun was barely waking when we were gathered in the assembly area with our maps. We were preparing for our day land navigation course necessary for the qualification for phase II OCS. The goal of the test was to find a minimum of five out of six points in four hours without getting lost.

In my head, I was remembering all the tough land navigation classes we had, then the tests from working with a compass and protractor, and properly plotting specific given points on maps. I had to use every second of every practice to learn as much as I could about the course. I did my best to get used to the terrain where we were practicing our pace counts. I knew we would run the same area for the test, not the same lanes, but on the same map sheet area.

Regardless, I was a bit concerned about my pace count. I wasn't sure if I had been walking at the right pace when we were practicing. Now I had to recreate the same speed and size of my steps in the unknown terrain. Another reason for stress was the fact that we would be evaluated during the entire test as the cadre would be out there watching us. They would be hiding in the woods and checking for cheating, like talking to other candidates or signaling others to a location point. If someone violated any of the rules, they would certainly be caught and possibly fail the test. I promised myself to keep a cool head during this time of tremendous stress while searching for my points. After all, this was a more mental than a physical challenge.

I believed our instructors and cadre had set us up for success. They were in the land navigation areas all the time and knew these woods like the back of their hand. I was hoping while they wouldn't be trying to make it easy on us, they wouldn't instruct us to do anything to lead us astray, either. Most importantly, they would definitely know how to find someone lost within our land navigation course. As I was thinking things through after plotting my points on the map, I decided to start my course by finding the farthest point first.

I immediately started running my first thirty meters on a dirt road. However, I didn't trust the road, so I had to choose the option of crossing the woods by relying only on my compass and a map. The bush was becoming thicker and eventually I had to slow down.

Suddenly, I walked into a terrain formed by two parallel ridges or spurs with low, fairly deep ground in between them. Days ago, in the classroom, we were told to avoid draws because it was easy to get turned around in them. I did a brief reconnaissance of the area and couldn't see any well-worn path cutting across, meaning no one before me had found the path of least resistance across the draw. I had to take a risk and cross it where my compass was leading me. I slid down and reoriented myself on the map. Then, I climbed out and reoriented myself again.

After twenty steps, I found a wooden four-by-four pole on the ground (marker) with a puncher hanging on it. With my heart pounding from effort and anticipation, I sped up. I checked the coordinates on an index card attached to the post. Just as planned, I found my first point. Relief. After quickly punching a star-shaped hole in my scorecard next to the matching coordinates, I felt more confident. I oriented myself to the next point I had designated on my map and then I turned around and started running in its direction.

To make sure that I wasn't getting distracted by the terrain, I was checking my compass every twenty to twenty-five paces. I was also constantly watching my timer. Because I'd spent a couple of minutes in the draw area searching for paths, now I had to run a little faster to make up for the lost time. I crossed the dirt road. After about twenty minutes of negotiating the thick bush, I came upon a pair of candidates walking together in front of me. I passed them silently and kept on walking in my chosen direction. I didn't want to create even the smallest impression that I was communicating with others, meaning cheating. A few minutes later, I found myself in a small island-like clearing. Another post. The coordinates matched my scorecard. I punched in the triangle shape.

I looked around to check the terrain and orient myself to the map again. I went according to the paths I had drawn on my map. My pace count was correct. I easily found the third marker behind a small cluster of bushes. Punched a square-shaped hole. Some people were right behind me. Immediately, after making sure I found the correct marker, I took off to avoid any contact with others.

From that point on, I was jogging on mainly flat ground. Because I found myself in a rare, nonrestrictive terrain where walking was easier, I took advantage of it. I stopped for a few seconds and, using my compass, I verified the direction I was going. As a reference point, I picked a lonely birch tree far in the distance and then started moving quickly in its direction. Eventually, I came up to the road where I found another marker on a sandy patch. I checked the coordinates and punched the round hole in the scorecard.

According to my map, the fifth marker was on top of a hill. Despite being in the shaded, wooded area, away from the scorching midday sun, I was sweating profusely. My helmet seemed heavier by the minute. I was trembling from exhaustion and stress. And now I had to negotiate the hill. Luckily, it wasn't very steep. I was leaning forward, patiently counting every step, marching. I was convinced that the marker would be somewhere on that hill. I was right. I found it near the top on a slope, fairly visible from where I emerged. The hole I punched was cross-shaped.

To find my last point, I ran downhill to a spot where I needed to take a sharp turn to the north to avoid a pond. I knew this detour would cost me some time, but I chose to proceed with caution. Besides, I had about an hour left to complete the course and I wasn't too far from the finish line. After walking for another twenty minutes and constantly checking my orientation to the map, I decided to speed up. I was still shaking from stress and exertion. Even though I was confident that I had found my previous points correctly, I was anxious about the last one. I couldn't just quit. I trusted my plan; however, my mind was playing games. I had doubts about the path I had chosen. On the map, my last point was literally in the middle of nowhere. As I pressed forward, approaching the marker area, I was desperately looking for something that could be nearby, signifying the designated point. A clearing, a post, a big rock, or a patch of sand or gravel. I couldn't find anything but trees. Then, guided purely by intuition, I came up to a large tree to check my map. The marker was right behind it. The coordinates were correct, so I punched my scorecard for the last time. I now had thirty minutes to walk less than half a mile. It was doable. I'd regained my confidence.

This time, once I found the road and verified that I was going the correct way, I began my airborne shuffle. Soon, nearly breathless, I started passing soldiers aiming toward the finish line, walking almost casually.

At the assembly area, I had my scorecard checked by a TAC. I'd made the course with a fifteen minutes margin and found all my points correctly. This test was my third victory in Alabama.

*　　*　　*

After a couple of hours to regroup, during which the TAC officers and NCOs were trying to locate and "rescue" the personnel lost in the land navigation course, those who completed the test successfully were released. After dinner, we were taken back to the woods for the nighttime navigation test. This time, we had to correctly locate a minimum of four out of five points in five hours.

"You will navigate from one marker on the ground to another during the night using only a compass. The flashlights with red lenses can be used only to read the requirements sheet and to write your test answers. You will not use flashlights to negotiate the course," the instructor's voice resounded calmly in the heart of the land navigation training course, submerged in the dusk.

I took a deep breath and looked at the modest patch of flat, open terrain around me. I wanted to remember as much as possible about this place before it dissipated in the absolute darkness. I plotted the points on my map and quickly decided about the itinerary. Although time was against me from the moment the sun vanished behind the ridge, I felt confident. I trusted my alliance forged with the Fort McClellan woodland days before. Nonetheless, with only a few hours to complete the course, walking was not an option. As soon as I visualized my path, I surged into the woods like a charged missile. I cut through the branches and dense foliage of shrubbery without counting my paces and ran ardently in a direction carved in my mind. Without any major problems, I correctly located my first few markers on the ground and continued my itinerary, energized more than ever.

Suddenly, I stopped as my breath was taken away by a vertical wall of a wooded slope appearing right in front of me. I found myself at the foot of the hill, which, according to my map and my calculations, was holding my last marker. I could go around and attempt to find a dirt road leading directly to the hilltop. The other option was to continue directly uphill, a definitely risky option considering there was a quite steep elevation on this side of the mount. Before I knew it, I was carrying on this almost vertical pursuit, with my arms and elbows ripping apart thick foliage, frantically trying to hang on to the branches or tree trunks around me. The ground covered with dense, damp leaves was extremely slippery and forced me to mount this unforgiving obstacle on my hands and knees almost the entire time. Nothing mattered anymore except keeping the pace and staying on track. I knew the marker was there on the top. Like a sightless maniac relying exclusively on my sense of direction and distance, I continued climbing the waterfall of leaves and branches cascading down on me as if they wanted to swallow me whole. Drowning in the thick bush, I made one more desperate and excruciating effort to pull my body up. Suddenly, I burst out of the giant leafy wave and landed on a perfectly flat surface, gasping for air like a fish thrown out of the ocean. Above me, the most fantastic firmament was graciously smiling with millions of flickering stars. It was the top of the hill. Just a few steps away, a familiar silhouette of a lonely marker appeared in front of me.

Immediately after punching the hole in my scorecard, with a sense of pressing urgency, I began my descent. Knowing that I had found my last point to pass the test, my heart rejoiced with relief. I practically slid downhill, taking the same route I used to climb up. Almost instantaneously, I was cutting through the darkness at the speed of light. As I was dashing through the woods again, the tree branches were bouncing off my entire body, slamming into my face, and grabbing my map case as if they were trying to stop me. I kept in mind the small clearing near the dirt road, my starting point. According to my map, I should be shooting straight at this field. Despite my enormous trust in my compass and my intuition, my heart grew anxious. I still didn't see my clearing. Suddenly, I heard some voices coming from the nearby shrubbery.

"Are you lost, soldier? Do you need help?" a mysterious male voice asked.

Without stopping for a second, I continued my pursuit. We were not allowed to talk to anyone during the entire course. Since I already found all my markers, the risk of being disqualified was too high. Even if I was lost, I still had time to find the right path.

"Would you like a burger?" the voice insisted enticingly, but I remained mute as a stone.

Time was still of the essence, so I kept on running more restless than ever before. The terrain became suspiciously unfamiliar, and I suspected that I might have drifted off my course. I looked at the map and the compass, corrected my body position, and, with a newfound energy and focus, exploded again across the dense forest. I didn't even care when I found myself in a small creek passing through. "Just don't step on the damn snake, now," I said to myself cautiously. Several more minutes passed before my energy would diminish. The enormous pressure, the darkness, and the fidgety run after the illusive ending of the course caused my body and spirit to break down. My uniform was drenched in sweat, my boots were wet from the encounter with the creek, and my face was scratched up by branches. I was trembling from stress, hunger, and angst. Just when I was ready to collapse from exhaustion, I noticed a change in the tree pattern. The trees became slender and more dispersed, with much younger plants dominating. A brand-new energy surged through my body. Tears burst from my eyes. I started running again, afraid that what I saw could disappear into the darkness forever.

After all those agonizing hours of struggle, I finally emerged from the woods. Dashing through the fantastically refreshing open space, I recognized a small area at the edge of the glade near the road where we started the course that afternoon. Barely catching my breath from physical and emotional exhaustion, I slowed down on the dirt road. My mind was still replaying like a tape the very recent encounters with the forest darkness, the hill, and the creek. At last, my nocturnal battle with the woods was over.

I continued running on the dirt road, trembling when it finally registered to me that I was done, that I made it through the night land navigation. I had twenty minutes left to meet my timing. At that moment, I absolutely needed to find Lieutenant Brown. I had a strong feeling that she wanted me to pass this test the first time around. My fourth victory in Fort McClellan.

Eventually, I made it to the end of the road to an assembly area where all successful candidates were getting their scorecards verified and gathering to enjoy their accomplishments. To my enormous disappointment, I couldn't find Lieutenant Brown.

"You did good, kiddo." Sergeant Mathis appeared in front of me out of nowhere and I appreciated it.

"Have you seen Lieutenant Brown anywhere?" I replied, breathless.

"She already left for the day. She'll be back tomorrow."

At that point, although the presence of Sergeant Mathis was reassuring, I didn't feel like talking to or seeing anyone else. I had to enjoy my small victory alone and peacefully amid the surrounding commotion.

* * *

After the land navigation tests, everything slowed down. I felt isolated and misplaced, uprooted once more. I replayed in my mind the recent moments of my journey, which suddenly seemed like a very distant past. Just a couple of days prior, I was in the field teaching my class "How to evaluate the casualty." Lieutenant Brown was telling us spectacular stories about her experiences from training with her chemical battalion. During the breaks, I was teaching Lieutenant Brown and Lieutenant Caldwell Polish phrases, and we all laughed hard at their attempts to pronounce the words, twisting their tongues in all directions. Lieutenant Brown would drop me for push-ups every time I saluted her using a Polish version of greeting. I remembered the omnipresent Sergeant Mathis from Illinois, who somehow always emerged from the crowd in my best moments. His presence would always give me much-needed support and reassurance. I especially liked how he called me kiddo, even though I was one of the oldest soldiers in the company. The last time I saw him in Alabama, he said, "Okay, kiddo. See you in four weeks." I sensed he was confident that I would succeed in phase II in Pennsylvania and come back to Alabama for phase III.

Almost too quickly, all of this was behind me in a blink of an eye. It turned into memories I wanted to cherish forever.

* * *

The day following the tests from the land navigation, in the afternoon, we had a leadership reaction course. Because we had passed all the required tests already, this course was conducted to keep us busy and entertained. It was a series of eight tactical exercises designed for us to practice our leadership skills while negotiating various obstacles. There were six giant wooden booths with tall walls on three sides. Each booth was designated for a specific "scenario," an obstacle involving a negotiation of certain elements, like a "broken bridge" or deep water, to transport several cases of ammunition and personnel. To help negotiate these obstacles, we had at our disposal some wooden crates, two ropes, and a couple of steel pipes. Each obstacle involved crossing the "river or a pond" represented by a waist-high pool of water within each booth. We had twenty minutes to come up with a strategy for how to build various structures from given materials and to perform the crossing operation. We had to use our imagination, physical strength, and skills.

In the beginning, it was a fun, challenging course. Everyone on my team of eight was dropping into the water as our structures were falling apart. The ammo crates were ending at the bottom of the pool. Our uniforms, including combat boots, were soaking wet. At one time, we were finally successful at crossing one obstacle without ending up in the water. Once we found ourselves on the other side of the "river," we were elated and started jumping for joy. However, our excitement didn't last long. We got hosed down by amused TAC officers and ended up back in the "river."

At the last obstacle, we were also doing very well. Although my uniform was heavy from water and slippery, I was bravely claiming a makeshift "ladder" made from two steel pipes while pushing the ammo crate in front of me. I was almost at the edge of the bank when I felt one pipe slide toward me, knocking me down and hitting the back of my knee. For a moment, I hung on the other pipe for my dear life, then plunged into the water. I felt a sharp pain in my leg. As in the old adage, it was all fun and games until someone got hurt.

It turned out I was badly injured. The knee swelled up like a giant balloon and because bleeding under the skin was severe, almost instantly magnificent bruises started forming around my entire knee. Without finishing the exercise, I ran to the medics for ice, but they were already relieved of duty. I had to remain in the deserted barracks to lie down and keep my leg elevated. Being injured at this critical point of the training was bad news.

* * *

Dear Alec,

Phase I is coming to an end inevitably and tomorrow, I'm flying to Fort Indiantown Gap, Pennsylvania. To some extent, I feel relief and pride from my successful mission completed in the last two weeks. On the other hand, I feel uneasy because I'm about to leave this place after getting used to people, places, and routines. All we have left at this time is packing our duffle bags to be shipped to Penn State.

My two weeks here went by fast. I'm very relieved that I survived the unforgiving weather and passed out only once, without any significant consequences. However, I'm pretty upset that yesterday during an obstacle course, I got hit on the back of my knee with a steel pipe. The pain is so bad that I can barely function. I will have to get it checked in PA as soon as I arrive. Other than that, I had no major or spectacular episodes.

The buildings are deserted. Most of the people from the traditional program left home as their annual two weeks have concluded. The sudden silence in the area and the emptiness of the barracks are palpable. I despise relocating. Fortunately, I got reunited with Arroyo and Mathia from Illinois, and if I get really lucky, maybe I will end up with at least one of them in my next platoon.

* * *

The following day was our last official full day of phase I in Alabama. Everyone was packing their belongings and returning books and equipment. The out-processing was in full swing. Because we spent the entire previous day in the water in wet combat boots, some of us developed athlete's feet, infections, or fungus. Mine were bad enough that after checking with the doctor, I immediately got a profile to wear sneakers with white cotton socks and to avoid water. In addition, because of my knee injury, I was given a "no physical activity" profile. Since the pain was not subsiding, I had to spend any time I could in the barracks resting.

Around lunch, we had an organized trip to the PX (post exchange, a military store on base) where we could buy all the articles needed for phase II of our training. I was elated at being able to find CamelBak, one in camo color for my BDU and a black one for my PT uniform. We were told that although in Pennsylvania we would be spending most of the time in school halls, we would also be exposed to extreme heat and humidity.

Just like in Alabama, staying hydrated was the key and hydration packs were a necessity.

The next day, I felt alone and confused in the unknown barracks, hunkered down in emotional and physical pain in the dark corner of the female bay on the first floor. The place was as dingy as the Alfa barracks. My heart was heavy because I realized that something had ended. I even felt a certain melancholy. In my imagination, I could still see the commotion in this now deserted place. I could still hear the war screams and the running footsteps of the previous inhabitants of the bay, which was now immersed in the hunting silence. I was anxious about having to adjust to the new barracks for only one brief night, then after arriving in Pennsylvania, having to adjust yet again, this time for four weeks.

* * *

At the end of each phase, we had our "peer evaluations" and I was a little anxious about it, knowing that females are usually evaluated very low by males. The males typically thought that women shouldn't be in the OCS program with the "hard-core guys." The captain who was counseling me at the end told me I was doing good, to take one day at a time, and to stay confident.

However, the one thing from Fort McClellan that resounded in my heart the most was my last conversation with Lieutenant Brown.

"I looked through your peer evaluations. The people in your platoon appreciate your leadership skills," she stated with a note of satisfaction. Perhaps her own opinion of me was validated by my peers. Being appreciated by my peers meant a lot to me.

"Thank you for everything. You saved my life," I replied, heartbroken and uplifted at the same time. Heartbroken because I didn't know if I was seeing her for the last time. Uplifted because she saved my life by sending me to the medics for an IV. If she hadn't cared, she wouldn't have done that, and I could certainly have died from heatstroke.

"I was just doing my job."

Of course, she did, because she had a heart and she cared about those under her command. And that meant that she was a genuine leader.

After a loaded pause, she continued, "You know, you are only as good as the people around you. Surround yourself with good people. Don't take anything for granted."

It sounded like a goodbye. Would I ever see her again?

"I want to be like you, Lieutenant Brown," I whispered, looking her straight in the eyes as if I were telling her a secret.

"No, you don't want to be like me," she replied, glancing away as if she didn't want me to see her teary eyes.

I wondered why she didn't want me to be like her. In my eyes, she was a role model, an ideal with no vices. Did she have a secret? Was she just humble?

* * *

At this stage, again, it was best to blend in and just be part of a giant, constantly moving human machinery. More than in basic training, I was exposed to a faster than ever pace of daily routines. Everything was more complex and included being responsible not just for myself but for others as well. I also found out how far I could push my physical limits. While mentally I was more or less fit to survive the officer's training, my body took a serious beating. The good news was that even being one of the oldest, I wasn't the weakest. I didn't excel, but I was in the safe middle, able to keep up with the demanding physical training.

I also learned how to accomplish a mission alone. The land navigation course, especially at night, reminded me that many times in my life, I would have to negotiate various obstacles alone with minimal tools. I would have to trust my knowledge, experience, and my instincts to succeed, just like one day others would have to trust me with their lives.

CHAPTER 18

PATIENCE, LEADERSHIP, AND KINDNESS

A somewhat turbulent flight from Southwest Airlines ended with a thump on the airport platform. After a nearly two-hour flight, we landed at the Harrisburg International Airport in Pennsylvania. The day was still young when we unpacked the plane from our duffle bags and arranged them in neat rows ready for pickup. Then our over two-hundred-strong group in uniforms walked across the platform and entered the gate.

Once inside, to our surprise, we were welcomed with standing ovations from the passengers throughout the facility, shouting, "Thank you for your service!"

We mounted the military white buses waiting for us outside, and after about a thirty-minute ride, we were approaching Fort Indiantown Gap. My thoughts were revolving around what was waiting for me in this new phase of training at this new location. As usual, facing the unknown, I was quite nervous.

From what we were told before, phase II was four weeks of training primarily in a classroom environment. I thought about all the classes I was about to get through, from leadership doctrine, combat service support, field artillery, military intelligence, to tactics. Would all the writing assignments and oral briefings be doable for me? I knew the expectations were high again; a mastery of the leadership skills about which I still was quite insecure. In addition, we were expected to complete a three, six, nine and twelve-mile road march, plus a two-mile run. How and when would I be able to run with my injury? Will it be a major obstacle for me in this phase? But most of all, the various leadership courses and field training exercises were to me a big mystery that I wasn't looking forward to because it was hard for me to imagine myself leading troops through the challenging tasks. Finally, there was the combat water survival training. What was that all about? I was sure that we definitely wouldn't be going to the beach. This was going to be a completely different adventure, and I didn't know what to expect.

I was also wondering how we were going to be treated here, what kinds of rules we would have to follow this time around, and which opportunities for getting "smoked" would prevail. Despite my angst, I was doing my best to stay calm and collected and not anticipate too much. My primary focus was to take care of my knee injury by going on a sick call as soon as possible.

At the reception building, we spent several hours standing in long lines, taking care of extensive paperwork. The atmosphere, at least for the time being, was casual and friendly.

At some point, I was approached by the posts' military reporter, a specialist, who asked me for a brief interview. I gladly agreed, as this was an excellent opportunity for a distraction from the mundane in-processing.

"Why did you join the army?"

"As an immigrant, I wanted to thank my new country for the opportunities I have been given," I replied. "I wanted to be part of the most powerful armed forces in the world, be part of a team of those who fight for the values of equality, liberty, and democracy for all," I added with pride.

Yes, I was proud to be part of something bigger than me and to have goals beyond the everyday tasks I used to have at home. I was proud that I had stepped up and said "yes" to my America. And since less than 1 percent of Americans were serving the country at any given time, I was proud to be part of the elite for whom doing extraordinary things was our job.

* * *

After the in-processing, we were allocated to our barracks and rooms. The red-brick buildings were fairly new, very well maintained, and reminded me of college dorms. We were assigned two persons per room within a two-room suite sharing a bathroom. There were no bunk beds, and the interior reminded me of a medium-class hotel. I was pleasantly surprised.

Later, I had some time to go to sick call to have my knee looked over. It was still badly bruised and fairly swollen. Luckily, I got some ice from the nearby DFAC. My profile was for no marching, no jumping, and no running. I could only hope for my leg to heal in time for me to pass the PT test and complete all required road marches. The first march was a three-miler and was to take place in one week. I needed to heal fast.

* * *

The next day, as I was leaving the DFAC, I walked into two TAC officers. Lieutenant Holmes and Major Effiert stopped me as I was slowing down to salute them and extend my greeting: "Gentlemen, Officer Candidate Rakowski. Good afternoon, gentlemen!"

"She's cool," said Major Effiert to the lieutenant.

"No," replied the lieutenant, "she's hot."

I took it as an innocent game of words. I wasn't about to debate if I was "cool" or "hot" because neither of these words seemed appropriate for a female officer candidate, anyway.

"She is aware of what time of the day it is," continued the major, referring to me in the third person as if I weren't there. "Teach these knuckleheads from Bravo (Company) the times of the day and a proper military greeting," he concluded, referring to my counterpart company.

"Sir, Officer Candidate Rakowski. Yes, sir."

"She's famous," continued amused Lieutenant Holmes with a hint of pride.

I used all my willpower to keep my composure and not burst into laughter. I had to be a quiet observer of this game.

"Oh yeah, why?" asked the major.

"She speaks like a million languages. What languages do you speak, Candidate Rakowski?"

"Sir, Officer Candidate Rakowski. I speak English, Polish, French, and Russian, sir."

"Great," said the major with relief. "Then teach the Bravos, *The House of Pain* in all languages you know." He giggled with satisfaction. "As you were, candidate."

Although I sensed that Major Effiert was joking about my task, the same afternoon, I went to the Bravo Company barracks and attempted to teach them *The House of Pain* in the languages I knew. I created the letter-size sheets with the phrases with phonetic spellings and passed them around until most of the soldiers got the hang of the words. Although on the surface this exercise seemed funny, this wasn't a laughing matter. We all had to be prepared for the worse at all times, be it physical or psychological punishment, for a good measure. And the Bravos didn't have it easy. From what I had gathered, they were more miserable than the Alfas because their TAC officers had more complex imaginations and therefore, the punishments were sometimes brutal. It made me appreciate my company more, where we just had to run and do push-ups and sit-ups at any given moment for any or no reason at all.

* * *

Soon enough, we had the change of command for the first rotation of the leadership positions in the Alfa Company. The new company commander, company executive officer, and first sergeant were now my fellow officer candidates. In addition, platoon-level positions (platoon leader and platoon sergeant) were also now assigned to the candidates. There wasn't much time to prepare, as these positions were only given a few hours before the change of command ceremony. The ceremony was fairly complex. The outgoing and incoming personnel at the company level would stand in front of four platoons in a specific configuration. Then the outgoing commander would symbolically relinquish responsibility and authority by passing the company colors to the incoming commander. It was to ensure that the unit and its soldiers were "never without" official leadership. Then the salutes were exchanged, and the new company first sergeant would address the company. The rest of the leadership would then take their specific posts within the formation, depending on who would be in charge of the company. I watched the first change of command with anguish. As the candidates in new leadership roles were attempting to complete the ceremony, TAC officers would surround them and try to "break them."

"And, Bradfield, do you know what to do? Then how can you be the company commander? What kind of example are you setting?" the TACs screamed in the new candidate-commander's face, trying to distract him from following the protocol.

"And now what do you do, do you salute or not? Just start crying or, better yet, go home now! This job is too hard for you!"

The candidates taking over the command were scrambling, trying to concentrate on the task at hand. The entire company watched in horror how one officer candidate was brought to tears and failed under pressure, unable to take charge as the company's new first sergeant. The entire company was in front of them, with four platoons of soldiers nervously waiting, watching the teasing, the psychological torture designed to break the bravest, the strongest, and the toughest. I knew that at any moment I could be chosen for the infamous role of first sergeant. There was no need to volunteer to be destroyed and publicly humiliated by the TAC officers in front of the entire company. I was praying to never find myself in that miserable position.

"Come on! Take the company colors, 'commander'! Just about now! Are you shaking? Are you scared?" TACs shouts and pacing around continued.

"Who wants the safety blanket, or a teddy bear, or maybe a hug?"

I trembled. This reminded me of my request for a hug in Alabama expressed as a joke. But here, there was no joking around. I wouldn't dare. Here, the intimidation and screaming seemed endless. Those candidates who could successfully survive this brutal assault had my attention. My lesson learned from observing this change of ceremony was to know the drill step-by-step with every detail. But most of all, keep a cool mind and don't let yourself get distracted or discouraged.

* * *

By the third day, I'd gotten used to the new fast pace of the school environment. Although we were spending most of our time on classroom instruction, we began our field exercises almost immediately. We would go to the nearby wooded area to practice our leadership, reasoning, and organizational skills during the exercises like SDLX (short-duration training exercise) conducted in a tactical environment. For example, we had an exercise on how to build "sand tables." The sand table was a shallow, four-by-four-foot wooden box without a lid and filled with sand.

In the box, we had to create a tridimensional "miniature map" of a specific battlefield based on an actual military map. Sand tables were used for military planning and wargaming, and training for military actions.

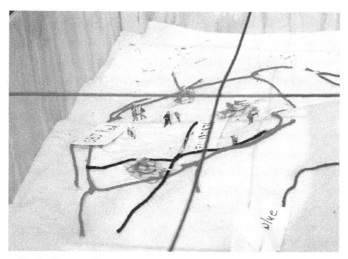

In the box, we had to create a tridimensional "miniature map" of a specific battlefield based on an actual military map.

The box reminded me of a construction painting, where in addition to paint and brush, various two and tridimensional objects could be used. Years ago, I'd built a painting like this for Chris. It was an abstract night landscape of a forest preserve where Chris lived. Dark hues of blue, purple, and green dominated the artwork. Five yellow plastic pieces represented the stars dispersed in the skies.

Now, at our disposal, we had sticks, cords (to mark supply lines), rocks (for defensive positions), ribbons (for main highways), flags (for ammo caches), matches (for barricades), stones (for terrain features), spiral wire (for concertina wires), miniature models of vehicles, as well as plastic models of other artillery and air defense weapons. At the end of the exercise, Lieutenant Jones gave me a positive review of my map-building skills.

"You have an excellent memory, Rakowski. You are building these maps like pictures. Everything is perfectly clear." This helped me gain some much-needed confidence. I constantly needed reassurance in this new environment, where I had so much to learn.

That same evening, Lieutenant Jones asked me everything about my background, then gave me a task to distribute the next day's operational orders to my class. I was honored to be entrusted even with the smallest tasks. It would give me an opportunity to demonstrate my readiness for the future big ones. At the end of the day, he ordered me to write a positive spot report for organizational skills. Spot reports were used to record cadre observations and form the basis for counseling. They were green cards to be filled out by candidates. We had to carry a stack of blank green cards with us at all times and use them when directed by a TAC officer. At the end of each leadership rotation, every forty-eight hours, these reports were collected by the cadre for candidates' evaluations. There was tremendous pressure to perform well and to collect as many positive reports as possible so that the final training evaluation would be positive, which was a condition to stay in the program. In addition, positive spot reports were an excellent confidence-building tool. And confidence in a future leader of troops was a key to success.

* * *

My next few days were filled with classroom instruction during the day and tests in the evenings. The classes were intense. Everything heard during the lectures had to be memorized almost instantly. There was no time designated for individual studies after school. I felt the pressure with this tempo. With every new block of instruction, I had doubts I wouldn't be able to absorb all the information fast enough and with almost no margin for error. I considered myself lucky that so far, I had successfully passed the tests of training management, operations, force XXI, and leadership. And that was enough to keep me going.

Even though we were mostly in the school hall, the time spent in the field was taking a toll on me. As a previous heat casualty, I kept in my mind that the scorching heat and humidity in Pennsylvania were my enemies. Our exercises were usually taking place in the middle of the day, the worst time for heat exposure. Wearing the heavy Kevlar helmet and load-bearing equipment wasn't helping either.

On day six, we had one of our many STXs (situational training exercises). Each iteration was called the "STX line."

In one of these scenarios, we were running through the woods as a platoon trying to locate our defensive positions near our weapons cache.

Time was of the essence because the enemy was fast approaching. Our task was to locate and retrieve the weapons and ammunition from the cache, then take our positions to meet the enemy and respond to possible fire. My movement reminded me of the day land navigation course I recently completed in Alabama. Anxious to keep up with the pace of my platoon leader, I was feeling weaker with every step. My legs were trembling from the effort every time my rifle was catching tree branches throughout the run, nearly knocking me off balance. After about ten minutes of running, I felt my head boiling under the Kevlar and my uniform drenched. Now, my entire body was quivering. As I continued my pursuit, I saw the trees closing in on me like the walls in a claustrophobic box. Various images from my recent past—the training in Alabama, the flight on Southwest Airlines, and the classrooms in Pennsylvania—started spinning in my brain in multiple colorful images, like in a fast-turning kaleidoscope. My sweat was burning my face, so I could barely keep my eyes open. In a moment of distraction, I caught a tree root protruding from the ground. Before I knew it, I was flying forward headfirst, then quickly landing with a loud thump with my face in the foliage. At first, because of my fiery headache, I didn't notice that at landing, my face hit something hard.

 Perez, who was running behind me, witnessed the entire fall, rushed to help, and called for medics in the process. He pulled me from the ground covered in leaves and dirt and looked horrified. I felt a cool, metallic liquid on my lips. I disregarded it, thinking that I had busted only my lip. However, once Perez lifted me, I felt the full extent of my injury. A waterfall of blood from my nose flew straight into my chin. He placed me in a sitting position against the tree, took off my helmet, and evaluated me for fractures. I wasn't able to stay in a sitting position for long and kept rolling down. Perez was making his best efforts to keep me calm, calling our location to the medics, who were approaching us with the stretcher. Then, with his handkerchief soaked in water, he padded my boiling face. When the medics arrived, quite a commotion had built around the scene of my accident. Judging by the look on my classmates' faces, my bloodstained face was disturbing.

 Shortly after, I was transported on the stretcher to the ambulance for further evaluation. There, I vomited all over the ambulance's floor and nearly collapsed from exertion and stress. It turned out that in addition to falling victim to heat exhaustion, I cracked the base of my nose. I was given an IV and quarters (time off) for the rest of the day. However, knowing that this afternoon we would have a test from leadership, I requested my platoon leader for help in getting to school for the afternoon classes.

* * *

On the morning of day eight, I received a clearance from the doctor for marching. My knee was almost healed, and I needed to build my strength for future road marches in the field. The morning air was crisp, and I was hopeful and energized about participating in the morning PT, which on that day was the two-mile run. Because I wasn't able to run yet, I joined a small group of other injured candidates walking behind the running formation. That day, for the first time since arriving in phase II, I was wearing my PT uniform: shorts and a short-sleeved T-shirt. I was in good spirits and kept a good walking pace, leading the "handicaps" group.

Suddenly, I heard a voice behind me: "What the hell happened to you, SKI?" I turned around to make sure that Major Moon's question was in fact directed at me. "Yes, what did you do to your knee?!" reiterated the major.

I realized that by wearing shorts, my injured knee was now exposed, and the view must have been quite dramatic.

"Yes, sir, Officer Candidate Rakowski." I stopped for a second so he could catch up with me. "No big deal. I just got hit with the steel pipe at the obstacle course in Alabama. It's healing nicely. You see? It's purple! My favorite color!"

The major giggled, most likely amused by my upbeat spirit. I enjoyed making others laugh.

"Good job for making a good effort! Carry on!"

* * *

That afternoon, knowing that we would have one of the most challenging blocks of instruction for me, which is field artillery, I was apprehensive. At first, I felt good at school. I was rehydrated; I had a fresh uniform, and my nose stopped bleeding the night before. The building was cool and quiet. As the afternoon hours were passing by, I did my best to pay attention and take copious notes. Despite the throbbing headache, I was determined to pass the field artillery test that evening. Field artillery was never my strength. Until now, my training was strictly focused on military intelligence, and I felt quite comfortable with this subject. Field artillery, on the other hand, was not only new to me, but it was also overwhelming. It was all about tactics, techniques, and procedures for the use of fire support systems in combat. The number of various types of weapons specializing in mobility, tactical proficiency, and short-range, long-range, and extremely long-range target engagement was staggering. All the guns, howitzers, and mortars were confusing. I was getting easily distracted by the extreme amount of information, like weapons' names, symbols, and applications. I felt that one afternoon of instruction would not suffice for me to retain all the material.

When I found out that I failed the test, I was devastated. I felt defeated and demoralized. I knew that these kinds of mistakes could cost me the entire phase II of the OCS. I just couldn't afford to add more stress to my journey. Regardless, I went to a study hall that evening with a small group of others who failed. We were afforded a second chance in the form of a retest the following morning.

For some reason, during the study hall, I felt more at ease. As if some burden was lifted off my shoulders. I kept a cool head and controlled my composure as much as I could. When I convinced myself that I would have a successful retest no matter what, I relaxed and studied hard. I asked questions and requested clarifications for areas I didn't understand.

"Good job, Candidate Rakowski," Major Roberts complimented my participation in our studies. "By the way, you are going to be an excellent intelligence officer because your reasoning and information analysis are spot-on."

I was thankful and uplifted. This comment gave me confidence in my abilities. I knew I would not disappoint Major Roberts the following morning.

It was day nine, Sunday. The entire group of those aiming for the "second chance" headed to school before dawn. The starry firmament and the full moon were our companions. After two hours of the most concentrated effort I could muster, I finally conquered the test with a minimum passing score. I was ecstatic. However, I promised myself to never allow the situation where I have to go through a retest again. Regardless of circumstances.

Later that day, Lieutenant Holmes stopped me on my way to the barracks and told me to write a positive spot report for asking for help during the study for the retest.

"I know English is not your first language. Always ask if you don't understand something. Good job."

He patted my shoulder. I had someone on my side, and it felt good.

Because my morning was dedicated to the retest, I missed the first company road march. Since it was a three-miler, it would have been a great opportunity to build up my physical stamina after being incapacitated for many days due to my knee injury. I grew anxious when I realized that the next road march was scheduled in only four days and unfortunately, it was a six-miler. At that point, I decided to use every viable opportunity to walk and exercise hard during our morning PT. I knew that physical strength and motivation were the keys to survival in OCS.

* * *

As much as I was able to exercise in the morning darkness before school, remaining in good shape during the midday field exercises had proven to be more challenging than I had anticipated. Knowing that I had become a heat casualty twice within a short period, every time we were in the field in the sun, I had to be aware of any symptoms leading to a possible heatstroke.

The day after my successful retest, we were practicing one of our "STX lines." This time, our task was to establish our individual fighting positions. After crawling through the woods, we had to spread out in an open field with minimal grass coverage. On my back, I was dragging the M60 machine gun, just over twenty-three pounds of weight, in addition to my helmet and load-bearing equipment. As I was negotiating the grassy area, I could feel the heat under my helmet and the all-so-familiar throbbing headache. I managed to crawl through the clearing to the wood line and was hunkered down by the bush. Keeping an eye on my weapon, I removed the helmet to catch some fresh air. I was sweating profusely and shivering. Attempting to control my body heat, I took one of my canteens and poured some water straight on my simmering head. Suddenly, I felt dizzy and nauseous. That's when I decided to signal my TAC officer about my condition. He instructed me to go to the ambulance with Candidate Michaud to get checked. Just as I made it to the vehicle on my cotton-like, shaky legs, I vomited violently on its rear tire. Minutes later, I had my IV drip installed.

I was dragging the M60 machine gun, just over twenty-three pounds of weight, in addition to my helmet and load-bearing equipment.

After this near-heatstroke episode, I went to sick call for meds for nausea and headaches. To my surprise, a crowd of nearly forty soldiers was filling up the entire floor. One of the platoons from the Bravo Company was in the emergency care waiting to be seen. It was Mathia's platoon. Apparently, a couple of days before, they had been punished for something by their TAC officer by crawling in a dirty dry creek bed. All candidates had infected elbows, forearms, and hands, and ended up with bandages one after another. I thanked the higher powers that my company's TACs were not as extreme.

* * *

On the evening of day ten, I took over the position of platoon leader. The change of command at the platoon level was informal. This time around, after my experience as a platoon leader in phase I in Alabama, I had more confidence in fulfilling my duty for the next forty-eight hours. Almost instantly, I had my hands full of new responsibilities. It quickly became overwhelming. I didn't even realize how many mundane activities required my full attention and how critical it was to make sure that everyone was accounted for and taken care of at all times.

During my second day as a platoon leader, I continued to monitor my platoon's accountability, remind them about hydration, and emphasize their physical and mental fitness. In addition, I received an assignment from Lieutenant Jones to prepare for him a briefing about motivating soldiers, operating actions, executing, and assessing. The goal of the assignment was to gain knowledge on how to build the confidence of troops from hard and realistic training. Although intellectually appealing and practical, the written assignments were time-consuming and a bit distracting from my schoolwork. However, as a future leader, I knew that the best time of learning from these assignments was during my leadership rotations.

Besides keeping an eye on my typical tasks as a platoon leader, I stayed focused on my school activities. This time around, we had a military intelligence operations class, which, for obvious reasons (being trained for months in Fort Huachuca as an MI soldier) was my favorite class. Because I felt comfortable with the material, it was very easy for me to stay engaged in a lecture. When the class was asked what military intelligence was all about, I couldn't help but raise my hand.

"Military intelligence is the information about the battlefield situation collected from humans, images, signals, and measurements used to provide guidance and direction to commanders to assist them in their decisions. The intelligence taskings are satisfied by collection, organization, processing, exploitation, analysis, and reporting of information," I recited almost in one breath.

"Are you sure you aren't the MI officer already?" asked our instructor, Major Rosier, amused.

The entire class applauded and was equally entertained. At the end of the instruction, I had the highest test score in the class from this block of instruction. The test not only validated my knowledge but also gave me the sense that I was belonging to the right place. This was my first and last opportunity to shine in school. I knew I wouldn't be able to become an expert in anything during phase II. Military intelligence was my comfort zone.

Although the military intelligence operations class and the test were the highest points of my day, just as important was to me the feedback I received from Lieutenant Jones during the counseling about my platoon leader's ending duties. I had earned some negative spot reports: for McFarlan not having water, for Polly going to a sick call without telling anybody, for low platoon motivation during the morning PT, and for a piece of blue thread found on my uniform at some point of the day. I also earned some positive reports: for the platoon being on time at every location as planned, for accountability after the sick call, for assuring the study materials were secured for those coming back from the sick call, for encouraging hydration, for leading by example by being active during the military intelligence class, and for achieving the highest score on the test. Overall, my rotation as a platoon leader was my first small victory in Pennsylvania.

At the end of the day, while relinquishing our duties to the next set of candidates taking over the platoon leader and platoon sergeant positions, both Michaud and I were proclaimed the 3rd Platoon's "dynamic duo" and the best pair of leaders thus far. Any positive feedback was helpful in shaping me as a future officer. I needed to perform well and having Michaud as a partner helped me in building my always-craved confidence.

That evening, the letters from the families and loved ones back home were distributed to my platoon. Unfortunately, since my arrival in Pennsylvania eleven days ago, I hadn't received any letters from Alec, and that made me worried. The only one in the group without a letter, I was wondering what could have been happening at home to prevent him from writing to me. Was he busy or forgot about me? I chose to think he was busy. Having so much on my plate here, I couldn't afford to be distracted by the situation at home. It was the best for me to believe that Alec's support continued.

*   *   *

America's birthday was my first opportunity to participate in a road march in Pennsylvania. While excited, I thought about my knee injury and the very minimal amount of physical activities I was performing so far. I also remembered that because of my field artillery retest, I missed my first road march, which would have potentially helped to build up my physical stamina. However, I was hopeful the injury had healed enough to allow me to be successful in this six-mile road march. I was also anxious about being able to march fast enough to stay with my platoon at all times without falling out of the formation. Being at the end was the worst imaginable situation, as it was hard in this position to keep up with those in the front with no one behind. It could quickly become a very lonely stroll. In addition, this march was especially important because it was a timed event—the fastest platoon would be the winner. The condition was that the entire platoon had to arrive at the finish line in a tight formation, with no one falling behind. I didn't want to be the reason for our platoon to fail.

At dawn, we formed in front of our barracks as a company and then we filled in the white buses, which were taking us into the marching area in the woods. On our bus, the driver turned on the radio and we heard the national anthem. With our arms enveloping the rucksacks on our laps, we sang along as if going to a battle.

The sun, in all shades of gold, was slowly rising among the tree lines. The soft clouds of fog were gently lifting above the ground, leaving the morning dew behind in our staging area. Waiting for a signal to move, we made a makeshift camp on the side of the road by arranging our gear in a circle. With our guidon proudly dancing in the morning breeze, we were sitting on the ground singing army songs to keep our spirits up. Before falling into our marching formation, I asked my platoon leader to put me in the front of the left row as a pacesetter. Being short and injured, it was the best position to keep up the good walking pace by actually setting it. This position would allow me to keep focused on marching forward and others following me without being distracted by the possibility of falling out of the formation. Setting a good pace for everyone behind me was an enormous responsibility that I was gladly willing to take on. The platoon leader, although skeptical at first, considering my size and knowing about my knee injury, let me convince him that designating me as a pacesetter was a good idea.

We formed up in two single files on both sides of the road in a staggered formation, with our weapons facing outward. Our TAC officers, Lieutenant Jones and Captain Kucera, started with me on the front. I set my watch and off we went. At the first mile marker, I knew that a healthy sixteen minutes per mile walk was my current pace.

After a while of marching on solid pavement, it started getting hot. Despite being protected from the direct sunlight by the foliage, I could feel the load of my gear and weapons weighing heavily. Because of the stiffness of my knee, I felt a lot of discomfort, but I pressed on. In the middle of the second mile, I sped up slightly to gain some timing before the three-mile turnaround point. I noticed that our TAC, Captain Kucera, was slowing down, so I encouraged her to keep up with me.

"Captain Kucera!" I waved to her. "Please join me at the front and let's win this thing!"

Then she jogged for a few steps to catch up with me.

"I can barely keep up with you, Rakowski," she gasped at every word. "Where did you learn to march like this?"

It seemed like she was genuinely interested.

"I did some hard-core competitive marching in Fort Huachuca last year."

And to keep the captain entertained, I told her the entire history of my German badge competitions.

Before we knew it, we reached the turnaround point, with everyone catching their breath. The platoon leader, Mayers, was delighted that we had made it this far in one intact group.

"We have no time for rest," I whispered to Mayers. "We need to walk right away. Just let them fill the canteens and let's go."

"Are you trying to kill us?" he whispered back, as if trying to keep our conversation secret.

"No, I'm trying to win!"

In a matter of a few seconds, we formed back up on both sides of the road and restarted our walk. Captain Kucera joined me promptly and promised to stay with me in the front. For the next three miles, I kept my pace of sixteen minutes per mile. However, I wanted to make sure that we won the competition. That's why when I saw the finish line about a hundred meters in front of me, I started my airborne shuffle. Captain Kucera nearly fainted when she noticed I was now jogging.

"Come on, captain, let's finish strong!"

I remembered the words of First Sergeant Owen from Fort Huachuca: "It doesn't matter how you start; it matters how you finish."

"Let's finish strong." More voices resounded behind me like an echo. Everyone followed my lead, and we got to the finish line double timing in a perfect formation.

We won that race. We received a streamer to attach to our guidon as a trophy. Everyone was elated by our success. People were thanking me for setting the pace for our victory.

"Some people run slower than your walking pace, Rakowski," remarked Captain Kucera.

I was grateful for this unexpected compliment. I never thought about my marching compared to running.

"And write yourself a positive spot report for setting a great pace and leading by example."

I felt good to hear it from Lieutenant Jones. After all, he was my TAC and role model.

The platoon leader came up to me to shake my hand.

"Thank you. We couldn't have done it without you!"

I knew that being in charge of a platoon was a lot of pressure for him, but he wasn't alone and knew how to appreciate it.

"You're an outstanding leader of a great team, Mayers."

My friendly wink was my way of appreciating him. For me, on the other hand, staying in front of the platoon was my second personal victory in Pennsylvania.

* * *

Dear Alec,

I had a very tough last forty-eight hours two days ago. I was assigned to a platoon leader position and was responsible for nearly forty people for two days. These rotations are very challenging, as I have to keep track of everyone at all times and make sure everyone's needs are met. In addition, I have to write spot reports pretty much about everything I encounter or about my qualities and shortcomings. It's time-consuming, but that's the game. Everything I do is constantly evaluated, especially when I am in a leadership position. I have to really pay attention to everything I'm doing. Luckily, I have some experience from phase I in Alabama.

Thank you for the care package you sent me. Since it contained candy (contraband), I had to give most of it to the platoon members. Fortunately, my fellow candidates didn't like the candy too much, so I still have plenty left for me. I absolutely love it because it's from you and it doesn't matter how it tastes.

Yesterday was the Fourth of July and quite a challenging day for our company because we had a six-mile road march in this extreme heat. You can imagine how afraid I was to march after my recent heat exhaustion. As a pacesetter, I walked my faster pace, but a bit slower than the Fort Huachuca speed. The platoon stayed very motivated the entire time and nobody fell out of the formation. We ended up winning the competition. Everybody was so excited that we were singing the entire way back on the bus. Later, our TAC officer said to me: 'Good job, Rakowski. You just set the new standard.' It felt good to hear that because I always try to make my best effort to keep the highest standards.

Today, we spent almost the entire day in the woods learning about army field communications equipment. Several long tables were set up, displaying machines and a variety of tactical radios supporting tactical communications and conducting large-scale combat operations. It was an interesting and fun block of instruction.

"Tonight was another change of command drill where a new set of candidates was taking over the company leadership. It was brutal. TAC officers managed to bring to tears two big men. One was taking over the company commander's role and when he was yelled at and teased, he couldn't render a proper salute. He quivered and then got dropped for push-ups. The other one was taking over the role of the company's first sergeant. This was even worse: he couldn't call the company to attention and forgot the drill and the commands. We could barely hear his voice of command because he was crying. He got dropped as well. At least he could do the push-ups. Under tremendous pressure, they both broke down and got eventually replaced, so the procedures could continue with more appropriate candidates. Either way, it was a horrifying sight, and I can't imagine being in this situation!

* * *

Eventually, I received a doctor's clearance for running. The timing was perfect as it gave me an opportunity to participate in my first run in Pennsylvania. It was a slow-paced, three-mile battalion run designed to improve candidates' physical endurance. I anticipated it for a while; however, I was a little apprehensive about my physical capabilities. By now, I knew I was able to walk everywhere at a normal pace and road march at a medium-fast pace, but running was still a mystery..

Even though it was Sunday, it was still a usual day. At dawn, we formed up on the quad as two companies. The run was taking place in a wooded area on a perfectly paved road. I was always the most anxious at the start line because tall men at the front liked to set a pace that was too fast for most of the candidates. An inappropriate pace would cause the formation to stretch out of proportion and cause slower runners to first fall to the back of the formation, then eventually fall out of the formation altogether. Since this was a battalion run, the idea was for the two companies to stay together.

Fortunately, the tempo was medium-fast, and I could stay with my platoon for most of the run. However, the last half of a mile was a struggle. Every twenty meters or so, I was slowly falling back. Eventually, row by row, I found myself at the end of the platoon. My legs were on fire, and I could barely catch my breath. Then I remembered my last battalion run in Fort Huachuca nearly a year ago. It was a grueling ascent up the Heritage Hill, where we were to assemble in the middle of the run for the change of command under a double rainbow. I remembered, despite the struggle with running uphill, how I stayed focused and positive and how, from the end of the formation, I had mustered enough courage and persistence to continue pushing forward. Finally, I remembered how I was doing everything in my power to prevent Geraldo from stopping and how we had run together until the end. These memories gave me a much-needed boost of strength. Now, I imagined that each terrain elevation was my Heritage Hill, to be conquered one at a time. I was about twenty meters behind the formation already and on my last breath, but I continued running. A few people behind me stopped running and opted for walking. I knew that if I started walking now, I wouldn't be able to pick up the pace on the last stretch. About fifty meters in front of me, at the finish line, the battalion was forming back up. Suddenly, I noted a silhouette dashing toward the group of stragglers and joining us. It was Major Moon, my company commander.

"Let's go, Rakowski!" I needed any support I could get, and his shouting in my ear was welcomed. "Some people are running sixteen minutes a mile and still falling out. I know you're faster than that." When we finally crossed the finish line, he said, "Good job for hanging in there." I loved when someone was helping me at the finish line, when I needed it most.

My head was throbbing, and I was nauseous from the effort. Before I could join the formation, I needed to dash behind a tree and vomit. Overall, because I endured and didn't stop running, this event was my third small victory in Pennsylvania.

Later that day, I went to a sick call, still with nausea and headache, where I met Lieutenant Holmes. He asked me how I was feeling.

"Sir, Officer Candidate Rakowski. I'm doing my best, sir."

That was the expected reply. I couldn't tell him that, in reality, I felt miserable. That would be disappointing, even for me.

"I know you're always doing your best. I can see that."

* * *

The following day, we continued our SDLX (short-duration training exercise) scenarios in a tactical environment (the wooded area on base). That morning was my turn to be in charge of our platoon in an assigned scenario. We were given a map of the area and the geographical coordinates of an alleged enemy ammo supply point. Our mission was to locate this ammo point and confirm its location. We were to stay put without engaging the enemy, then retreat and report back to the command. A whistle from one of the TAC officers was a signal for the end of the exercise.

At the tree line, our starting point, I gathered my platoon and plotted the ammo point, as well as our current location, on a map. In my head, I quickly designed a tactical approach to my mission. I choreographed it like a dance.

We started with marching for about fifty meters through a thick brush in a single file formation, straight toward the target. I was leading from the front. About twenty-five meters from the enemy's location, I gave the sign to stop, and from this point on, I was giving signals for the single file to split. While continuing the move, one soldier would go about thirty degrees to the left and one to about thirty degrees right, flanking the enemy in semicircles from both sides. There was about a ten-pace distance between soldiers. Eventually, we surrounded the enemy in a complete circle and through a line of trees, we could see them moving around their area, arranging the boxes of ammunition. The enemy's location was confirmed. I gave my platoon the sign to get down on the ground and stay put. Leading by example, I assumed the prone position with my rifle pointed at the enemy. The enemy (three TAC officers playing the roles) was unsuspecting and continued their activities. I waited for a few minutes to observe the area. I was ready to give the signal to retreat the same way we came to the target, then meet with Lieutenant Jones in the clearing by the tree line. Suddenly, to my surprise, my platoon members started coming out of their hiding positions, charging the enemy. We were close enough to surprise them and even engage in hand-to-hand combat. Every soldier involved in this confrontation was "killed" and we "lost" half of our people. I called the headquarters on the radio to give a situational report and was ordered to retreat. The whistle sounded off.

I was disappointed with the results of my mission because my fellow candidates acted directly against my orders and against the overall mission.

During the after-action review, Captain Robins (one of the enemy role players) admitted that they were all caught by surprise at the ammo point.

However, because they had the power as instructors, they punished those who charged by "killing" them.

"This was a well-designed and thought-through tactical approach," said Lieutenant Jones, and I believed he was objective. "And if they had listened to your orders, there wouldn't have been any casualties. Great job."

"You have to listen to your leader," added Captain Robins, addressing the platoon. "You can't just do your own thing and charge the enemy because it seems like a good idea. By making your own decisions, you just undermined the orders of your leader." It wasn't a good feeling to be undermined, and I was glad that the captain pointed it out.

"And Rakowski's orders were very clear," added Lieutenant Langford (another role player). "Confirm the location and retreat. No engaging the enemy."

That's right. Even though I had a distinct Polish accent, my English wasn't so bad that they would not understand my orders.

Everyone listened in silence.

"Otherwise, this was a good exercise."

I was glad that Lieutenant Jones's overall conclusion was positive. In my mind, I marked the event as a fourth small victory in Pennsylvania.

As we were walking out of the area, Michaud patted my shoulder.

"I know why these knuckleheads didn't listen to your orders."

"Because I don't have a dick," I interjected with frustration. I remembered from my previous peer evaluations that females were unwelcomed by male candidates and perceived as weaker kind.

"But that doesn't mean you don't have balls." His wink provided much-needed reassurance, especially coming from a male.

* * *

Later in the evening, I was informed by Lieutenant Jones that in twenty-four hours, I would be taking charge of the company as first sergeant. The dreaded company-level position. Despite all my worries about ever finding myself in this position, at this moment, I had no other option but to embrace it. Deep down I thought that if I fail, it would be a failure in something significant and challenging and it would be an excellent lesson learned. Failing in an easy position would just be an embarrassment. On the other hand, there was always a possibility of success. And success in something significant and challenging would be priceless.

"I don't know why, but I like you." I sensed he meant it in a good way. "And I'm giving you a homework assignment as preparation for your first sergeant role. I need you to study the 'command voice.' Report back to me with the results no later than 2100 hours."

I realized I had received this assignment to learn how to effectively address the entire company as the company's first sergeant. My natural voice was relatively quiet, and it would be impossible for over a hundred people in a formation to hear my mousy voice and execute my orders properly. Besides, I needed to sound like I was in command of the troops, decisive and convincing. That's why I could use any help I could get. I couldn't afford to stand in front of the company and embarrass myself and my TAC officers, so I studied my drill and ceremonies training circular extremely diligently.

Before reporting to Lieutenant Jones, I went to the small area behind the barracks and surrounded by a few trees. I practiced giving commands slowly, prolonging syllables and keeping control of my voice. It was an entirely new experience, as I never had to address a large group of people outdoors and without a microphone. At the same time, I was looking forward to discovering the new me through my voice.

* * *

The following day was a special day. First, it was finally my time to pass my first and only PT test in Pennsylvania. I wasn't too worried about my push-ups and sit-ups because we had our morning physical training every day. We were also frequently dropped by our TAC officers to do push-ups for no apparent reason, any time of the day. The most stressful, however, was the thought of running two miles. I remembered how, just two days prior, it was extremely hard for me to complete the battalion run. Nonetheless, that morning, I went to the PT test, hopeful and determined to pass it the first time around. As I was hoping, the push-ups and sit-ups didn't pose any problem. However, during the run, I had to constantly remind myself to keep a steady pace, relax my body, breathe, and sprint the last fifty meters. In the end, I accomplished all that with good timing. I added this test to my imaginary list of small victories in Pennsylvania. This one was the fifth.

The second reason that day was special was because that evening, I was taking over our company as the first sergeant. I dreaded it. By now, I observed on several occasions the infamous change of command ceremonies, as well as all methods of teasing and intimidation by TAC officers thereafter. To prepare for my ordeal, I kept replaying in my mind the proper procedures and drills, and most of all, how to stay calm, collected, and confident. All these were to be expressed by my new, powerful command voice.

* * *

As usual, for the change of command ceremony, the company was in column formation facing the building, with platoons in line, centered, and facing the company's outgoing commander forming the unit.

The platoons stood in anticipation, hopeful that the procedures would go as planned and they wouldn't have to be punished with push-ups. Ready for the show, the cadre started swarming around the outgoing leadership. The commander called the company to attention, then to parade rest. The TAC officers did everything to distract him, but he was unwavering.

Candidate Jackson, the incoming company commander, as well as the new executive officer, Candidate Remy, were called to the front and center, ready to take charge. From my third rank in the third platoon, I watched with growing nervousness the transfer of the company colors to the new commander. I was praying for it to be successful and not to enrage the TAC officers too soon. While watching the transfer of the flag, I was moved and started tearing up. Then I realized I needed to keep my bearing, so I wouldn't be perceived as weak. If that became the case, I could quickly become an easy target for TAC officers' tormenting activities in front of the entire company. The voice of the new commander brought me back to reality: "Post!"

The outgoing first sergeant and the company executive officer took their positions at the back of the formation. One of the TAC officers called out, "Officer Candidate Rakowski, front and center!"

To boost my courage in the face of a challenge, I whispered to myself, "Showtime!" Hoping that no one heard me, I snapped to the position of attention.

"Sir, Officer Candidate Rakowski. Here, sir!" I shouted, confident through the ranks.

I stepped out of the ranks and double-timed to take my place at attention in front and center of the commander. It was my time to shine. I was now on stage performing my solo in front of an anticipating audience.

I felt like the good old days when I was a ballerina in my blue tutu, dancing the role of Princess Florina from the ballet *Sleeping Beauty*. Except now, my blue tutu was replaced with my green-brown-black BDU, my ballet pointe shoes with combat boots, and there was no fairy tale but full alert and tension of 120 actual soldiers.

"Bring the company to attention," said the commander.

I saluted him with an energetic snap, then I turned around to face the company.

Anticipating the barrage of words from the TAC officer already pacing around me, I was telling myself, "Keep cool, follow the procedure."

Suddenly, one TAC officer got in my face, screaming, "Now what, Ra-kow-ski!? What do you do?! Can you take the pressure?"

Although he was relentless, I didn't want to give it to him. Not so quickly, anyway.

"She's gonna break!" the other TAC screamed in my left ear, jumping like a monkey.

I stood motionless, concentrated, thinking about my next move. "Call the company to attention, that's it." My body was getting warm and sweat drops started forming on my forehead. "Just don't show them you're shaking inside," I thought to myself.

"If you can't take the heat, go home now!" The TAC's screams resounded in my ears like a drum.

Seconds seemed like hours. I thought about home. No, I wouldn't allow myself to think of home. That would weaken my resolve. I couldn't be weak. Not now.

"Or give us a good show and start crying!" The other TAC laughed in my face. I'm not from those who cry, except when I cry from joy. I'll cry when it's all over, I thought.

That was enough for me. I mustered all the courage and screamed from the top of my lungs using my freshly acquired command voice: "Com-pa-ny! Atten-tion!"

With relief, I observed the company snapping to attention in a split second. Silence. It worked. My command voice worked. They all heard me and executed.

Then I addressed the platoon sergeants with an equally powerful voice: "Receive the report!"

When the platoon sergeants were ready to give me their reports, the commotion around me came to a halt. The TACs froze and continued to watch me in action, stupefied.

I resumed the procedure by addressing the platoon sergeants using the proper inflection and power: "Report!" I shouted from my diaphragm, surprised at the power of my voice.

The platoon sergeant from the first platoon on my left-hand side saluted me. While I was returning his salute, my right hand went to the position of attention quickly and sharply enough to inadvertently brush the uniform of the TAC officer standing beside me. He jumped away in shock.

"That was one crisp salute!" he said with satisfaction and moved farther away. He needed to stay away from me because I had three more sharp salutes to return, and he could get struck again if he didn't keep his distance. I took it as a compliment and continued my reporting procedure. "She's good to go," the TAC added.

The other TAC officers surrounding me made a couple of steps back as well. The silence ensued, and the intimidation was over. One for me, zero for the TACs, was my summary of the match. A tiny victory for now. I just set myself up for success for the rest of my rotation.

After I received all the reports, I took a deep breath and did an about-face to face the commander standing behind me. I saluted him and reported, "Sir, all accounted for."

The company commander returned the salute and commanded, "Post!"

After that, I did an about-face and marched to the rear and center of the company, halted, and turned around to face the commander again. The outgoing first sergeant was relieved from his post and took his place in the second platoon. The commander was now in charge.

Only now could I breathe calmly. Although I was still shaking inside and my palms were sweaty, I didn't let anyone see my stress. The most important thing now was the fact that the change of command ended successfully without me breaking down despite the enormous pressure. I could almost hear the sigh of relief throughout the platoons.

For the rest of the evening, I was meeting with new leadership, taking directions from Jackson, the new commander, and communicating with my platoon sergeants regarding the next day's company activities. Lieutenant Jones, impressed by the change of command procedures he had just witnessed, instructed me to write a positive spot report for successfully taking over the duties of the company's first sergeant.

When Captain Kucera approached us to congratulate me, my TAC officer said with pride, "I'm talking with a squared-away soldier." I liked that expression. It gave me a warm and fuzzy feeling that I was doing okay.

* * *

The next morning was the beginning of my first full day as a company first sergeant. When I stepped out of the building to call the morning formation around 5:30 a.m., everyone was already outside. The cadre was also pacing around my post, waiting for my actions. The cadre company's first sergeant, First Sergeant Todero, was also closely monitoring the situation.

I received the reports from my platoon sergeants and took detailed notes of the information I was given. These notes were the basis for writing my own "accountability reports" to be submitted to First Sergeant Todero. From then on, about every two hours, I was to submit to him on special yellow cards my "company status reports."

As I was going through my routines of the day, I heard the familiar voice of Major Moon, who was always observing my actions in my new role. "Keep doing what you're doing, First Sergeant Rakowski. Testosterone!" He made sure everyone could hear. I noticed how the cadre started calling me "first sergeant" instead of "officer candidate," and I took it as a positive sign I was accepted in this role so early in my forty-eight-hour journey.

During lunch at the DFAC, the TACs continued to tease me in a friendly manner: "Rakowski, I've heard that you're doing so well as first sergeant that they are extending your duty one extra day!" Lieutenant Jones giggled, sincerely amused.

"Can you give the commands to the company in Polish?" added Major Moon, curious. I thought this was a phenomenal idea, but I only responded affirmatively to Major Moon's question. I instantly came up with a plan to shock the entire company the next day, including the TAC officers.

Later that day, one of my platoon sergeants reported that a couple of soldiers in her platoon were hungry. I directed all four platoon sergeants to take count of how many people were hungry in their units. It came out that over twenty people needed to be fed. With this report, I went to First Sergeant Todero's office to request MREs (meal ready to eat).

That night, under the starry skies, I was in front of the barracks looking for my pen I inadvertently dropped on the ground earlier.

Suddenly, I heard Lieutenant Jones beside me: "Who did you piss off to get this first sergeant position?" I knew he joked because his face was serious. When he was serious, he had a smile on his face. I could read him because I operated the same way.

"Sir, Officer Candidate Rakowski. I thought this was a reward, sir."

"That's the right answer," interjected Captain Kucera, returning my smile. "You're doing a great job, first sergeant." Her warm voice sounded like home with freshly baked bread.

* * *

On my second day as the company's first sergeant, the first accountability formation for that day took place at 5:45 a.m.. As usual, the TAC officers were monitoring me at the exit from the building.

I took my usual post in front of the company and yelled with my distinct command voice, which was well-practiced by now: "Kompania! Baczność! Sierżanci, przyjąć raporty!" (Polish: Company! Attention! Sergeants, receive the reports!)

The silence ensued. Soldiers were looking around in consternation, confused. The TAC officers and First Sergeant Todero started giggling like schoolchildren and left me alone. I was glad that I could finally use my Polish to my advantage. Some laughter came from the platoons. Then, to everyone's relief, I repeated the commands in English.

We loaded the white buses at 6:00 a.m. for our road march. We formed up as a company in the clearing in the nearby woods. As usual, we marched on both sides of the road in a staggered formation, with weapons drawn and pointed to the outside. The morning was crisp, and the company was in good spirits. At the front, I've put the short people as pacesetters. I remembered from my recent experience as a pacesetter when our platoon won first place that being short didn't have to mean slow or worse yet—the last. This was an opportunity for the shorties to shine. My place was in the middle of the road, centered between two single files of soldiers, each stretching about seventy meters, and between the second and third platoons. My role was to oversee the marching from my position. I had to constantly run up and down the formation to check on every soldier without paying attention to my heavy rucksack and my legs burning from the effort. The biggest challenge was naturally every hill that we were encountering. Every time I was negotiating a hill, I had to lean forward for better balance and control of motion. I had learned this trick the hard way in basic training, when marching uphill was common. After the break at the half-point, I formed up the company, keeping short people on the front because they were doing a phenomenal job.

Lieutenant Jones and Captain Kucera were also on the front and every time they saw me, they would resound with a reassuring, "First Sergeant Rakowski, hard-core! Keep up the good job!"

At the end of the event, I had the entire company arrive in tight formation and in good spirits. Out of over 120 personnel, I had only two heat casualties and no other incidents.

"I think differently about shorties now," admitted Jackson, the six-feet-tall company commander. "They can be really 'high-speed'!"

"We *are* high speed!" beaming Michaud corrected him and gave me a double high five.

Michaud was the shortest male in our platoon, so it meant a lot. This march was my sixth small victory in Pennsylvania.

* * *

After returning from the road march, my day as a first sergeant continued. During the lunch formation, Sergeant Wood, Captain Kucera, and Captain Roberts admitted I was doing a great job as a first sergeant and asked me to write a positive spot report for my leadership during the road march. In addition, I later received compliments from my fellow candidates, which helped me realize I could step up and be the leader that others expected me to be.

"You did better as the first sergeant than I would ever do," said Mulchany, a timid and soft-spoken man who rarely uttered a word.

His handshake reassured me that at least some males in this male-dominated world respected me. As a representative of merely 8 percent of the female population within our company, I felt good being valued.

"It takes a lot of guts to be in charge of over a hundred people," added Michaud. "And you definitely have it. That's hard-core!"

Later in the afternoon, I called the company to the last formation of the day, during which the next change of command ceremony took place. As I stood there waiting to be relieved by the incoming first sergeant, I realized how fast these last two days went by, how my hands were full, and how successful was the road march under my command. Although I was tired and still shaking from emotions, I thought that overall, I enjoyed this role. My self-confidence skyrocketed. The rotation as the company first sergeant was my seventh, but this time, a big victory in Pennsylvania.

The change of command was brutal. McFarlan was called for the role of the company's first sergeant. She wasn't able to keep her composure and call the company to attention. Her voice was quiet, and she quickly became invisible. I rejoined my platoon's third squad as Officer Candidate Rakowski and was now a spectator with all my fellow candidates.

* * *

Despite the unsuccessful change of command the night before, the TAC officers decided to give McFarlan another chance and continue to be in charge. This meant that while she desperately needed to prove herself, the entire company would suffer every time she was underperforming. When the company wasn't able to hear her commands, no one knew what to do. This would create lots of confusion within the platoons and a lot of commotion around her. The TAC officers were relentless in their teasing and shouting. When things were not going well, the formation time would extend, and we had a little time left to go to DFAC for our meals.

During that morning formation, we were all in our front-leaning rest positions, ready to do push-ups. Everyone, including me, was getting smoked for the past fifteen minutes and frustration was reaching the boiling point. Then I heard a voice coming from the ranks of a platoon next to me.

"Rakowski, get up there and be the first sergeant!" a fellow officer candidate cried out.

"Yeah, First Sergeant Rakowski. Hard-core!" sounded off another voice.

Hearing "hard-core" boosted my self-confidence.

"First Sergeant Rakowski, we need you!" echoed more voices.

I smiled to myself, amused. I appreciated being recognized for my former role as the first sergeant. At the same time, I was relieved that my duty was over and that I fulfilled it to the best of my abilities. Now, I was enjoying not being responsible for over a hundred people and just being punished with push-ups with everyone else.

* * *

After breakfast, we were going to the nearby swimming pool for our long-anticipated and somewhat dreaded CWST (combat water survival training). I wasn't sure about swimming in my uniform. The last time I was swimming was a year ago and in my swimming suit, and still, it wasn't easy back then. This time, it was all about "survival," so I was convinced that it would be much harder and probably some obstacles or challenges would be involved.

On this sunny, hot day, we lined up on three sides of the pool in groups. Each side of the pool represented a station for a different water activity. I ended up with the group going to the diving board first. I wasn't looking forward to being in the water in full uniform, in combat boots, and with a weapon, but there were no other options. As I was moving in line, I was growing anxious. Never in my life had jumped into the pool from a board three meters high above the surface. This side of the pool was the deepest, and there was no way I would touch the bottom after the plunge. The depth alone was giving me shivers. I had jumped into a swimming pool or a large body of water from the rope before, recreationally, in comfortable clothes, and with no pressure. Here, there was nothing recreational about the jump I was about to perform.

I listened to the instructions and watched with full attention the soldiers before me, one by one, performing the drill. At the beginning of the board, we were first blindfolded with a white cloth. Then, with a weapon in both hands above the head, we had to walk to the end of the board. Finally, we would take a step forward and plunge into the water with crossed, straight legs. Once on the surface, we would grab the white cloth and swim with the weapon raised above water out of the pool. Besides the first few courageous ones, most of the people in line were apprehensive. The exercise didn't look that appealing to me either, but the jump had to be done sooner or later. I watched, trying to learn in my mind the entire maneuver.

Eventually, I mustered the courage to step on the board and say goodbye to the dry uniform. A TAC officer put the blindfold on my eyes. With an M16 in my hands, I started advancing on the board. "Small steps," I thought to myself. "Step away from the board and don't catch it with the back of your skull. I could easily break your neck and drown." The board was bending more as I moved forward. Then I heard: "Stop now! Ready? One-two-three go!"

I took a deep breath, hoping that it would last me long enough to make it through this evolution. My legs were like cotton, with my entire body in spasms. One step forward.

The flight seemed like an eternity. I hit the water with a splash. As I was going down, I could hear a massive swoosh and feel the water enveloping me like a cold blanket. The blindfold fell off on impact. Completely underwater, I kept my eyes closed, still holding my initial breath. While the water was closing on me, I remembered my first serious encounter with the water when I was a little girl growing up in Poland. I was sitting on the pier with my father nearby. When someone accidentally pushed me, I fell into the water without realizing that I was drowning. My dad's quick reaction saved me once he noticed the red bow on my ponytail submerged in the water. Now I had to count on myself. As I was losing my breath from impact and stress, I started moving upward to the surface with my rifle raised. Once I broke the surface, I shook my head around a few times to gain a better view. When I located the blindfold, the water was still swirling and foaming around me. I grabbed it and swam to a designated exit. Soaking wet, I could barely pull myself on the ladder. Then I moved to the next station. I was now officially primed for two more water exercises.

While waiting my turn, I noticed that on the shallow side of the pool ("kiddy pool") there were several candidates who desperately needed to learn quickly how to swim. We were told that each candidate had to complete all three exercises, with no exceptions. I wouldn't want to be in their position and try to learn how to swim in full uniform, then jump blindfolded into the pool. The pressure was enormous.

The next exercise was about "ditching" the load-bearing equipment in the water. This station wasn't very popular either because the exercise was more complex than a simple plunge. Besides, the water on this side of the pool was just as deep (twelve feet) as in the area with the diving board.

With all the gear secured to my torso, I took my position at the edge of the pool, facing away from the water. Before I knew it, I was pushed violently into the water backward. After a second of shock, I regained my bearings, and while holding my breath, I pointed the rifle at the "enemy" (a TAC officer on the edge) and pulled the trigger. In the next second, I was engulfed by the cold water, bubbles forming all around me. For a moment, I thought that this time around I would drown for sure. But I surfaced somehow. I was now holding my rifle in my left hand while using the right hand to undo with great difficulty the clasp of my LBE belt. I shook my head vigorously a few times. The wet uniform and combat boots were pulling me down. "Breathe and keep moving," I thought to myself. Just like during my dancing years, when I was learning new steps, I had a tendency to hold my breath. Now I had to muster all my physical strength to stay calm and continue swimming without panicking. Once I resumed my breathing again, I pulled myself up the ladder.

Even though it was a hot and sunny day, by the third exercise, I was trembling from the cold and, most of all, from stress. I took a quick look at the "kiddy pool" area. Not much progress was made there. As soldiers were rotating between stations, completing their tasks, the non-swimmers were struggling, and I felt sorry for them.

At last, I was at my last station, anticipating my most challenging task. This station was the toughest one because it involved a straight fifteen-meter swim with a weapon. I watched as some people before me were swimming across the pool with ease. Others had to be "rescued" midway. Before I jumped into the water, I quickly thought about my strategy. I decided to swim on my back with my right hand pulling the water and with the left holding the weapon on my chest. Once in the water, I thought about my swims in Fort Huachuca. I felt confident because the backstroke was my proven forte. I followed my strategy until I lost track of how far I was swimming. Apparently, I drifted a bit toward the wall of the pool but was quickly corrected by a nearby TAC. "Stay calm, breathe," I kept telling myself as the water was trickling in my ears. Because of my wet uniform and boots, I had an uneasy feeling I was swimming in place. I could barely move. I looked behind me and noticed the TAC officer at the end of the line.

"You're almost there, Rakowski! Hard-core!" I could barely hear his voice echoing through the swooshing waves.

Then a familiar voice of Lieutenant Jones resounded, "Rakowski, I didn't know you were such a good swimmer!"

I didn't know that either. I didn't realize what it took to complete this training. Until now. I was good enough, and that mattered to me.

I made it out of the water on my last breath and near a physical and mental collapse, but with a great sense of accomplishment. Exhausted, I ran to the changing rooms to put on a dry, fresh uniform. When I came out of the building, the sun was already setting and the "kiddy pool" was still full of non-swimmers. With relief, it finally dawned on me I didn't break my neck after all and didn't drown. I survived. I could taste the sweetness of my eighth victory in Pennsylvania.

I decided to swim on my back with my right hand pulling the water and with the left holding the weapon on my chest.

* * *

After the combat water survival training, I met with First Sergeant Todero to brief him on the homework assignment he had given me the night before as a conclusion of the counseling about my leadership role. This time, I was to present the topics related to confident leadership as the most essential element of combat power, providing the purpose, direction, and motivation in combat. After First Sergeant Todero heard my briefing, he said that I would be a great noncommissioned officer, but I would be a fine commissioned officer. Then he concluded, "It will be an honor for me to salute you when you are in Fort Indiantown Gap. You gave 110 percent again and I see it even when others give only 90 percent."

"It was an honor and privilege to be your company's first sergeant."

* * *

We spent the entire following day in the field near the barracks negotiating the LRC (leadership reactions course). The course was composed of eight stations, separated by twelve-foot walls. Each station was built to represent a specific scenario. The structures inside were constructed from wood and steel pipes. Sometimes we had a rope, a ladder, or a makeshift stretcher available to help transport everything. Some fragments of the structures were painted red, meaning they were off-limits because of them being broken, booby-trapped, or otherwise nonfunctioning. Each rotation at any station had a duration of thirty minutes, which included the time to receive the mission, coming up with the strategy to negotiate the obstacle, and execution. We had to be creative, as some obstacles seemed impassable.

I ended up being a squad leader at the ammo transportation station. The structure in that station was made from three steel pipes forming an upside-down letter *u* ten feet above the ground. The legs had fragments painted red on the bottom and the pipe parallel to the ground was painted red in the middle. A box of ammo was to be transported across the structure using a relatively short rope. Several tall fellow candidates jumped at the opportunity to climb the pipes, and it looked like they were enjoying it. At some point, one person hung straight down, and another had to use his shoulders to help climb back up. Then another person on the ground received the rope from up top and tried to tie to it a heavy ammo box. This box had to be hoisted up, then moved to the other side of the pipe on top, now holding four candidates. It was extremely hard for me to direct from the ground people hanging for dear life. I wasn't able to help much, except to offer moral support and encouragement. I felt inadequate in this situation, but I did the best I could.

It was extremely hard for me to direct from the ground people hanging for dear life.

My biggest enemy, however, was, as usual, the heat. On that day, the heat index was nearly 120°F and as the day proceeded, it was harder and harder for me to stay focused. As a previous heat casualty, I got permission from Lieutenant Jones to swap my Kevlar helmet with a soft cap and to unblouse my pants. At first, I felt some relief, but after a while, I started feeling nauseous and dizzy and I had to go to the ambulance. I was still able to walk on my own, but I was ready to collapse any minute. In a cool, air-conditioned vehicle, I was eventually cooling down. My uniform was drenched, my entire body was shaking, and I definitely had a fever. Finally, I received an IV and calmed down. I was worried about being a heat casualty for the third time in Pennsylvania because each instance of heat exhaustion was draining me of so much needed energy.

Later in the afternoon, during our recall formation, the TAC officers relentlessly "smoked" us until we were completely exhausted. McFarlan was still in charge of the company, failing miserably. We were continually dropped for push-ups, or we were doing side-straddle hops for good measure. It was to teach everyone that the first sergeant's job was to be taken seriously. McFarlan herself was getting dropped for push-ups as well, which made it for her so much harder to shout commands from the front-leaning rest position. In these situations, everyone grew frustrated, discouraged, and demoralized, but the show had to go on.

*   *   *

It was the last Sunday of our phase II in Pennsylvania when we received an assignment from Captain Lloyd for our next day's field trip to Gettysburg. In teams of two, we had drawn from a list of key points of the famous battle a topic to discuss. We were to write a two-page essay about historical figures and tactical maneuvers to be presented during the trip as vignettes.

The next day, after lunch, we loaded the buses and were on our way to the Gettysburg National Military Park Museum. For about an hour of the ride, we could rest mentally and physically from our demanding routines on base. It felt good to wear our PT uniforms and relax by not carrying any equipment at all times. By visiting a historical site of such magnitude, we were transported into the history of our nation and lived through the most significant moments of the Battle of Gettysburg. The goal of the trip was to teach us the art and history of leadership while allowing us to fully comprehend academic concepts with practical application on the famous battlefield.

Our bus followed the "car tour" itinerary. We were accompanied by a licensed battlefield guide. We would stop at the most significant landmarks and terrain features, and in teams of two, gave the rest of the platoon brief presentations of the battle events related to the location. At the high-water mark of the Confederacy, Michaud and I delivered our presentation about Pickett's Charge. Although we were well prepared, I was quite uncomfortable with giving my presentation in English. From sheer nervousness, I kept injecting Polish words into my speech. It seemed like nobody paid attention to my mishaps, so I pretended I did it intentionally.

As the sun was setting above the battlefield of Gettysburg, I was thinking about all those who had lost their lives in the battles of freedom, equality, and democracy for all. And that one day, I could find myself in a situation where my values and beliefs would be put to an ultimate test on a battlefield somewhere in the world.

* * *

Dear Alec,

Thank you for your last two letters. Yesterday we spent the entire day until late evening at the Gettysburg National Military Park. For me, it was a very intense educational experience, a big lesson in American history, which was unknown to me. As you know, in Poland, I didn't have much opportunity to learn much about it. Our history lessons usually evolved around European countries. Gettysburg Park is huge and very impressive. Historical cannons and a multitude of monuments commemorating the efforts of those who perished in the battle were present everywhere.

I have the last three days here and on Friday, we are going back to Alabama for the final two weeks of training. So this is probably my last letter from Pennsylvania. In the past few days, since we last spoke, time went fast and furious. We've gone through some pain and suffering for good measure. We also had wonderful moments, though. Most of all, I'm glad my forty-eight-hour "leadership position" rotation as the company first sergeant is over.

The only thing we have left here is tomorrow's twelve-mile tactical road march with all the gear in the field. On Friday, we will have a small graduation ceremony, during which perhaps we will be granted the official status of "senior officer candidates." This would be the equivalent of being the third lieutenant, almost an officer.

These four weeks in Pennsylvania were very tough, but after looking at the schedule for the remaining two weeks (Alabama), it will not be easy by any means. We will spend most of our time in the field. Most likely it will be humid and nasty. We will be carrying all the gear and weapons on us at all times in the woods, 'playing war.' Everything will be serious as an actual war, except for the blank rounds in our rifles.

I am extremely tired, and I miss you, Sznurek, and our home. I often think about you and how you conquer the heat and humidity while riding your bike daily through the Chicago suburbs. Do you still ride across the forest preserve in Glencoe to Lake Forest? Sometimes your entire loop would take you fifty miles in a single day. I always admired that. I miss seeing your hair all sweaty and wrinkled after you took off your helmet at the end of a long ride. I was always making fun of it because you looked like a porcupine.

* * *

The last Wednesday of our phase II was about the final big event for this period, a dreaded twelve-mile road march. As usual, given my recent heat exhaustion, I was worried if I still had it in me to complete this required event. It was almost the distance I had last marched in the desert landscape at the feet of the Huachuca Mountains for the German

Badge. This time, however, although I wasn't injured, I was extremely tired physically and mentally. Regardless, I had to push forward just to prove to myself more than anything that I was still capable of this tremendous effort for the last time.

This time, instead of being transported by the buses to the woods, we marched out directly from the barracks in a tactical formation staggered on both sides of a paved road. The darkness was fighting with the daylight. Our column of shadows with weapons at the ready and the "Army Song" on our lips, we marched with purpose through the morning fog.

At first, the miles were disappearing fast and before we knew it, we found ourselves at the tree line just before disappearing into the woods, which were slowly awakening from the peaceful rest. I started my journey on the front, remembering that this was the best spot for either pace-setting or at least for staying with formation. I was going strong for the first half of marching. It was extremely hot, and my uniform was retaining more and more sweat in high humidity. At the midpoint, we took a break. I used it to eat an apple I took from DFAC at breakfast and to put on a fresh T-shirt under my uniform and a dry pair of socks. Only then, I realized that after taking my combat boots off, it was nearly impossible to put them back on because my feet swelled up. After a few good minutes of struggle and extreme discomfort, I finally succeeded.

Shortly after the turnaround point, I started to lose my pace. It was harder and harder to keep up with the front. I fell into the middle of the formation, but I was still in relatively good spirits. I was carried by the wave of strong marchers around me. Singing cadences with the entire company was still helpful.

After a few more miles, I slipped further into the back of the formation. My legs were rebelling, and the rucksack seemed heavier with every step. I literally dragged my feet. Every once in a while, I would pour some water from my canteens on my head to cool off. However, under the heavy Kevlar, my brain seemed to be boiling in this extreme heat. The ambulance was riding a few steps behind me. The temptation to get in it was strong, but I had to push hard until I couldn't push anymore.

After a while, I walked like in a dream, half-conscious. Nothing really mattered. I continued fighting the temptation of giving up and catching the ride in the ambulance.

Finally, we reached the familiar bridge about a mile from the entry to the woods at the small clearing. The formation was already falling apart for a while, and I was almost at the end of the column with a small group of stragglers in the middle of the road. Soon, the exhausted people were slowly passing me by. The bridge was stretching into eternity and for a moment, I was nearly collapsing on it; it would be the end of me. "One step at a time," I kept telling myself. Then I heard behind me a familiar voice of one of my fellow candidates: "Come on, first sergeant, you can do it!" This gave me a much-needed energy boost. I was being remembered from my glory days when I led this same company to success on the nine-mile march just a week ago.

I mustered all the courage and strength I had left in me and pushed on. At that moment, I decided to finish this event on my own legs, no matter the struggle. I didn't want to disappoint those who still believed in me. I continued to fight myself and the elements, the exhaustion, and my hallucinating mind, scraping from the pavement the debris of my willpower. I finally crossed the never-ending bridge. The woods on both sides of the road were closing on me like a dark cell. I walked through a forestal tunnel, fighting off the intrusive thoughts about giving up and catching the ride in the ambulance.

At last, a clearing opening up to the main road leading to the barracks began appearing two hundred yards before me. It took all my willpower and whatever was left of my strength to travel this last stretch. After nearly four hours of marching, I finally reached the barracks, with a small group of people struggling along. It was a beautiful, sunny midday, with 97°F outside. At last, here was my ninth victory in Pennsylvania.

After lunch, before I could go to the barracks to change, I found out that I was assigned to clean the weapons used in the road march. At first, I was frustrated because I was counting on getting some well-deserved rest. Then, when I realized I was entrusted with this task, probably because someone thought I would do a good job, I took the situation as a compliment.

The cleaning of weapons was taking me long hours, mainly because I was exhausted. All the people who were also assigned to this task had already done their part and left the weapon storage area. I was sitting in front of the building and conversed with First Sergeant Todero about his experience with candidates at Fort Indiantown Gap Training Center. I could barely follow his monologue or concentrate on my task, but I desperately needed to stay awake and alert.

* * *

The sun has set already, and the stars began shining on the firmament. A multitude of insects as tiny as the particles of dust was twirling around in the beams of the building lights. I took apart the last rifle to be cleaned. When I arranged all the parts on a white cloth, through my tired brain, I started seeing the parts dancing in a joyful formation. The smallest ones had lined up in the front and the bigger ones followed to finally close the circle. Then the circle split in half to create two parallel rows on both edges of the cloth. This reminded me of many choreographies I had seen on the stage of the Great Opera in Warsaw. Lines, circles, and swirls of dancers and their graceful movements. Just like that time at the Great Opera in Warsaw, in August 1992.

It was the beginning of the opera season which Chris and I had been looking forward to the entire summer. We walked into the Great Opera through neoclassical interiors with marble columns and magnificent gilded chandeliers to see the production of the beloved *Swan Lake*. In some sense, the Great Opera was our home because we both once had a common dream of becoming a ballet dancer. A dream that for Chris had never come true. For me, shortly after it became true, it had been brutally disrupted by the political scene in Poland in the 1990s.

For three years since the fall of the communist regime in Poland in 1989, the borders were open and Eastern Europe's political world was upside down. The old socialist order of privilege and certainty was no longer there to subsidize the arts. The lavish productions with magnificent sets and the wide-ranging repertory disappeared, marking the hard times for previously state-supported theaters and operas. During the challenging financial crisis, repertories had tightened as directors desperately attempted to hold down the high costs involved in staging various productions.

"Did you know," I asked Chris while we were sipping red wine in the luxurious lobby before the show, "that last year, fifteen dancers from the Opera quit and left for Germany?"

"Indeed, it's a massive exodus these days. I've read in the newspapers that one time, the Poznan state ballet company went to Italy on tour and one-third of the company refused to come home," Chris replied with sadness.

"I can't imagine how tough it must be for the dancers now. They literally don't have enough work or enough variety."

"Thank God we can still enjoy the good old *Swan Lake* with Wiech and Wozniak. Do you remember Wiech from school?"

"Of course, she was eight years my senior. She was finishing school the same year I started. She was always meant to be a star," I added with melancholy.

We took our seats in the center of the mezzanine, the best seats in the house. Soon, the spectacular setting of the famous ballet, accompanied by Tchaikovsky's fantastic music, transported us into the fairy tale.

Act II where prince Siegfried found himself alone by a lake, with the swans gently floating in the moonlight, was always my favorite part. I especially liked the scene in which the prince was mesmerized by the emergence of the queen of swans from the dark. Then the most impressive pas de deux choreographed in the nineteenth century would begin. Although the original choreography was preserved, the now-decimated ballet corps could fill the enormous stage as it would normally do in the good old days. The only thing left from these days was the legend. The legend of the two lovers by the lake and the legend of a long-gone splendor of this ballet production.

As the curtain went down at the end of the show, my eyes opened, and I came back from my reverie. I put back together the now perfectly clean rifle. The insects continued their dance in the beam of light.

*   *   *

Toward the end of phase II, time was flying fast. For the first time, the PT in the morning was pleasant. We did some yoga stretches in a relaxed, casual atmosphere. Almost suddenly, everything came to an end: the activities in the field, the school instruction, the marching, the yelling, and the teasing. The base was calm and almost too quiet.

On the last day, we were invited to an auditorium for a screening of *Saving Private Ryan*. The motion picture *Saving Private Ryan* embodied the military policy regarding the "sole survivor" in the family. Until now, I hadn't had a chance to see the movie, so I was looking forward to it.

The action of the film was taking place in Normandy (France) during World War II. The film was so realistic it was hard for me to watch the opening scene on Omaha Beach, representing the Normandy invasion by U.S. troops. The action demanded me, instead of being just a spectator, to participate with those young men who had never seen the battlefield. After the credits, I remained in my seat, captivated and wordless. I felt as if I had just survived a horrifying battle. I remembered the exercise in basic training called Omaha Beach (the last part of the night infiltration course), where we had to crawl for 150 meters through thick sand with simulated artillery and ground shaking. Now I understood we had to learn this maneuver not only to be better soldiers, but also to pay respect to the legacy of our predecessors from Normandy.

I thought about everything I had learned in my officer training. Would it be enough to succeed in a battle like this? Would I have enough strength and confidence to lead others and save lives? I pondered what it really meant to be an American soldier when duty calls for an ultimate sacrifice.

* * *

Impressed and moved by *Saving Private Ryan*, I decided to thank Lieutenant Brown, my TAC officer from phase I in Alabama, for inspiring me to be the best version of myself, to always give a hundred percent as an officer, and to lead by example. I wrote her a letter expressing my admiration for her.

Dear Lieutenant Brown,   July 19, 2002

"I keep thinking about my two weeks spent in Alabama OCS Phase I. I remember my confusion, sadness, and loneliness. I was afraid. I wanted to stop time and rethink if I was ready to be there. But it was too late to look back.

"Everything at the beginning seemed so blurry until that one evening. You stopped me in a hallway and said that I was 'squared away'. This one comment built me up better than anything. I started regaining my self-confidence.

"Now I want to thank you for all you've done for me, even though you said it was your duty as an officer. I felt you did it, more than anything, from your heart. I will never forget the day I was in the ambulance because of heat exhaustion, and I heard your voice asking medics about me. 'Someone actually cares,' I thought. I will never forget that you had arranged for me an additional medical treatment the next day, that you brought lunch for me, and gave me a purple Gatorade. I will always keep in mind all these moments when you motivated me to push myself harder or made me laugh or cry. But most of all, I will remember that you kept me focused. Now I know for sure again that I want to be *like you*.

"Because you gave me strength and inspiration. Because you showed me how to maintain high standards and how to take care of soldiers. No manual or training would ever replace my experience of being your student and seeing how to do the right thing and how to do things right.

"During the last four weeks in Pennsylvania, I thought about what you had told me on the last day in Alabama. I consider myself lucky to be under your command. I could only wish I was surrounded by people like you throughout my entire military career.

"I realized again why I am in the army and why I want to be an officer. Because of people like you who inspire by example—by the way, they are and who they are: role models, leaders, and genuine officers.

"Thank you again for everything,
Officer Candidate Rakowski"

* * *

After the movie, we stayed in the auditorium for the phase II OCS unofficial graduation. The end of this phase marked an important milestone in our training. Now, only the best and the strongest prevailed by successfully completing this part of the training. The commander of the 2nd Battalion, 166th Regiment (OCS), Regional Training Institute, delivered his speech. The best student, Candidate Lyles from Illinois, received an Army Officer Saber as a symbol of excellence he displayed throughout the program. After all, we were all given the "senior officer candidate" status.

In the afternoon, we had the final counseling sessions with our senior TAC officers. My grader, Lieutenant Laiosa, reviewed all my grades, tactics' evaluations, and various reports from my leadership positions.

"Your performance was excellent. Your decision-making process is outstanding," he said. Then, looking me straight in the eyes, he added, "Although you're not six feet tall like Jackson, you have a command presence that is admirable. You have it and I don't know how you do it."

This was the most valuable feedback I'd heard during the OCS. I could almost feel myself blushing like a schoolgirl. The successful completion of phase II was definitely a big victory, the tenth and last victory in Pennsylvania.

* * *

Accepting a failed test wasn't a simple task, but life wouldn't stop there for me to ponder the situation. I still had so much to learn about the various forces and components of the army. Patience and kindness to myself was the key. Being patient helped me survive the mentally challenging, stressful time while in charge of troops. When people looked at my every move and waited for my commands, I had to perform the part of a role model. It was a frightening and rewarding experience. As a future officer, I understood how to be a successful leader. This time, command presence and confidence were essential. A timid mouse tucked away in a secluded corner had to step up and execute.

CHAPTER 19

LOOKING DEATH IN THE EYE

The plane landed in Anniston, Alabama. As soon as we exited the airport building, the hot steaming air filled my lungs, and the sun was already setting. The white school bus pulled over to the airport exit. I sat down quietly, hugging my duffle bag, trying to picture what the future events would reveal. We drove for an hour outside the city limits. My heart was pounding from angst and excitement, but at the same time, I was full of hope that this last phase of OCS would be somewhat calmer, and we would be treated better than the first time we were here six weeks ago. The driver finally dropped us off in front of the two familiar barracks. This was our last OCS stop.

I was assigned to the 3rd Platoon, Alpha Company, 2nd Battalion (OCS), 200th Regiment. Luckily, I landed in the same barracks as in phase I and was finally reunited with Mathia and Arroyo from Illinois. It was good to see their familiar faces again.

I immediately started looking for Lieutenant Brown, but I only managed to find Lieutenant Coldwell from phase I. He told me she would like to meet with me. He promised to give her the message that I was looking for her.

* * *

Dear Alec,

I'm back in Alabama already. It feels really weird to be here again because it's like being a different person visiting a place from the past. For now, it's not too bad. We are being treated differently than before. No more TAC-ing. Now it is like mentoring. We don't have to run everywhere and be stressed out. We will train in the woods—tactics, leadership, command presence, troop leading procedures, and operational orders. Hopefully, it's going to be a nice training. Many people from the cadre from phase I remembered me from six weeks ago. Even medics when I bumped into them!

Unfortunately, my feet are pretty messed up from the constant heat and moisture in my boots. They are cracking badly and painful wounds form. It's because we were spending twenty hours a day in combat boots in the heat.

I started thinking about coming home pretty soon. I just need to survive these days in the field and the hot and humid weather without a shower. I have so much to tell you, but also need a normal life to rest and relax. I can now let myself imagine us sitting on our purple and pistachio green patio sipping wine in the evening and Sznurek eating a steak stolen from the dinner table.

* * *

For the first five days, our training was to entail only field exercises in a tactical environment. We packed our rucksacks, put on our camo makeup, and left the barracks into the woods on deuces. The only food available to us was three MREs per day.

We set up the camp with a large gate secured with concertina wires. Our sleeping quarters were flat areas with clusters of bushes throughout the camp. Our beds were sleeping mats and sleeping bags. As my "room," I selected a decent-size lonely tree, which served as my pillow and semi shelter. We were now living in the camp, sharing our forest floor with chiggers, poison ivy, and poison sumac. For the first time, I learned how important it was to tuck my pants tightly in my boots. It was to keep the bugs away. Even though theoretically, the crawlies shouldn't be able to get into our skin, practically, they had managed to do so with splendid success. Despite duck-taping our pants to the boots and covering our sleeves, they were eating us alive.

Several times a day, we were to march short distances in platoons, then split into squads to arrive at our respective tactical areas where the leadership exercises were organized. Each of these two-hour operations was to be evaluated by a TAC officer as. In my squad's case, it was Lieutenant Jones, who had arrived with us from Pennsylvania. In each exercise, there were thirty minutes to receive the mission, prepare the strategy for an advance, and assign positions. The rest of the time was for mission execution and, at the end of the exercise, for an evaluation by our instructor. It was important to plan the mission within a prescribed time. However, Lieutenant Jones allowed an exception. If a leader was running out of time and asked in time for an extra minute or two, they wouldn't be disqualified from the exercise.

Each candidate had two chances of getting evaluated and it was done in two different scenarios for consistency of results. However, only one "go" was needed to pass OCS. We had to attain either an "E" (excellent) or an "S" (satisfactory) on the FLX II (field leadership exercise) evaluation to graduate from phase III.

* * *

On day two, it was drizzling since the early morning. It was my turn to be a platoon leader for Operation Tiger 2. At noon, I led my platoon out of the camp, going north on route 134 in tactical formation. Two miles later, we stopped at the intersection of 54 and Barrage Road for instructions from the higher-ups. At 1200 hours, an RTO (radio telephone operator), Michaud, received the mission from the headquarters.

Next, I rallied my platoon sergeant and all four squad leaders while the rest of the platoon was guarding the perimeter with their M16s at the ready. I plotted all the enemy and friendly positions on the map. With Michaud's assistance, I gathered all the necessary materials to put together an improvised sand table by a cluster of young trees.

Once the mission was planned, I briefed Lieutenant Jones, then the squad leaders were given the time to disseminate the plan to their squads. Finally, I orchestrated a brief rehearsal to make sure everyone understood where their respective positions were, how smoke colors would be used, and the goal of the missions. I ordered the inspection of gear, especially ProMasks in case of a chemical attack.

We moved out on a violet smoke signal to cross Barrage Road at 12:45 p.m. In fifteen minutes, we reached the intersection of Maine and Route 54, nearly a hundred meters east of the enemy position.

Shortly after we had split to encircle the enemy, two shots were fired, and I heard loud battle cries throughout. The enemy was scrambling and caught completely off guard. I hesitated. Once I had a visual on the enemy, I threw a can of red smoke, which was a signal to attack. Through the violent sounds of the battle, the shooting of machine guns, and the cries of the wounded, I couldn't make out who was attacking. I prayed it was my platoon.

Once the smoke cleared, I assessed the situation and found my soldiers closing in on the armored vehicle, shooting at the enemy left and right. Suddenly, a tear gas canister landed near my feet. "Shit! Tear gas! Tear gas!" I yelled quickly. While holding my breath with my eyes closed, I grabbed the can and blindly threw it deeper into the woods behind me. With my hands shaking, I put my ProMask on my face and made sure I had suction. Some gas had gotten into my eyes, so for a few seconds I couldn't see much. Shortly, I regained my bearing and started advancing toward the enemy. From the corner of my eye, I could see that some of my soldiers were struggling with their masks but still had managed to keep actively attacking the enemy.

When the tear gas cleared, I assessed the situation again. A few enemies were shooting from the west side of their vehicle that wasn't covered. I dashed to the unprotected part of our circle, jumped into the trench, and shot several rounds toward the enemy. Then I yelled from the top of my lungs, "Take cover!" Two seconds later, my grenade was flying between the trees toward the armored vehicle. I ducked into the trench. As the grenade reached the armor, I could hear a characteristic snap, a sign that the grenade "exploded." I waited a few seconds inside the trench for the debris (as if it were the case of a real grenade) to settle. I assessed the situation again. I desperately needed to see my soldiers and take accountability. The shooting stopped. I called for squad leaders, and they quickly emerged from the bush.

The entire third squad appeared to my left, with four prisoners tied to one another. Apparently, the squad members bumped into them while they were patrolling their line of departure about ten meters from their vehicle. The enemy surrendered after a few shots were exchanged. Four members of the first squad appeared to my left and reported finding two more enemies in the trench area. They were also detained after surrendering. With the members of the second squad, I approached the detonated armored vehicle to look for survivors. Instead, I found ten enemy bodies. We confiscated the weapons. After collecting the remaining reports from the squads, I found out that we sustained one casualty and two soldiers from the fourth squad were wounded. I had Michaud call for a medevac, and we started retreating toward the east.

Once we reached the clearing by Main Street, we sat down in a circle for the evaluation of the mission, listening to the TAC's comments. The overall mission was completed successfully. The advance was good, and the tactical aspect of the advance was designed well. However, I left the enemy's west flank uncovered, and they could defend their position from there for a while. The signal for the attack was a bit delayed. We had one casualty. I agreed with all that was being said. Shaken up by stress and anxiety, I could barely hold my weapon. I was drenched from sweat and the drizzle. As I reflected on everything that had just taken place, I was hoping I'd achieved the overall desired mission results. The troops followed my orders. I had a feeling that they were fully engaged, and afterwards, they were satisfied with the outcome of our mission. This first small victory in phase III was, however, overshadowed by sustaining one casualty. It was hard to accept.

After the review, we hunkered down in the rain and talked with Lieutenant Jones about what it would be like to come home after all our training was completed. Here and now, home seemed like such a distant concept. It almost felt like a sacrilege to think of home while in the field. The field was our home now and everything else was a sin.

* * *

For the remaining three days, we continued our leadership training in the field. I could breathe easy because I received a good rating in my first scenario. I was evaluated once more and received a satisfactory rating as well. Overall, I received a "GO" for this exercise.

After the first part of the FLX II was over, we took one day off. People with "GOs" went to the barracks to refresh, shower, do some laundry, and repack their rucksacks for the last part of the exercise. Those with "NO GO" had to be relieved from the program and sent to their home state for evaluation by their Regional Training Institute commander for possible recycling. My heart went out to these candidates. On our day off, everything was happening in a much more relaxed atmosphere and partnership, and we were treated almost like officers. We departed to the field the next morning.

For the last five days of this part of the training, we moved into a new, more secure camp. My friend from Illinois, Mathia, was the company commander. She was the best candidate, as she had over sixteen years of experience in the army before the OCS. She was squared away, hard-core, and had a tremendous command presence. In addition, she was highly respected by TAC officers and fellow candidates.

The perimeter was well secured by various barricades and barbed wires and was guarded in shifts. Many of us were burned by poison ivy and poison sumac and struggled with bandaged arms in the humidity and heat. The small missions continued for four days. I was assigned a company-level function of S2 (intelligence officer) in the company headquarters because of my intel background. I was working twelve-hour shifts in a large tent in the middle of the camp. In the corner of the tent was my little workspace; a makeshift "desk" made from a stack of empty wooden ammo cases and a folding metal chair. During my nonworking hours, I was sleeping under a large tree just outside the tent.

In this scenario, my role was to provide commanders with intelligence assessments and estimates. I was also responsible for performing intelligence preparation of the battlefield and for advising the commander and subordinate units on the enemy, weather, and terrain. I felt at home in this role. Fort Huachuca now seemed like a warm memory of learning about my job as an intelligence professional.

* * *

My second day in the headquarters was my busiest day of intelligence collection. In the morning, a prisoner of war was brought to me for interrogation. It was a deserter from the enemy motorized company stationed in the vicinity of Dormantville, just two kilometers south of our defensive positions. Private Donvan fled his company because he wasn't being taken care of as a soldier. Food was scarce. They'd been on the road for a long time without rest, and he missed home. He was captured while running across the woods straight into our patrol's custody. At first, he wasn't exactly ready to talk, but I remained patient. I pulled out an MRE and started preparing it right in front of him. With his eyes fixated on the food, he started salivating and swallowing heavily. I waited for the food to heat up, asking him control questions to which the answers I already knew. He was telling the truth. I took some crackers from the MRE and offered them to Donvan. He devoured them in a split second, then he started choking. I offered him water in a plastic cup. He drank it just as fast. I asked him about the position of his unit, but he seemed distracted by the now-warm food on the table. I pushed the MRI packet toward him and gave him a fork.

"Eat and speak," I said. "I don't have all day."

He didn't need more encouragement and answered all my questions concerning his unit positions, strength, equipment, and mission. After the interrogation, I released him to the guard. Immediately, I prepared my first intelligence report about the upcoming likely attack of the enemy Bravo motorized company at the rear of our defensive positions around Mount Vernon. I recommended a reconnaissance mission around the perimeter of Hill Vermont and Stony Creek trenches to check for the presence of other enemy units. Since I sensed that more critical information was needed, I sent a counterintelligence agent from my unit disguised as a local civilian to connect with James, our informant in the nearby town of Dormantville. For hours, the attempt at contact seemed futile. In the meantime, our radio operators intercepted the enemy communication about an attack at 6:00 a.m. on Mount Vernon. However, the date and other details were unknown.

The next morning, the reconnaissance mission was completed, resulting in two more enemy units found in the vicinity of Mount Vernon: the Delta motorized rifle company near the Stony Creek trenches and the 54th rifle detachment occupied the bridge on Stony Creek, northeast of the trenches. As bits and pieces of information were coming from various sources, the PIR (priority intelligence requirements) were the strengths of units and the time of the attack on our defensive positions. I reported everything I had so far to the battalion commander, but I still needed my PIRs for the report to become actual intelligence. This information could only come from the informant James, who was nowhere to be found.

Another several hours had passed before my counterintelligence agent showed up with the news. He found James that morning hanging with his buddies at the local pool hall. Apparently, he had some information for us the day before, but was too drunk to report it immediately. From James, I finally had the strength and the time of the enemy attack on Mount

Vernon. The enemy was planning the attack on our defensive positions on Mount Vernon on 31072002 at 0600 hours. Enemy strength: Bravo motorized company with three BTR60 (1.6 kilometers to the West of Mount Vernon), Charlie chemical company with one BTR60 (800 meters southwest of Mount Vernon), Delta motorized rifle company with two BTR60 (800 meters north of the Stony Creek trenches), and the 54th rifle detachment with eighteen x RPK47 (on the bridge on the Stony Creek, 1.6 kilometers northeast of the trenches). I quickly completed my final report for the commander.

* * *

In the evening, after delivering my last report of the day to Commander Mathia, I lay under my tree to process all the information I had received so far to get some rest. It was all now in the battalion commander's hands. I was lying restless for a while, vigilant, and hugging my M16. Just as I drifted off, suddenly the ground shook as if a missile just landed within yards of my position. I grabbed my rifle and leaned against the tree, aiming in the direction where the single shots were now coming from. I heard the commotion in the tent behind me. Then the silence. Later, I was told that there was an attempted attack on our battalion headquarters, but fortunately, it was intercepted by our units patrolling the perimeter. Either way, the enemy was closing in and we had to begin our preparations.

That night was a sign of tough times approaching. Out of nowhere, the thunder started piercing the cloudy skies. The ominous wind was blowing through the trees and shrubbery. For the time being, the headquarters were dissolved, and everyone had to return to their respective platoons. When I arrived at my platoon location at the edge of the woods, I noticed the resentment of my fellow candidates toward me. I could tell that they hated the idea that I wasn't with them engaged in short daily missions. Perhaps they thought I was just spending a pleasant time in the headquarters tent, excluded from the daily tasks. No one would speak to me, and they barely even looked at me. I felt lonely and detached more than I had ever felt before.

We had to evacuate the forest as a company. We walked through the darkness in tight single files until we reached the main road. There, several DEUCEs were waiting for us, providing temporary shelter from the storm. The rain and thunder were relentless. Packed like sardines, we spent a few hours stationary, waiting in the vehicles for the weather to calm down.

On my mind were our defensive positions on Mount Vernon and the enemy approaching. We had only one day left to reinforce our fortifications and the security around the perimeter. Time was of the essence, and that worried me greatly.

* * *

As I was drifting deeper into my thoughts about the defense, I was transported back to a different time in my life when I was on a defense. I was going to defend my master's thesis at the University of Warsaw and at the National Music Academy.

In June 1993, the traffic in the midmorning hours in Warsaw was tight. It seemed like everyone got into their cars at the same time to drive somewhere. I was extremely nervous that I would be late for the defense of my thesis at the National Music Academy. Fortunately, I left the dorm early enough to make it through the crowded city. When I arrived at the school, I still had time to stop by the school coffee shop to get a shot of fresh espresso for courage.

I entered a large conference room with a long table covered with a white cloth. Twelve people from the school faculty, including my chairperson, were awaiting me. We were not sitting down for dinner. They were all there to grill me and squeeze out of me every bit of information to prove that I deserved to be there. Some of the faculty were specializing in dance and some were in music. However, none of them spoke French or knew linguistics. Just like ballet and linguistics, French was my strength. I felt confident. This was my time.

For an hour, I was answering all the questions pertaining to ballet terminology and jargon with ease. I was in my element. It felt like the music specialists were learning from me about ballet, linguistics, and French. Those specializing in dance asked lots of questions about linguistics as well, perhaps because it was never a subject of a master's thesis at the academy. Typically, the thesis evolved around music and musicians or dance and dancers. My defense made everyone interested in the subject of ballet terminology. I passed the exam with flying colors. I was now officially holding the title of master's in fine arts in dance pedagogy.

Two days later, I repeated the process at the university. Before I entered the school, I stopped briefly by the pub Harenda next to the building. A shot of gin was a good starting point for my second defense. Here I was much more nervous because Chris, as the reviewer of my thesis, was also part of the examination committee.

This defense took place under somewhat intimate conditions compared to the academy. There were only five people in the small conference room with dimmed lights. Since everyone in the room was an expert in French and linguistics, most of the questions asked of me were about ballet. Ballet was never a subject of study at the French Philology department. Again, I was in my element and enjoyed explaining to the committee the structures of ballet terms and even demonstrating a step here and there.

An hour later, I came out of the room as the official holder of the title of master in liberal arts in French philology. The next day, I showed up at school with flowers and asked for Chris at the dean's office. It was a common practice to give professors flowers after a successful defense.

"These are for you," I said with satisfaction. "Thank you for everything and especially your support in the hardest times."

We hugged openly in the hallway for the first time. Hugging was not common, but now that I wasn't a student anymore, our friendship became official.

* * *

The last two days of July were designated for wrapping up our operations, cleaning the area, and packing. Then the third platoon was taken to Mount Vernon to set up defensive positions on top of the hill.

Before we were shipped to the battlefield, I stopped by the perimeter gate to check my gear and noticed Lieutenant Jones sitting against a tree, relaxing.

"You know, Rakowski, I want to go to Poland and find a hard-core woman like you," he stated somewhat melancholically. He was smiling, which meant that he was actually serious.

"That seems like an easy task," I replied with a smile. "There are plenty of women like me in Poland. See you at the hilltop, lieutenant. I'm ready for the battle of the century!" I added, rubbing my hands.

Lieutenant Jones only giggled, shaking his head.

* * *

We were dropped off about half a mile from Mount Vernon. It was a beautiful afternoon for marching as the heat of the day started subsiding.

For the last time in OCS, we had to walk a distance. It didn't bother me anymore because I was more anxious about our defensive positions, our strength, and the battle. The enemy three companies plus a platoon-size detachment (all played by the remaining three platoons of our actual company) were advancing toward the hill. They were to reach our defense line the following day and attack at dawn, in the dark.

The march uphill wasn't as easy as I originally had thought. The paved road ended, and we had to negotiate a dirt road covered with gravel and rocks. I felt like I was walking in place. This reminded me of my marching for the German Badge in Fort Huachuca almost a year ago. In Fort Huachuca, I was fighting pain in my feet, the scorching heat, and the games my mind was playing with me. When I felt something wet in my boots, I had serious doubts about the purpose of my suffering. Now I was feeling the same anguish.

"I heard you are hard-core, Rakowski," a sudden comment from Lieutenant Kohls passing me by brought me back from my reminiscence. It was nice to be called "hard-core," especially at the time of near despair. "How are your feet?"

"My feet are okay and I'm hanging in there." My typical response annoyed me. Was I really hanging in there or persevering? I'd prefer perseverance and tenacity. It sounded much better than "hanging," more elevated. Regardless, it was nice that he asked about my feet, even though I suspected he couldn't care less.

We reached the top of Mount Vernon a few minutes after sunset. We set up our tents for a quick night with relentless chiggers who were ignoring the duct tape on our boots and a special bug repellant. Just like the advancing enemy, they wanted our blood. With my rifle tight against my chest, I was lying on the hard ground, shaking from anxiety and fear. I was looking at the starry skies above me, thinking about our upcoming last battle in OCS. I wasn't sure if I was prepared mentally for this kind of engagement. Would it be realistic? Would the enemy surprise us with artillery and heavy guns? How many soldiers would be attacking us? Were my intelligence reports accurate? Would I be able to react properly to open fire? How would I know if I was killed or wounded? How will the cadre act? All these intrusive thoughts were invading my mind, like the chiggers invading my tired body.

After a long restless night on the hill, the crisp morning was very welcomed. Immediately after eating our breakfast MREs, the commander briefed us as to the activities to prepare for battle. We studied the maps with the current suspected enemy positions. We reviewed the principles of war: Mass Objective Security Surprise (MOSS) and Maneuver Offense Unity of Command Simplicity Economy of Force (MOUSE). I liked the second one better because it reminded me of home, as this was the nickname Alec had given me one day. Except now, the mouse was a transformed beast, a tiger waiting with a weapon for the enemy, ready for the last enormous battle.

We spent the entire day setting up our fighting positions. Michaud, Arroyo, and I dug our foxholes next to each other. In front of us, around the perimeter, we dug three more holes shallower than the foxholes to slow the enemy. In front of these holes, we stacked the tree logs we had managed to find in the vicinity. Finally, in front of the logs, we stretched a decent amount of concertina barbed wire. More wooden barricades were placed mid-hill. The rest of the platoon followed suit and built similar structures all around the hilltop. At the end of the entire day of digging, I developed blisters from my entrenching tool. I was drenched from physical effort and drained by psychological tension.

To relieve some discomfort, I "took a shower" by using baby wipes wherever I could and put on a dry T-shirt and fresh socks. At dusk and after a dinner MRE, I fixed my camouflage makeup and made sure that my weapon was clean, put several magazines in my cargo pockets and on my LBE. Since the hill defense was to simulate a real battlefield environment, I donned my MILES (multiple integrated laser engagement system). MILES was the training gear which used a laser module mounted to the barrel of an M16 loaded with blank cartridges, a blank-firing adaptor for the weapon, and sensors on the soldier's helmet and on the load-bearing equipment harness. When a blank shot was fired by a weapon, the laser would fire a burst in the direction where the weapon was aimed. Then, if that burst was picked up by the sensors on the "hit" soldier's harness or helmet, the gear would beep to signal they were "killed". Theoretically, the beeping sound of the harness meant that someone was aiming at me, while a loud, flat tone and flashing sensors indicated the kill. After being shot, the hit soldier was required to lie on his back to stop the noise and signal others that he is "dead". I didn't want to be "killed" so I was reluctant to wear this equipment. I wanted to fight until I had no fight or bullets left.

I fixed my camouflage makeup and made sure that my weapon was clean.

As the night fell, everything quieted down. We took our positions in the foxholes with weapons at the ready. I waited for the enemy, motionless, sweating from anticipation. I was scared. Genuinely scared. But I needed to stay put and survive.

* * *

At dawn, everything was happening in slow motion. Delicate clouds of fog barely lifted off the ground. They seemed to be moving slowly toward me like an invisible, powerful force that kept me still, barely breathing, my heart pounding. "Don't shoot too soon," I continuously repeated to myself. "Wait. Don't give up your position." Then, from the clouds, I saw shadows approaching; however, they looked dispersed as if a gentle breeze was carrying them through the bush. I wasn't sure if these were the enemy forces or an illusion of a tired mind. Regardless, I breathed slowly and quietly, suspended in the anticipation of the worst and hoping for the best. The dawn was late; the darkness of the night wouldn't surrender. The shadows were coming. "Let them come closer, be patient, trust your instinct," I quietly whispered to myself like a prayer. I tried to pinpoint the pause between my breaths, the sign that it was time to shoot.

Before I could take a deep breath before firing, a sudden barrage on the outside perimeter began like thunder shaking everything and everyone in the vicinity. The weapons shooting, bullets whistling, and the bursts of white and red fire and lasers in the darkness seemed unstoppable. The brass casings raining on our heads bouncing off our bodies. Friendly forces hiding in foxholes in front of me were attacked, and the fire was now coming from both sides. The enemy was approaching relentlessly. The fire exchange was moving forward like an ear-splitting storm. The sounds of beeping sensors were overwhelming. I could see the tree logs being crossed and the barbed wires cut and dismantled. Then I noticed the silhouettes jumping over the stacks of tree branches, charging.

By now, we were all firing tenaciously. Arroyo and I were shooting our M16 rifles, standing up in the foxholes. Michaud, in a prone position between us, was shooting using his M60 machine gun. His shells were flying off the cartridges from a disintegrating belt of M13 links. Mathia was right behind us with her M16, shooting at the enemy as well. For a few moments, alarming thoughts invaded my brain. What if somehow one of the enemies had live rounds? What if the action on Mount Vernon just looked like training, but it had the potential to become an actual battle with people dying? I thought about the movie I saw a few years back called *Opposing Force,* where a situation like this actually happened. I remembered the final shooting scene on top of a hill. Several people died. Overwhelmed by panic, I thought anything was possible. We could actually die, here and now, defending our hilltop. I shook my head vigorously a couple of times to chase this vision away. I closed and opened my eyes and took a deep breath to regain focus and come back to reality. In this reality, I didn't want to die.

Eventually, part of the positions on the outside perimeter and one inside layer of the camp were compromised. The enemy was charging toward the center of our camp toward the strongest defensive positions. All around me, the sensors were lighting up like Christmas trees; however, it was impossible for me to discern if it was the enemy being shot or my fellow soldiers. Some silhouettes with brightly lit sensors were advancing through the camp. They should have been down. On the other hand, some silhouettes with beeping, illuminated sensors were attempting to stand up or still fire from the ground.

"Stay down, you're 'dead'!" someone from the cadre with a black cap shouted.

"No!" a voice rebelled. "You're 'dead'! I'm only wounded!"

I could just see in all the commotion the instructor pushing his boot against the rebelling soldier's chest. I realized perhaps all bets were off and the rules didn't apply anymore. Here, during the battle, it could get physical and no one would dare say anything in this chaos. Holding the soldier down on the ground, the "black cap" furiously yelled through his teeth, "You're 'dead'! Stay down and stop shooting!"

The chaos continued. I couldn't differentiate who was the enemy because we all had the same uniforms. Helmets were flying as soldiers were going down after being shot and "killed." Arroyo's hole seemed empty from my position. I peeked and saw only the top of her helmet inside. I couldn't see her sensors. Thinking that she might have been injured, I started crawling out of my foxhole to drag her back to safety. As I approached her, I realized she was 'dead' against the wall, her harness sensors beeping. A few steps to my left, I heard Michaud yelling while frantically spraying the battlefield now with his rifle, bullets flying in all directions. His machine gun was near me, abandoned without bullets. I attempted to take cover under the brush to my right since the chaos was overbearing and I needed to assess the situation and regroup.

I was crawling low and had almost reached the brush when I heard a ping. Before I could register what was happening, I was shot in my back. All sensors on my torso lit up. In the last desperate effort, I turned on my back, aiming at and looking at the shooter straight in the eyes. It was Lieutenant Kohls. There was no time to feel any resentment as he shot me again in my chest. "Traitor!" a thought went through my mind. My rifle fell out of my hands from shock, my helmet tumbled to the ground. I lay there on my back, looking at the sunny skies, 'dying' in broad daylight.

The sounds of the battle slowly subsided. Those still on their feet were now collapsing from stress and physical effort. The weapons and helmets were being tossed.

The only thing left in me was the sense of pride that we were holding strong against the forces three times our size for as long as we could. In the end, we were surrounded and overpowered. This time, there was no victory, only a complete defeat. We all 'died' in the fiercest battle at the officer candidate school.

* * *

After we'd cleaned the battlefield from all brass, filled in all the foxholes, and dismantled our defensive positions, we were taken by the buses back to the barracks. Almost immediately, we started out-processing, cleaning weapons and gear, and packing.

In the afternoon, we were allowed to wear civilian clothes for the first time since we had first arrived in Alabama eight weeks ago. The special treat at the end of the training was a trip to the nearby town of Anniston to have fun and relaxation at the motel until late at night. Hotel Express was a fairly low-standard motel about half a mile from the Fort McClellan gate. However low the standard, it was better than the dingy barracks on-post. As a reward for completing OCS, we were invited to use the swimming pool and the hotel's facilities. I spent the entire afternoon sunbathing by the pool. Finally, wearing anything but my military uniform, I watched how my fellow soldiers and some cadre had fun in the pool, playing with water like schoolchildren.

I didn't stay long at the swimming pool. I was extremely tired and overwhelmed. In my mind, the images of our fearless defense of Mount Vernon were replaying like a film. I could still hear the battle cries, the shooting, and the sensors beeping. It was all too real to forget. Emotionally, I was completely drained, even though the pressure was gone. Perhaps too suddenly. I needed a quiet moment for myself to organize some of my thoughts and acknowledge certain feelings.

The taxi dropped me off by the barracks. From there, I took a short walk to the parade field. The sun was setting above the horizon, enveloping the field with its golden arms. I stood there alone, mesmerized by the serenity of nature around me. The freshly cut grass was surrounding me like a vast ocean. On this very grass, everything started just eight weeks ago. It seemed like the ages had gone by. Back then, I was a brand-new, scared officer candidate among a few hundred others. I had no confidence in my abilities and no experience of being in charge of troops. Back then, on this very field, I was getting "smoked" with everyone else, trying not to stand out. Throughout the training, however, I learned how to stand out in a good way as a leader, a future officer leading by example. I had endured a tremendous amount of pain, four heat exhaustions, a broken finger, a broken nose, an injured knee, and multiple infections of my toes. I'd been eaten by chiggers and burned by poison ivy. I survived obstacle courses. I led two out of four road marches: one as a pacesetter and the other as the company's first sergeant. I'd passed ten theory tests and two practical land navigation tests. I successfully performed in six different leadership positions. I led the troops in offensive operations, and I defended the hill with others. When troops were hungry, I took care of them. I inspired others. I had achieved all these in just eight weeks, and despite the struggles at every stage, I stayed in the program. But most of all, I had become a different person. I grew confident in my skills and abilities. I had a new command presence, and I believed in myself. And now the struggle has ended only to bring forward new opportunities and challenges. My big victory was to successfully complete phase III of the OCS. While reminiscing about all that I had gone through within the past eight weeks, I sensed someone's presence next to me.

"You will be an outstanding intelligence officer, Rakowski," said Major Effiert. "Go to your Illinois and do great things. They should be very proud of you."

"Yes, sir," I replied, and we shook hands.

We stood there for a few moments, watching the sunset in silence.

* * *

Children are wonderful at role-playing games—doctor, house, police, war, or pretending to be superheroes. When I was little, I played a detective searching for clues to solve cases. It was fun and rewarding because I got to ride my bike really fast to catch the bad guys. I got to climb the trees to conduct my clandestine observations. Now, as a real soldier, to learn the art and craft of war, I was wargaming, which was no child's play. I was using a real rifle in real, tactical conditions with artillery simulators, playing real war scenarios. Often I had that uneasy feeling that there could be a real bullet in one of the weapons, in which case I was looking death in the eyes.

I believed that my intense tactical, every day training was bringing me closer to the reality of war that I could face one day. Waiting in the trenches for the enemy, without seeing much in front of me, only trusting the orders of my superiors was a frightening experience. Their judgment based on the battlefield information and proper decisions were a matter of life and death, and as a future officer, I had to be prepared for that.

CHAPTER 20

A LEADER WITHIN THE GREATER PROFESSION

Once I came back to Illinois, the day of graduation from OCS arrived at last. The day prior, Alec took me back to Springfield, Illinois, to the Regional Training Institute to take care of out-processing paperwork, equipment turn-in, and preparation for my "walk" on the stage.

While on the base, I was revisiting in my mind all the places from my previous encounters. I remembered the big auditorium in the main area of the compound. That was where, nearly two years earlier, as a freshly enlisted soldier, I attended the welcome ceremony for the new recruits. That same weekend, I experienced for the first time what it felt like to be a soldier. Prebasic training was only two days, but they were intense enough for me to picture what the real basic training would look like. I was mentally prepared.

Sixteen months later, I was back in Springfield to attend a preliminary meeting with those who expressed their interest in attending the OCS. There were generals and institute cadre giving speeches about the reality of training and how much responsibility comes with being an officer in the U.S. Army. That afternoon, in this large classroom where the meeting was held, I promised myself that I wouldn't bail out when the times get hard and I would do anything in my power to persist.

One month later, I came to Springfield for the "introduction to the officer candidate school." This time, I was learning how harsh was this training environment. We were yelled at and openly discouraged to quit the program at the beginning. This was a challenging time; the pressure for speed and accuracy in everything we were doing was tremendous. I remembered the tree under which, as the new candidates, we stood in platoon formation, studying the officer candidate guide. We were so focused and scared, we remained motionless, like under a spell. The tension was palpable. We could only pray for a better time. During this visit, I found out enough about the process and was eager to start pursuing my dream.

Phase 0 of the OCS commenced a month later in April. Here I was, back again in my state capital. The training was getting more demanding with every step. I was worried about having to drive to Springfield for eighteen months. Luckily, I was presented with an opportunity to complete the OCS via the accelerated "501" program. I applied and in May, I received an acceptance into the program.

In June, Alec drove me to Springfield for my physical performance test before shipping to Alabama. I remembered the maze of small streets on the base, my run around the pale structures, and my push-ups on the grass near an office building.

And now I was back again for the last time to receive my officer's commission. This time, I was more of a witness than a participant in the training events. As I watched the candidates from traditional OCS struggling and scrambling around the base, being yelled at and scared, my heart went out to them.

* * *

The graduation took place in the Illinois State Capitol, a magnificent nineteenth-century structure at the center of Springfield, Illinois. The auditorium was packed. We were waiting just outside the room. There were fourteen of us new officers: six from 2002 accelerated 501 program and eight from the traditional program which began the year prior. The Color Guard entered the auditorium with the sound of a military march.

We entered the room and took our places in the front row. After the national anthem, there were speeches, awards, and more speeches. We stood up and turned toward the audience to take the "officer oath of office," which signified our appointment as a second lieutenant in the United States Army. We promised to support and defend the Constitution of the United States just as I promised when I enlisted nearly two years ago. But now, I was finally accepted as both a member of the U.S. Army Officer Corps and a leader within the greater profession.

After the main ceremony, we were finding our loved ones so they could pin our golden bars to the uniform epaulets. I was happy to see my husband, who supported me through the entire OCS, finally with me at the graduation, proud. Alec and our friend Nick were pinning my bars.

Per tradition, an NCO (noncommissioned officer), in my case Sergeant Mathis (from phase I OCS in Alabama), was the person to render my first salute. I was elated that he was there for me in the audience. I respected him tremendously for this honor. He approached me and saluted with satisfaction. I returned the salute, and in gratitude for the valuable assistance and constant support during my most challenging times in Alabama, I rewarded him with a 2002 Silver Eagle dollar coin. That was my "silver dollar salute."

I was accepted as both a member of the U.S. Army Officer Corps and a leader within the greater profession.

"You did great, kiddo," he said, beaming with pride. "Congratulations!"

It seemed like it had been ages since Sergeant Mathis called me "Kiddo." I already missed it. It felt like it was coming from an older brother who was always looking out for me. Having this nickname was also giving me a sense of comfort and peace, even as a commissioned officer.

* * *

I had a similar sense of comfort when my French boss Yves called me by my nickname, Asia (Ashia, a diminutive of Joanna in Polish) back in 1993. I just started my first job at a French company in Warsaw after graduating from university. Yves was just a few years my senior, and from the beginning, he was treating me more like his younger sister than his employee. Being called Asia felt like a family. It was endearing, and I appreciated it. But I appreciated it even more when, one October day, Yves decided to take me on a business trip to Belgium. After the conference in Brussels, we were going to stop briefly in Paris before going back to Warsaw. Luckily for me, the trip coincided with the time when Chris was in Paris working on a research project. I was looking forward to this meeting with Chris.

That night, Yves and I arrived from Brussels at the train station in Paris. The City of Lights looked especially beautiful. It was a celebration of a special moment in my life when everything was falling seemingly into place. Being in Paris felt like being in love with everything that was surrounding me, even in the middle of the night.

Yves wanted to spend a weekend in Paris and visit his friends. I had a mission of my own. He dropped me off at 74 Rue Lauriston by the stylish iron gate of the eighteenth-century building from the Napoleonic era. A big brass plate right above read: "Centre Scientifique de l'Académie Polonaise Des Sciences de Paris" (Scientific Center of Polish Science Academy in Paris). I stood there for a moment, listening for the steps on the stairway behind the gate. I was sure that I would hear these steps soon.

"Are you sure someone is going to open the gate for you?" my boss asked carefully.

"Yes, I'm sure. I've made the arrangements. Thanks for the lift. I will see you tomorrow at the airport."

A couple of seconds after he left, I finally heard the steps.

"Jo, I wasn't sure if you would really come to see me here, in Paris."

"I told you I would come—here I am. I'm so glad to see you, Chris."

The entire City of Lights was pulsating in my chest with energy, color, and stars.

We went back upstairs to the room where Chris was staying. I pulled out a bottle of Belgian champagne I received after the conference the previous day. Chris and I drank almost the whole content using plastic cups. The night was still young, so we left the building and took a long walk on Champs-Élysées, "the most beautiful avenue in the world," connecting the Concorde and Arc de Triomphe. That night, Champs-Élysées, the place of the blessed in Greek mythology, seemed a truly blessed place for us. My dream finally came true. I was meeting Chris in Paris. I wanted to celebrate our secret moment openly, on this grand avenue. It was a secret that I wanted to share with the entire city, with every passerby as a witness, in the middle of the night. When we reached L'Arc de Triomphe, I gently pulled Chris to my heart and tenderly kissed those beautiful, half-closed eyes, smiling at my face. Our heartbeats were singing in perfect harmony with all the lights around us and the stars on the high black firmament...

* * *

Enduring OCS was not only a matter of physical and mental strength and confidence. It was also about teamwork and the trust of those under my command. It was about taking care of others and simple responsibility for their lives. But the biggest part of my evolution was the ever-present support of my trainers and counselors. I appreciated the importance of mentorship and encouragement, so critical in becoming a warrior and a leader.

PART VI

MY FIRST OVERSEAS TRAINING:
U.S. ARMY EMERGENCY DEPLOYMENT READINESS EXERCISE, POLAND

CHAPTER 21

SOMETHING BIGGER THAN MYSELF

In the spring of 2003, I was mentally preparing myself for my military intelligence officer basic course (MIOBC) in Fort Huachuca, starting in the last week of June. In the meantime, I received information from my Chicago unit that they were looking for Polish-speaking volunteers to go on an overseas training mission. Because the timing was appropriate and the mission would end just before my MIOBC, I volunteered without hesitation.

Being part of both NATO and the European Union Poland was the chief European ally of the United States, and one of the strongest Continental partners in promoting international security and wealth. Consistently throughout its history, Poland was a pro-American nation in the world, with eighty percent of its citizens perceiving the U.S. favorably in 2002. In 2003, Poland became part of the American-led Iraq War coalition, providing one of the largest contributions in terms of troops to the Iraqi war. Poland-U.S. relations were the key to maintaining peace and security in Central and Eastern Europe and to providing immediate assistance in response to any aggression against NATO members. Hence the collaboration between the two countries and military readiness exercises in Poland.

My team of Polish linguists from our unit met at O'Hare airport wearing civilian clothes and with bags full of uniforms and gear. This was my first intercontinental flight as an officer in charge, thus I was nervous.

Fortunately, the trip to Italy was uneventful. We were picked up from the airport in Venice and taken by van to the U.S. base. We were stationed with the Southern European Task Force (SETAF) headquartered in Vicenza, Italy.

For the first three days, all we had to do is to hang out with the full-timers on base and wait for the rest of the team to arrive from the U.S. The base didn't look much different from the ones I was used to seeing in the States. There was a U. S. Post Office, Shopette, PX, and a Burger King.

Because we still had the entire two days of waiting, I wanted to do something special for my team. I approached my commanding officer, Captain Greenly, with the idea of taking them on a brief trip to see a few Italian cities. We would leave on Tuesday morning and come back by the end of the business day the next day. He agreed and had me promise we would be back in a timely manner. We had a deal. That same day, I purchased a travel guide for Italy in English, and we immediately started planning our trip together. Using the enclosed maps, we laid out the itinerary.

The next day, we left the base early in the morning to catch the train to Rome, passing through Padua, Ferrara, Bologna, and Florence. We boarded the Italo bullet high-speed train and after two and a half hours, we landed in Rome at the Termini station at the heart of the town.

In Rome, we were practically running through the city, only stopping for a few seconds in front of major landmarks like Colosseum and statues. However, my team, being all born and raised in catholic Poland, had an especially important mission in Rome. We wanted to visit the Papal Basilica of Saint Peter in the Vatican to honor our Pope.

I was nine years old when Cardinal Karol Wojtyla, Archbishop of Krakow, Poland, was elected the 263rd successor to Saint Peter and chose the name John Paul II. This election of a man from behind the Iron Curtain evoked powerful emotions around the world because the conclave broke the rule that the Supreme Pontiff had to be Italian. For the Poles, it was a tremendous deal not only because he was the first ever Slavic pope elected, but he was also Polish.

In 1979, the year I started ballet school, the Pope visited Poland for the first time as the head of the Catholic Church. Back then, I was too young to understand the significance of his visit. Only years later I could appreciate the Pope's role in Poland's political future. Having a powerful influence on Polish society when the Church was the major force protecting the citizens against the communist regime's pressure, the Pope was a huge symbol of hope and inspiration to his countrymen. As a spiritual authority for the devout Polish Catholics, he was credited for his contribution to the collapse of communism. It was no surprise that immediately after his inauguration, the pilgrimages to Rome began increasing. And now my team had an opportunity for its own pilgrimage to Rome. We had just enough time to enter St. Peter's Basilica and see the magnificent interior, including its dome designed by Michelangelo.

In Rome, we were practically running through the city, only stopping for a few seconds in front of major landmarks like Colosseum.

The sun started setting above the hills of Rome. We desperately needed to find a place to spend the night. No hotels were available in proximity to our location. We had no option except to continue running and stopping by every hotel just to find out that all rooms were sold out for the night. At last, we found a place that had a suite available just enough for the four of us.

After spending a quick night at the hotel, we headed toward the train station. At lightning speed, we made it to the station in less than half an hour and boarded the first train going toward Venice. We decided to stop by Florence to spend a few hours in the capital city of the Tuscany region. After a two-hour ride on the train, we ended up at Santa Maria Novella, one of Italy's busiest train stations by the Santa Maria Novella church. I had a mission of my own to see something very specific in this city.

When I was little, there was an enormous book in my parents' library called "In Renaissance Florence". Its size alone—it was bigger than all the other books—was attracting my attention. I was also intrigued by its cover, a photo of a bird's-eye view of hundreds of little buildings packed among the narrow streets with one immense dome dominating the picture. I was wondering for years until I could read what this was and why it seemed so odd. How was it possible that all these buildings around the dome were so small, and why this one enormous structure was so unproportional, I wondered? Ever since, I wanted to go to Florence and see for myself if something was wrong with that picture. As we were moving at a fast pace through the narrow and crowded streets of Florence, the first thing that stood out was the city's most iconic sight, the Duomo, also known as Santa Maria del Fiore Cathedral, a giant structure with a terracotta-tiled dome. Now I finally had the opportunity to see the largest structure in Florence.

Indeed, the Duomo was dominating the cityscape and was surrounded tightly by the smaller buildings. In front of it was the famous Piazza della Signoria, a beautiful city square surrounded by several important buildings, including, Palazzo Vecchio, the Loggia della Signoria, the Palazzo degli Uffizi, the oldest art museum in the world, the Palace of the Tribunale della Mercanzia, and the Palazzo Uguccioni. In the Piazza della Signoria we visited the well-known loggia with statues, recalling important events in the city and important myths. We admired several 15th and 16th century famous works like a replica of the David, Perseus, Hercules and Cacus, and the fountain of Neptune.

I was especially excited about visiting the nearby famous Ponte Vecchio, a historic bridge buzzing with life, and full of mesmerized tourists. I knew about it from my music history lessons in ballet school. We studied a famous piece of music by Giacomo Puccini, "O mio babbino caro" ("Oh my dear Papa"). It was a soprano aria from the opera Gianni Schicchi (1918). It is sung by Lauretta after tensions between her father Schicchi and the family of Rinuccio, the boy she loves, had reached the point of threatening to separate the lovers. She begged her father to let her marry Rinuccio or else she would throw herself from the Ponte Vecchio into the river Arno. At the bridge, we were lucky to witness this aria being performed by a casual singer, as if she wanted to live through a genuine moment from the opera. I was moved by her beautiful, convincing singing.

It was just past noon, and the weather was extremely hot. However, being soldiers with experience in fast marching in the most unforgiving conditions, we didn't encounter any problems. Our biggest enemy was time. We were moving at a fast pace through the narrow and crowded streets of Florence. Eventually, we stopped by the Caffe Duomo restaurant for lunch near the Ponte Vecchio. It was a perfect place for traditional regional meat and pasta dishes and Tuscan wines. The pizza we had was light and tasty, with a very thin crust golden on the edges. Nothing like Chicago-style pizza. I preferred the Italian version. After lunch, we hopped on the train from Florence to Vicenza. At last, a bus took us to the SETAF base. The visit was intense, but quick. I promised myself to return there one day and truly enjoy this wonderful city.

It turned out that we had another day available before the departure on the mission to Poland, so with the approval of our captain, we took a train to Venice and landed at the train station called Stazione di Venezia Santa Lucia. Because our time was limited, our plan was to see the major landmarks from the boat without stepping on the ground. We bought the tickets for the waterbus called *Vaporetto* at the vending machines.

From there, we sailed under the Rialto Bridge, the oldest of the four bridges spanning the Grand Canal in Venice. The Grand Canal, the major waterway of Venice, was lined on each side by Renaissance and Gothic palaces and churches. From the water we saw an impressive St. Mark's Square, the principal public square of Venice. We stopped briefly by Saint Mark's Basilica, the cathedral church of the Catholic Patriarchate of Venice. We also saw St Mark's Campanile, the bell tower of St Mark's Basilica, the tallest structure in Venice. From there, we sailed by the Venetian Gothic style Doge's Palace, and passed by the Bridge of Sighs, a white limestone structure over the Rio di Palazzo canal. From the water, we also noted the Basilica Santa Maria Gloriosa dei Frari, from where San Giorgio Maggiore, an island with its Palladian church, was visible in the distance.

After sailing through Venice for a while, we continued the sightseeing on foot, as it was the fastest and most efficient way to move around. We walked through the mazes of narrow streets with clotheslines stretched between the buildings. At almost every shop, with souvenirs, stunning carnival masks were displayed. It was a magical world.

* * *

The following day, we packed our bags, changed into uniforms, and headed toward Poland. After a twenty-five-hour ride on a luxury coach, we found ourselves near the Drawsko Pomorskie training area, where our training was to take place. We were part of the U.S. Army Emergency Deployment Readiness Exercise (EDRE) designed to test a rapid transfer of troops across the Atlantic as part of NATO's allied assistance to European countries. The exercise involved American, Polish, and British paratrooper units.

For most of the days, we worked twelve-hour shifts in giant tents in the field. In the evenings, we were spending time with Polish soldiers stationed at a base in well-appointed barracks.

Eventually, we connected with more members of our team: two colonels from Washington, D.C., from the Civil Affairs branch. My team played a critical role in conducting liaison activities with the Polish civilian population. One day, the entire team was invited to visit the primary school in Drawsko Pomorskie. The director, the entire school staff, and all the students were anxiously waiting for us in front of the school. The kids were mesmerized by the American soldiers of Polish origin. We gave them plenty of stickers with U.S. Army emblems and the American Flag.

Then we had a conference in school, during which the staff and kids were asking us countless questions, taking pictures with us, and even taking our autographs. The school personnel were equally intrigued by seeing us in American uniforms. This reminded me of a time in 1991, when I was traveling through Germany with my university's dance ensemble. During a stop to refuel at one of the gas stations in Stuttgart, I saw a military truck with an American flag. I ran up to it like a child in a toy store and asked a friend of mine to take a picture of me with two American soldiers who emerged from the truck. I was in awe that I had this special opportunity to have a photo with heroes I looked up to. Back then, I wouldn't have dreamed that one day, I would be one of them and someone would want to take their picture with me. And now, here I was, surrounded by schoolchildren like a hero, admired and respected.

I asked a friend of mine to take a picture of me with two American soldiers who emerged from the truck.

We were later invited to the local high school, where we met the young cadets in Polish Army uniforms, eager to know details about us serving in the U.S. Army.

In the early afternoon, we had a celebratory lunch prepared at school. Received as very important guests from across the ocean, we enjoyed phenomenal food and translated conversations. We were told about the school's roof falling apart a few years back and how the American soldiers had fixed it. A large commemorative bronze plaque was mounted on the building wall outside, just by the front entrance for everyone to see. The staff and our team were equally proud of this gesture.

After lunch, we were invited by the school director to her house for dessert, where we continued friendly conversations and answered more questions about America and the U.S. Army. Later that day, we visited the area filled with WWII-era Polish armored vehicles, tanks, howitzers, and monuments. Then we headed back to the barracks on base to return to our training the next day.

Although for a short period, it was good to visit the old country.

My team played a critical role in conducting liaison activities with the Polish civilian population. Drawsko Pomorskie, Poland

* * *

After returning from Europe, just before my departure to the officer basic course in Fort Huachuca, I was back at my Chicago unit to receive my first official officer evaluation by my unit's commanding officer, Major Larson. I was nervous. While driving to the city, I was trying to recall everything that was related to my military duties and conduct that could influence my evaluation. But my mind was a mess. Images from the past year of being an officer were scrambled like an overused videotape. My mind was racing. It was extremely important for me to have a positive evaluation in my early officer career to help me in my future advancement as an intelligence officer. Typically, before being promoted, these reports were studied closely by the senior officers to determine if a candidate was promotable.

That Friday, it was almost the end of duty day when I finally arrived at the Chicago armory on Calumet Avenue. I met with the commander in the same room where we had our first conversation after my enlistment. Back then, he asked me if I was ready for the basic training, and I enthusiastically replied that I was as ready as could be. And now, I was getting my first officer evaluation.

The commander had a stack of papers from my brown personnel folder in front of him. My report contained the details of my duties, specific aspects of my performance, performance potential, and future assignments.

Major Larson recommended me for a promotion and that was crucial to me.

We talked briefly about the nature and purpose of the report. I skimmed through the section regarding my duties. During my monthly drills, they included leading a translator/interpreter team of one officer and four enlisted translators/interpreters in Polish and French. I was responsible for the training, welfare, discipline, and accountability of a team of soldiers and their equipment. I was also acting as a provisional company S3 (managing and tracking current operations and organizing training).

Regarding the specific aspects of my performance, I was nervous like a schoolgirl awaiting the scores from a math or science exam. I was hoping to receive a good "grade", like a "center mass". I knew I wasn't outstanding, and a center mass grade was typical. But performing well as an officer was both math and science. Logic, precision, and proper execution were keys to success in everyday tasks.

With trembling hands, I took the third page of the report and first scanned quickly for any negative signs. When I didn't find anything alarming, I took my time to read the whole thing again slowly. In his comments about my performance, the commander said that "2LT Rakowski is a very proactive, self-motivated young officer. While serving as a provisional S3 for C Company, 2LT Rakowski devoted a great deal of time to assisting in the planning of this year's language exercise. 2LT Rakowski's passion for language prompted her to volunteer to serve C Company as the command language program manager (CLPM). In that capacity, Lieutenant Rakowski traveled to Washington State to meet with the CLPM of the 341 MI Bn (LINGUIST) to participate in one-on-one CLPM training. This training inspired her to become more knowledgeable about CLP operations and procedures. In addition to gaining valuable training, she acquired many valuable training support tools, some of which she implemented at the unit. This raised the overall DLPT average of C Company to the point that the unit enjoys one of the very highest DLPT averages of any unit of its kind in the army. Additionally, 2LT Rakowski spent a great deal of her own time and resources to develop a packet on recruiting materials such as business cards, posters, pamphlets, and a website to promote C Company."

I was pleasantly surprised. Until this review, I didn't realize how busy I was during the monthly drills with my unit in Chicago since the OCS. It seemed like my efforts were appreciated by the leadership and I was moving forward in my career, constantly challenging myself. I believed everything was slowly falling into place. After this evaluation, I was inspired and energized to tackle the MIOBC and become the best intelligence officer I could be. I was obsessed with the idea of progress and couldn't think of anything else.

On that gloomy afternoon, I drove through the streets of Chicago with my heart fluttering from joy and a sense of accomplishment. I was relieved and uplifted. Even the stalling traffic on the highways seemed like a pleasant adventure. The shining red back lights from the slow-moving cars in front of me looked like lava from a volcano without a beginning and an end. I could almost feel an overpowering heat surrounding me as the smell of hot exhaust was suffocating me behind the wheel. But I didn't mind, I was happy.

*   *   *

For the first time in my life, I finally felt that I was part of something bigger than myself. I understood the cooperation between the ally countries as part of NATO. It wasn't only about the tactical or strategic operations on the battlefield. It was also about developing relationships with the local civilian Polish population, a wholehearted supporter of American presence in Poland. As American soldiers, we were their beacon of hope.

PART VII

MILITARY INTELLIGENCE OFFICER BASIC COURSE:
LEARNING MY JOB AS AN OFFICER

CHAPTER 22

HEARTACHE AND LONELINESS

Since coming home from the OCS, I was thinking about the next step in my military career. I had to attend the officer basic course in Fort Huachuca to become an expert in military intelligence at the officer level. The slot for the intelligence officer was already assigned to me in my unit and was waiting for me to finish my MIOBC. I wanted to take care of it as soon as possible, so I scheduled it ten months after the OCS.

In June 2003, Alec and I drove my car to Fort Huachuca because I was staying on base for over four months and needed a personal vehicle. This time, I also had to bring with me a lot of personal items, like a computer, a printer, a bicycle, etc. During the trip, our situation at home was on my mind. After my return from Fort Huachuca, I stayed home for seven months and did everything I could to keep Alec happy. I was an easygoing, cheerful, devoted wife who was gladly driving Alec home after a night of drinking beer and playing pool at our favorite Polish tavern in Chicago. I was happy to attend gatherings with our friends and be his companion at family functions. Still, I had an uneasy feeling that I was an annoyance at home, like I couldn't be myself anymore. It was easy to volunteer for the mission in Poland just before the MIOBC. Of course, it was a lifetime opportunity from my military career perspective, but part of me just wanted to give Alec some space, and get out of his way. Six days after Poland, I packed again. This time, I was going away for over four months. Since Alec was to drive with me, we had his parents take care of our two yorkies, staying with them while we were gone. Although I had a good relationship with my in-laws (they calmed down a bit seeing that I returned to Alec after each of my military trainings), I could sense some resentment from them. I imagined how much it had to bother my conservative mother-in-law, that instead of being at home, as a good cooking and cleaning wife, pleasing my husband, I was "playing a soldier." This was putting unnecessary pressure on the relationship between Alec and me. But for the time being, I thought Alec was on my side.

After driving for almost 1,800 miles in less than three days, we finally arrived at the Fort. It was a hot Saturday evening.

On the surface, everything seemed to be the same since the time I was there two years ago. The same streets, the same buildings, and the same reddish sand and rocks. The same hot air. The only thing different about Fort Huachuca was the feeling I had about being there. I felt independent and grown up. Becoming an officer gave me a sense of confidence and internal balance. I felt like I was in the right place at the right time.

This time, I was staying at the Army Lodge on the higher elevated ground by the Old Post. It was a pleasant hotel. The rooms were spacious and well-equipped, which included a small refrigerator, a microwave, and a decent-size television. The most important for me were a personal phone, a computer desk station, and an internet connection.

Although this was our last night together before several months of separation, we managed to have an epic argument about my idea of having a family after I came back home. Alec didn't want to hear any of that. I didn't want to argue all night long, so I gave in. My heart was shredded to pieces when I realized we would never have children of our own. Not a little boy riding a blue tricycle at the age of three nor a little girl with Alec's curly hair and my green eyes. At the beginning of our marriage, we discussed having six of them. I was willing to compromise and have only two kids, but none? I didn't want to believe that things had changed, but Alec was adamant about the matter. Was it something about me? Perhaps I wasn't a suitable material for a mother?

I felt as if someone had pulled a rug from under my feet and I hated having to give in. What else was I supposed to do? I just didn't know what could be done in my situation. From my perspective, at this moment, we'd become prematurely separated. I was trying to understand that we'd been under a lot of pressure as a couple, family watching our relationship closely, if we would survive constant separations. This was our fourth long-term separation since I joined the army. It had to be hard for Alec.

Nonetheless, with a heavy heart, I took Alec the next day to Tucson for his flight home. On my way back to Fort Huachuca, I suddenly felt lonely, sad, and empty without Alec's support. The thought of being lonely for so many months far away from home was debilitating. I needed a remedy and promised myself to do something about this feeling of isolation.

* * *

In addition, I had this familiar feeling of anxiety about everything new waiting for me. I had to adjust to wearing my uniform daily. I had to get used to spending a lot of time in a school hall. It had been ten months since I graduated from OCS, the last time I was in school. I had to get used to my being independent on the base, where I could move freely throughout the post and go off-base any time I felt like it. My car was my best companion in this independent life. At all times, I was solely responsible for myself. I had to make myself comfortable living in the hotel for so many months. I never spent in any hotel more than four days at a time. Here, it was to become my true home away from home. Having lots of personal time was also new to me. I came from a life where I had a full-time job at Pfizer, a part-time job at Home Depot, and monthly drills with my unit in Chicago. I practically had no life besides work. Here, after school, I would wear civilian clothes, go anywhere, and spend my free time as I wished. New daily routines were also a mystery for me. I was wondering what my schedule would be like, what responsibilities I might be given in class, and what activities we would be engaged in as a class besides schoolwork. I also thought about all these new people I would meet in class. Would there be many? Were they going to be friendly? Would they be my age? Until now, in basic training, advanced individual training, and the OCS, I was always one of the oldest soldiers.

Finally, I had to learn how to take care of my basic needs in this new environment. I had to buy my food, take care of my car, pay my bills, buy my uniform if needed, run errands, and establish a P.O. box for my mail. I was doing all these things at home, but here everything seemed new.

Anxiety about getting familiar with the unknown was, as always, my primary concern. However, deep in my heart, I knew it was only a question of a short time to alleviate this feeling. But most of all, I knew that I would have to do something about the heartache and loneliness. Something useful and fulfilling.

* * *

As anxious as I was about my new life, for the rest of Sunday, I was waiting for the school with the anticipation that everything would work out. I had to focus on the next step of my career path and get myself into the mindset that I would enjoy classes and successfully conquer tests and various written assignments. I liked learning and was always welcoming with excitement the opportunities to gain new knowledge. This time, I was about to learn what it meant to be an intelligence officer. I knew that the selection for service in the MI Corps was highly competitive. I felt lucky that I was in this prestigious field with a guaranteed slot in my unit. And now, I was only one step away from becoming a member of the Intelligence Officer Corps. I had imagined being able to do this job after the "officer basic course" and this gave me a boost of faith.

The first day at school, June 23, was dedicated to organizational and administrative affairs. We met our cadre, Captain Pettigrew, the class TAC, and his assistant, Staff Sergeant Wills. We had a platoon-size (forty-four personnel) group, including seven females and five international students. They came from the Czech Republic, Slovakia, Hungary, and Egypt. We also received our classes, activities, and holidays schedule for the upcoming four months.

What caught my attention, however, was the activities were entirely different from the typical military ones. Captain Pettigrew encouraged us to take part in volunteering activities on and off-post. Apparently, the two hundred hours of volunteer service would earn someone a "Military Outstanding Volunteer Service" medal. I was ready to embark on this potentially exciting journey. I believed that being engaged and useful would reduce the feeling of loneliness.

The first proposition for volunteering was to serve as a coach for the German Armed Forces Proficiency badge. The only condition for this job was to be a recipient of this medal.

"Who has the German Badge?" Captain Pettigrew addressed the class.

I slowly raised my hand. Suddenly, all eyes were on me. Apparently, I was the only one in class to have the badge.

"Impressive. Where did you earn this award?"

"Here in Fort Huachuca, two years ago, sir."

I never thought that I would be back in Fort Huachuca to be a coach and organizer of the events for the badge. I felt honored.

* * *

The first Saturday of June, I woke up rested and energized. Since the day was very young, I figured I could go for a bike ride around the Old Post. The day was barely waking, and the early morning sun was gently caressing the snowy peaks of the Huachuca Mountains. I stopped for a moment to admire the view and ponder what Fort Huachuca would look like under the snow. There could be snow at the foot of the mountains during the Christmas season, I imagined. I thought that the Old Post buildings would look very charming, covered with white fluff and holiday decorations. Then I thought of one Christmas in Poland.

Although I was never a big fan of Christmas, there was one time when this season was quite special for me. It was December 1994, the second time in my life that I saw Alec in Warsaw.

For over a year, Alec and I were writing letters to each other. A year prior, back in Chicago, he came across an interview with me in a Polish magazine where my photo was included. He liked what he saw and looked me up in Poland. He called all the sources he could find and finally gained my Warsaw address. After exchanging several letters, we eventually met briefly in Warsaw.

That Christmas, the city of Warsaw was beaming with holiday energy. Crowds of shoppers were roaming the streets in search of perfect gifts. The garlands of lights and tridimensional decorations were filling up the city. Gentle snowflakes were dancing in the air.

Chris was very excited to hear about my friendship with Alec and insisted that I brought him with me to Chris's party for the celebration of the new year of 1995.

Days later, Alec and I drove through the snowy suburbs to the Kampinos National Park, where Chris lived. Chris wanted to hear Alec's story with every detail. Alec was born in Chicago and raised there by his Polish parents. He was often visiting his grandparents near Warsaw. He was a proud owner of a bicycle shop in Northbrook, Illinois, where he lived. Within the first year of writing to each other, we became fast friends. This time, Alec was in Poland again for his first official visit to get to know me better.

After the party, I told Chris that Alec and I were going to visit the town of Zakopane in the south of Poland. When Alec was younger, he was training in Zakopane with the U.S. National Cycling Team. Now, he wanted to show me around and visit the places he had fond memories of.

A few days later, after our visit to Zakopane, Alec flew back to Chicago, and I was happy to see Chris again. With excitement, I was telling Chris how Alec was a perfect gentleman and fun to be around, that we had a great time together in Zakopane, that it was extremely cold outside, and how we were drinking hot tea with rum to warm up.

Suddenly Chris's face saddened.

"The ring . . . " Chris noted, submerged deep in thought. "You got engaged?"

I stretched my fingers briefly, then removed my hand from the table, as if trying to hide the obvious. The engagement happened fast indeed. I imagined it must have been a shock to Chris. It was quite a shock to me.

"Yes, we did. Apparently, Alec was planning on marrying me for a while. I was caught completely off guard by this proposal and at first, I didn't know what to say. But eventually, I said that I would spend the rest of my life with him. I can hardly believe what just happened, but it's true."

I could see that Chris listened but grew anxious.

"This is happening fast . . . When and where is the wedding? Have you made any plans yet?"

"Yes, we have no time to waste, so the wedding is in four months in downtown Warsaw. You are invited, of course."

Indeed, I thought that prolonging the wedding would be a waste of time. I was eager to start a new chapter of my life. I was getting "old." In Polish culture, a woman unmarried after the age of twenty-five was considered an "old maid." Although I hated this stereotype, deep down, I knew my clock was ticking. I was over twenty-five already.

"And then what?"

"Then I'll go to Chicago."

"You don't want to see America first and check how you would like it there?"

More of a waste of time.

"No, I would rather commit and go and then figure things out as they proceed."

Life is too short for experiments and hesitations. I was almost getting irritated. Almost.

"You're jumping into the pool without checking if the water is there."

"I know it's there. What I don't know is the depth of what I am getting myself into. But I'm willing to take that risk for my future, for my dreams."

I didn't want to and couldn't live in Poland anymore. I wanted to spread my wings and fly, even if it was across the ocean. But most of all, I desperately wanted Chris to understand and be on my side.

I raised my glass of wine and clinked against Chris's.

The morning bugle call on the parade field brought me back from my contemplations. The flag was being raised with the reveille resounding throughout the post. I saluted the flag with my right hand over my heart. I felt at home. America was my home.

* * *

I was extremely excited about volunteering as a German Badge coach. I intended to run this show exactly the same way it was ran when I was competing. As an organizer, I had to first get an approval from a German liaison, Colonel Schaeffer. He was very pleased that my class would have the opportunity to earn the award. I figured out the schedule for the first set of activities, like sprint, distance run, and swimming. I selected two assistants—proctors for all the events—Johnson and Martin, who didn't participate in the badge. My classmates were very enthusiastic about the badge too. Over half of the class signed up. I enjoyed working on my computer at the hotel, setting up a schedule for the events and planning reservations for the sites and equipment.

It was the beginning of July when I learned that in the Army Family Team Building (AFTB) office, there was a bulletin board with different volunteering opportunities advertised. I had to go check it out. The classes at school were, at least for now, pretty straightforward and not very demanding, so I had a lot of free time after school. I wanted to be busy, so I wouldn't feel lonely. I found two exciting opportunities. The first one was for graphic design services for the AFTB; they needed an advertising package for their upcoming classes. I immediately volunteered for this and had a brief interview with the head of the organization. I had a great experience in designing a variety of advertising and publication materials from working for Wolters Kluwer publishing company before joining the army. For a few years, I also was running my company from home, designing and producing marketing materials for my clients. Finally, having a computer, a printer, and a scanner, plus all the necessary graphic design software, I was a good match for the job and was eager to start.

The second volunteering opportunity that caught my eye was the floor renovation at the Sportsman's Center on base. This one was intriguing, so I had to research it. I called the place and was immediately invited to see and assess the situation with the flooring.

The range was on Garden Canyon Road in the middle of the desert. A decent-size terrain around was sprinkled with wooden barricades for paintball shooting and the shooting targets throughout. The range was busy with players running around the bushes as well as "clay" shooters in the area. The center was a one-story building, reminding me of a bunker with windows. It was of light pink color, like most of the buildings on post. Mick, the range manager, showed me around. The place was divided into two main areas. One area was a lounge with comfortable club chairs and coffee tables. The main part was the store area filled with cases full of weapons, accessories, and bullets. I had never been to a place where you could buy a rifle or pistol, so the store seemed very exotic to me. By the walls, the vending machines full of drinks and snacks and coffee maker were set up. I was surprised to see a vending machine with beer. I was wondering if shooting the weapons under the influence wouldn't pose a safety hazard.

Then I saw the floor in its overwhelming disaster. Apparently, the project of renovating the floor began several months prior. In the lounge area, the old, filthy carpet was partially removed and by the window area, almost two rows of the new ceramic tiles were set. The veterans who took this project on had to abandon it because it had proven too challenging for the older men's physical condition. The materials were there; the Home Depot donated a sufficient amount of tiles, mortar, and grout. Indeed, the project seemed very challenging, mainly because the old carpet still had to be removed, and judging by the sheer size of the area, that was the most time-consuming and physically taxing part.

I imagined that this project was doable for me. After all, I had experience in laying tiles from our house in Northbrook, where I completely remodeled the entire bathroom. The only difference was that Sportsman's

Center amounted to nearly five hundred square feet, while my bathroom was less than one hundred. The good news was that I had a lot of time (many upcoming weekends) to complete the project. Mick accepted my proposal with relief and gratitude. For now, I was then booked for three volunteering endeavors and felt like I was going to be quite busy. Hopefully, less lonely.

* * *

Sometimes, you revisit a familiar place yet find no comfort. Like with the river, you come back to the same spot cherished all those years ago, but the water is now replaced by a fresh stream. A patch of grass turned into a pile of sand. The small tree by the edge grew exponentially. The big rock by the bend is now polished by the patient water. A little bridge had collapsed and appears abandoned in the background. That's how I felt in Fort Huachuca. I had to relearn how to love it, re-engage in it, and to call it home again.

CHAPTER 23

LIFE IN SLOW MOTION

I spent the Fourth of July weekend organizing materials for the flooring project. With excitement, I discovered where Home Depot was located. I didn't remember seeing it in 2001, so they must have built it recently, as if especially for me. Since back home I had worked at Home Depot, I was familiar with the store layout and merchandise. I purchased the Homer orange bucket and all the necessary supplies. I felt like a kid in a candy store. I could sense my dopamine skyrocketing; I could barely contain my excitement. For me, Home Depot was a place of therapeutic properties, especially the lumber section. I loved walking around and smelling the fresh wood throughout the store. It reminded me of home.

Because of the long weekend, I had plenty of time to visit the range and meet with Mick to discuss my proposal for the floor renovations. I wanted to concentrate on laying out the tiles. He agreed. Once the volunteers scraped the floor, I would come in and immediately begin the tile work. I would start with the main entrance of a fifteen-by-fifteen-foot surface area in a nook. I proposed a tile mosaic representing a target, which would be done from white and black tiles on a terracotta background. Since the design was drawn on my computer, it was fairly easy to explain my idea. After the main entrance was finished, I would work by sections to allow the furniture to be moved around as more areas were done. I couldn't wait to start, so I came in on Saturday to help scrape the floor. The personnel of the center, along with veterans and some local high school kids, were helping. For the time being, I felt like I was a part of a family.

* * *

Dear Alec,

I'm slowly getting used to my new life here. On the last Friday of June, we had a so-called "icebreaker." Our TAC invited us to a half-day hike in Huachuca Mountains and into the Coronado National Memorial. The area is in the southeastern line of the range near the Mexico–United States border. We visited Montezuma Pass at an elevation of 6,575 feet. We also met the coast guard patrolling the border. They let us use their giant binoculars on tripods to look at the area and spot illegal immigrants crossing the desert. As I thought about those crossing the desert in the scorching heat and without water, I imagined how desperate and determined they must have been in search of a better life on the other side of the border.

After the hike, we went to dinner and shopping in Sierra Vista, where I purchased a pair of awesome-looking Harley-Davidson boots. I've always wanted to have boots like these.

I decided to throw myself into volunteering on-post. So far, I volunteered to be a coach for the German Armed Forces Proficiency badge, the same one I was fighting for so fiercely two years ago. That's a serious project involving lots of planning, administrative paperwork, accountability of participants, and rentals of spaces and equipment. Everything is extremely formal and under the strict supervision of the German officers on-post. I never expected in my wildest dreams that I would have this opportunity to help others earn the badge. The Army Family Team Building organization was where I also volunteered as a graphic designer. I am designing for them typical advertising materials. It's a pleasant activity that allows me to use my design skills and creativity.

Finally, the best volunteering opportunity I found on-post is the floor renovation at the Sportsman's Center. People go there to have fun, shoot targets, buy guns and bullets, and socialize while drinking beer. Most of the customers are military retirees and veterans. Young people come mostly to use the paintball ranges. The visitors are having difficulty believing that I will be doing the tiling all by myself. I just smile at them. Even though this flooring project is a colossal task, I'm very excited about it. It already makes me feel like I'm doing something useful.

My new address here is actually a P.O. box because the Lodge doesn't distribute personal mail to its residents. I love letters from you with the cartoons of us and Sznurek chasing the raccoons and hunting for cheese. It makes perfect sense. After all, I am Mouse the Hunter.

After the hike, we went to dinner and shopping in Sierra Vista.

* * *

One afternoon, I went to ride my mountain bike. I never had an opportunity to do it in the actual mountains. The sun just began setting. The skies looked like a melting slice of a fruitcake with jelly. The entire post was shimmering with orange dust.

I took a tour along the post's gates and then back to the Old Post. In my memory, I traveled to the times when as an enlisted soldier, I journeyed the routes of the Fort. Back then, I was collecting the change from the streets and saving it for taxis to travel off-post. I was lucky when I could catch a bus with a transfer option for half the taxi price. Now, I was free to drive my car everywhere and even ride my bike recreationally.

I stopped by the Inspector General building by the parade field and looked for "my" picnic table. It was still there and still had traces of my initials with the date of June 2001 carved in it. It was exactly two years ago when I sat there, anxiously awaiting a meeting with Major Johnson. I had so much to tell him back then.

I rode away toward the mountains to watch the sunset. At the split of a tiny dirt road, I couldn't decide which way to go, so I crashed into the wooden post in the middle. I dragged my bike onto the grass and lay down to watch the skies, trying to absorb the peacefulness of the moment without thinking too much about anything. Tiny insects were dancing in the rays of the departing sun. I looked at a scar on my calf and thought about the time, six years ago, back in Northbrook, when Alec and I rode our bikes to see our potential new house just listed on the market. It was the first one we would own as a married couple. I was so excited to see that house that I lost my balance and crushed my bike into a steep curb. The chain dug into my calf and left me with a bleeding wound, but I didn't care. Alec and I laughed about this incident for years while drinking beer in the backyard of our first house.

"Excuse me, do you need help?" I suddenly heard a voice next to me.

It was a man on a bike wearing a helmet with red-white-blue stripes. I tried very hard to remember why his face and voice seemed so familiar to me.

"Colonel Keller!" I almost shouted with excitement. "How wonderful to see you again! I'm Lieutenant Rakowski. Two years ago on my AIT with Echo Company in your battalion."

"Of course, I remember you. What are you attending now, MIOBC?"

"Yes, sir. Just started a few days ago."

"Congratulations on becoming an officer. I suspected that you would be back here again."

"I'm glad to be here. I think I have four interesting months ahead of me."

We started walking in the darkness toward the main road.

"Where is your headlight?" the colonel noted.

"I don't have one because I normally don't ride in the darkness. I know, it's silly."

I sounded a bit careless. This was such a lame excuse, but I couldn't come up with anything better.

"Then I guess I have to keep you company."

With the colonel's headlight leading our way, we walked our bikes around the Old Post's parade field, then uphill toward the Army Lodge. He told me that his tour of duty in Fort Huachuca just ended, and as he was leaving the next day for his next assignment in D.C., I realized how much I would miss my guardian angel.

"This is home," I said once we reached the Lodge and shook the colonel's hand.

"Home away from home."

His wink assured me that everything would be okay.

* * *

By the second week of July, besides schoolwork, I was preoccupied with the German Badge. I was meeting with the German liaison officer to get my schedules and plans approved. Before I knew it, we had our first preparatory swim session. There were over twenty people eager to pass this event. However, half of the people didn't pass the swim and became discouraged. Some felt that they needed to practice more, while others decided to leave the competition. In the meantime, I organized the sprint and the next day, a distance run. Sprint posed some challenges for those over thirty years old, so they opted for shorter distances. Since it was a *"go"* or *"no go"* event, it didn't matter which distance was run as long as the timing was within the prescribed limits. Two people withdrew from the competition because they weren't able to make the sprint. Now I had twenty in my badge group, plus Captain Pettigrew and Sergeant Wills, who also were pursuing the badge. Everyone passed the distance run with flying colors.

In the evening, we went to the track and field to throw shot puts and to qualify for a short or long jump. These events had proven harder than most expected them to be. I was patiently raking the sand after each long jump, encouraging my classmates to continue until they succeeded. It reminded me of the time when Drill Sergeant Britting was doing the same for me two years before on this very field.

* * *

While waiting for the old carpet to be removed at the Sportsman's Center, I figured I needed more activity in my life on-post. At the AFTB bulletin board, I found another interesting opportunity. It was building the houses for Habitat for Humanity in Sierra Vista. Apparently, there were lots of people in need of affordable housing in the area. Home Depot was donating all the building materials. Since I'd never been involved in building an actual house, I thought it would be interesting to try something new, so I signed up. The following weekend, I showed up at the site. The foundation for a little two-bedroom house was already set and the first vertical two-by-fours of the framing was already installed.

I thought about the future inhabitants of the house. What was their story? Would they like the house? Would it make a difference in their lives? I was hoping everything would turn out well for them and this would be their "lucky house."

* * *

My schedule started filling up quickly. I was happy that I had relevant things to do besides schoolwork. My flyer and poster for the AFTB were practically done, the German Badge activities were in full swing, the Sportsman's Center was prepared, and I was ready to start the next weekend. Now, I was building a house.

I was engaged in my volunteer activities on weekdays while no testable courses were in school, and on the weekends for physically demanding jobs. On the second Friday of July, I couldn't wait for the next weekend, and since I wanted to see the progress at the shooting range, I grabbed my tool-filled Homer bucket and showed up the next day. Significant progress was made. Over half of the lounge was stripped clean and the old carpet and baseboards were removed. The area near the main entrance needed some more cleaning. I grabbed the scraper and got to work. Puzzled veterans were passing me by, wondering what I was about to do there, a petite figure in camouflage pants and tiny yellow work boots. Everyone was trying to help in any way they could. Some were removing chairs from my work area and some were sweeping as I was scraping. Soon we had an audience of two dozen people watching the operations.

I stood up from the floor and shook my hands, warming up for the next activity. The commotion in the center settled. Everyone watched me with anticipation. The magic show had begun, and I was the magician.

I took my bucket and posted it in the middle of the room. One by one, I started removing all my tools and accessories, showing them around for everyone to see. Then I took a yellow tape measure, shook it, and jokingly pressed it to my ear as if listening to a seashell. I pretended to hear from the tape measure. I showed my thumb up, and I gave a nod to the amused audience that the project was officially started.

First, I measured the area several times to designate a square for the "target design." I took my chalk line and showed it to the audience, who were now in a semicircle near me watching the magic happen. I pulled out some chalk line and blew on it, creating a small cloud of blue dust as if I were doing a magic trick. I taped to the floor the end of the line at the center point of the entry, gently pulled the line off the floor, and snapped it. A perfectly straight, fluffy blue chalk line appeared on the floor. Standing ovations erupted. I giggled and bowed to the appreciative audience.

I took a printout of my "target design" and showed it to the men who were watching me with curiosity. Some nodded after seeing the design. I laid down the tiles according to my design to have an initial dry layout. I marked the tiles and went to the back to cut them with a wet saw. I poured water into the container to cool the blade and turned on the machine. Through the corners of my goggles, I could see that the audience had followed my every step. I was in my element, getting all dirty and wet from the saw and making a lot of construction noise.

I placed the cut triangles into their respective spots on the floor. This time, I nodded with satisfaction and bowed to the entertained, applauding audience. Then I disappeared with my orange bucket at the back of the building. Three veterans couldn't help but follow me. There, sitting on the log with the bucket between my knees, I started turning the mortar mixture with a piece of wood lying around. I earned some nods again. I took the bucket inside and announced with a smile, "Now we wait fifteen minutes . . ."

I placed the cut triangles into their respective spots on the floor.

At that time, everyone resumed drinking their beer. Once my mortar started thickening, I proceeded with laying out the tiles. As I was making trowel notches in a wave pattern, I could see from the corner of my eyes that the audience was intrigued again.

"Are you a contractor?" someone asked.

"No, I am a volunteer. I'm in Fort Huachuca for my officer training."

"Are you a captain?" I remembered the last time I was in Fort Huachuca, Mike from the food truck called me a captain. Perhaps I still had this "captain aura."

"No, lieutenant, but someday, I hope to be a captain." If they only had any idea how much I wanted to be a captain. I could probably achieve it in two years if everything went as planned.

"Where did you learn all this tiling stuff?" asked a man in a leather vest. He seemed genuinely interested. It wasn't just small talk.

"I did some tiling back home, renovating my house." That was an understatement.

"So you're Lieutenant Magic, small but mighty!" I was definitely small, but wasn't sure about this "almighty."

* * *

By the end of July, I'd gotten to know most of my classmates. Many of them selected to live off-post in the local motels to have more freedom. I preferred to live on-post at the Lodge because I felt safer and the place was cheaper, fitting my budget and allowances from my unit in Chicago. Another reason for living on-post was my resolution to keep away from daily partying and drinking. Some people referred to these activities as "good old college days." For me, partying and drinking weren't all that appealing. In the past, every time I attended any party, the next day I felt hungover and had a throbbing headache.

One day, however, I was invited to a special occasion party to celebrate Johnson's birthday. The entire class, including Captain Pettigrew and Sergeant Wills, gathered in one of the local motels. We were occupying the entire swimming pool area. Most of the people were sitting on the pool chairs, enjoying their beer. I was drinking a fake drink made of water and a lemon slice.

At some point, someone came up with an idea that it would be fun to jump in the pool to see who could make the biggest splash. After a while, someone noticed that some of us who didn't wear bathing suits were outside the pool, dry. The men started throwing every bystander into the water, fully clothed with drinks and all. The bottles of beer and plastic glasses were floating everywhere.

I was wearing my new Harley boots and the thought alone that I could be thrown in the pool in my clothes made me nauseous. I didn't want to get wet and then be cold for the rest of the evening in wet clothes. I had to act, so I put away my drink and headed inside the hotel. Soon, I heard behind me a group of voices pursuing me. I started running, looking for the nearest exit. The layout of the hotel was not user-friendly, causing me to reach the dead ends of the hallway. I kept turning into different passages and for a moment, I thought I was lost. The guys following me were closing in on me. I took another desperate turn and right in front of me I noticed an exit door with the sign "emergency exit only." At this moment, I considered my situation an emergency, so I dashed toward the door. I burst through it like thunder, triggering the fire alarm, which for a couple of seconds slowed down my pursuers. Once outside, I immediately spotted a chain-link fence surrounding the property. I needed some momentum to get on the fence, so I made a few gigantic steps forward and caught onto the fence. I barely climbed to the top when the group caught up with me. They tried to grab my left boot, but I managed to wiggle it out of their hands. Then they attempted to shake me off, to no avail. I desperately needed to stay on top and avoid breaking my neck. I didn't want to fulfill my mother-in-law's infamous prophecy and get injured. My hold was firm. Being on top of the fence reminded me of a time in Warsaw years ago when, as a university student, I was coming late to the residence where I was renting a room. The gates of the compound were usually closed for the night. Instead of waking up the landlord, I would opt to climb the fence with my giant school bag. One time, my long coat caught the barbed wire on top and I had to rip off my coat lining to be liberated. I always had to hurry to avoid someone calling the police on me. This time, however, I was on the fence trying to save my boots from being ruined by chlorinated water. I also was saving my dignity.

I finally crossed the fence and landed on the other side. Not sure if the pursuit would continue, I started running toward the parking lot, frantically looking for my car. Once I found it, I took off like a rocket; the tires screeching. With my heart pounding from the effort, I promised myself that I would avoid pool parties at any cost.

*   *   *

I was a misfit, disconnected from people around me, and lonely. It was a big surprise because this time my age was comparable to my peers, who were in their thirties and were married, sometimes with children. Some were older than me. Yet, I felt like an outsider. Sadly, with time, I'd gotten used to the idea that I wouldn't develop any long-lasting friendships.

Everything seemed futile and temporary. In my previous trainings, I was adjusting to an ever-changing environment and conditions fairly quickly, like a well-programmed machine. It was probably because of the fast pace of these trainings. Now everything was happening, seemingly in slow motion. I had to accept it and figure out how to function without feeling guilty about not being as active as I used to be.

CHAPTER 24

SURVIVAL BY VOLUNTEERING

The beginning of August was marked by GAFPB weapon qualifications. I reserved the range on Garden Canyon Road near the Sportsman's Center for Friday and Saturday. Out of five lanes, four were set up for practice shooting and one for qualifications. Two range control sergeants were supervising the process. From the beginning, I noticed that a few people were very good at shooting and were hitting five out of five almost every time. This was very important as the 9-millimeter handgun results would determine what level of road march for the badge a person would qualify for: gold, silver, or bronze. We were shooting in the afternoon's blazing sun until sunset, just to come back the next day for more chances. This time, the group was smaller. Two people didn't make the cut and left the competition. Now I had a group of eight classmates, the captain, the sergeant, and four international students, who all qualified for the next steps of the competition.

I spent the rest of the weekend in town for the Habitat for Humanity project. The roof was almost done, framing was completed, and the exterior walls with Tyvek house wrap were being finished. As soon as the drywall was delivered, volunteers jumped at the opportunity to help with the interior walls. I was in the group with Cindy, who was helping me measure the boards and make cutouts to accommodate the shape of the walls inside. The work was proceeding fast and by the end of the weekend, the house's major structure was completed. However, we still had lots of work for the following weekend: patching the walls, priming everything inside, installing the flooring, and painting the interiors.

* * *

Later that month, we started the class about the equipment used in military intelligence. We were mostly learning about vehicles with mounted radars. There was a multitude of information to retain mainly because of different equipment structures, capacities, and designations. One day, we visited the area of the base where these radars were set up in the desert. As we walked around the perimeter admiring the impressive equipment, I started feeling nauseous. Partially, it was because of the desert heat and partially because I was overwhelmed. This class reminded me of the field artillery class in the officer candidate school where I had to learn a lot within a short period. The information was escaping me, and I couldn't keep up with the fast pace of learning.

As I predicted, I failed the test the next day. It was a significant blow because until then, I was passing all the tests with high scores. I was afraid that I could never memorize so much information and this highly technical knowledge. I was also wondering how so many partygoers from my class had successfully passed this test.

Nevertheless, I had to gather all my energy and intellectual power and attend an evening study hall along with eight others who didn't pass. In my head, I had a whirlpool of specialty vehicles, radars, and helicopters.

Once at the hotel, I threw off my uniform and changed into my sweats. On my bed, I spread out my notes and handouts to study for the practice tests. My stuffed reindeer, whom I simply named Reindeer, wearing a "Fort Huachuca l♥ves You" T-shirt, was supervising my studies. For good luck and knowledge absorption overnight, I placed the most important handouts under my pillow. I didn't remember falling asleep, but I woke up covered with papers and the Reindeer sound asleep on a pillow next to me.

My stuffed reindeer, whom I simply named Reindeer, wearing a "Fort Huachuca loves You" T-shirt, was supervising my studies.

The retest was early in the morning before classes. I was extremely tired and nervous. Oddly enough, once the test began, everything started coming back to me and I grew confident in my ability to conquer this test. I ended up with a much higher score than my original one. I hated the setbacks, but now felt liberated.

* * *

For the next three days after the intelligence equipment retest, we had classes about target development. As usual, the course was packed with tons of information crammed into seventy slides. Fortunately, this was not a testable material, so I didn't have to stress too much. However, the recent failure gave me a lot to think about. I needed to learn how to deal with intense material without creating too much tension in my mind. The pressure at school was killing my brain. I needed a relaxing activity that would allow me to focus on the task without unnecessary pressure.

The opportunity to do just that arrived sooner than I expected. One day, I stopped by the company commander's office to deliver some paperwork. The commander was talking about the company mascot to a few people in his office. Apparently, he decided that since the company was C (Charlie), we needed a new mascot (an animal) starting with the letter "C." Someone suggested a cobra, and the commander agreed with the choice.

"I want a large painting of our new logo to be posted on the main wall. Who can paint?"

I thought about cleaning the sink stained with paints two years ago in Fort Huachuca. Back then, I wondered if perhaps one day I would paint a company mascot. Who knew that I would have this kind of opportunity? But I hesitated because I worried it could be too big of a project to undertake.

Everyone looked around stupefied, but for some odd reason, all eyes were suddenly on me, standing by the doorframe.

"Can you paint, lieutenant?"

I thought really quickly about my experience with painting and drawing in college while studying graphic design. The last time I painted something significant was about five years ago. However, despite my initial hesitation, I had a feeling that I could still do a relatively good job. This was a chance to revive my skills.

"Yes, sir, I can. When do you need it?" Game on. No need to hesitate anymore.

"Mid-October for my change of command ceremony. That's about two months from now. Can you handle it?"

"Yes, sir. Consider it done." I agreed with enthusiasm, already planning in my head a trip to Home Depot and getting the hardboard cut on the spot. Was I too eager? Perhaps, but after all, I was an officer and needed to act confident.

The first Saturday after the conversation with the company commander, I was already at the library searching for books with exotic animals, where I could find some snakes. After selecting one that would fit my concept best, I designed the initial layout. The general idea was to paint a giant coin with an inscription around it that read: "C CO, 304th MI BN, Fort Huachuca, Arizona." In the middle of a circle, on a background of a waving American flag, was a portrait of a cobra standing up with its mouth wide open and fangs showing, ready to attack. The cobra was wearing a dog tag with the word "Cobras." I knew that this project would be a good creative outlet for my anxiety and insecurities.

* * *

On the third Saturday of August, after the morning bike ride, I packed my toolbox and the faithful Homer bucket and rushed to the range. The visitors were enjoying their morning coffee before going to the ranges. In a matter of minutes, the work at the Sportsman's Center was in full swing. To bring tiles into my work area, I had a little red wagon at my disposal.

Pulling the red wagon around in my little yellow work boots and green work gloves, I looked like a child having the best time of my life. But the work was not child's play.

I was laying tiles methodically from the center of the design out, making sure that the lines were straight and proper distances between tiles were maintained. I was mixing my mortar in small batches, just heavy enough for me to carry the bucket back and forth. With a friendly audience of veterans and other customers as a company, the work was progressing nicely. In a few hours, the target design was all laid out and now needed twenty-four hours to set. In the meantime, I had to prepare the main area of the lounge for the tile work. The veterans were eager to help in moving the furniture around.

Wagon by wagon, I was bringing the tiles and stacking them in piles of five along my new chalk lines. The audience was anxiously awaiting the next part of the show. I got on my hands and knees and poured some mortar onto the floor. The spectators admired my technique of spreading the mortar in wavy patterns. I had such a good time that before I realized it, I completed three long rows of tiles for the first quarter of the lounge.

While driving back to the Lodge, I noticed I could barely hold on to the steering wheel. My hands were shaking and on fire from the effort. Once at the Lodge, I ran to the ice machine at the end of a hallway. With both hands submerged in ice buckets, I could finally rest in my room with my Reindeer keeping me company.

I had to work at the Sportsman's Center on Saturdays and set as many tiles as possible. Then the tiles would dry and set throughout the week while my hands and back were recovering. I just needed to be careful not to injure my back by heavy lifting and bending. I realized I undertook a massive project all by myself and for a few moments, I had some doubts that I would complete it before my departure. But the show had to go on.

* * *

A few days later, I found out that the Habitat for Humanity house project was completed. Along with many volunteers who contributed their efforts, I was invited to an open house. There was a project manager from Habitat for Humanity of Sierra Vista, the town officials, and a local chaplain. After the speeches and the blessing, we had a small reception with pizza, snacks, and soft drinks.

"Thank you for building my home." I suddenly heard a familiar voice next to me and turned around.

"Cindy!" I recognized the woman who was helping me with cutting drywalls and painting. "I didn't know . . ."

"I feel so blessed that Habitat accepted my application, and I wanted to help as much as I could. This was my chance of a lifetime to finally have a decent place to live."

"Sometimes life throws a curveball at you and before you know it, everything falls apart."

"And that's what happened to me. My husband and I never had too much to call our own, and with four kids, one disabled, it was already hard to make ends meet. Then we lost our previous place because we couldn't pay the rent."

"That's awful. How did you manage?"

Cindy told me all about her hardship. I could hardly hold my tears, but things looked better for her now because she just got a job, and she could take a bus to work.

"I can finally afford to live in an actual house. It's all thanks to Habitat and volunteers like you."

I was ecstatic that Cindy's story had a happy ending. What for me was a project to combat the feeling of loneliness, for someone else, was a beacon of hope for a life with dignity.

* * *

The end of August was nearing, and I had to figure out the topic of my battle paper. I was interested in the WWII era, but I wanted to write about a lesser-known American battle involving the Polish Army. The inspiration came from a Polish war song I had learned back in Poland as a child, "The Red Poppies of Monte Cassino." The song made an unbelievably big impression on me as it was talking about the poppy flowers drinking Polish blood on the battlefield. As a little girl, I was wondering how it was possible for the flowers to get their intense red color from feeding on the blood of dying soldiers. This somewhat terrifying image of bright red poppies blooming on the war-torn fields had stuck with me for years.

I was lucky enough to find in the local library an entire book about the Battle of Monte Cassino. I was pleasantly surprised that a book like this could be found in the remote military base of Fort Huachuca.

The Battle of Monte Cassino was a series of four assaults made by the Allies against German forces in Italy during World War II in 1944. After several months of battles, one Polish unit conquered the monastery on the hill of Monte Cassino.

As I was writing, I thought about the tremendous efforts and sacrifices of Allied troops fighting for the values of democracy and freedom for all. I imagined what it was like for the Polish soldiers to win the battle for Monte Cassino and place the Polish flag in the ruins of the monastery. I closed my eyes and thought about the sound of a Polish bugler playing the "Hejnał Mariacki" (Saint Mary's Trumpet Call, a traditional Polish bugle), announcing victory. I closed my eyes to process these events in my mind.

Before I knew it, I was running with my rifle pointed at the enemy swarming in front of me on top of the hill. The ground, thorn up by the explosions, was sucking me in and I felt like I stood in place. The poppy fields around me were plastered with bodies covered with blood and debris. The ground was shaking every time a missile landed nearby. Shrapnel was flying around with ear-splitting noise. Then the flowers were growing tall, obstructing my view. The stems were enveloping my body in a deadly embrace. I kept on running as fast as I could, cutting through the blood-crying poppies, now as thick as the bush. Then I found myself surrounded by the enemy. Blindfolded, bound, and on my knees, I felt the barrel of a gun against the back of my skull.

I woke up drenched and covered with papers next to my Reindeer. Through an open window, I could hear the Taps signaling lights out for those on post and commemorating all those who were sound asleep for a long time.

* * *

In the fourth week of August, I returned to activities related to the German Badge. I had the ten strongest competitors left in the game. There were two events left: a relatively easy practical test from first aid and an extremely hard road march. From the organizational perspective, the first aid test was not posing any problems because it was short, and it was possible to administer it during one lunch break. The organization of the road march was an entirely different story because it involved the reservation of a nineteen-mile long-range area for marching. Because the range was a busy place on the weekends, it was hard to find a good fit for an early-morning event. The class had to march on a Saturday to avoid missing hours at school. Eventually, I scheduled the range for mid-September. I prepared the route on a map, listed the required supplies, and wrote detailed operational orders for Captain Pettigrew and the range control. Finally, I had to submit all the paperwork to the German liaison, Colonel Shaeffer.

On one of the usual sweltering days, I was going to the Riley Barracks, where the German officers were located. The distance to travel seemed reasonable, so I went on foot. I was walking on a paved sidewalk when I noticed that the hot asphalt was shimmering in the sun. Then it started moving in waves right under my feet. I found myself walking to a grassy area with no sense of direction. I drifted off while walking, then I suddenly heard a noise and felt something hot and rigid on my forehead. When I woke up, I realized I had walked into a metal dumpster. I turned around and, with my back against the structure, slid hopelessly to the ground.

* * *

Dear Alec,

Even though I'm tired by the end of each day, I still have trouble sleeping. Because of that, I'm sleepy during the day and what's worse, during school. Forget about concentrating on any subject at school. I found myself falling asleep while walking and I often lose focus while driving. I don't know where it all came from because I don't have too much stress here. I should be able to sleep at night. I think that if it continues, I'll have to see a doctor.

How is August in Northbrook? Are you going to see the annual classic car show in Village Green? You know I've always wanted to own a classic car, perhaps a 1955 Cadillac. If you go, perhaps you will see a purple one for me, one with large fins and white leather seats? If you do, take some wonderful photos, and send them my way.

* * *

In contrast to the OCS, which was like a high-speed train, MIOBC was a slow ride without scenic views. Volunteering became my way of surviving in Fort Huachuca. Giving my time and effort to causes outside of school felt good, as I needed this kind of fulfillment. Although it seemed like I stood still, I had to accept this ride as it was. And that was okay, because slowing down let me appreciate where I was in life and who I was becoming.

CHAPTER 25

DISCONNECTED COG

September came fast. Two days before the big road march for the German Badge, I received the approval of my operational orders and got clearance from the range control to conduct the march. The next day, I went to the range with Johnson and Martin to set up the route. We had to place along the route eight single-mile markers in the form of small flags and water jugs. The first four-mile markers were equipped with light sticks ready to be deployed. We also set up three turnaround points for different levels of marching: 9.35 miles for the gold, 7.8 miles for the silver, and 6.25 miles for the bronze. I marked the start/finish line with orange spray paint and set up the trash bags in the area. Finally, we marked with flags and taped the areas where the paved road was changing into a dirt road to keep the marchers on track. I remembered when two years before, I was marching alone on this very dirt. My feet were hitting the rocks and sometimes it felt like I wasn't making any progress. This was by far the most challenging part of the march. Now, even driving my SUV through this terrain was quite difficult. To compensate my classmates for the effort, I filled my car with an ample supply of Gatorade.

The next day, I woke up excited about the event. It was a few minutes after 4:00 a.m. when I arrived at the location. I immediately started setting up a check-in station.

Soon, the vehicles started pulling up to the parking lot. At the table, I was checking in with everyone and we weighed the rucksacks. The participants were given the scorecards to be signed at turnaround points. Finally, I gave the safety briefing and asked everyone to pet the Reindeer sitting on the table for good luck. I lit up two light sticks at the start line.

We synchronized our watches and set the timers, and the march began at 4:30 a.m.

Once my classmates were en route, I drove ahead and one by one, lit up the first four one-mile markers to be visible in the dark. I figured it was better to march toward some light, especially the green one, the color of luck and health. Johnson and Martin were also roaming the road, checking if everyone was safe.

About one and a half hours from the start, I sent Johnson to the earliest turnaround point at the 6.25-mile marker for the signing of the scorecards for those going for the bronze medal. An hour later, I sent Martin to the second turnaround point at the 7.8-mile marker to do the same for the silver medal. Finally, about two hours from the start, I headed to the farthest turnaround point at the 9.35-mile marker to wait for the gold medalists.

The sun had risen, and the desert heat quickly became unbearable. Some people managed to continue at a fast pace with the "airborne shuffle," but some were struggling. I used the same technique Captain Hamilton once used with me during my road march for the German Badge. I would drive off twenty-five yards in front of the marchers, step out of the car, and encourage them to catch up with me. Then I would drive off again. Once they picked up the pace, I would go to a different group and do the same.

After a while, the first two people for the bronze showed up on top of the last hill. All three of us—Martin, Johnson, and I—ran up the hill to cheer on the first bronze medalists while running with them to the finish line. Then we waited for the next group. Once they showed up on top of the hill, we did the same drill. Those who had already finished joined us on this last stretch. The gold medalists were scattered, so I drove up to the last one, Mendoza, and gave him a power bar for extra energy. He had very little time left, so I repeated my drill by driving off and encouraging him to run faster. On top of the hill, he poured his last water on his face, spent. I could see in front of me the entire group of those who had finished, with Martin and Johnson leading the way to meet Mendoza. At this point, I got out of my car and joined everyone on the last run to the finish line.

At last, everyone made it within their prescribed times, and it was time to celebrate. The Gatorade was pouring, and the uniform coats and caps were flying in the air. A group of ten, including Captain Pettigrew and Sergeant Wills, were now fully qualified to receive their German Armed Forces Proficiency badges. I could also breathe with relief because organizing all the German Badge events was very stressful, and I wanted to do a good job. The most important for me was that we didn't sustain any casualties, and the winners were all in good spirits and satisfied.

A group of ten, including Captain Pettigrew and Sergeant Wills, were now fully qualified to receive their German Armed Forces Proficiency badges.

* * *

After cleaning up the road march route, I went back to the Lodge to rest and regroup. My plan was to spend the rest of the weekend at the Sportsman's Center.

"Welcome home, Lieutenant Magic!" I heard a friendly voice once I set foot in the center. "What kind of magic we're doing today?"

"It's nice to be back! Today we are doing the grout by the front door and the rest of the lounge. And if I have energy left, I'll start setting up the area in the middle. Then it all has to dry and set."

The lounge was nicely cleaned up and prepared for the next stage of work. Even though I grew tired, I was determined to lay down at least four rows of tiles. A few hours later, that part was completed and nearly the entire lounge area was ready to set and dry. Because this was a significant milestone and the floor was taking a nice shape, the manager wanted to have a small celebration. He bought several pizzas, and everyone enjoyed a relaxing time. I was extremely spent, so I made me some coffee to keep myself awake. The coffee was awful. I suspected that the coffee machine hadn't been cleaned for a while, hence the nasty aftertaste. Not having eaten all day since I woke up at 3:30 a.m., I was also starving. I welcomed the pizza with an open heart. The veterans were very pleased with my work and complimented my efforts.

I was standing by the counter struggling with the terrible-tasting coffee when I drifted off. Suddenly, I noticed that the tiles in the entrance area started peeling off the ground and rising one by one. I was watching with horror my "target design" being ruined. The black, white, and terracotta tiles started spinning, creating a mini tornado. Then the tornado was shifting around the lounge and lifting the freshly laid tiles in the air. As the spinning whirlpool was moving to other areas, I was running in circles, trying to catch the tiles. Once I caught one and placed it back in place, in seconds it would lift off again to continue the mad dance with the other tiles. Suddenly, it was raining. I panicked, knowing that the freshly laid tiles should not have contact with water. Then, the tiles fell to the ground, shattering into pieces. I stood there watching a muddy pile of broken tiles.

Suddenly, I felt something hot on my chest. I woke up realizing that I spilled the coffee all over myself. I was evidently tired and sleep-deprived. The vision of the broken tiles in my dream was unnerving. I'd paid attention to dreams and was convinced that dreaming about a particular scenario always had some meaning, that it was happening for some specific reason. What could be the reason for a dream about the destruction of my work, as if it was a fragile house from cards falling apart? What would be the reason for rain and shattered tiles? Perhaps my shattered dreams? God forbid. Since these visions were all negative, I abandoned the investigative monologue in my head. At that point, I faced a choice: going home and rest or continuing the work. I decided on the latter. It was mainly because it was too dangerous to drive in my state. On the other hand, as counterintuitive as it sounded, working would keep me moving and mentally active, so I would have a better chance of staying awake for a while.

My next step was to grout the entrance area with the "target design," then proceed with the lounge. I liked grouting a lot. It was a bit like painting, moving the grout around, then pushing it with a foam trowel in the gaps between tiles. This part was messy, as the grout that was spread on the tiles was drying fast. This excess had to be promptly removed before setting. I was practically running around, bringing buckets of clean water to wash off the tiles. My faithful audience was around me, with some people still nodding with approval. A few hours later, the grout was done. I swept the bigger chunks of dried-out grout debris.

Eventually, it was time to call it a day, and I went to the Lodge. My thighs and hamstrings were sore. I could barely press the pedals in the car. My hands and arms were on fire, making it hard to hold on to the steering wheel. When I arrived at the Lodge, I practically fell out of the car, spent. Even undressing was a challenge. I finally ended up lying on my bed with both hands submerged in buckets of ice. My Reindeer looked at me with reproach, as if he was saying, "You definitely overdid it this time."

* * *

The following week was going fast, especially after a Monday test from IPB (intelligence preparation of the battlefield), which I passed with flying colors. However, still having plenty of time on my hands during the week, I wanted to do more toward my career. After researching the matter, I discovered I could take the MICCC (military intelligence captain's career course) online. The course was designed for the reserve component commissioned officers, 1st lieutenant and above, who completed the military intelligence officer basic course. Apparently, the correspondence courses could be finished in advance and before the graduation from the MIOBC and before the first active duty for training.

I jumped at the opportunity with new enthusiasm. I knew it would be much harder to do correspondence courses while at home, with life getting in the way and other distractions. Here, I had plenty of time in the afternoons, and being in the "learning mode," I could achieve reasonable progress. Besides, if I wanted to advance in my career and be ready to become a captain, I would have to take these classes sooner or later. This was enough motivation for me to sign up and order my first study materials.

* * *

During one of the lunch breaks in school, Mendoza and I went to Sierra Vista to grab something to eat. We stopped by Subway as the fastest option. As usual, the line was long, and I was apprehensive about staying there. Since we didn't have much time to drive around in search of better options, we stayed. I was tired and not in the mood for a conversation. Mendoza patiently stood by me, trying to entertain me with stories about his personal life. Back home in Washington state, he was into real estate. He was buying and flipping houses. His business was flourishing, and he was anxious about his affairs when he wasn't home to supervise the projects. I was mildly interested in real estate, as I had no experience with flipping and selling houses. It seemed to me like a complicated endeavor. Nevertheless, I expressed my admiration for all the skills and tenacity he had to grow that kind of business.

At some point, I lost my focus on the matter and all I could hear were indiscernible whispers and a buzzing noise around me. Staring at the cases filled with deli meats, I remained motionless. Suddenly, I felt a hand on my right shoulder, tapping me gently.

"Are you okay, SKI?" Mendoza sounded alarmed.

With difficulty, I came back and realized that it was my turn to place an order and everyone was waiting for me. Embarrassed from holding the line, I finally ordered my Italian BMT.

"You fell asleep standing with your eyes closed," noted Mendoza once we sat at the table. "It worries me. Are you okay?"

"I don't know what exactly is happening with me, but lately I tend to drift off in the least expected situations." My daytime sleepiness worried me too.

"Do you sleep at night?"

"Not really. Something keeps me up and I'm usually restless in the morning."

"It would probably be good to see a doctor."

I hated seeing doctors. I didn't want to be sick. There was too much to do. I was afraid that I could receive an unwanted diagnosis. But I knew he was right. I needed to get help, perhaps sleeping pills for the time being.

"I agree. I've been putting it off for a while, but I'm getting where this sleeping during the day is getting dangerous."

I felt like I was admitting to having an addiction. I was vulnerable.

* * *

The following day, directly after school and still in my uniform, I went off the base to run some errands in Sierra Vista. I had barely any energy and a massive headache from the daytime heat. It was getting dark when I pulled up to the main gate to enter the post. I was stopped by the guard for an identification check. Satisfied with my documentation, the guard saluted me and gave me the signal to proceed. Without realizing it, I started driving and ended up on a high curb in the exit line. Luckily, I missed the booth in the adjacent line.

"Are you okay, ma'am? You just drove into a curb."

It sounded surprising to me when the guard called me "ma'am." I wasn't used to being called that, but after all, I was an officer, so I should get used to it. Now, however, I had a bigger problem. It was dangerous for me to drive in my state, but I needed to get to the Lodge. I was grateful that he didn't suspect me of driving under the influence and perform a sobriety test. This would have been embarrassing.

"Yes, I'm just extremely tired. Let me get some fresh air."

"Please pull over to the parking area if you need time."

I pulled over cautiously and got out of the car. I grabbed a bottle of water and sat on the curb, contemplating my next move. I knew that somehow I had to get to the Lodge, but it wasn't safe. I could take a taxi, but then I would have to leave my car at the gate. One last option was Mendoza. Because we became friends since the road march for the badge, I was hoping he could help me. Minutes later, he was at the gate.

Our plan was to drive in a mini convoy formation where he would be in front, leading me with the emergency lights. I had to drive behind him, trying to focus on his red blinking lights. The operation was successful.

Once in my room, I dropped on my bed fully clothed, combat boots and all. I was worried. The Reindeer, awakened by my sudden arrival, looked at me with compassion. I knew exactly what he was trying to tell me. The incident at the gate was the proverbial last straw. I had to seek medical help as the instances of falling asleep during the day kept occurring. I promised the Reindeer to take care of this issue as soon as possible.

The following morning, I went to the doctor and received Ambien for sleep. I was to use it for four weeks, then check back with the doctor. It worried me that I had to be on prescription medication. I felt like I was slowly falling apart.

* * *

The time was passing by fast and before I knew it, the fourth week of September had arrived. We started the wargaming course where we were divided into small teams and worked in booths. We were given daily scenarios and played the roles of a unit commander and his/her intelligence team. At the end of a scenario, we would give Captain Pettigrew our briefing about our proposed actions for evaluation.

On the first day of the wargaming, an announcement was made for all teams. It was about the contest involving a design of the opening page of the website for Team Sentinel, the name of our brigade. The project was due the next day. I couldn't resist the opportunity to volunteer for something that nobody on my team desired or had the tools to complete.

After school, I began the work with great enthusiasm. I researched the images of modern battlefields, soldiers, and equipment. As a patriotic factor, the American flag had to be part of my design. I designed a blend of images transitioning smoothly from one scene to another. The skies were depicting the waving flag.

The next day, all teams submitted their designs and, after a brief review by the cadre, the winners were announced. Our team took first place. As a reward, we were offered a pizza, and the design made it to our class website.

* * *

The third day of wargaming was extremely hot. To make matters worse, the air-conditioning in the entire building went out. Before we knew it, the rooms became so hot and stuffy that we could barely breathe. At some point, our captain proposed taking off our BDU tops, but only under the condition that the females were agreeable to taking off theirs. It was all or no one. The six ladies in the class promptly agreed, and we worked in our T-shirts.

I was preoccupied with plotting enemy positions on a map when I felt someone's eyes on me. I looked behind me and caught a glimpse of Palermo quickly turning away. Later, when I was sitting at the desk, the same thing happened. I looked at my chest to check if perhaps I had a greasy spot from the pizza. Nothing identifiable was there. When I looked up, I caught Palermo again, but this time his eyes were on my breasts. Obviously, my bra was visible under the tight T-shirt and that must have been an unusual view for males who were accustomed to seeing females in rather loose BDU tops with pockets on the chest.

"Anything interesting you see, Palermo?"

My tone of voice was serious. I was hoping Palermo didn't think that I was flirting with him. I knew better and wanted to send him a proper signal.

"Hmmm..."

He only blushed and turned away. I was glad that there was no need to continue the dialogue.

* * *

At the end of the week, I submitted my hours to the volunteer office. I completed over three hundred working hours as a volunteer in many activities. Since I exceeded considerably the minimum requirement of two hundred hours, I was a candidate for the Outstanding Volunteer Service medal. But my volunteer work was far from being completed.

The weekend immediately after the wargaming, I was excited again. It was time to go back to the Sportsman's Center to continue my favorite activity. The main entrance area and the lounge were finished. I proceeded with the store section, and once this section was covered with tiles, the only tiles left were the borders around the entire place. I had to cut a tremendous amount of tiles to fit in the edges. Finally, by the end of the day, all drenched from the wet cutting saw and with my hands in grout up to my elbows, I finished the work. To celebrate this part of the project, pizza was ordered again and everyone at the center enjoyed a peaceful time eating and drinking beer.

Once at the Lodge, I gave the Reindeer a high five, and I stuck my hands in the ice buckets. I couldn't wait till next weekend to do the final grouting.

* * *

Dear Alec,

My time in Fort Huachuca is flying fast. The classes at school are mostly exhausting because of the endless PowerPoint presentations. They make me sleepy at best and bored at worst. Regardless, I did very well on the intelligence preparation for the battlefield test. The flooring project at the Sportsman's Center is going well and starting next week, I will have my weekends back.

I started working on the Cobra painting. Today, I purchased at Home Depot a four-by-four feet hardboard and primed it white. I already drew the sketch of the entire design and I'm ready to paint.

I had some incidents of falling asleep while standing, walking, and driving. Eventually, I saw the doctor, and he gave me Ambien for sleep.

I don't exactly have a diagnosis, but apparently, my daytime sleepiness is caused by a lack of sleep at night. I have to admit my nights are not exactly restful, but I think it's probably because I am mentally and physically too tired to be able to sleep. To make things worse, I often have nightmares, which keep me awake, sometimes for hours. I'm a little concerned with Ambien, however. This drug is designed for short-term use because I could quickly develop a tolerance and would possibly need higher amounts to achieve the same effect. For now, I don't even see any effect in terms of better sleep. But my follow-up appointment is in two weeks, so I have to wait a little longer to see if it helps.

The good news is I was just notified by my unit in Chicago that I received some medals and ribbons. The first is the Army Reserve Component Achievement medal for three years of exemplary service in the National Guard and the second is the National Defense Service medal for serving in the Armed Forces during a period of armed conflict or national emergency (current war on terrorism). I also received the National Guard Military Attendance ribbon for continuous perfect attendance over a period of twenty-four consecutive months, and finally, I was authorized for the Army Reserve Components Overseas Training ribbon for my training in Poland earlier this year. Although I didn't expect any medals, I have to admit that I'm happy that my efforts were rewarded, as it was a lot of hard work to get to this point.

* * *

Because of my declining health, I felt exposed, like a disconnected cog with broken projections. The fast-moving human machinery was nowhere to be found. I missed the team mentality and the dynamics of pursuing a common purpose. Although I stayed busy, something was off. I should have been happy for being a fully independent grownup responsible for my well-being. Yet that only deepened my loneliness.

CHAPTER 26

BROKEN AND VULNERABLE

The first days of October were marked by my intense work on the painting of Cobra. I worked slowly as it involved a lot of details. For several days, I was working on the project in the afternoons when the light in my room was best for my eyes. This activity was not physically demanding and was extremely relaxing mentally. I had always loved painting and drawing, as they would transport me to distinct realities and let me focus on positive feelings resulting from the process.

The first time I remembered drawing was when I was in kindergarten. My mom signed me up for art classes where we would draw, paint, and create various types of artwork with available materials. I liked the creative part of the process and enjoyed the activities tremendously. One day, one of my drawings was entered into a competition without my knowledge. After I won, I was made aware that my picture with a family of bears was the winner. As a grand prize, I received an inflatable pontoon boat for two. It was a pretty big deal for a six-year-old. This encouraged me to pursue drawing, and I would use any opportunity to draw, especially cartoons with my favorite characters from bedtime stories on TV. Throughout the entire ballet school, I was drawing for leisure, often volunteering to draw portraits of famous Polish writers and artists for classroom displays. However, it wasn't until the time when I was studying graphic design after coming to America that I was exposed to proper painting and drawing techniques.

Drawing class was especially exciting because we were learning a variety of techniques. I remembered practicing at home, drawing in my block anything I could lay my eyes on: furniture, flowerpots, kitchen utensils. At school, we had a locker full of a wide variety of solitary objects, mostly throwaways. Each student had their favorite junk. Mine was an old beat-up violin without strings, and it was depicted on my first black charcoal drawing. I also was learning how to draw from live models. For that assignment, I chose black and white charcoals to draw a shoulder of a nude man posing for the class. The drawing gained rave reviews from my classmates, as it was deemed so realistic, with some describing it as a vintage black-and-white photograph. I received an A+, and the drawing was mounted and displayed in the school gallery.

And now, I was again creating something for display. This time, a representation of our company character as compared to a powerful, wild animal with patriotic flair.

* * *

In the meantime, the flooring project at the Sportsman's Center was finished. On the first Saturday of October, I successfully grouted the remaining tiles around the entire perimeter. As a gift, Ryan, my helper from a local high school, made for me two bricks. A gray one from a leftover mortar and the brown one from a leftover grout. He embedded in the bricks "2LT (lieutenant) Rakowski." Once I finished grouting, the furniture was placed back where it belonged. As usual, we celebrated with a good old pizza and some beer. I was extremely happy to complete the project within a reasonable time before my departure. I didn't even care that I was sore, and that night I skipped the customary buckets of ice. The Reindeer just shook his head as if he was saying, "You're gonna regret it."

I didn't have to wait long for his warning to materialize into a fact. The next day, I sat at my computer to design an invitation for our class dining in, planned for mid-October. It turned out I wasn't even able to open my laptop, as my hands were on fire. I ended up with buckets of ice, after all. As a result, I couldn't do any work on my computer anyway, because my hands were literally frozen red.

I could continue working after just one day of rest. I spent the entire week and the long weekend of the Columbus Day holiday on the cobra. The animal I painted had his mouth open and his fangs exposed. The only thing left was to install the back framing necessary for attaching the hooks holding a string to hang the painting. For that, I needed to visit my favorite store, Home Depot, to purchase my very first Black and Decker drill. It was a small women-size tool with a power cord for charging as I didn't want to deal with charging removable, large batteries. I also bought a small handsaw for cutting the mitered edges of the wood to be mounted on the back as a frame. After the project was finally completed, I went back to my dining-in materials. Once the invitation was designed and printed, I quickly put together a PowerPoint presentation to be shown during dinner. The presentation contained various funny and serious photos of my classmates I had taken throughout the program. This was my last contribution to volunteering. I was spent.

* * *

By mid-October, my studies for the MI captain career course were well on the way. When not painting the cobra or doing my schoolwork, I was spending my time on correspondence courses. I was making significant progress and enjoying the process. I had the study materials sent to me by mail, then the tests were done online with instant results. It was a very satisfying activity, as it was bringing me closer to achieving my ultimate goal of becoming a captain.

I was in my room when the phone rang.

"Are you ready?" It was Mendoza.

"Good thing you called. I almost forgot. Let me put on my uniform really quick and I'll meet you by the back door in five minutes."

"Good plan. I'm driving."

It was the award ceremony I was invited to attend a few days earlier. I was to receive my Outstanding Volunteer Service medal at the Murr Center. It was a battalion-level celebration for those who had completed the required service hours. When we arrived, a good amount of soldiers, their loved ones, and friends were gathered, socializing.

I felt blessed that Mendoza agreed to go with me; otherwise, I would have been there all alone. Mendoza and I were helping each other out the best we could. Like myself, he was a loner and chose not to socialize with other people in our class. In addition, just like me, he wasn't a partygoer or a drinker and preferred quiet time with friendly conversation about life.

After the ceremony, there was a small reception with snacks and wine. Mendoza and I opted for Chinese food off-post.

"Congratulations, my friend. You really outdid yourself with these volunteering projects." As usual, he sounded sincere.

"I tried to do something that would make a difference in the civilian community."

"I'm sure that what you did will never be forgotten, unlike some people giving out towels at the swimming pool." He laughed. We were definitely on the same page.

"I know, but in the end, it's the conscience that matters. I did everything to help wherever help was needed, and that was enough for me."

"We wouldn't have the opportunity to do the German Badge without you." He remembered. I felt like he truly appreciated it.

On our way to the car, we wanted to stop by a little shop with leather goods. I was especially interested in some good old-fashioned cowboy boots. Suddenly, the skies turned black and out of nowhere, it started pouring. A severe thunderstorm was coming to town from the Huachuca Mountains. The ear-splitting sounds of angry skies were unbearable, with low dense clouds just above our heads. In a matter of seconds, the streets turned into raging rivers. It was too dangerous to drive through this flash flood.

We sought shelter in the nearby Walgreens, which was already full of stranded shoppers waiting out the downpour. By the time we entered the store, we were soaking wet. To make our waiting time more pleasant, we bought ourselves some ice cream from the fridges.

"How is your sleeping these days?"

I knew he would eventually ask. He was a kind friend, and I appreciated his being concerned.

"It seems like the Ambien I got from the doctor isn't exactly working as it should. I'm still mostly tossing and turning at night."

"How long have you been taking these meds?"

"Over a month now. Just yesterday, my doctor increased my dose, so I'll have to wait and see what happens. My concern, however, was that Ambien shouldn't be taken long term, as I could develop a dependency on this drug. But I have no other options."

"Let's hope this won't be the case."

After I arrived in my room, I looked at the Reindeer, who was just waking up. When he saw me, he seemed remorseful. "Sorry I missed the ceremony. Congratulations." Then he turned around and fell back asleep. I wished I could sleep day or night as easily as he could.

* * *

I wasn't looking forward to the dining-in event. It was mostly because of the uniform. Although the invitation stated that the dress code was either Class A or Army Blues, I'd heard the cadre encouraging the Army Blues. As a member of the National Guard, I wouldn't have many opportunities, at least for a long while, to wear the Army Blues. Buying the expensive set for just one occasion, especially when it was not required, didn't justify the cost. Besides, there wasn't enough time to buy it and get the uniform tailored appropriately in time. Despite feeling sick and tired, that evening I put on my Class A and went to the class dinner at Lakeside Activity Center, a walking distance from the Lodge.

When I arrived, I noticed I was wearing my "Army Greens" with just one other person from the National Guard. We definitely stood out in the worst possible way. Throughout a stiff, formal dinner, I felt extremely uncomfortable and out of place. Fine dining in uniform was not my activity of choice. However, it was a requirement, and I had no other option but to be part of it.

After dinner, we had a relaxing time in the hall. My PowerPoint presentation with the pictures of my classmates was displayed on a big screen. Everyone enjoyed the memorable moments from the past months we had spent together as a class.

Then there were little poems written by two classmates about each of us. They were mostly funny and harmless. When it came to what my classmates thought of me, I wasn't amused. They were making fun of me, pointing out that I was busy doing lots of things outside of school and that I always had some paperwork and errands to take care of. I was applauding the clever but painful comments with tears in my eyes. I never felt more alone among nearly fifty people. At that time, I sensed that I didn't belong in this unappreciative crowd, especially after I'd done everything in my power to have my classmates earn their German Badge. No one mentioned a word about it.

After mingling for a while, I realized that there was nothing for me to do at the event, which I wasn't enjoying. It turned out that so far, everything I was doing to feel less isolated, instead of bringing me closer to people, it created even a deeper crevasse between me and the world.

At last, I found just the right moment to sneak out and head out to the Lodge. The stars sparkled in the low firmament. I could almost touch them. I made a wish upon the closest star to never feel this alone again.

Suddenly, I heard Taps being played, announcing the end of the day. I turned toward the Old Post, where the sound was coming from and saluted the flag in the darkness, alone.

* * *

In the third week of October, we started the last block of instruction, called Basix (battlefield simulation exercise). It was conducted in twelve-hour shifts in giant tents set up in the middle of the base near our school hall. In this five-day exercise, we were conducting battlefield-simulated operations based on different scenarios. My shift was, unfortunately, during the night, from 7:00 p.m. to 7:00 a.m., and interfered with my sleeping schedule, which I was desperately trying to establish for weeks using Ambien.

From day one of Basix, things were not going as planned. Our night shift did not end at 7:00 a.m. as per instructions, but was extended for a couple of hours. At first, I thought it was an exception because we were just starting operations. On the second day, however, our shift got extended even longer. This time, I thought the cadre was pushing us to develop more strength of character.

What I needed the most was the sleeping schedule, and it was nearly impossible to accomplish that while my body had gotten used to taking Ambien at night. In this situation, I had to take the medication during the day for a few days and then force myself to stay awake during working hours at night. As a result, my internal clock was disturbed. To make things worse, the ever-extending night shift prevented me from getting rest after work, when theoretically I should be released. For the time being, I was suffering in silence, hoping that I would manage to somehow survive these five days.

On the third day of Basix, again, we were not released on time. Because of that, I barely made it to the Sportsman's Center, where I was invited for a grand opening after the renovations. The company commander told me that my presence there was mandatory. Besides, I wanted to see the place after everything was done. It turned out there was a big ceremony. Veterans and guests gathered as the chaplain was blessing the place and the company's first sergeant was giving a memorable speech. Then I received an "Eagle Award for Excellence" for the completion of the flooring. I was moved to tears when the dedication took place and the plaque with my name was placed on the wall. It felt good to be recognized for all my hard work. However, for me, the main reason for pride was to be a volunteer and provide services where and when they were needed.

*   *   *

After this uplifting experience, I had no time to rest because my night shift was starting soon. I only had time to take a quick shower, put on a fresh uniform, and polish my boots. During my shift, I had trouble concentrating and found myself drifting away. I was making every effort to stay awake, but it proved futile. I couldn't remember the operations we were conducting; the information being briefed, and even the big picture of the scenario we were working on.

In the third week of October, we started the last block of instruction, called Basix (battlefield simulation exercise).

At last, the morning came, and I had high hopes that I could go to the Lodge at a decent time and get some rest. Instead, the change-of-shift briefing dragged on. Since the day shift had already arrived, the tent was crowded and hot. Two hours later, the night shift was still in the tent. At some point, I took a chair and sat outside to get some fresh air. After a while, one of my classmates came out of the tent to check on me. Apparently, I was found on the ground in a fetal position with my head under the chair, half asleep.

When I went back inside, I was dizzy and nauseous. Without sleep and food, I was pushed to the limits. The briefing was still going on. Desperate for help, I searched for Captain Pettigrew and told him about my situation. He said that the briefing should be over within minutes. Another forty minutes later, I lost hope and had to use the "open-door policy" and speak to the battalion commander. Captain Pettigrew tried to stop me, but I was determined. I'd reached the breaking point. I didn't care about anything anymore.

The office of the battalion commander was just a few steps away from the tents, so I made it there fairly quickly and was directed to the colonel immediately. I told him the entire story about sleeping issues, ever-extending shifts, Ambien, feeling sick, and not being able to focus. He listened with compassion as I broke down in tears. He told me not to worry and sent me to see the doctor right away.

After hearing about my situation, the doctor seemed concerned.

"Ambien reduces natural brain activity, causing drowsiness, which then results in intense sedation." No wonder I was in a foggy state of mind lately.

"My shifts are during the night, and I have to be awake for twelve to fourteen hours straight."

"If you take Ambien and force yourself to stay awake, you can find yourself doing things that you have no recollection of later. In addition, another dangerous side effect of that is amnesia."

That scared me. I didn't want to have amnesia. I needed to be healthy. There was still so much to be done. Amnesia would ruin everything for me.

"I have no way of making up the sleep during the day because there is no time; my shift starts at 7:00 p.m.," I interjected.

"You have to sleep at some point. I'm giving you quarters until tomorrow morning. Go home and get some sleep."

Since I hadn't eaten for a long time, I went to the commissary and bought a whole roasted chicken. Once at the Lodge, I devoured it in a matter of one hour. The Reindeer was observing me with astonishment as if he was trying to say, "How can you eat as much chicken at once?" I knew that he would prefer some fresh and juicy grass.

After resting for the rest of the day in the evening, I was back in the tent, ready to tackle the night shift. I survived the next twelve hours despite dealing with a splitting headache and trouble concentrating. We were released only one hour later, and I could go to the Lodge and try to sleep.

During the last night of Basix, I was experiencing brain fog again. Everything was confusing, and I didn't remember the battle positions, enemy strength, or friendly courses of action. Therefore, I failed the last briefing, which was testable. This was alarming because the school was officially over, and the only thing left in Fort Huachuca was the out-processing and graduation the following week. I was worried that I could become a holdover and wouldn't be able to graduate and go home. Fortunately, I was not the only one in this predicament. The retest was scheduled for Monday morning.

I was studying all weekend long as if my life depended on it. On Monday, I was extremely nervous. I thought that after all the hard work I'd put into my studies throughout my stay in Fort Huachuca, and very good scores until now, I needed and deserved to graduate. But for the time being, I felt singled out and unworthy.

The retest took place early in the morning before the rest of the class showed up at school. This time, despite my tremendous anxiety, I passed the test with flying colors. In class, one cadre stopped by the last row where I was sitting to congratulate me and brought me fresh coffee. I was a bit surprised by this friendly gesture. The most important, however, was that I could finally breathe with relief.

* * *

Reaching my boiling point was exhausting. In sheer desperation, in my awful position, I had to stand up for myself. No one else would. For the first time, I was forced to muster all my courage and complain directly to the battalion commander, skipping the chain of command. It was a bold move, and that scared me. To my surprise, it didn't empower me. It was exactly the opposite. My self-confidence plummeted. I was different again. I hated being broken and vulnerable and needed to hide it from the world, as if I were ashamed.

CHAPTER 27

INTELLIGENCE PROFESSIONAL SECOND TO NONE

Finally, the graduation came, and I was happy that I finished yet another training, a significant milestone. Yet, it seemed like I didn't fully appreciate my success. During the past four months, I'd been through so many ups and downs dealing with my health issues, being a misfit, and my loneliness that I barely noticed that I was making progress toward my biggest goal. I couldn't figure out why I almost felt like I didn't accomplish anything at all. Was it because my mind hadn't settled yet from all the struggles? Or perhaps I was taking my success for granted?

I hated the fact that I wasn't giving myself enough credit for finishing the MIOBC. As if I didn't deserve it, as if it was just a formality. I didn't enjoy this moment of success as fully as I should have, partially because Alec wasn't around to celebrate with me. However, I knew it shouldn't have mattered if he was there because my achievement was unquestionable, and Alec's absence shouldn't diminish its value. Yet, deep down, I wanted him to be there for me because *he* did still matter to me.

As I walked outside the building after the ceremony, I realized that despite many obstacles, I had pushed hard to achieve my dream. And although it mostly felt like I was doing it alone, I still reached for the stars. Ever since I had joined the army, these stars seemed so distant, but I kept reminding myself that one day they would be within my reach. I just had to persevere. At last, my hard work and tenacity had paid off, and now I was a full-fledged U.S. Army intelligence officer. My journey was ending, but I was feeling like a piece of me was still missing.

The next day, as Alec and I were leaving Fort Huachuca, I still felt uneasy that another big chapter of my military career had ended. I was suddenly a misplaced piece of furniture that had to be moved to an unfamiliar room because it wasn't matching the new paint on the walls anymore.

To console myself, I thought about what it would be like to come back to Fort Huachuca yet again to complete my onsite portion of the captain's course. The Reindeer on the dashboard only shook his head.

Finally, the graduation came, and I was happy that I finished yet another training, a significant milestone.

* * *

I knew that after my MIOBC I would begin a new chapter of my military career, possibly being deployed overseas for several months of combat operations in Iraq. I was looking forward to it and was mentally ready to embark on a life-changing mission.

I had a similar feeling of readiness and longing to cross a significant threshold back in the spring of 1995 in Warsaw, when I was also ready for a big change in my life.

That spring was uncharacteristically cold. The winter would not give in, and spring was reluctant to arrive. As if lifeless, the trees were still asleep in deep slumber. The sun was shy, only occasionally peeking through the clouds. Nature wasn't ready for the new season and new life.

I, on the other hand, despite the weather, was more than ready for the next chapter of my life. Ever since our engagement in January, Alec and I were writing to each other and speaking on the phone almost daily. I fell in love with Alec and couldn't wait to start our new life together in America.

We ended up having two different wedding ceremonies on the same day. One was at the church with music and a church choir, and the other at the city hall in a more casual setting. Alec's parents and sister flew in from Chicago. His grandparents and other family friends from Poland were present as well.

During the wedding party, Chris, as well as the author of the magazine article, which brought Alec and me together, were my guests of honor.

At some point, I noticed Chris was submerged in deep thoughts, mindlessly watching the dancing and drinking crowd. We just got served more vodka, so I took our shot glasses and gestured for Chris to go with me outside.

The skies just cleared, and it felt good to be out of the building, away from the noise and festivities.

"What's wrong?" I was concerned. "It doesn't look like you're having a good time."

"No, I am enjoying everything . . . " I sensed that this wasn't exactly true. "It's just . . . " Chris tried to continue with the glossy eyes. "It's you leaving that makes me sad. I feel like something is ending for us. You are going to be so far away. We won't be able to just go out to dinner and talk through the night like we used to."

"It's far, but there are still letters, remember? I'm used to writing to you for so many years of our friendship. Even if we are far from each other, it won't make any difference. It will just take a little longer to receive them."

"I always knew that you would leave Poland sooner or later, but I thought you'd be closer. Like Germany. You liked Germany, didn't you?"

"Yes, but Alec is from Chicago, so I am going with my husband. I love him. We have a life together in America, where he is established. We don't have to start from scratch." I desperately tried to explain. I hated having to explain my life choices. Even to Chris.

"What about the language? You don't speak English."

I didn't speak German either, so what was the difference? I was convinced that Chris was now growing desperate.

"That's okay, I can learn it just as I have learned French. It will be all right. It's just a new challenge for my new life." I decided to just be polite to avoid arguing with Chris.

I lifted my shot glass and clinked against Chris's.

"To your new life." Chris smiled through tears.

"To my new life."

I felt like I finally received Chris's approval to go to America. It was an uneasy feeling because, in fact, I didn't need anyone's approval. Even from Chris.

*   *   *

I was finally a fully qualified "intelligence officer second to none", like in the good old MI soldier's creed. So what now? Instead of elation, I felt restlessness. For the past three years of my journey, I was longing for the stars, watching their shimmering glory, searching the firmament on a cloudy night, reaching for them. Now when I finally captured them, I looked at my hands, hoping for the golden stardust. Only to find that I was holding the remnants of my faded dreams. Self-judgment and incessant internal monologue, a destructive power of self-doubt, were consuming my resolve to continue. Yes, I had plans to become a captain, but there was nothing immediate I could do about it. I would be eligible for a promotion in three years.

PART VIII

MY SECOND OVERSEAS TRAINING:
DANGER FOCUS II EXERCISE, GERMANY

CHAPTER 28

BELONGING AND FITTING IN

During the three-hour ride from Stuttgart to Grafenwöhr, Germany, I had plenty of time to think about my military career. I was satisfied with the way it was going so far. For most of the three years of my service, I was busy fulfilling all my required training. Ever since I became a soldier, I achieved my goals of completing the prebasic, basic training, advanced individual training (intelligence specialty), then the goal of becoming an officer, and being trained as an intelligence officer. I completed one overseas training in Poland. I was also awarded a new military occupational specialty, 97L (linguist) in addition to my original MOS as an enlisted soldier, 97E (interrogator) and my current MOS as an officer, 35D (all source intelligence analyst). I finished the correspondence portion of the military intelligence captain's career course. I was also given a new function in my Chicago unit, command language program manager, and was responsible for orchestrating language exercises during our monthly drills. In addition, I was tasked with the compilation of the Bosnia and Herzegovina country study to prepare the unit for an upcoming deployment to that area for peacekeeping operations. Finally, I received an excellent officer evaluation report with a recommendation for promotion from my unit commander.

Although I felt a bit worn out from all my trainings and very minimal presence at home, I gladly volunteered for another overseas annual training mission in Germany with my Chicago unit, taking place in the second half of November 2003. Things between Alec and me were good. Although a bit reluctant, he agreed with me that I should take advantage of every opportunity to learn as much as possible. This would help to gain valuable experience to prepare myself for the rank of captain. Besides, training was only two-weeks long. I loved having his support again.

It was already dark when we arrived at Grafenwöhr's U.S. military base, filled with military vehicles, signal equipment, tactical tents, and buildings. Our mission, Danger Focus II, was a training designed to build leaders in combat operations the following spring in Iraq. We were training with the famous U.S. Army 1st Infantry Division and the Multinational Division Central-South (MND-CS). The 1st Infantry Division, also known as "The Big Red One" after its shoulder patch, was a combined arms division of the Army, and the oldest continuously serving unit in the Regular Army. At that time, the division was headquartered in Germany. Multinational Division, on the other hand, was a newly created unit (September 2003), and supported by NATO, as part of the Multinational Force Iraq. Headquartered in Camp Echo, Iraq, it was under Polish command with the largest Polish contingent.

Shortly after the arrival, my team of Polish linguists was introduced to our new commanding officer, Lieutenant Colonel Ellson, and his team of three majors from Nebraska. As we stood there conversing casually, someone asked to speak to Colonel Ellson. When he came back, he announced that the three majors were just called to Iraq. With their still-unpacked bags, they left the rest of us immediately.

"You are the only officer left on my team now," said the colonel, looking at me. "You are going to take over the majors' responsibilities and be my battle captain for the duration of the mission."

I was stunned, but gladly accepted the challenge. This was my chance to shine as a newly minted U.S. Army intelligence officer. Not only would I have to perform the job of three people, but they were also two ranks above me. This was my chance to prove myself more than anything.

* * *

Our team worked at a tactical operations center (TOC) in an enormous tent next to our building, equipped with giant screen monitors of the battlefield. A TOC was a command post coordinating military operations from battalion level down to companies and platoons. The focus of the command's responsibilities was tracking operations on the battlefield, relaying information, assessing results, and assisting in planning new operations.

Grafenwöhr's U.S. military base, filled with military vehicles, signal equipment, tactical tents, and buildings.

As the battle captain, my role was to supervise two specialists and help monitor and track friendly troop movements. Every time new information was reported to us from the battlefield, my task was to assess it, analyze it, and transfer it to the command at TOC. I ran back and forth between the center and our building several times a day with newly processed reports and with new taskings received from the command.

I enjoyed this work tremendously. Especially intriguing was the battlefield analysis, plotting operations on maps, and generation of reports for the command. Our information was then used to assist in the decision-making process on the battlefield. The battlefield was a simulation of the war operations near the building's compound. More often than not, I could hear the sounds of artillery coming from the field. The ground was shaking from explosives day and night. These simulations of operations on the battlefield reminded me of my MIOBC training in Fort Huachuca. It was a perfect continuation of what I had learned during my previous trainings.

I had a strong feeling of belonging and fitting in. Although I worked the night shifts, I was fully engaged in my job. At some point, I became so good at it I could "read" the mind of Colonel Ellson and act proactively, analyzing field reports. As a result, I gained an endearing nickname: "the colonel's mini-me." It was funny and flattering.

We also worked with two Polish colonels attached to the Multinational Division of American, Polish, and British troops. My team of linguists was also serving as liaisons between Poles and American forces. We had opportunities to exchange and compare battlefield information and create final reports for the command. Finally, knowing the Polish language had proven not only useful but crucial in relations with the Multinational Division members. I felt well enough in this environment that I openly expressed my interest in going to Iraq in February of the following year to be part of combat operations with the 1st Infantry Division and the Multinational Division.

The only issue I had was the lack of sleep. I was on Ambien for nearly four months now, with inconsistent results. In the current conditions where I worked the night shift, I had to switch taking my Ambien from nights to days again. However, the barracks where I lived were extremely noisy during the day and I wasn't able to get any rest. At least our shifts were twelve hours square without holding us over.

Because the work was going great and my Polish linguists were performing a tremendous job in our intelligence operations, I recommended each member of my team for the Army Achievement medal. Colonel Ellson, as approving authority, agreed and recommended me for the medal as well. The official orders described my achievements. I was especially proud of achievement #4: "2LT Rakowski functioned as a battle captain coordinating planning operations for the entire Multinational Division. While preparing numerous reports, she oversaw the Polish as well as the British Division personnel. On numerous occasions, 2LT Rakowski's knowledge, control, and leadership were commended by the maneuver control cell commander."

I came home with a great sense of accomplishment and couldn't wait to be deployed to Iraq and work again with the Multinational Division and the 1st Infantry Division. I wanted to contribute, and I felt I knew enough basics as an intelligence officer to undertake a new challenge from which I could learn and become an even better specialist in my field. Most of all, potentially being part of a multinational intelligence team in Iraq, I had the confidence that I could function in this environment to my full intellectual, mental, and physical capacity. After all, I was a qualified intelligence officer.

PART IX

ENDURING THE DARKNESS:
THE END OF MY JOURNEY

CHAPTER 29

BROKEN KALEIDOSCOPE

Thanksgiving festivities in Alec's family were coming to an end. I was looking forward to our trip to Door County, Wisconsin, in mid-December. After not being home for almost six months, I wanted to do something special for Alec. I organized the trip to spend some relaxing time with our friends from Indiana, away from everyday hustle and bustle. I was enjoying being home again, knowing that I had a while before being deployed to Iraq the following spring.

In December, on Alec's birthday, everything changed. In the middle of the party, I received a phone call from my unit that I was being called for active duty to Bosnia for eighteen months of peacekeeping operations. At first, my heart dropped. When I heard that I have to report to Marseilles the next day for a predeployment in-processing, I nearly passed out. My plans to go to Iraq were no longer valid as there was no other option but to comply with the orders and go to Marseilles.

Alec, when he heard the news, was livid. He didn't want me to go anywhere, especially for that long. He was angry with the army for sending me away again. I tried to explain to him it came with the territory of being a soldier, that deployments happened all the time. Especially during times of war or other international conflicts, even the National Guard and the Reserves were being called for duty to serve overseas. He didn't want to hear any of this. I was torn between Alec, who preferred to keep me home, and the country, which needed me to stand for the values of democracy and freedom in Bosnia. Being committed to the officer oath, I chose the latter.

I drove to Marseilles with a heavy heart, distraught. In my memory were the times when I went to Marseilles for my phase 0 of the officer candidate school. Back then, I was excited to be there to start a new path in my military career. This time was different; I was anxious about being deployed in such a short time. I was especially worried about my health.

I spent two days in lines with hundreds of soldiers, waiting to be seen at different processing stations. Just like my team members from the training in Poland and Germany, who were also called, I was stressed out. We were filling out a tremendous amount of paperwork, direct deposit pay, arrangements for deployment, disposition of financial affairs, and the will. The latter made me realize I could potentially never come home from this deployment. It was an uneasy feeling, but it was part of the job.

The review of my medical records was very thorough. The doctor pointed out that I had several issues that needed to be taken care of. My feet (I had plantar fasciitis in both feet) and my left hip desperately needed physical therapy, and my left knee was a mess. However, the biggest problem was my sleep situation. I'd been on Ambien for several months now and this raised a red flag. Because of these circumstances, I was given a ninety-day no-duty profile, non-deployable status, and the recommendation for a sleep study. I was to resolve all issues in ninety days.

When Captain Flores, temporarily in charge of my Chicago unit, heard the news, he was enraged. He accused me of trying to get out of deployment and ordered me to fax to the unit my treatments' reports every two weeks. I was to fill out formal paperwork with the progress and prognosis signed by each respective doctor.

In order to regain good health, I started with physical therapy for my feet. The therapist tried everything: muscle strengthening, cold and hot therapy, massages, electrode stimulations, ultrasound, orthotics, taping, and even special boots for sleeping. I was also treated for my hip.

In the meantime, my knee was getting worse. It came to a point where I wasn't able to take the stairs to get into my house. To get to the second floor, I was climbing on my bottom backward. Finally, in February, I was scheduled for surgery at the beginning of February 2004. Although this was the very first surgery in my life involving full anesthesia, I was desperate to have my knee fixed. I was determined to recover from it as quickly as possible. I'd been injured many times before and was used to pain and discomfort. Recovering from surgery would be the same thing.

Suddenly, taking care of all these health issues in such a short time became a true ordeal. I was stressed out and overwhelmed.

* * *

"The anesthesiologist will be with you in a few minutes, but it's possible that you will be out by then."

A few moments after the injection of the anesthetic, the nurse's face faded away and my eyes closed heavily, remembering the dimming lights on the ceiling. Nothing mattered anymore. The pain disappeared, and I felt an incredible lightness taking me away from reality.

I woke up in the hospital bed, groggy and confused. My knee was bandaged, and the bloody dressing made me nauseous. I didn't feel any pain yet, but I was told that it would happen soon after the anesthetic wears out. Reluctantly, I accepted taking codeine for pain relief. I was afraid the medication taken on an empty stomach would make me sick, like the infamous cough syrup I received during my training in Fort Huachuca. Knowing that the pain would be unbearable, I had no other options.

I was wheeled out of the hospital, straight into Alec's arms. He was happy to see me and so was I. After all, I survived a surgery with full sedation.

* * *

On our way home, I couldn't stay awake. My chaotic thoughts about disconnection from the world around me were roaming lazily through my brain. It was the same feeling I had back in the fall of 1999 in Warsaw. When I saw Chris, I realized that a worrisome separation between us started appearing.

It was the first time I traveled to Warsaw since my departure to the U.S. in 1995. It was a big occasion. The ballet school I graduated from in 1988 was celebrating two hundred years of existence in Warsaw. Knowing how much Chris loved ballet, I thought we should spend some quality time in a ballet environment together. My heart was still broken about leaving Chris in Poland, but at least we had letters and phone calls. I also had promised I would visit whenever an opportunity arose because I missed Chris dearly. Now seemed to be a perfect time to get united for a brief while.

Since I set foot at the Warsaw airport, something about Chris bothered me. I couldn't put my finger on it. Chris seemed detached and distracted, as if the four years of separation made us strangers. I felt uncomfortable, but after shrugging it off, I went along. Perhaps we needed some time to reacquaint ourselves with each other.

Although we enjoyed our time at the ballet school during the festivities, as well as the performances at the Great Opera, our conversations lacked the passion and emotional engagement they used to have. We were both tense and even stressed out to a point that I couldn't talk to my beloved childhood ballet teacher, whom I didn't see for sixteen years. I felt rushed and out of place in my world. My relationship with Chris suddenly felt awkward.

It was the time when I had just learned how to build basic websites. As a gift, I had created one for my school to assure their presence on the internet and to promote the institution.

"The website has the entire school history dating back to the eighteenth century, when the school was established as part of the Great Opera," I reported, all excited.

"Why would they need a website?" Chris asked apprehensively.

"What do you mean?" I was stunned. "Everything is now on the internet for the entire world to see. Besides, the school has a lot to be proud of and so do its alumni all over the world. I'm sure they would like to see their alma mater from any place in the world, read the latest developments, see themselves on the register of graduates, and show school photos to their children and grandchildren."

I hated explaining such a simple concept to someone so intelligent.

"I don't know what this internet thing is all about, but I don't believe in it. It won't last for long."

I wasn't sure if Chris was serious or just pushing my buttons in mischief. I used to know the difference, but that was no more. I felt helpless because it seemed like I wasn't able to share with Chris the simplest things, like my enthusiasm for the internet. Apparently, we lived worlds apart in two distinct realities. At some point, I realized that perhaps the seventeen-year age difference between us finally caught up with us and divided us for good.

* * *

I woke up in the car halfway home with stomach cramps and severe nausea. We had to stop in a random parking lot as I was vomiting violently.

Once we made it home, I had to climb the stairs with my crutches. Drowsy from the drug, I ate some food, then didn't remember anything afterwards. For several days after that, I was in a fog, barely registering what was happening around me, spending most of my time stretched on the bed semi hallucinating.

A week after the surgery, I began intense physical therapy for my knee three times a week at the nearby Illinois Bone & Joint Institute. First week Alec drove me there, but with time he grew more reluctant and impatient. It must have been hard for him, I understood, as he was trying to grow his insurance business. I didn't want to burden him and put any strain on our relationship, so I started driving on my own. Every time I drove there, I was praying for a speedy recovery. Although going to Bosnia was out of the question, I was hoping perhaps I could still go to Iraq with some intelligence units in the summer. I hated being broken and had no patience for these kinds of setbacks.

* * *

Once I was in better shape, I underwent a sleep study. Spending a night in the hospital with my entire body connected to electrodes was borderline frightening. It turned out that during the six hours of my sleep observation, I would stop breathing over three hundred times, which amounted to waking up roughly every seventy seconds. As a result, I was diagnosed with severe obstructive sleep apnea. This explained my sleepless nights in Fort Huachuca. I was terrified when another sleep study was recommended, this time with a CPAP (continuous positive airway pressure) machine. This study didn't provide the expected results; I was struggling with breathing through the hose attached to the machine and with the air pressure, which was unable to keep up with my breathing patterns. Seemingly, the machine was blowing air with a delay, which caused me to stop breathing, regardless. Eventually, I was fitted with the auto-adjusting machine, which was supposed to follow my breathing automatically. I was devastated. The thought alone that I would have to sleep with a noisy machinery connected to my face was nauseating. It wasn't helping our marriage, either. I was now damaged goods, and I couldn't help it. I felt more vulnerable than ever before.

* * *

Shortly after my diagnosis, Alec announced he needed to take a brief break and go to Europe for a couple of weeks. He planned to go to Holland and visit his friends in Poland. I didn't object, as I understood that my recent health issues could have been a burden for him. With my heavy heart, I watched him packing. At the last moment, without Alec being aware, I put in his bag my faithful friend, the Reindeer. This was to remind him of my love for him and about home, where I would be patiently waiting for him.

He came home in good spirits, happy that his mission was accomplished. Right away, I noticed the Reindeer missing. When I inquired about him, Alec told me he gave him to a child in an orphanage he visited in Poland. My heart sank. Alec never mentioned any plans about visiting an orphanage, so it was hard for me to buy his explanation. I suspected he gave the Reindeer to one of his friends in Poland, which he had often talked about. Although my heart was broken because I just lost my companion from Fort Huachuca, I tried to understand. I didn't want to press the issue, but deep down in my heart, I had this uneasy feeling that something was off between Alec and me.

* * *

In the meantime, I received more bad news. Pfizer was closing all sites in Illinois and moving its operations to New York. Along with nine thousand people, I found myself without a job. All I had left to do was to go to my former workplace to return my ID card with access to the building. When I arrived at the site, my card didn't work anymore. I found the building empty, and its parking lots deserted. Somehow, I found a guard at the back entrance and gave him the card. I felt as if I were visiting an abandoned ship. Just months ago, this place was bustling with activities, meetings, town-halls, celebrations, and open-houses. People working, talking, eating. Now it was just a skeleton of this former life. The day when during my OCS training, I found out that I landed a job at Pfizer was now a distant and bittersweet memory.

* * *

By the end of spring, after sending all my health reports to my unit in Chicago, I received a dreaded letter from the Department of Military Affairs. I was found unfit for duty and, therefore, I was being honorably discharged from the service for medical reasons. My military career was officially over. There was no place for discussions or negotiations. This was an official order. I was discarded like trash. This time, not in a "recycle bin," but regular trash from which there was no return. No chance to rise from the ashes, no chance to be reborn. I no longer had the right to dream my dream. I would never become a captain. My heart was broken again. A void in my chest, emptiness in my soul. A sudden silence in my brain. Everything I worked so hard for; all my struggles and victories were now dismissed. I was no more.

I was also disappointed in the army that it was so easy for them to disqualify me after all this intense training I endured. It made me feel unworthy, as if I wasted mine and everyone else's time and resources. Suddenly, achieving my goal of becoming an army intelligence officer didn't matter anymore. It didn't mean anything even to me. I discarded myself, along with my dreams and ambitions. There wasn't much to hang on to anymore.

* * *

Although distraught by the recent news, I was barely hanging on, suffering in silence, not to trouble Alec. After all, I had my husband of nearly ten years and believed that I could start over with his support like in the good old days. One evening, I took him out to dinner at our favorite restaurant to spend some relaxing time in a casual atmosphere. We had a good time joking and talking about the future. The plans for the construction of our dream house were approved by the Village and the loan was secured. Although Alec wasn't too excited about the house, I figured it was just stressful for him and it would pass once the project started.

The next day, it was a beautiful, sunny Saturday morning. I was planning a brief retreat for us to a picnic at the nearby forest preserve, where we used to ride our bikes or walk our two Yorkies. It'd been a while since we spent some quality time in nature, so I was looking forward to this excursion. I just got out of the shower when I heard the garage door opening. In my robe and hair wrapped up in a towel, I went downstairs, curious about what Alec was up to. To my shock, I found the door wide open, and a truck pulled up backward. The garage was half empty. Alec was vigorously packing. For a moment, I thought he wanted to put some of his belongings into storage to make space in the garage for his workshop and tools. Then I went to get the mail from the box around the corner. There, I picked up a letter-size orange envelope addressed to Alec.

"This is for you," I said and gave him the envelope.

After a quick glance at the content, he put the papers back inside and said, "No, this is for you."

It was a "petition for the resolution of marriage." Stunned, I needed to run upstairs, get dressed, and flee the house to avoid watching my life shattering into pieces. No need to read the paperwork. I already knew what was in it. I'd seen divorce papers on TV before.

My mind was racing as I couldn't figure out what had transpired. I hated the surprise factor in this situation and started blaming myself for not being around for months at a time. Had I been naïve thinking that our marriage was good despite its low moments? Was I such a terrible wife? What did I miss? I deserved to know. My head was spinning in despair. I felt betrayed.

I understood days later that our marriage fell apart because of the army. For the past few years, I lived in denial and simply was rejecting the idea that we were slowly growing apart. That's why I continued to write letters to Alec from each of my trainings. However, my letters were becoming shorter and there was less tenderness and vulnerability in them.

I also realized how much I had changed during my military career. My journey had shaped me to be a stronger, more confident person than I was at the beginning. I wasn't that fragile, romantic ballerina I once was. I became a hard-core soldier. Apparently, this new me didn't fit the model of our marriage anymore. And now I had to accept the brutal truth. As a married couple, we were no more. I had to let Alec go.

* * *

A couple of months later, after the divorce, our purple picket fence house was sold, and with my Yorkies, I was moving to a different place to start everything all over again on my own.

The house was already empty when I picked up the last box with my hands shaking from emotions, ready to leave. The box fell, revealing its content. There was an empty Gatorade bottle with a white cloth tape inside, my souvenir from the OCS in Alabama when I fell victim to heat exhaustion for the first time. Lieutenant Brown gave me the purple Gatorade back then.

I also noticed a suspicious stack of unrecognized letters tied together with a rubber band. All of them were from Chris written within the past four years. I read a few of them with my heart pounding. I had no idea Chris was writing to me all these years. All the while, deep down in my heart, I had those recurring images of our relationship first flourishing, and then abruptly falling apart. For all these years, instinctively, I was trying to pick up the pieces of our friendship like parts of a broken kaleidoscope.

Next to the box on the floor was a book from Chris with the paintings of ballerinas by the French nineteenth-century painter Edgar Degas. It was dedicated to me. Chris gave me this book a long time ago when our friendship was thriving. As I was flipping through the book, remembering our multiple discussions about ballet matters, between the pages, I found a purple envelope addressed to Chris. It was the letter I wrote on the day of my enlistment in the army. How was it possible? I'd been convinced for years that I had sent this letter. Until now.

* * *

"My dear friend,

"It is extremely hard to keep me from writing to you. Since I am back in Chicago, everything seems to be deranged. Nothing makes sense anymore. The last time I called, you said that *it's never really a good time to talk*. It was like a dagger in my heart.

"Over the last thirteen years, I have created an ideal image of you, and I believed in it so hard that it almost became true. Perhaps all these years I've been seeing you as a character in a fairy tale. Perhaps I am too romantic. I might be too sensitive and fragile, and this jeopardized our friendship.

"We are so far away from each other again, and it's not just because you're in Switzerland right now. We don't listen and don't understand each other anymore. You didn't even notice that I haven't written a single letter for six months. You don't think that anything happened at all. You just don't care. It looks like everyday life just caught up with you and I don't exist for you anymore like I did all these years. I don't want to start a discussion online or a hasty exchange of ordinary, meaningless, and superficial e-mails. I have to tell you how I feel about us. This time, however, I won't use any figures of speech or metaphors, as they came out to be a horrible entrapment device for both of us.

"I'm tired of constantly having to defend my American way of life, my American dream, which I never would have had a chance to fulfill in Poland. I love where I am, and I don't feel like I should have to explain why. America is all my home now. My home is where my heart is.

"Unfortunately, I can't write to you anymore. I don't want to pretend that everything is fine. I just realized that when you said to me that I shouldn't offer you all my passion because you didn't deserve it—you were right. I should have followed your advice. You don't need to distance yourself from me, as we are already far enough from each other. There is nothing left of our friendship but distant memories. Goodbye, Chris."

I folded the paper, kissed it, and pressed it against my heart. I thought that perhaps because Chris had never received my goodbye letter, there was still hope and my four-year-long grief after what I thought was a lost friendship could be still resolved.

I stood in front of the empty house. Everything old was gone. Everything new was a mystery. "I will endure the darkness because it shows me the stars," I thought to myself, looking at the skies. The moon was smiling at me in his white and cynic glory. The stars on the high firmament, my faithful companions for all these years, were still there for me. As I wondered if the four years of my military career were worth everything I'd lost, I could hear the stars whispering to me.

Even though I had never seen the battlefield, I was still a hero. I had the courage to pursue my dream as far as it would take me. I had the courage to change and reinvent myself, from a fragile ballerina to a hardcore U.S. Army intelligence officer. And now, I would have the courage to change again.

EPILOGUE

Two months after the divorce, I went to a job interview for a marketing position. To check my writing skills, the interviewer set me on his computer and asked me to write a paragraph-long piece of creative writing. I wrote this:

"I looked upon the skies, cold and shivering, curled up in the deep and sandy hole. It was the beginning of spring in South Carolina when a freezing and unforgiving night was about to reveal the beginning of my life's next chapter. I looked at the moon, full, smiling in his white and cynic glory, and I saw my purple house in the middle of the night. Suddenly, I woke up from my live dream and I realized that I would have to go to a battle very soon. I could get hurt or die. And I might never see my purple house again."

The interviewer, who was an English major, couldn't believe I just wrote this from my head on the spot. I couldn't either. But I knew that one day I would write a book about my military experience and this fragment would be part of it. I got the job.

About that time, I went back to school for my MBA with a concentration in finance at DeVry University in Chicago, then two years later for my Master's in Project Management. Immediately after that, I completed three years of studies at Benedictine University in Lisle, IL for my PhD in Organizational Development. During this time, I visited my beloved Florence again.

In the meantime, I located Lieutenant Brown, who became a captain, completed two tours in Iraq, and just came back home to Alabama. We talked briefly on the phone about the OCS. I sent her my letter written at the end of Phase II in Pennsylvania.

In 2006, I finally mustered the courage to get in touch with Chris. There was a lot to explain. I went to Poland without an announcement. I stayed at a hotel right next to the French Studies building. My plan was to locate Chris's car by watching the parking lot early in the morning and leave my army photo with a brief letter behind the windshield. Like the good old days. While leaving the hotel, I noticed Chris with a juice box crossing the street, walking in my direction. We froze in a tight embrace right in the middle of the street. We rekindled our friendship.

Alec and I became close friends and since he was now living in Dallas, Texas, we maintained a long-distance relationship, talking on the phone for years. I decided to stay single; it suited me better.

Later, I worked for some time for the Department of Defense, at USMEPCOM (United States Military Entrance Processing Command) a joint headquarters of all military recruiting stations nationwide. I was a Change Management Lead in the Strategic Planning Directorate. After that I worked for several years for the Department of Veterans Affairs' two hospitals in their research departments. I was reviewing proposals for research studies before their approval by the Institutional Review Board committee.

At some point, with my mom visiting from Poland, we went on a ten-day trip through central and northern Arizona. We drove over four thousand miles, stopping by the Grand Canyon and all the places I saw with Coleman in 2001.

Now that over two decades have passed since I had shipped to basic training, I think about those long-lost days with melancholy. Life is a continuous cycle, full of glorious moments of light and moments of darkness. You never know where a new passion for life will come from, either as someone or something you fall in love with. Then you become that passion which defines your existence. You become someone new and as you grow with love and within it; it fills all the voids in your heart and heals the wounds. Eventually, you find your daylight.

The End

REFERENCES

Beyerle, Dana. "War on terror has taken toll on Alabama National Guard." Published 12:01 a.m. CT Sept. 11, 2006. Tuscaloosanews.com. https://www.tuscaloosanews.com/story/news/2006/09/11/war-on-terror-has-taken-toll-on-alabama-national-guard/27687403007/

Center for Army lessons Learned. n.d. How to master wargaming. Commander and staff guide to improving COA analysis. Center for Army lessons Learned. https://usacac.army.mil/sites/default/files/publications/20-06.pdf.

Company B (OCS) 2nd BN (MOD TNG), 166th Regiment, RTI Officer Candidate Guide US Army National Guard. 2009. Company B (OCS) 2nd BN (MOD TNG), 166th Regiment, RTI, Fort Indiantown Gap, Annville, Pennsylvania.

Garlauskas, Markus V. "Intelligence Support for Military Operations." Https://Apps.Dtic.Mil. 2002. Accessed October 10, 2022. https://apps.dtic.mil/sti/pdfs/ADA524838.pdf.

Gilbert, A. "Battle of Monte Cassino." https://www.britannica.com. Accessed January 10, 2023. https://www.britannica.com/topic/Battle-of-Monte-Cassino.

Headquarters Department of the Army. 1998. Army Regulation 840–10, Heraldic Activities. Flags, Guidons, Streamers, Tabards, and Automobile and Aircraft Plates. Headquarters Department of the Army Washington, DC., https://armypubs.army.mil/epubs/DR_pubs/DR_a/ARN30056-AR_840-10-000-WEB-1.pdf.

Headquarters Department of the Army. 1998. Oath of Office. Military Personnel. DA Form July 1999. Headquarters Department of the Army Washington, DC.

Headquarters Department of the Army. 1999. Army Leadership. Field Manual No. 22-100. Washington, DC: Headquarters Department of the Army. https://www.armyheritage.org/wp-content/uploads/2020/08/FM-22-100-Aug99.pdf.

Headquarters Department of the Army. 2001. Army Correspondence Course Program Catalog. Department of the Army Pamphlet 350–59. Washington, DC: Headquarters Department of the Army. https://apps.dtic.mil/sti/pdfs/ADA402745.pdf.

Headquarters Department of the Army. 2006. Human Intelligence Collector Operations. Washington, DC: Department of the Army. https://irp.fas.org/doddir/army/fm2-22-3.pdf

Headquarters Department of the Army. 2021. Drill and Ceremonies. Training Circular 3-21.5 Washington, D.C.: Headquarters Department of the Army. https://armypubs.army.mil/epubs/DR_pubs/DR_a/ARN32297-TC_3-21.5-000-WEB-1.pdf.

Headquarters Department of the Army. United States Training and Doctrine Command. 1999. IET Soldier's Handbook. TRADOC Pamphlet 600-4. Fort Monroe, Virginia, Headquarters Department of the Army. United States Training and Doctrine Command.

Headquarters, Department of the Army. 2020. Techniques for tactical radio operations. ATP 6-02.53. Headquarters, Department of the Army. https://armypubs.army.mil/epubs/DR_pubs/DR_a/pdf/web/ARN20819_ATP_6-02x53_FINAL_WEB.pdf.

Hempen, Jacob. "Daytime Land Navigation: In One Word." https://futurearmyofficers.army.mil, June 2, 2019. Accessed October 3, 2022. https://futurearmyofficers.army.mil/2019/06/02/daytime-land-navigation/.

http://asc.army.mil. The Instrumentable-Multiple Integrated Laser Engagement System (I-MILES). Accessed February 17, 2023. https://asc.army.mil/web/portfolio-item/instrumentable-multiple-integrated-laser-engagement-system-i-miles/.

http://www.mosdb.com. "Army Human Intelligence Collector. Enlisted. 35M MOS." Accessed: November 22, 2023. http://www.mosdb.com/army/35M/mos/2192/.

https://fas.org. "Military Intelligence Captains Career Course Seminar." February 26, 2008. Accessed March 14, 2023. https://fas.org/irp/agency/army/mipb/2008_02.pdf.

https://asc.army.mil. High Mobility Multipurpose Wheeled Vehicle (HMMWV). Accessed: January 22, 23. https://asc.army.mil/web/portfolio-item/cs-css-high-mobility-multipurpose-wheeled-vehicle-hmmwv/.

https://Wikipedia.org. "Pope John Paul II," n.d. Accessed February 25, 2023. https://simple.wikipedia.org/wiki/Pope_John_Paul_II.

https://www.armystudyguide.com. "Human Intelligence Collector (97E). Army Study Guide." Accessed March 11, 2023. https://www.armystudyguide.com/content/Prep_For_Basic_Training/army_mos_information/human-intelligence-collec.shtml.

https://www.classic.com. AM General Humvee (1984 to 2021). Accessed: January 22, 2023. https://www.classic.com/m/am-general/humvee/.

https://www.military.com. "Land Navigation Is Coming Back to the Army's Basic Leader Course." Accessed October 10, 2022. https://www.military.com/daily-news/2022/04/19/land-navigation-coming-back-armys-basic-leader-course.html.

https://www.nps.gov. Gettysburg National Military Parke Pennsylvania. Accessed on: October 16, 2022https://www.nps.gov/gett/index.htm.

https://www.romereport.com. "40 years ago, John Paul II's first visit to Poland that brought the collapse of communism. JOHN PAUL II." 2019. Accessed: February 25, 2023. https://www.romereports.com/en/2019/06/04/40-years-ago-john-paul-iis-first-visit-to-poland-that-brought-the-collapse-of-communism/#:~:text=John%20Paul%20II%20first%20visited,Paul%20II's%20visit%20to%20Poland.

https://www.thefirstnews.com. "US Army to Test Emergency Deployment Readiness in Poland.," July 10, 2020. Accessed November 8, 2022. https://www.thefirstnews.com/article/us-army-to-test-emergency-deployment-readiness-in-poland-13986.

https://www.thefreelibrary.com. "Reserve and Active Components Military Intelligence Captain's Career Course Comparison. U.S. Army Intelligence Center and School." 2018. Accessed October 23, 2022. https://www.thefreelibrary.com/

Reserve+and+Active+Components+Military+Intelligence+Captians+Career...-a0537983424.

https://www.westpoint.edu. "A Brief History of West Point." Accessed March 2, 2023. https://www.westpoint.edu/about/history-of-west-point.

https://www.wikipedia.com. Multiple integrated laser engagement system. Accessed January 25, 2023 https://en.wikipedia.org/wiki/Multiple_integrated_laser_engagement_system.

https://www.wikipedia.org. "Battle of Monte Cassino." Accessed October 21, 2022. https://en.wikipedia.org/wiki/Battle_of_Monte_Cassino.

https://www.wikipedia.org. "Saving Private Ryan." Accessed October 18, 2022. https://en.wikipedia.org/wiki/Saving_Private_Ryan.

Hymers, Dallas. 2012. The U.S. Army leadership manual. EADM 424 Book Summary. https://static1.squarespace.com/static/5df3bc9a62ff3e45ae9d2b06/t/5e666dc8c8831f128e870aff/1583771087409/US+Army+Leadership+Field+Manual.EBS.pdf.

Keegan, J. "Normandy Invasion." https://www.britannica.com. Accessed January 18, 2023. https://www.britannica.com/event/Normandy-Invasion.

https://military.history.fandom.com. "Creed of the Military Intelligence Corps," https://military-https://military-history.fandom.com/wiki/Military_Intelligence_Corps_(United_States_Army)#:~:text=Charlottesville%2C%20Virginia-,Creed%20of%20the%20Military%20Intelligence%20Corps,and%20never%20lose%20the%20enemy.

Roy, Sally. Italy Travel Guide. Edited by Jackie Staddon. 2nd ed. AAA Publishing, 2002.

USAG-WP, Dir Plans, Tng, Mob & Security. 2018. U.S. Army Garrison-West Point DPTMS – Range Operations Policy & Procedures. Standard Operating Procedure Anzio Obstacle Course. DPTM-SOP-AOC, Revision: 3, USAG-WP, Dir Plans, Tng, Mob & Security. https://home.army.mil/westpoint/index.php/download_file/844/663

https://www.history.com. "This Day in History. May 18. Pope John Paul II Born." Accessed February 25, 2023. https://www.history.com/this-day-in-history/pope-john-paul-ii-born#:~:text=On%20May%2018%2C%201920%2C%20Karol,position%20since%20the%2016th%20century.

3 1491 01434 7268

Niles-Maine
District Library

FEB 0 8 2024

Niles, IL 60714

Printed in the USA
CPSIA information can be obtained
at www.ICGtesting.com
LVHW030514280124
770020LV00001B/15